f8

D1766374

ENGLAND'S MAIL

Two Millennia of Letter Writing

What printing presses yield we think good store
But what is writ by hand we value more.
Translated from John Donne's Latin elegiac Doctissimo Amicissimoque, by Edmund Blunden.

'When all else has been said, narrative history depends especially upon letters, which express opinions and directions at the time of writing.'
Sir Maurice Powicke, The Thirteenth Century, page 739.

To put your hand on a letter, to see its address panel and seal, to read the text and signature, is to come as close as you can to the essence of our history.
Chapter on Sixteenth-Century Letters.

ENGLAND'S MAIL

Two Millennia of Letter Writing

PHILIP BEALE

TEMPUS

Front cover: Georg Gisze, London merchant, by Holbein. Letters hang in racks with a string holder, scales, crystal ball, seal, inkwell and quill pen. The Latin motto translates as 'No joy without sorrow'. The notice dated 1532 reads, 'The picture you see here records the features of Georg. Such are his lively eyes, such is his face.' Courtesy of Bildarchive Preußischer Kulturbesitz, Berlin.

The back cover shows an English Herald receiving a letter from King Edward IV and delivering it on the continent. Taken from the manuscript The Legend of St Ursula by courtesy of Stad Brugge Stedelijke Musea.

Dedicated with gratitude to the late Frank Salter and the late Dr Ralph Bennett of Magdalene College, Cambridge

This edition published 2005

Tempus Publishing Limited
The Mill, Brimscombe Port,
Stroud, Gloucestershire, GL5 2QG
www.tempus-publishing.com

© Philip Beale, 2005

The right of Philip Beale to be identified as the Author of this work has been asserted in accordance with the Copyrights, Designs and Patents Act 1988.

All rights reserved. No part of this book may be reprinted or reproduced or utilised in any form or by any electronic, mechanical or other means, now known or hereafter invented, including photocopying and recording, or in any information storage or retrieval system, without the permission in writing from the Publishers.

British Library Cataloguing in Publication Data.
A catalogue record for this book is available from the British Library.

ISBN 0 7524 3491 8
Typesetting and origination by Tempus Publishing Limited
Printed in Great Britain

CONTENTS

PREFACE

From Roman times until the twentieth century much of the administration of England has been carried out by sending letters, either in the form of written instructions or authorisations to deliver information orally. They were addressed to the recipient and authenticated by a seal or signature, often having a greeting and a personal conclusion. Also included were copies of laws, regulations and summonses to courts. Without an efficient messenger service there could be no effective control of the country and no means by which government could be informed of events taking place. Separate postal services were also developed to meet the needs of the nobles, the church, the merchants, the towns and the public. This book discusses letters, those who carried them, and the means of distribution, being three meanings of the word 'post'. It shows that the postal service established throughout England by the medieval kings continued until 1635 when it was officially extended to the public, thus starting its amalgamation with the other services.

My interest in this subject started when I read with great pleasure Mary Hill's *The King's Messengers 1199–1377* and realised how extensive the medieval sources were for a study of the royal post. So began several years of reading and visiting archives. Encouraged by Mary Hill and then by Dr Ralph Bennett, who with others read the early drafts, I put together this book. Our national records are so extensive that it is possible to describe the development of postal services that were essential to the administrative, social and industrial growth of the country.

The opportunity to revise a book published seven years ago has enabled me to add much new material, to introduce two new maps and have another redrawn. Some corrections have been made, new illustrations introduced and the number of colour plates increased. The title has been changed to distinguish it from the former *History of the Post in England from the Romans to the Stuarts*.

Philip Beale

ACKNOWLEDGEMENTS

For the original research I have many people to thank apart from Mary Hill and Dr Ralph Bennett. I was then helped by Professor Alan Bowman, Dr Gerald Harriss, and Michael Scott-Archer, who have again helped me with improving sections of the book. Dr Christine Carpenter kindly advised on one chapter. John Taylor gave me advice on early English letters. It will be obvious that I am particularly indebted to M.T. Clanchy's *From Memory to Written Record*, to contributors in Rosamund McKitterick's *The Uses of Literacy in early Medieval Europe* and to John Taylor's *English Historical Literature of the Fourteenth Century*. Dr J.W.M. Stone's *The Inland Posts* provided a valuable calendar of Tudor and Stuart sources. I must also thank Louise Wheatley, assistant archivist at the York Merchant Adventurers, and her successor, Jill Redford; Peter Field of the former Post Office Photographic Library; Edward Tilley of the Public Record Office; and all those who have so courteously replied to letters. Recently Shirley Bayliss, archivist of Postal Heritage, Robin Harcourt-Williams, archivist of the Marquess of Salisbury's Library, and Paul Johnson of the National Archives have guided me in obtaining illustrations. Hugh Davies has provided the Antonine Itinerary map and Dr Paul Hindle has supplied the medieval road map. In commissioning the Elizabethan postal routes map I am indebted to Dr Mark Brayshay's articles and maps on the subject. In researching both books I am grateful to the Rossiter Trust which has made grants.

When working in libraries I have been kindly received and must thank in particular E.B. Nurse, the librarian of the Society of Antiquaries, and his assistant librarian, A.C. James. The staff at the British Library's Department of Manuscripts, the Guildhall Library, the Corporation of London Library and Cambridge University Library were unfailingly supportive. To all these people I give thanks and trust they will forgive any errors they note, which will all be mine.

PRIMARY SOURCES WITH ABBREVIATIONS

APC	Acts of the Privy Council
CCR	Calendar of Close Rolls
CChR	Calendar of Charter Rolls
CIMisc.	Calendar of Inquisitions Miscellaneous
CIPM	Calendar of Inquisitions Post Mortem
CLR	Calendar of Liberate Rolls
CPR	Calendar of Patent Rolls
CSPD	Calendar of State Papers Domestic
CSPDF	Calendar of State Papers Domestic & Foreign
CSPF	Calendar of State Papers Foreign
CSP Milan	Calendar of State papers Milan
CSP Venetian	Calendar of State papers Venetian
PRO	Public Record Office [now National Archives]
RS	Rolls Series. Chronicles and Memorials of Great Britain
RCM	Royal Commission on Historical Manuscripts
TRHS	Transactions of The Royal Historical Society
Rolls Series	Chronicles and Memorials of Great Britain
Sec. Com.	Report of the Secret Committee on the Post Office

I also quote from Calendar of Letters and Papers relating to the affairs of the Borders of England and Scotland 1560-94 and Correspondence relative to Scotland and the Borders 1513-34.

The Calendars typically give a short account of the state papers to which they refer so in some cases it has been necessary to go to the original documents in the National Archives. The reader should be aware that there has been more than one edition of several of the volumes listed above and also reprints so that the same reference may appear on differently numbered pages. The titles of some editions differ slightly from others. However, all volumes are well indexed and locating a reference should not be difficult. There are also Addenda volumes to State Papers. In the references I often give short titles for books. Full titles will be found in the Bibliography.

Dates

Until the year 1752, March 25, known as Lady Day, or St Mary's Day in Lent to distinguish it from other festival days of the Virgin Mary, marked the beginning of the legal year. Documents dated between 1 January and that day may give different years according to whether the calendar or the legal year was used. I show such dates as, for example, 1566/57, 1556 being the legal year and 1557 being the calendar year. If I refer to events that took place between the calendar years 1556 and 1557 they are shown as 1556-1557.

From the accession of King Richard I royal letters are dated by the sovereign's regnal year, the beginning of which was the day of the sovereign's accession. The regnal year is therefore not the legal year and not the calendar year. Statutes and Proclamations become dated by the regnal year. The first number in a Statute is the number of the regnal year and this precedes the name of the sovereign. Statutes in the period covered by this book usually include a great number of disparate topics. Each one has a separate chapter for which I use the abbreviation ch. They are shown in the form 22 Henry VIII, ch.5.

1
FROM THE ROMANS TO THE NORMAN CONQUEST

The Romans, who made their first reconnaissance to Britain in 55 BC, brought with them the art of letter writing, an efficient postal system and the skills required for building paved roads. They had already established highways from Italy to the English Channel and, as their army advanced, so the same pattern of regular posting stations, bridges, fords and river transport was extended here. Construction work started in southern England about AD 43 and was largely completed by the year 81. Roads extended from London throughout Britain to Devon in the south, across much of Wales and into East Anglia, reaching as far north as Carlisle and Corbridge on Hadrian's Wall, approximately the centre of Britain. Those that were constructed in Scotland between the 80s and 160s as far as the Antonine Wall, which ran from the Firth of Forth to the River Clyde and then beyond it to Inchtuthil, were abandoned by the end of the second century and only used for occasional incursions thereafter. Along the main roads, many of which were to remain in use until modern times, were placed milestones commemorating the emperor of the day, showing distances and destinations. The miles were a little shorter than our present measurement, being based on 1,000 strides of 5ft taken by a runner, equivalent to about 1,660 Imperial yards.

Before the Romans came, there were some roads, for Julius Caesar notes in his account of the campaign against Cassivelaunus that the British king sent his chariots 'by all the well-known roads and tracks'. Caesar moved so quickly that it seems he must have used them. During the centuries that followed the Roman departure, their style of letter writing survived and, while the people spoke Celtic and later Old English, the ability to read and write Latin was to remain part of the formal education of all professional English people until the twentieth century. It was the only European international language.

The Roman postal system was established during the Republic but its final structure is attributed to the Emperor Augustus. Our knowledge of it comes almost entirely from literary sources though, as will be shown, some original

English letters written on wood have survived. In 20 BC Augustus had been appointed as commissioner of the roads near Rome. Each trunk road had its curator and at the hub of the system in Rome he erected the so-called 'golden milestone', a column bearing plaques of gilded bronze on which were inscribed the names of the chief cities with their distances from the capital. At this time along the main routes there were post stages about 8⅓ miles apart where horses were kept and refreshment was available. At every third station was a night quarters, enabling a courier to travel 25 or 50 miles a day according to weather conditions and time of year. There are exceptional, well-recorded accounts of far greater distances being covered, including one when Augustus sent Tiberius through Rhaetia and Germany to visit Augustus's dying brother Drusus. He travelled 200 miles in a day and a night. Cases are known of men travelling 140 miles a day for several days using two-wheeled carriages – speeds that were not improved upon until the advent of the railway.[1]

In setting up the system of couriers, at least two basic models must have been considered. The courier could hand over his letter to another at a stage and thus fresh messengers and horses would ensure the quickest possible transmission of the post. On the other hand, the courier might take regular rests and deliver his message personally. The first model was used and then changed to the second. In Suetonius' life of Augustus there is this account of the postal service and the Emperor's use of letters:

> To enable what was going on in each of the Provinces to be reported and known more speedily and promptly, [Augustus] at first stationed young men at short intervals along the military roads and afterwards post-chaises. The latter has seemed the more convenient arrangement, since the same men who bring the letters from any place can, if occasion demands, be questioned as well. On passports, despatches and private letters he used as his seal first a sphinx, later an image of Alexander the Great, and finally his own image. This his successors continued to use as their seal. He always attached to all letters the exact hour, not only of the day, but even of the night, to indicate precisely when they were written.[2]

Later the Emperor Hadrian placed the military road system under imperial control with its costs chargeable to imperial funds, and an office was opened in Rome under an equestrian *praefectus* to administer it.

The method of delivering letters by a messenger who took mail from the sender to the recipient continued to be used until modern times. Speed was not the main consideration; it was the certainty of arrival and security of the letter that mattered most. The conversation between the messenger and the recipient of the news could be an essential part of the process. Equally important as delivery of the letter was the verbal reply that would come back by the same messenger. Many letters that we know of from early times are primarily letters of introduction, the bearer being able to pass on the important news by word of mouth, thus ensuring both confidentiality and a reply.

The army which used the roads in Britain may have numbered 60,000 at the height of Roman power, far larger than any force assembled by an English medieval or Tudor sovereign. However, it is likely that the population of Roman Britain reached between 4 and 6 million at its peak, perhaps twice that of the time of Henry VIII.[3]

As the legions advanced they built links to their base and thus they constructed their roads. The roads were not built to join the British towns together, for they normally avoided them. Their purpose was military and political. The centre point was London with roads linking it, like spokes on a wheel, to the legionary fortresses at Exeter, Wroxeter, Colchester, Lincoln, York, Chester and Caerleon, to the bases of local administration and to Hadrian's Wall. The Ordnance Survey has produced a splendid map of the roads, which provided facilities for the traveller that were superior to any until the eighteenth century. They followed the most direct routes available and so were not the ways usually traversed by the local population, who would take the ancient tracks that linked their towns and religious centres. For example, the old route known as the Icknield Way, a series of local roads running along the Berkshire and Chiltern escarpment, is not in origin a Roman road; neither is Peddar's Way in East Anglia.[4]

An exception to the pattern of routes to and from London is the Fosse Way. This started at Topsham near Exeter in Devon and linked it to Bath, Cirencester, Leicester and Lincoln, thus crossing the island from south west to north east. Though it is not regarded as having been intended as a frontier, it seems likely that the first wave of the Roman advance stopped at these points, thus taking military operations to the natural boundaries of the Severn and the Trent. It marked a period of consolidation during which settlements were linked together, making a supply road which served the needs of local rather than through traffic.

The main trunk roads, which must be distinguished from minor trackways, were at least 14ft in width, sufficient to allow two waggons to pass each other, although their main purpose was to provide for marching soldiers and their baggage trains. They were firmly constructed with a gravel surface, usually with side ditches. In towns they would be paved. Unstable ground was secured by wooden piles, brushwood and occasionally concrete. Even the minor roads could be regarded as all-weather routes. Bridges, fords and culverts were soundly made and today many of their foundations can still be seen. Each main road in its final state had its inspector in chief known as *curator viarum*, while the minor crossing roads were put under local control. Traders were subject to duties of 2½ per cent charged at customs posts. The survival rate of low-value Roman coins is such that there must have been considerable commercial business. Roads were kept as straight as possible but would divert if any substantial obstacle was met, as with Silbury Hill in Wiltshire. Such a road was best for the marching soldier, less likely to harbour an ambush and helpful to the drivers of vehicles which had no movable joint between the pairs of wheels.

There was also water-borne traffic. Dover, Lympne and Richborough served as cross-Channel ports, and the Tyne communicated directly with the

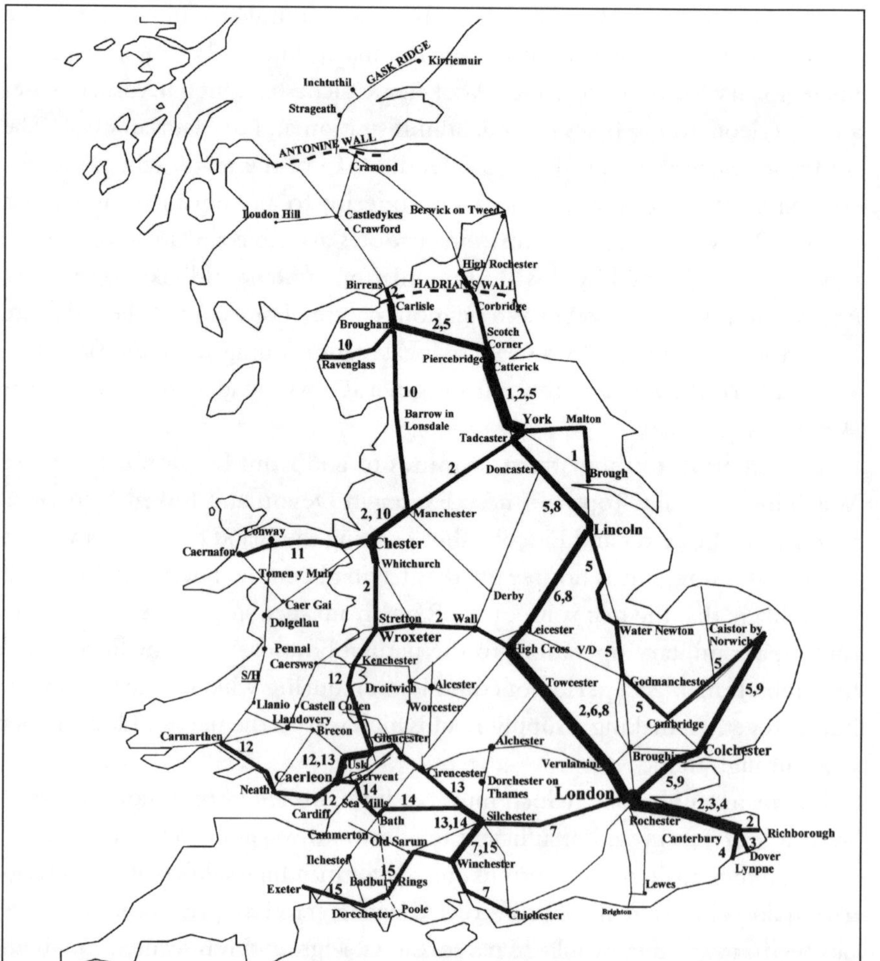

1.1 Map of routes on the Antonine Itinerary and other Roman roads. (Hugh Davies, from *Roman Roads in Britain*)

Rhine. Otherwise, continental trade came to depend mainly on the harbours of London, Southampton and the Humber. The realisation that the port of London was not tidal in Roman times, and that this would have suited sailors used to the almost tideless Mediterranean sea, helps to explain the dominant position that the port of London achieved.[5]

Inland rivers were used as much as possible for the transport of heavy objects; the Foss Dyke linking the Trent with Lincoln is thought to be a Roman canal. The oysters that are typically found in profusion on Roman sites imply their fairly rapid distribution, for unless they were carried quickly in water tanks they would have soon deteriorated.

Much of our knowledge of British Roman roads comes from archaeological excavation but there are other sources. There is one important map, the medieval Peutinger Table, which is believed to be based on a Roman one. It is named after a sixteenth-century owner, Conrad Peutinger of Augsburg. Originally it consisted of twelve sheets of parchment but now there are only eleven, the missing section having covered most of Britain. All that remains are some routes in southern England. Some minor information comes from parts of Roman bowls which list the forts along Hadrian's Wall in northern England. They could have been made as souvenirs. Far more valuable, however, is a Roman road book, The Antonine Itinerary, thought to date from the third century AD, which has a British section often indicating journeys that do not follow the direct military ways or the shortest routes but which take the traveller through tribal capitals like Winchester and Silchester.[6]

It lists fifteen British journeys and records over a hundred place names. Collingwood and Myres suggested that this volume is really a description of the routes of the Roman postal system and their view has been supported by more recent studies.[7]

The state-organised service for the use of those officials who held warrants for the carriage of letters, goods and equipment was at first known as the *vehiculatio* and then the *cursus publicus*. Travel along the roads was open to the public with priority given to official transport. The Itinerary does not describe all the Roman roads and so seems to be a record of fifteen actual journeys undertaken by officials. Parts of some journeys are duplicated in other ones, being shown by thicker lines on the map (Fig. 1.1), the thinner lines on the map indicating roads not mentioned in the Itinerary. The numbers shown refer to the fifteen journeys. They extend through much of England with London the town most frequently mentioned; Silchester, High Cross and York are important junctions. The two most northerly places are just beyond Hadrian's Wall.

The journeys in the Itinerary refer to *mansiones* and occasionally to *mutationes*, which were both places for the use of travellers holding warrants authorising them to use their facilities. Information about such buildings can be found in the Theodosian Code, a third-century compendium of legislation. The *mansiones*, which replaced what were previously called *praetoria*, were regularly spaced at about 12 miles apart, providing overnight accommodation, stables and refreshment. For reasons of safety they were often placed within a settlement. The *mutationes* appear to have been smaller in scale, probably with facilities for changing animals and for rudimentary overnight shelter. Each *mansio* was in the charge of an official known as the *manceps*, who might also be responsible for one or two *mutationes*. He had a staff of grooms, carriage repairers, veterinary specialists and slaves, and he maintained a considerable number of animals. In many respects *mansiones* resembled eighteenth-century posting inns with a central courtyard and a range of adjacent buildings. The *mansio* would need to be able to accommodate an important official with a train of mules and horses, or serve several vehicles carrying bullion and valuable goods accompanied by an escort. Its size would depend upon the expected traffic. When fully developed, the town site at Letocetum in Staffordshire had an elaborate complex with buildings extending over an area of 20 or 30 acres, including a large bath-house and a *mansio* which comprised an entrance hall and a courtyard round which ran a colonnade with access to eight ground-floor rooms. The substantial foundations indicate that there would have been an upper storey, probably with a balcony. Excavations suggest that there was a garden outside with a statue; the amount of window glass and plaster found suggests a building of some aesthetic quality.[8]

Those who used the *mansiones* required an official warrant, of which several types are known. A *diploma* (plural *diplomata*) was a letter, folded double, which allowed the holder passage on the *cursus publicus*. At first *diplomata* were only issued by the emperor, who supplied them to provincial governors for their allocation, but by the second century the governors were authorised to provide them. They were granted to couriers, magistrates and other officials. There were two types of *diploma*: one related to waggons pulled by oxen, the other to lighter vehicles and animals. Lodging with full board would be allowed and each *diploma* had an expiry date. Other types of warrant were *evictiones* or *tractoriae*. Both appear to be impersonal documents allowing the holder to travel on public or military roads and to use the facilities of the *mansiones*. They would be suitable for a regular courier. Warrants indicated the use that could be made of overnight accommodation, some allowing as many as five nights which might be needed by a convoy of vehicles that needed repairs or by officials collecting local taxes. No warrants are known to have survived but they are mentioned in literary sources such as Pliny's Letters, as well as in official codes.

At first the *cursus publicus* was intended for the rapid transmission of messages, but gradually it became used for other purposes. Two divisions were set up: the express post, known as the *cursus velox*, and the slower waggon post, the *cursus clabularis*. The express post provided changes of mules, ponies or horses, two-wheeled carriages and four-wheeled waggons, the driver returning the vehicle to the posting station. It was used by couriers, officials travelling on business and for the carriage of valuables. The slower post used ox-drawn waggons for the transport of such military supplies as armour, clothing and grain, or stone and timber for public works. Maintaining so large a posting service was extremely expensive and was a major charge on the revenues of each province. It involved the feeding of animals that were replaced every four years, the costs of the staff, and the maintenance of the buildings. The army had its own transport services but how these were integrated into the *cursus publicus* is not understood.

It is difficult to identify any of the many buildings found along the Roman roads with the *mansiones* or *mutationes* because they have no obvious distinctive feature, but many sites have been excavated which have buildings that could have served the *cursus publicus*. Vindolanda on Hadrian's Wall has a military fort with what seems to be a *mansio* built outside it. There is a series of buildings on Watling Street which are spaced between 8 and 16 miles apart. It is likely that *mansiones* served a variety of purposes in addition to providing accommodation and stables. Some probably provided a place for policing an area and also served as collecting centres for taxes. Buildings that may be granaries could be stores for grain and foodstuffs that were handed in as payment. Legal codes stated that *mansiones* should hold weights and measures. It has been suggested that some important villas such as Chedworth served as public hostels. They may even have extended their use to double as *mansiones*, but excavation of the likely *mansiones* and their adjacent buildings indicates that accommodation for the public had developed alongside those for the officials.

A variety of vehicles was used on the Roman roads. Most common was the two-wheeled *birota*, pulled by two or three mules, and the four-wheeled *raeda*, a cart used for loads of bullion or people. Heavier loads were taken by the *angaria* which had four wheels and was pulled by four oxen. The specified loads are very light by modern standards but this is presumed to be because of the poor system of harnessing animals that was used and the difficulty that the larger vehicles had in turning. The horse collar had not been invented and there is no evidence for brakes. Other small two-wheeled vehicles were used for rapid transport. The post horses, known as *veredi*, had strict weight limits placed on each part of their equipment, saddles, bridles and saddle bags. A type of sandal, of Celtic origin, was sometimes used to protect the feet of oxen and mules but there is no evidence that horseshoes were used in Roman Britain. The hard surfaces of many Roman roads made them unsuitable for unshod animals and steep, straight inclines would give them no purchase.

The Roman postal service was not available to the public except by favour. They had to use private couriers or make arrangements with carriers. The letters that were sent would be written with a pen on papyrus, wood or parchment, though for disposable messages wax was spread on a tablet and the writing made by a stylus – the tablet could then be erased and reused.[9]

Tablets of the last-mentioned kind dating from about AD 100 have been found at Vindolanda on the Stanegate frontier road south of Hadrian's Wall. They measure about 15cm by 10cm and are about 0.5cm thick at the rim, the centre being hollowed to take the wax. They are made of larch or spruce, which indicates that they had been imported. Slots along the back may have been intended to take the seals of witnesses when needed and notes could be written along the rim. A number of these could act like a set of modern files. Other wax tablets of this kind dating from about AD 600 were found in the Springmount bog in Ireland, two tablets being bound together with the waxed sides facing each other. Further Roman examples have been found at sites including Caerleon, Carlisle and London. In almost every case the wax has perished and it is almost impossible to decipher any lettering on the wood underneath. Writing was done by using a pointed metal stylus with a blunter opposite end which could be used for erasing.

That the Romans in Britain used wood as a writing surface for correspondence was shown by the discovery of writing on wood as thin as veneer at Vindolanda.[10] The letters vary in thickness from 0.25mm to 3mm, being cut from alder, birch or oak trees, which grew then, as now, in the area. The writing is in ink made of carbon, gum arabic and water, usually in a cursive hand, sometimes using a Latin shorthand. The text is normally in two columns starting on the left, the leaf being folded between the columns with the address on the back of the right hand half. Exceptionally, in one example, the first column is found on the right and it is presumed that the writer was left handed, the arrangement of the columns ensuring that the writer's hand did not obscure what had already been written. Wood was a writing medium to be obtained at little cost and the find of deposits of letters, accidentally preserved, suggests that this was the normal means of correspondence used for all but the most important documents. Such use has not entirely disappeared: on a visit to the Cherokee National Park in the United States the

1.2 Roman wooden writing tablet inset for taking wax. (British Museum Romano-British dept PS 200270)

writer was intrigued to buy postcards made from two slivers of wood glued together.

The surviving letters that can be read refer, as would be expected from their provenance, mainly to military matters such as the movement of troops, but others concern more mundane details like the purchase of clothing or an order for beer. We can see military reports and even a list of kitchen equipment. Some involve women correspondents – one group consists of letters to Sulpicia Lepidina, wife of the prefect of the ninth cohort of Batavians, from three women friends. An elegantly composed invitation to a birthday party from Claudia Severa to Sulpicia declares: 'You will make the day more enjoyable by your presence,' and ends in her own handwriting with 'Farewell, sister, dearest soul as I hope to prosper, and hail.' (Fig. 1.3) Its date, estimated from the context of its discovery, is about AD 100. A letter addressed to 'Your Majesty' complains of a beating that a tradesman, possibly a Roman citizen, had suffered, perhaps at the hand of a soldier. Exceptionally, writers quote from the poet Virgil. As with other Roman letters, they begin with the name of the recipient and the sender and close with a brief greeting, probably in the sender's own hand. Such finds, mainly written by the senders rather than by scribes, suggest a greater incidence of literacy in the Roman world than had previously been thought possible and provide a fascinating, sometimes intimate, picture of the people who lived at that time. In later Roman Britain there is evidence that many people in towns could read and write in Latin although few countrymen achieved that level of education. It was hardly necessary for letters to be enciphered in Britain, but the Romans are known to have used ciphers and Julius Caesar occasionally wrote using Greek letters to protect the security of his correspondence.[11] The larger British landowners became Romanised, building magnificent villas and acquiring a taste for a culture that involved the use of correspondence.

Where there are addresses, the Vindolanda letters give the name of the addressee in the dative case and the address is often in the locative. When translating from Latin into English it is necessary to add a preposition to show the effect of the case ending, so the words 'to' or 'deliver to' are understood before the name of the person and 'at' before the name of the place. Letters are known addressed to London and York. The correspondence shows that writers used the opportunities provided by travellers to send letters to distant places, but that officers would send soldiers to closer destinations.

As well as these letters, the text of one written by the secretary of a British governor has survived. It is described as being of a remarkably high standard and we can presume that it is typical of the thousands of administrative letters that must have been composed in Roman Britain.[12]

We know very little about the details of the transport of parcels and freight, but numbers of lead sealings survive which were probably attached to the packets and letters. Thirteen oblong sheet lead tags were found in 1973 in a pit in the Neronian fortress at Usk. They had been inscribed with a sharp point on both sides and had evidently been attached to packages, giving the number, the weight in pounds, the value in denarii and presumably the contents.[13]

1.3 Letter on wood from Sulpicia Lepidina to Claudia Severa, wife of Cerialis, inviting her to a birthday party. (British Museum Romano-British dept PS 192782)

1.4 Letter on wood from Niger and Brocchus to Flavius Cerialis, commander of the eighth cohort of the Batavians at Vindolanda. (British Museum Romano-British dept PS 3134591)

By the third century Christianity had become established in south-east England and when the Romans started their withdrawal, the new religion was to be the provider of culture and education. Roman control had begun to wane before 350. The Emperor Theodosius restored order after the barbarian attacks of 367 but in 408 invaders overran the country. Rome itself fell to Alaric in 410. By about 440 the remnants of the Roman army had left Britain, leaving the country at the mercy of Germanic invaders, who occupied much of England. The language which we call Old English evolved to replace Celtic as the common tongue except in Cornwall, which was not occupied until the ninth century, and Wales, which retained its independence until the conquest of Edward I. The invaders made use of the Roman roads after the *cursus publicus* and its *mansiones* had fallen into disuse. They had served an administration that had departed and required a basis of local taxation that no longer existed.

The two centuries that followed the Roman departure are the most obscure in British history, as hardly any contemporary documents are known. While there was much warfare, yet there is evidence to show that cultural life continued. For example, a book composed by Fastidius in Britain about the year 420, *On the Christian Life*, is in simple and elegant Latin. A number of letters exist in copy form from popes addressed to Britain at this time, which implies that there were replies. These contacts culminated in the mission of St Augustine to Canterbury in 597, and in 601 Pope Gregory the Great set up the two provinces of the Church in England. In 669 Pope Vitalian sent Theodore, who came from Asia Minor, to be the archbishop of Canterbury. The English historian Bede had many papal letters copied for him by a friend on a visit to Rome and some of them are incorporated in his *Ecclesiastical History of the English Nation*, completed in 731. We know also that St Patrick, who was born in England, wrote letters.[14]

Political contact with the Continent also continued: in the sixth century, King Aethelberht of Kent had married Bertha, the daughter of the king of Paris. The splendid jewels and plate found in the seventh-century Sutton Hoo burial of an East Anglian chief show that there were contacts with places as far away as Byzantium, as well as an appreciation of fine possessions.

A curious incident is related concerning the use of writing in Ireland.[15] St Patrick, who had come from Britain, was nearly killed when the writing materials that he and his followers were carrying were thought to be weapons. We can only surmise what these were. Wax tablets would seem unlikely and the thin wooden letters of the type already referred to as found at Vindolanda could hardly be thought to be offensive. It has been surmised that what the party was carrying were sticks engraved with runes or, more likely, ogham script. This originated in Ireland and is a method of representing the letters of the Latin alphabet by notches and grooves. Such sticks have been discovered in excavations of medieval Bergen where they were then used for carrying messages, the letters being cut on the smoothed sides of the sticks. There is a reference to one in an Anglo Saxon poem, *The Husband's Message*.[16]

Perhaps such sticks were in common use in England and Ireland at this time. After all, it was unknown until recently that the Romans wrote letters on wood and British inscribed sticks may some day be found and recognised. Medieval wooden tally sticks, discussed later in this book, were used as receipts until the eighteenth century, and had smoothed sides on which were written details of the transaction.

By the eighth century, when more stability had been established, the British Isles started to have a profound influence on Europe through both its Christian missions and scholarship. It is the century of the magnificently illuminated Lindisfarne Gospels and the time when the saga of Beowulf was written in a literary form. There are surviving collections of letters including 150 from the Anglo-Saxon Continental Archbishops Boniface and Lullus, and 350 from the Englishman Alcuin who became head of the Emperor Charlemagne's palace school. His letters discuss astronomy, music and natural history. Bede's *Ecclesiastical History* quotes a considerable number of earlier letters in full. One is a detailed reply to nine questions put by Augustine which describes the practice of the Church in respect of such matters as the ordination of bishops, punishments, and the relationship of dioceses with one another. The letters are headed in this form: 'To his most reverend and holy brother and fellow Bishop, Augustine; Gregory, the servant of the servants of God'. That concerning the future Bishop of London ends 'dated the 22nd of June, in the nineteenth year of the reign of our most lord and emperor Mauritius Tiberius, the eighteenth year after the consulship of our said lord' (i.e. AD 601). Bede quotes in full two interesting letters, dated 625, from Pope Boniface to King Edwin and his wife Ethelberga exhorting the king to become a Christian and urging the queen to encourage him to do so. The latter ends:

> Having premised thus much, in pursuance of the duty of our fatherly affection, we exhort you, that when the opportunity of a bearer shall offer, you will as soon as possible acquaint us with the success which the Divine Power shall grant by your means in the conversion of your consort [...] We have, moreover, sent you the blessing of your Protector, St Peter, the prince of the apostles, that is, a silver looking glass, and a gilt ivory comb, which we entreat your glory will receive with the same kind of affection as it is known to be sent by us.[17]

Another letter quoted in full by Bede is from Honorius, Archbishop of Canterbury, in 634 dealing with the vexed matters of the date of Easter and the spread of the Pelagian heresy.[18]

During the seventh and eighth centuries England was divided into a number of kingdoms, which must have made long-distance travel difficult. Nevertheless, when the monastic church at Wearmouth was being built, masons were recruited in France and messengers were sent with letters to obtain workers in glass. Furniture and vestments were ordered from the Continent. In 672 it was possible to summon a national synod of clergy to be held in Hertford. By now large numbers of pilgrims were travelling to Rome taking letters of recommendation to ensure exemption from customs duties. One extant letter from Charlemagne, ruler of most of Europe, to King Offa refers to traders who evaded customs under the pretext of being pilgrims. Pilgrim routes across Britain and the Continent were becoming well established, with halts at towns, monasteries, shrines and churches. Willibald, a Wessex man, travelled to the Near East in about 720 and later an English nun wrote the *Vita Willibaldi*, the earliest travel book composed by a native of this country.[19]

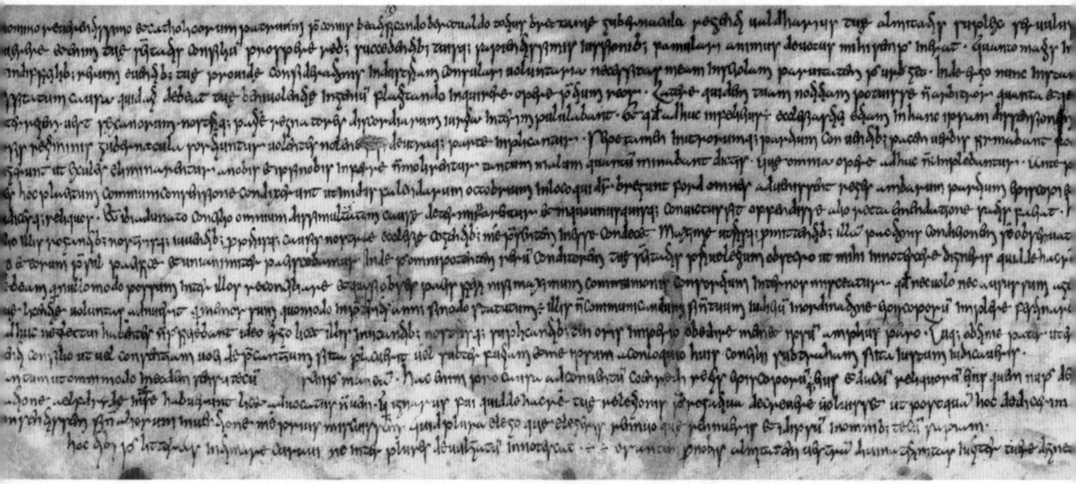

1.5 Letter from Waeldhere, Bishop of London, written in 704 or 705. (British Library Cotton Augustus II f18)

After reaching Rome, Willibald went on to Jerusalem, travelling alternately by ship and on foot. The overall picture given from his account is of a society that was surprisingly well organised. Ships crossed the Channel regularly, captains collected fares, travellers took tents and expected to pay tolls on the way.

The earliest surviving medieval letter in northern Europe was written by Waeldhere, Bishop of London, to Archbishop Brihtwold. Although it bears no year it can be dated from internal evidence to 704 or 705. It is preserved in the British Library among the Cottonian manuscripts and has been described in detail by Pierre Chaplais.[20]

The letter, which is considered to be in the Bishop's own handwriting, is written in Latin on a piece of vellum measuring 363mm wide by 145mm high. Faint lines were ruled to assist the writer. It was folded twice vertically and also twice horizontally, thus producing nine rectangular sections. On the outer side is the address written with a blank part in the middle so that a tie would not obscure any part of it. A strip of vellum was probably used to hold the folds firm and this would be knotted tightly. The letter has no seal and is therefore not what is called a 'letter close', which was so secured that the seal had to be broken before the letter could be read. It begins by addressing the recipient by name and giving that of the sender.

Later, during the ninth century, an ingenious method of securing letters came into use. The scribe would cut a strip from the end of the parchment leaving it still attached. This formed a tongue which was then wrapped tightly around the folded letter, looped through itself, and then knotted. It would be most difficult to undo the tie without separating it from the letter. Letters and charters exist with the stub of the tie remaining at the foot of the document. A later variant of this is found by the time of Henry I when two strips were sometimes cut from the foot of the letter, the upper to receive the seal, the lower to act as a tie. Another very early letter which survives was written in Old English to King Edward the Elder explaining the history of an estate at Fonthill in Wiltshire. As it originated early in his reign it can be dated soon after 900.[21]

The eighth-century missions to parts of pagan northern Europe had been led by clerics from Britain, and the correspondence of Boniface is the most important historical source for those times. It is a significant period in the history of British letters and documents as it marks a shift from the almost exclusive use of oral evidence to the acceptance of written documents. Monasteries and abbeys received charters, which were deeds in letter form, and within a century we see regal writs, letters from the king to individuals granting them rights over a particular area of land. References to charters granted to lay nobles are known for the eighth century, though all the original documents have perished. The existence of these writs and charters suggests that rulers may have had a *scriptorium*, employing clerics to write on their behalf. However, it is more likely that the comparatively few Anglo Saxon royal charters and letters were written by those clerics and bishops who happened to be with the court or who lived nearby, rather than that the monarch had an office like a later Chancery.[22]

Ingulph's *Chronicle of Croyland* states that the abbey's earlier abbot Turketal was appointed Chancellor by Edward the Confessor.[23] One royal scribe in the time of King Aethelred, the thegn Aelfwine, is known to have received a grant of land in 984, and charters in the time of King Edward the Confessor name two others and another Chancellor, Regenbald.[24] However, the Latin word for Chancellor, *cancellarius*, may mean no more than the keeper of the treasure chest at this time and so not describe the important officer of state of later times.

A great impetus to scholarship and the use of writing was given by King Alfred's translations of celebrated books from Latin into Old English. He arranged for the distribution of copies to bishoprics and schools between 892 and his death in 899. It was his intention that all in authority should be able to read. There is an interesting comment in his translation of St Augustine's *Soliloquies* where he writes:

> Consider now if your Lord's letter and his seal come to you, whether you can say that you cannot understand him thereby or recognise his will therein.

This shows that in the late ninth century a lord might write to someone on his estates, attaching his seal to the letter and expecting that it would be read.[25] Indeed, it implies a common practice that was well established, indicating that letters were composed by laymen as well as by royal or clerical persons. There are enough copies of letters surviving from the ninth and tenth centuries to show that their use was replacing oral messages, just as the written law was beginning to replace law based solely on memory. At the same time the written will was starting to replace those relying only on witnesses. The most celebrated letters of this period are those written by King Alfred to Bishop Asser, his biographer, and the two letters sent by King Cnut on a return journey from Rome.[26]

Details of royal expenditure before the Conquest have not survived, so we have no written information about the messengers employed at court. Obviously writs and charters had to be conveyed from wherever the king happened to be. One aspect of the work of the clerks and their messengers is shown in surviving legal texts from the reign of King Aethelstan (924–39). In the words of Simon Keynes, who has described them:

> One could hardly wish for a better view of the administration of justice during Aethelstan's reign, or for a better demonstration of the use of the written word: the king sent written instructions to his reeves who were responsible for administering the law in their localities; written texts of royal decrees were sent to the shire courts, where they were duly published; the officials of the shire courts sent written reports back to the king, to assure him that they were fulfilling his instructions; and local bodies drew up their own written statements of their own local practice, augmenting them with other relevant records.[27]

The evidence from monastic records indicates that the cleric who carried a letter was the one thought most suitable to convey the news and discuss it when delivered. This principle also applied to royal letters. The more important the missive the more important would be the bearer. Obviously, messengers were needed for all legal processes and carrying letters was probably a feudal obligation long before the Conquest. There is a surviving memorandum made by Oswald, Bishop of Worcester, quoted by Stenton during King Edgar's reign, in which he sets out the terms he expects his tenants to observe.[28]

He regards them as mounted retainers bound to ride on his errands and lend their horses as required. An indication that this obligation to carry messages was a common one is shown in a writ that survives from Lowther Castle. In this case, the obligation is specifically withdrawn. The writ is from Gospatric, probably between 1041 and 1064, and declares that Thorfynn has judicial and financial rights over certain lands in Cardew and Cumdivock, near Carlisle, free from the obligation of providing messengers and witnesses.[29]

Letters of this period are composed in the same format as those we read in the New Testament or from Romans such as Cicero, which is evidence of some continuity since those times. They begin with a protocol or introduction naming the person addressed and the sender, and they usually end with a date. Royal writs were sent to a variety of people: to sheriffs, who were the financial agents of the king; to *ealdormen* or earls, who had administrative and legal functions; to thegns of the shires, who were local lords; and to archbishops, bishops and abbots. Being from the king and often granting rights over land, they were kept and copied. Other letters rarely survived. The survival rate of papyrus in northern Europe was poor, so if it was used, there is little evidence remaining. Vellum and parchment could be scraped and reused as palimpsests; this would be the usual treatment for letters that were not considered to be of importance. The passage of time, the work of rodents, the reuse of skins, together with the destruction wrought in the eighth and ninth centuries by Viking invaders who had no respect for Christian monasteries or abbeys, in addition to the many fires which took place in those days, account for the destruction of almost all letters and documents written before the Conquest.

2
THE ROYAL MAIL IN THE MIDDLE AGES

After the Conquest the king's writs came from the Court that travelled with him in England and France, or from those parts of it that had become detached and settled in Westminster. The writs were usually short letters of instruction composed in the vernacular sent to royal officials or subjects, with an address written on the reverse side or on a tag attached to the foot of the document. Under the Norman kings they came from a government which moved around the country, and those who wished to see the king had to find him. Under later monarchs the Court settled in stages into a permanent location. The first section to separate was the Exchequer, which had been formed in the reign of Henry I (1100–35) as the place where the royal accounts were managed and monies received. It moved in the reign of Henry II (1154–89). A royal messenger service was needed and was controlled by an official called the Usher, who was compensated by a grant of fees and lands. Fitz Nigel's account, written in about 1179, describes the Exchequer as sitting twice a year, though by the time of King John (1199–1216) it was in continuous session and its messengers had become a charge on government.[1]

Chancery was the other major part of the household, dealing with most royal letters, grants, patents, leases and treaties. It was a distinct section of government by the time of Henry II and developed into a law court, dealing with matters of equity – matters of natural justice that lay outside the common law. Its move to Westminster, completed by the end of the thirteenth century, was not an abrupt one, for parts of the household had stayed there temporarily whenever the king had travelled to France or made a journey to the north.[2]

Like the Exchequer, Chancery needed royal messengers who were still a part of the king's messenger service. It appears also to have used a variety of other messengers, as shown in this entry from the Liberate Rolls for 1243:

> To Adam de Haunfeld, clerk of the Chancery, £7 11s 1d paid in divers items to divers couriers going on the king's errands to divers parts of England, Ireland and Scotland.[3]

Later in the century, in the reign of Edward I (1272–1307), the Issue Rolls show a gentleman at Court taking Chancery documents:

> To Lawrence, the son and heir of Roger, formerly Usher of the King's Exchequer, 12s, for taking twenty-four of the King's summonses to divers counties of England.[4]

After their moves from the Court, the Exchequer and Chancery were like minor households of a semi-collegiate kind. This was to change later when their members became laymen and lived out with their families.

The king's law courts of King's Bench and Common Pleas were the highest tribunals after the King's Council. They too moved to Westminster, as did the Privy Seal Department, so that in stages an administrative capital evolved. When Westminster Hall was rebuilt by Richard II (1377–99), the King's Bench normally used the dais and Common Pleas sat alongside the west wall, their fittings being removed for ceremonial occasions. The Royal Council had a room on the east wall and other sections of government occupied rooms in other parts of the palace. The Privy Seal was the part of government responsible for sending the royal commands to the Chancery or Exchequer, and its clerks took those letters. It also dealt with summonses to Parliament and instructions concerning the issuing of licences and pardons. Until 1234 the cost of providing for all the messengers required by these parts of government was paid for by writs of *liberate* or *computare* sent from the Chancery to the Exchequer. During the development of the Royal Wardrobe between 1234 and 1342, it took over the control and payment of all riding and foot messengers, though the Exchequer still had an overriding financial control because it passed the Wardrobe's accounts each year. After 1342 the Exchequer resumed direct financial control of messenger expenses. These arrangements for the transport of documents and for the payment of the messengers lasted until the latter part of the fourteenth century.

The king's writs which originated at the court now used the seal of the signet. A travelling law court developed, the Court of the Verge, which not only kept control over the household but over the verge, an area of 12 miles surrounding the Court wherever it might be. Because the court moved frequently it was often in conflict with local jurisdictions. The king's household, whose travels are described in Chapter 3, grew from about 100 persons under the early Normans to as many as 500 in the late fourteenth century, so the arrival of what was in those days a small town's population, with all the demands it made upon the local area for food and accommodation, was bound to cause friction.[5]

When Parliament began, it was summoned by the royal messengers to wherever the king decided to hold it. Although it became recognised as the supreme court of the land, it was in origin part of the royal household and its legislation required royal approval. Increasingly, the later medieval monarchs chose to spend more of their time near London, often staying for weeks at Windsor, Sheen, Eltham or King's Langley, so that Parliament was held mainly at Westminster.

From all these institutions there flowed a continuous stream of documents which would have been of little value unless they could be delivered to the appropriate recipients with reasonable speed. The problems of communication that could arise are illustrated in a letter from Henry I to Archbishop Anselm in 1100. On Henry's accession Anselm was on the Continent and the royal consecration took place in his absence. Henry wrote in a very dutiful yet firm manner:

> I would, indeed, have sent you some [messengers] from my personal suite, and by them I might have despatched money to you; but owing to my brother's death the whole world is in so disturbed a state all around this realm of England that it would have been utterly impossible for them to reach you in safety. I therefore advise and enjoin you to come by way of Witsand and not through Normandy and I will have my barons at Dover to meet you, and money for your journey and you will find means by God's help, to repay any debts you have incurred.[6]

The letter is witnessed by various bishops and nobles.

The procedures involved in sending royal documents can be illustrated by an example. In July 1290 a parliament met which made a financial grant to the king, known as a fifteenth of movables. The news was taken to Edward I, then staying at his hunting lodge in King's Clipstone, so a writ was issued there on 22 September to arrange for the collection of the money. The writ went via the Privy Seal Office to the Barons of the Exchequer requiring them to commission groups of men to serve as taxers and collectors in the counties. They in turn sent writs to the sheriffs dated 6 October, instructing them to send the men to take their oaths and receive their commissions between the 18th and 29th of the month. The sheriffs then sent their messengers to the collectors they selected and sent their returns to the Exchequer.[7]

Should a patent be required, an instruction would be despatched through the Privy Seal to the Chancery in Westminster where it would be issued under the Great Seal and, after careful checking and usually the payment of fees by the recipient, it would be sent by any available messenger. If necessary, the administration could move quickly. A study of the dates on fourteenth-century Remembrance Rolls, those made by an official known as the King's Remembrancer at the Exchequer, give an example of a letter from the Prior of Coventry arriving at the Exchequer in 1316 and a reply being sent back with the prior's messenger on the same day.[8]

Details of times and expenses allowed for royal messengers are given in the *Red Book of the Exchequer*, a thirteenth-century remembrance book referring to events back to about 1135, full of information about the royal household and of feudal services. There are detailed tables of the allowances payable to messengers to the various counties. Those travelling to Surrey, Sussex and Middlesex were allowed one day for travel and were paid twopence for their diet, while those travelling to the furthest destinations of Northumberland, Cumberland, Westmorland and Wales received over twenty pence for an eight-day journey. A similar table is shown for journeys from York should the Court or the Exchequer be there.[9]

Calculating the total volume of mail sent out by the Chancery or Exchequer during the Middle Ages is difficult because complete records do not survive. One estimate of the number of letters written each year in Henry I's Exchequer between 1100 and 1135 has been made by Clanchy, who conjectures that there was an average annual figure of 4,500.[10]

By examining the records of wax accounted for in the next century he shows that there is a steady progression in its use by Chancery, for it seems reasonable to relate the use of wax to the volume of letters despatched. At the beginning of 1226, in Henry III's reign, the Chancery used about 3½lb of wax each week, but by 1271, at the end of his reign, it was using almost 32lb.[11]

The royal letters and documents produced during the Middle Ages are often attractively written, sometimes even elegant in appearance if addressed to an important person. Many use small strips of parchment. Even though Roman numerals were used, the tedious arithmetic is very rarely incorrect. At the end of the Middle Ages we have an interesting account of the work involved in writing the royal writs. Thomas Hoccleve's poem *The Regement of Princes* describes the working conditions in the Privy Seal Office in the fifteenth century where he worked for thirty years without promotion. After an imprudent marriage, he left his quarters for a 'humble cot' and when he was on a pension he had difficulties in getting it paid. He describes the pay in these lines:

VI marc, yeerly, and no more than that
ffadir, to me, me thynkyth is full lyte
Consideryng, how that I am nat
In housbondrye, lerned worth a mite.

Certainly, 6 marks (or £4) was a poor salary for one who had to be able to read and write in Latin, French and English. However, there were some tips and gratuities to help, and at the end of his employment he had both a pension and a corrody, that is a place in a monastery. He compares the clerks' labours with those of an artificer:

This artificers, se I day be day
In the hottest of al hir bysynesse
Talken and syng, and make game and play,
And forthe hir labour passith with gladnesse;
But we in labour in trauaillous stillnesse;
We stowpe and stare upon the shepes skyn
And keepe muste our singe and wordes in.[12]

At that time he had worked for twenty three years in silence, the stooping over the documents having resulted in pains all over his body and the spoiling of his eyesight. Despite his self-pitying words he was evidently a thorough worker, for he left behind a Formula Book which gives examples of all the types of documents used by the Privy Seal Office.

The habit of dating writs and letters is a modern one and in early times was not considered necessary. Without a diary or newspaper the writer might not know the day, month or even the year. Reference was often given to a recent event. As late as the twelfth century royal writs and charters are not dated, though the practice of using the regnal year (dating from the current monarch's accession), starts at the reign of Richard I (1189–99).[13] Signatures were not important; it was the seal that mattered. No full royal signature is known before that of Richard II in 1386.[14]

Occasionally, extraordinary methods were used to authenticate a document and Corner mentions the use of rings, knives, crosses, and staffs. An extraordinary one was used by Edward III who bit the wax with his long tooth, and an equally bizarre one occurred when William Earl of Warenne had his hair and that of his brother cut by the Bishop of Winchester as he confirmed the grant of the church of St Pancras at Lewes.[15]

Edward III authenticated letters to Pope John XXII by adding 'Pater Sancte' (O Holy Father) in his own hand to distinguish them from others sent by officials. One such letter, part of his secret correspondence with the pope written by his secretary Richard de Bury in 1330, has the two words added by the king and is the first example of English royal handwriting.[16]

A thirteenth-century closed writ was written on parchment from the foot of which a strip was partially cut, broader at the free end. This acted as a tie to secure the document and the destination was written on the wide end. The writ was then folded at least once horizontally, according to its size, and then vertically. The tie was wound round the document and hot wax was poured over the place where the tie crossed itself, the seal being applied there. Occasionally, two cuts were made at the base, one being used for the seal, the other as a tie. A further variant came later, when a slit was cut in the document allowing the tie to be passed through it.

The sealing of letters continued throughout the Middle Ages. While most writs and letters bore one seal, important documents could have a great number. When the Hundred Rolls were stored in about 1278 they became

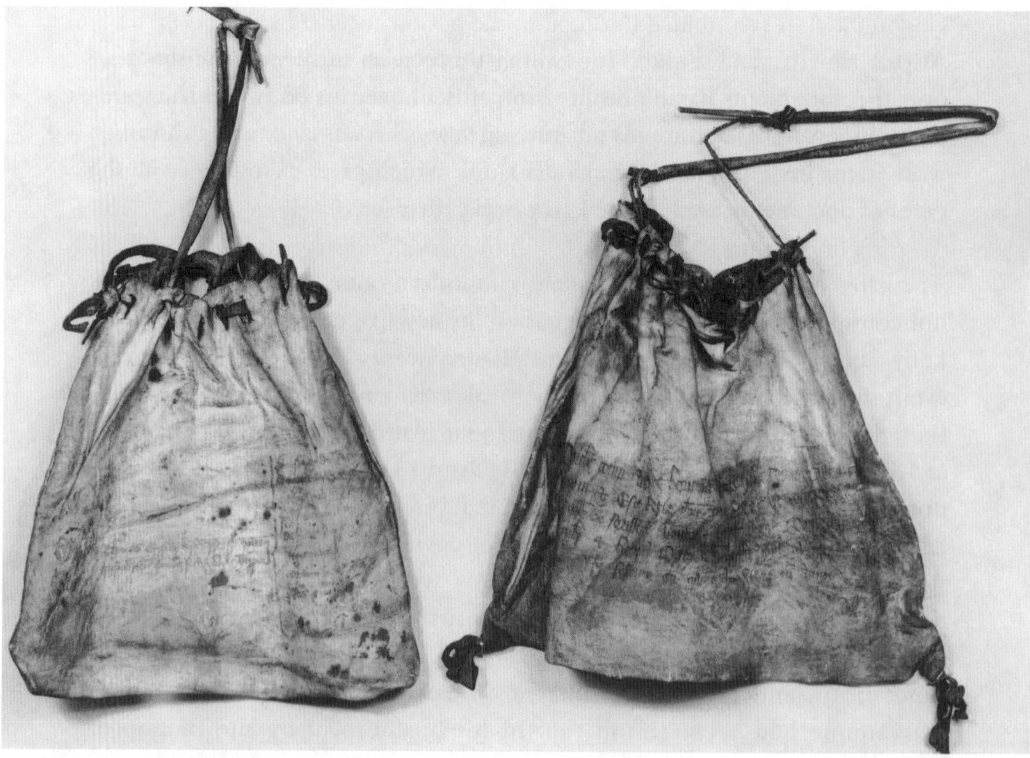

2.1 Medieval leather bags for carrying letters. (National Archives 50/59 no.^921)

known as the Ragman Rolls from the mass of attached seals.[17] In the Public Record Office there is a letter drawn up by the Parliament of Lincoln in 1301 and sent to Pope Boniface VIII bearing the seals of eighty-seven Lords.[18] Letters Patent, as their name implies, were unsealed documents.

Most royal writs and letters went to the sheriffs, who were the king's agents, and kings did all they could to ensure they were their men, supportive when disputes arose with Parliament. In royal boroughs the mayor was regarded as having the authority, if not the title, of a sheriff because he derived his authority from a royal charter. Before the Tudor period, by which time the office had usually become unwelcome, there were many struggles over the terms of appointment. There had been sheriffs before the Conquest but after 1070 their importance increased; they were among the most powerful individuals in the land, inferior only to those in the Royal Council, of which some even became members. Through them the king would hope to influence elections of members of Parliament. Even though their authority gradually declined because of the growing power of the knights of the shires, the coroners and the justices in eyre, and by Tudor times the lords lieutenant, their role as the chief officer of the king in the shires continued throughout the period covered by this book.

Each sheriff maintained a substantial office with a considerable number of clerks, usually at the county's royal castle. Few sheriffs' records survive from medieval times, but we can reconstruct much of the work undertaken from Chancery and Exchequer documents. There are also some lists of writs enrolled and rolls of pleas made at sheriffs' courts which, taken together with the royal documents, show the scope of the work undertaken. The sheriff had an exchequer where the receipts and dues of the county were received, and similar procedures were followed as at the national Exchequer.[19]

In medieval times there was an average of twenty-eight sheriffdoms covering thirty-seven counties, some men controlling two of them. This total excludes the sheriffs appointed to large towns. An entry in the Liberate Rolls of Henry III lists eight messengers 'going on the king's errand to all the sheriffs of England with the king's letters concerning the aid granted to him 12s 3d', thus showing the number of men required to take routine circulars to the sheriffs in the thirteenth century.[20]

The sheriff was president of the County Court, collector of the king's revenue unless this was dealt with by a special commission, captain of the local feudal army until Tudor times, and generally the royal representative. Consequently, he received most of the royal mail that arrived in his shire. It came by messenger to his office where it would be recorded on rolls, stored and acted upon. Often this required a great deal of clerical work, for a typical medieval ordinance or statute ended with directions that it should be sent to the sheriffs 'to be proclaimed and published in cities, boroughs, towns, fairs, markets and notable places within your bailiwick'. By the terms of a writ in 1361 concerning the Ordinance of Labourers sent to the sheriff of Lincolnshire, he was not only required to have it read in all public places but to copy it to all justices of the peace.[21] Letters that needed to be redirected were taken by the sheriff's own messengers to their destinations.

For the counties of Bedford and Buckingham there is a surviving enrolment of writs received by the sheriff from June 1333 to November 1334.[22] Although much is obviously missing, 2,000 writs are recorded and these indicate the considerable numbers of letters and other documents that must have been received and despatched each working day. The office was modelled on the royal equivalent at Westminster, its furniture containing stocks of soft white leather used to make up the pouches in which the correspondence was sent. On the pouch the clerk wrote a note of the county, the date and contents and then tied its thong. A number of these medieval pouches still survive at the National Archives. (Fig. 2.1) Hazel wood was preferred for the tallies that recorded payments. The rolls on which records were made show the names of the sheriff's messengers, the expenses they incurred and times they left. Two of them are called *nuntii*; three others were evidently official messengers; and a further five were presumably reliable men who happened to be travelling to the right destinations.

The procedure was that when the king's messenger arrived and handed over a bundle of letters and writs he was given an official receipt bearing the sheriff's seal. Each letter was enrolled, that is its details were entered on a roll of parchment, and the original was retained. Many letters required action by the sheriff's agents, known as *ministri*, his bailiffs, reeves and constables, and so copies would be made and forwarded. Through these men he collected the royal revenues, an arduous task that required keeping a staff of several clerks, under two seniors who headed his exchequer and chancery. Copies of all legislation were sent to him to be proclaimed at his court. Twice a year, at Easter and Michaelmas, he received a royal summons for him or his deputy to attend the national Exchequer and render his accounts. The Pipe Rolls, so called because they resembled pipes when bound and stored, contain records of these accounts. They usually consisted of two or more skins stitched or tied together of up to 2m in length. A year's accounts were piled on top of each other and secured by cords, the result being far easier to handle than a continuous roll such as was kept at one time at Chancery. Even so, it would have been more convenient to have kept records in books; presumably it was tradition or cost that prevented a change.[23]

The medieval shire was divided into hundreds, in some places called lathes, rapes or wapentakes, each in charge of a bailiff who was answerable to the sheriff. In the reign of Edward I (1272–1307) there were about 628 hundreds.[24]

Even in those hundreds which were not royal but private, feudal dues would normally be paid to the sheriff's bailiff. Exceptionally, there were private liberties such as some hundreds in the Palatinate of Durham, the Earldom of Chester and lands belonging to great abbeys where the lord could claim to make payments directly to the Exchequer, though sometimes their writs and letters might come through the sheriff's bailiff. The bailiff needed an office in his own house, and in order to send his letters and the writs from his court he required clerks and messengers who, like the sheriff's messengers, often took private documents and letters for a fee. The larger hundreds usually held courts at three-weekly intervals. Helen Cam describes the riding bailiffs who travelled through the shire carrying the sheriff's documents and whose main task was the conveyance of writs which would require endorsing and returning. She points out that the riding bailiffs also carried writs from tenants and so acted as occasional postmen for the rural community, and made a part of their income from the payments received.[25]

Coins often had to be taken to the royal treasury or to some castle nominated to receive them. The original Norman treasury was at Winchester, but by Henry II's time money was being stored at a number of castles spread throughout the land so that the king was never far from a supply. Obviously, the arrangements for the transport of treasure, and the nightly accommodation of its escort, were complex. Until the reign of Edward I the only coins minted in England were silver pennies, apart from the rare gold penny of Henry III, which was worth twenty of the silver ones. Smaller sums were paid by cutting pennies in half or quarters. A large stock of silver pennies was so cumbersome that a train of horses with carts might be required for their movement. As we shall see later, supervising the movement of the money was often entrusted to the royal messengers. Edward I added round halfpennies and farthings, but no larger coins appeared until the reign of Edward III (1327–77). Transporting coin was a typical feudal duty. In Herefordshire the manor of Marden had the obligation of conducting the king's treasure to London and similar obligations applied throughout the shires. The Calendar of Inquisitions shows many such entries, of which this is typical:

> 28 October 2 Edward II [i.e. 1309]. Sutton. Arable land held of the king in chief in sergeantry, with other tenants, of conveying the king's treasure from Sutton to London at his own costs rated at 6d yearly.[26]

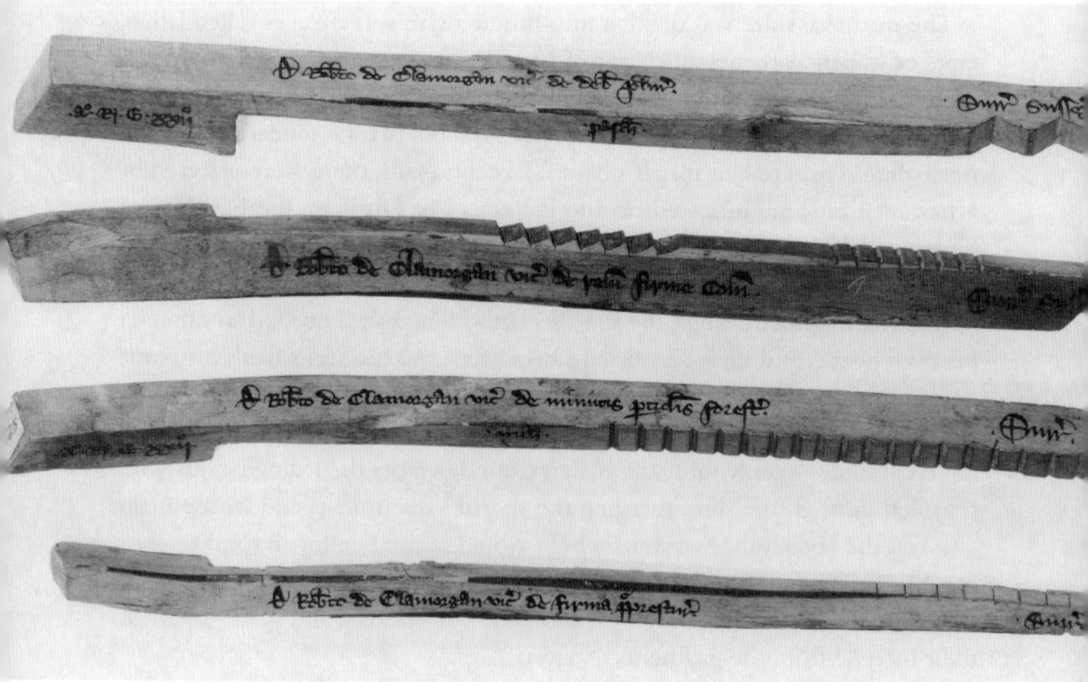

2.2 Medieval wooden tallies. The words name those who paid the money into the exchequer, the notches indicate the totals. (National Archives E402/3A Tray 2)

The use of letters of credit did not begin until later in the fourteenth century and was then very limited in use.

Wooden tallies, shafts of hardwood incised with notches to indicate a sum of money and with details of the transaction written on a smoothed edge, were commonly used as receipts, a most useful method in a partly literate age. (Fig. 2.2) A detailed description of their cutting and use is given in the *Black Book of the Exchequer*, completed by Richard Fitz Nigel, Bishop of London and Treasurer of the Exchequer, about 1179. They were split in two, the payer and the payee each retaining a half. Should it be necessary, the two parts could be produced in court to prove a payment. They have similarities to another medieval practice of making two or more copies of documents called chirographs with a word such as *cirographum* inscribed in a gap between the two. The document was then cut into two through the word and the two parties concerned each kept one of them. This explains the use of the word 'indenture', referring to the wavy edge of the cut. Enormous numbers of tallies were later stored in the basements of the Houses of Parliament and the deliberate burning of some of the later ones in 1834 led inadvertently to the destruction of the buildings. The same principle of similar parts was often applied to seals: the 1285 Statute of Merchants recommended that royal seals used in courts should be made of two interlocking sections so that two matching documents could be produced in cases of dispute. This applied in the customs service, and as late as 1600 the new Charter of Newcastle upon Tyne required a seal of two pieces to be used in court for sealing recognizances of debt – one part for the mayor and one for the clerk.[27]

Each royal messenger had a round for routine business. He covered about four counties with regular places to stop overnight. Both mounted and unmounted messengers were in use from at least the beginning of Henry III's reign (1216–72). It was usual for them to arrive at least once a month, to deliver documents and take back the answers to those which had been delivered previously.

Apart from the routine visits, there were other occasions requiring deliveries. Some royal documents required a large number of copies for the messengers to carry. One such from Richard I in 1190 concerning wrecks is headed:

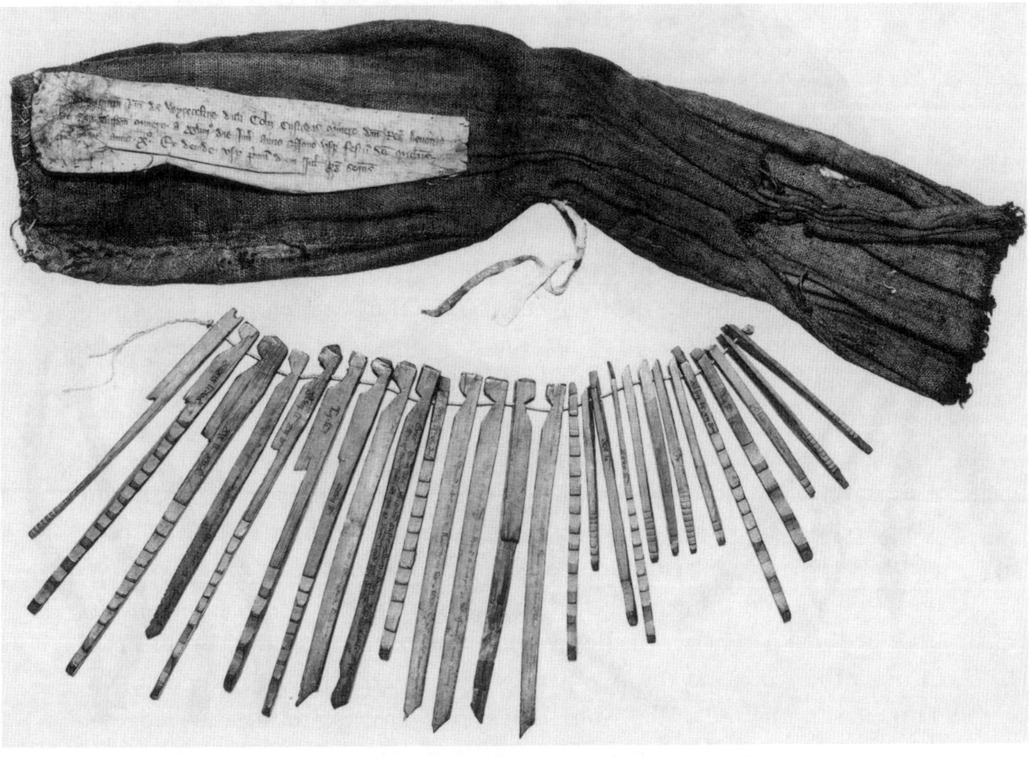

2.3 Set of tallies with storage bag. (National Archives E101/261/21 (3))

2.4 Royal sealed documents. (National Archives. King's Orders)

> Richard by the grace of God, King of England, Duke of Normandy, of Guienne, and Anjou, to his archbishops, bishops, abbots, counts, barons, justiciaries, sheriffs, and all bailiffs and faithful subjects to whom this present letter may come: Greeting.[28]

Special occasions also involved many similar letters. When Edward V was preparing for his coronation in 1483, fifty similar letters went out requiring each recipient 'to prepare and furnish yourself for the noble Order of Knighthood', an instruction that would no doubt be received with mixed emotions for the fees were considerable.[29]

Letters to France, when English kings owned extensive lands there, went mainly to the king's Gascon officials; the Seneschal of Gascony and the Constable of Bordeaux acted much like English sheriffs. The Captain of the town of Calais acted in a similar way. They received the letters at their offices and sent them on by their messengers, the expenses being accounted for to the Exchequer. The series of Gascon Rolls gives many references to messengers, their names, destinations and expenses. Usually the messenger on a long journey would stay for a few days until answers had been written on the matters referred to in his letters and any oral messages had been entrusted to him. When an envoy or ambassador was travelling abroad he took one or more royal messengers to bring back despatches and take letters to royal agents. The diplomatic mission to Italy in 1286 involved a great number of messengers who were required to visit the kings of France, Aragon and Sicily, as well as the pope. In the previous year envoys were sent to Paris on two occasions to enquire into rumours concerning the health of King Philip III of France.[30]

An envoy to Aquitaine in 1327 sent in a claim for over £19 spent on twenty-one private messengers, employed while he was on the Continent. At that time there were no English ambassadors resident abroad and it was not until the early sixteenth century that some were appointed.

A study of fourteenth-century envoys records ninety-five accounts enrolled between 1327 and 1336.[31] During this period, the Wardrobe authorised payments of £547 3s 9d for their *nuntii* and other messengers plus a further £156 2s 4d for *nuntii* including payment for cloth. About half of their expenses was advanced before their departure. As envoys and ambassadors travelled more slowly than the messengers, they would expect to be met on their return at Dover enabling letters to be brought swiftly to the court.

There was correspondence with the Channel Islands, where St Peter Port in Guernsey attracted much foreign and English shipping. Their security was a continuing problem as they were only a day's sail from France in good weather. The accounts of the Great Custom show that 487 foreign ships called there between Michaelmas 1329 and August 1330, raising large sums for the customs. Le Patourel's *The Medieval Administration of the Channel Islands 1199–1399* lists correspondence between the English Court and the wardens and others on the islands, which would usually pass through Southampton or Poole.

Other royal households existed apart from that of the king, for the queen and princes each maintained a considerable staff. They provided training grounds for future royal messengers. An enrolment of 791 letters of Edward, Prince of Wales, son of Edward I, for the year 1304–05 has survived. It shows that he employed a staff of 100–200 persons, including a secretariat of a dozen clerks. His *valetti* or yeomen included many young men of good family who often carried his letters depending upon the importance of those who would receive them. Letters went to the pope, the papal nuncio, ecclesiastics, sheriffs, bankers and merchants.[32]

Royal marriages involved continuous correspondence. Eleanor of Castile, the wife of Edward I, had letter carriers travelling to and from Spain. Her accounts show that she had two or three *nuntii* and five lower-ranking *cursores*. Isabella, the wife of Edward II, wrote regularly to her family in France. She had two mounted and eleven unmounted messengers.[33] For Queen Philippa, the wife of Edward III, there are some letters extant which date from 1328 to 1360.

Royal messengers might travel long distances. The Liberate Rolls of Henry III are a source of much information on payments to messengers. For 9 March 1227 there is an entry detailing sixty-six journeys made by twenty-two different messengers and four envoys, while another reference lists fourteen different messengers by name. The people and places they visited are also named and include sheriffs, archbishops, bishops, abbots, earls, constables and bailiffs, together with various ports. Costs for journeys varied from 2d to 3s 6d. The Rolls list many messengers who arrived at the Court from abroad, including those from the emperor, the kings and queens of France, the kings of Norway, Castile and Aragon, and from many counts and European nobles. It was customary to reward them well. An entry dated 7 October 1241 authorises payment of 100s (£5) to Hubert, messenger of the king of Almain, Frederick II. The year is that of the height of the Mongol invasion of Europe and their defeat of the German army, so the news was doubtless fascinating. One letter from Edward I dated September 1290 quoted in the Close Rolls is addressed to Argon, king of the Tartars. Argon had been converted to Christianity and sent envoys who, after visiting the pope, travelled on to England. They promised Edward gifts of horses and equipment when he reached the Holy Land on his projected crusade. Edward's letter was taken by Sir Geoffrey de Langley to Tabriz with a gift of falcons and jewels.[34]

Considerable collections of letters to foreign countries survive; one from Richard II (1377–99) consists of 252 letters.[35] In the early fifteenth century there is a series of letters from Henry IV sent to such potentates as the emperor of Abyssinia, the doge of Venice and the kings of Cyprus and Armenia. Some letters to Constantinople were taken by the archbishop of the East, an Englishman, John Greenlaw, who had been appointed archbishop of Sultania in Armenia by Pope Boniface.[36]

Chancery records contain copies of the writs sent out to summon medieval parliaments together with the returns of those nominated to attend. The former are typically narrow strips of parchment about 1½ inches in depth and the replies are in a squarer format.[37] A messenger could carry the writs for a number of counties in a small wallet or pouch. Even town charters could be very small documents.

Royal letters survive in considerable numbers from the time of King John in the early thirteenth century. Nearly 700 letters from the reign of Henry III have been printed.[38] Others have been edited in the Rolls Series and in the collections of royal letters by Ellis, Steele and Crawford, with others in copy form in the London Letter Books. One such was written on 22 October 1356 at Bordeaux by Edward, Prince of Wales, the Black Prince, describing in detail the progress and strategy of his army in France and ending with the victory at Poitiers:

> Whereupon battle was joined on the eve of the day before St Matthew [21 September] and, God be praised for it, the enemy was discomfited, and the King was taken, and his son, and a great number of other people were both taken and slain as our very dear Bachelor Messire Neele Loereng, our Chamberlain, the bearer hereof, who has very full knowledge thereon, will know how more fully to inform you and show you.[39]

Such accounts are part of a new type of letter, the newsletter, stimulated by the Hundred Years' War. Several such were written by the royal clerk, Michael de Northburgh, describing campaigns in Brittany, and others were dictated by Henry V.[40]

A further, extensive, group of royal letters was addressed to the pope concerning such topics as ecclesiastical appointments, monastic houses and the various payments due to him. Many of these can be found in the *Calendar of Entries in the Papal Registers relating to Great Britain and Ireland Vols 1-4*. Correspondence with Rome and Avignon was so extensive that several bishops and abbots had messengers who were familiar with the routes and the English clergy resident there. In 1302 the king approved the drafts of various letters to the pope. They were to be sent to one of the messengers of the bishop of Chester who was an envoy to the Court at Rome.[41] Mention of others is made in the Paston letters, which are described in Chapter 6.

The Roll of Expenses of King Edward I at Rhuddlan Castle gives a picture of mail from the royal household when it was in Wales.[42] There is an entry 'To William the messenger, carrying letters of the King to London, which were to be sent to the Court of Rome, for his expenses. 1s.' Another reads, 'To a boy bringing letters to Aberconway. 3d.' Edward II's Wardrobe Accounts show some much larger payments, such as 'To Sir John de Weston-Subedge, knight, sent by the King and Council under the great seal to divers parts of the Kingdom. £48 10s.' Messengers who arrived from the nobility received a gift and were accommodated until a reply was ready for them to take back: 'Messengers from the Lord Archbishop of Canterbury, the Earl of Pembroke, of Sir Bartholomew de Badlesmere with letters and returning with letters. £1 each.' Messengers from lesser persons received smaller sums: 'Adam Shirlock, coming to the King with letters from Sir Gilbert De Midelton, Knight, and returning to the same with letters from the King. 6s 8d.'[43]

Those who brought important news could expect to be well rewarded. The Wardrobe accounts include 'News of the surrender of the castle of Knaresborough and returning with letters. £2.' Personal information was the most welcome: 'To Sir Eubolo de Montibus first bringing the news to the King of the happy delivery of the Queen of her son John at Eltham £100.' The more important the bringer of a letter, the greater would be his gift. When Edward received news of the election of the pope from Lawrence of Hibernia, messenger of the Bardi of Florence, bringing letters from them, he was given £1 in payment, but when the Pope's own envoy arrived later with the same information he was given £100. These accounts list the routine messenger journeys in a separate section showing dates and names with destinations. For example, the eleventh year shows the number of journeys to be 387. The average annual cost is £86, excluding those sent abroad.[44]

Royal officials could hire messengers and later ask for payment, for we see such entries in the Liberate Rolls as:

> 18 May 1239 to the Earl of Lincoln, Constable of Chester, 18s 7½d expended by the king's order on messengers hired to go on his messages for his affairs in Cheshire.[45]

This was one of many messenger costs incurred by him.

As we have seen, a great variety of people carried the letters of medieval kings and their sheriffs. In the earlier period some were carried as part of the feudal system of messenger sergeantry. Letter carrying was an obligation frequently placed upon those holding a virgate of land, that is about 30 acres, or more. Land held in this way carried specific obligations to the feudal lord. It was hereditary and, in theory, was indivisible. Under it many tenants could be required to carry letters. This is a typical entry taken from the Calendar of Inquisitions:

> 23 October 4 Edward II [1311]. Mardfield South. A capital messuage and three virgates containing 51a of land, held of the king in chief by sergeantry of carrying, together with his partners, at their own costs, the king's writs for forty days in England on the king's summons, which sergeantry is rated at 15s yearly at the king's Exchequer by the hands of the sheriff of Leicester.[46]

Such feudal obligations could be for as little as one day a year. Another entry from an Inquisition reads:

> 15 October 1266 for Ralph Brian who held half a manor by service of going one day's journey at the summons of the king or his bailiffs with arms if needful [...] within the county only at his own cost and no more unless at the king's cost.[47]

The system was gradually commuted to cash payments and by 1300 had fallen into disuse. Cam records that in the late thirteenth century Bassetlaw in Nottinghamshire replaced its six sergeantry messengers with three riding bedels, two grooms and three bedels on foot. At this time such surviving services merely supplemented the royal messenger service.[48]

As we have already seen, the king's agents in the counties and the hundreds had also developed their own messenger services. The king's messengers and his agents could use the royal right of purveyance to demand the use of a horse or a cart if they needed one. This right was, inevitably, unpopular but it remained until Stuart times. In November 1392 the justices of the King's Bench were in York. It was their practice to take the rolls of the court with them when travelling and they instructed their keeper to convey them to Nottingham. The weather was atrocious and the carts bearing the documents stuck in the mud at Norton near Welbeck. Two horses were commandeered in the name of the king which provoked an angry response from the villagers, who came armed with swords, sticks and bows. Arrows were shot through the rolls and the keeper with his men were chased through the night to Warsop. It is surprising that when the wrongdoers were brought before the justices in the following February they were granted a pardon.[49]

The royal messengers, the *nuntii*, were supplemented by a class of lesser messengers called *coquini* or *cokini*, who travelled on foot. During the thirteenth century they became a permanent force of lower-ranking employees. In the reign of Edward II their name changed to *cursores*. Their status improved and the *nuntii* were often recruited from their ranks. It is possible to estimate from records the numbers of *nuntii* and *cursores*; this has been done by Mary Hill. The *nuntii* numbered fifteen or sixteen in the reign of King John (1199–1216) and twelve at the end of Edward II's reign (1327). The *cursores*, who are first listed as numbering nineteen in 1264, rose to a maximum of forty-one at one point in Edward I's reign and totalled thirty-seven by the death of Edward II. Under Edward III the *nuntii* declined to seven and the *cursores* to fourteen. Times of war or crisis called for more messengers, and the state of the royal finances also affected their numbers.[50]

Most royal mail was taken to the sheriffs for their messengers to deliver, but use was made of messengers from bishops, nobles and mayors who had brought letters and waited until replies were ready. As we shall see later, letters to sheriffs and mayors and others were sent for onward transmission.

The Lord Treasurer's Issue Roll of 1370 shows a great variety of messengers being employed. William Chamberleyn, valet of the Treasurer's household, was paid 3s 4d for carrying letters to the Bishop of Ely. Frank de Hale, knight from the retinue of the Duke of Lancaster, was paid £73 6s 8d for employing messengers 'to watch the desires and actions of the French enemies'. Valets and others from Westminster received £8 1s. A royal sergeant at arms, John Basynges, was paid £2 for taking letters to Calais, and a royal valet, Simon Holbrok, travelling to the North of England with letters that included requests to 'the Abbots of St Albans and the Blessed Mary of York to make processions and prayers for the peace and estate of the Kingdom of England', had 16s 8d.[51] It must have been convenient for many minor court employees to carry letters if it enabled them to be paid for a visit to their own locality.

One indication of the trust given to the *nuntii* is shown in the amounts of money they might carry along with the mail. In 1274 the papal nuncio authorised one of them to collect all the money arising from the collection of the tenth of the revenues of the Bishopric of Lincoln, which was deposited at Oxford, a result of the ruling of the Council of Lyons to collect money for a crusade: the king guaranteed the transfer. Large sums were needed during wars in France and Scotland, so messengers often supervised the movement of considerable amounts. As an illustration, in 1307 Robert Manfield, a messenger, was put in charge of £4,000 in coinage (i.e. 960,000 silver pennies) to be taken from London to Carlisle. Four carts were needed, each pulled by five horses. Robert hired twelve men at arms at 1s a day and sixteen archers at 3d a day who took eleven days on their journey. £1,330 6s 8d was then loaded on pack horses to be taken to the army in Scotland and the rest was placed in the royal treasury. The total costs involved came to £28 19 1d. Even short journeys required escorts; in 1377 three messengers received extra expenses of 8d 'for porterage of gold and silver from the Treasury to the Exchequer of Receipt'.[52]

An interesting use of two royal messengers is recorded during the reign of Edward I. He sent them with accounts of his Scottish campaigns to all abbots, priors, and men of religion, his purpose being that they should record his deeds in their chronicles. The messengers received 7s for their tours.[53] A macabre but not uncommon task was the carriage of the head and quarters of those executed for treason, so that they could be displayed in public places.

Another messenger duty was to escort foreign ambassadors. These were often received with suspicion and it was felt necessary to see what letters they brought and received. Foreign letter carriers are occasionally mentioned in medieval records. Richard II issued a safe conduct in 1396 allowing a messenger from the Duc de Berri with his three attendants and their belongings to travel without hindrance to Scotland. They were on a mission to obtain greyhounds for their master.[54]

Such men would be escorted and exactly the same treatment was given to English royal messengers abroad, unless they succeeded in passing themselves off as merchants or pilgrims, but that was a risky venture. The messengers could often be required to make confidential enquiries when calling with letters. During 1370 William Fox, a royal messenger, was sent with letters to Winchelsea and asked to check the accuracy of the returns from the mayor and bailiffs relating to the ships in the port. Another messenger, John Eliot, was sent to Ireland in 1376 with letters summoning barons to the council, but his real purpose was to bring back a report on the state of the country.[55] Cases are also recorded of messengers being required to escort prisoners while travelling on their rounds, a duty which, like carrying letters, had its origins in messenger sergeantry.

The Wardrobe accounts for 1286 show the messengers in yet another role. There had been many outrages committed in the royal forests and a force of knights, sergeants and squires was assembled in Oxfordshire, supported by archers and mounted foresters. In midsummer they entered the forests of Bernwood and Weybridge, where they made arrests. Their bill included fetters for sixty malefactors with escorts to Newgate and other prisons. The expenses of the messengers who were intermediaries between all involved are shown in the accounts.[56]

Another group of men who might assist in carrying royal messages were the porters who accompanied the king's travelling justices. During the fourteenth century there was a great extension of the work of the King's Bench and Common Pleas, when the justices travelled into the counties, usually three times a year. The first duty of the porters was the transport of the copies of the court's rolls and the statutes in addition to which they could be required to perform other tasks. Fees for court officials are laid down in section 44 of the 1285 Statute of Westminster. The judges were preceded by the porters and the vergers, carrying ceremonial wands, administering the oaths and proclaiming the verge, an area of 12 miles of peace around the court. They were paid 10d for each assize with extra payments for additional duties. Clerks received 1d for writing a writ and the cirographers 4s for a chirograph. [57] The justice could use the messengers employed by the sheriff but his own staff would help with the delivery of additional writs, escorting prisoners and proclaiming the peace.

This description of the work of the royal *nuntii* shows that they were primarily bearers of letters and documents, but were able to carry out a range of other carefully specified duties entrusted to them. They were never ambassadors or diplomatic envoys and were not able to commit their master to anything to which he had not previously consented. Before ambassadors were appointed abroad in the sixteenth century, distinguished men could be sent as envoys to foreign courts. They might be known as *procuratores*, or in English proctors – men who were given the authority to negotiate on behalf of their master. An example of the work of *procuratores* occurred in 1286 at Westminster when a dispute between Flemish and English merchants was settled by proctors who had letters empowering them to act on behalf of their masters.[58] Senior papal representatives in this country were often described as *nuntii et procuratores*.

During the fourteenth century another category of men, the heralds and pursuivants, began to take royal letters. The first reference to heralds is in the Wardrobe Accounts for 1290, where the cost of robes is given for two Kings of Heralds, the most senior rank.[59]

In his chronicles Jean de Froissart describes the arrival of the Herald Carlisle from Gascony at the Court of Edward III on 13 April 1338. He brought letters from Spain and also from the lords of Gascony. On being welcomed by the king he replied:

> My lord, read or cause to be read, if it please you, these letters, and then I will tell you more, for there is news in them that touches you closely.

So, the chronicler tells us, began the Hundred Years' War.

Heralds had traditionally been regulators of tournaments, scrutinising the arms of competitors, but their functions grew to include the regulation of ceremonies, the granting of coats of arms, carrying letters and even acting as ambassadors. There were six fourteenth-century heralds and seven pursuivants. By the end of the century they were the regular carriers of important letters abroad. William Bruges, created the first Garter King of Arms in 1415 and answerable directly to the Earl Marshal, travelled on missions abroad almost every year until his death in 1450. He went to France, Normandy, Brittany, Flanders, Hainault, Scotland, Spain, Portugal and Italy. His status was such that in effect he acted as an English ambassador as there were no permanent appointments abroad. He entertained the Emperor Sigismund in his own house in Kentish Town and had lodgings at Windsor Castle. Other heralds were much used by Henry V, who sent his Aquitaine King of Arms to take a letter to the Emperor at Constance and Gloucester Herald with letters to the Kings of Castile, Portugal, Aragon and Navarre. The heralds were granted their own seal in 1420, royal in appearance, and received a Charter from Richard III in 1483.

The pursuivants were trainee heralds, performing duties of lesser importance. They often carried important letters to nobles. The status of both these royal servants was higher than that of the Chamber, Exchequer and Chancery messengers, and it was possible for a man to rise through the ranks. Thomas Hawley was a Chamber messenger who was appointed Pursuivant Rouge Croix in 1509 and eventually became Carlisle Herald.

Our survey of royal messengers shows that soon after the Conquest a royal postal service was established throughout the country. Messengers left the Court and Westminster with mail for the sheriffs. The sheriffs in turn developed a separate royal messenger service which took the post on to local destinations and to their bailiffs who employed men for deliveries within the hundreds. Direct deliveries were made to those members of the royal family and the Council not at Court, whose own messengers were available for local deliveries of the royal mail.

As we will see later, the towns were brought into the network and could be instructed to use their messengers to carry royal mail when required to do so. The service steadily expanded as the volume of mail grew but it did not work to a precise timetable except for the regular summons of sheriffs and customs officers to the Exchequer. So many men were employed in deliveries that it must have been unusual if a late thirteenth-century sheriff did not receive a royal messenger each week.

The great nobles maintained households very similar to those of the king, and their servants carried letters to and from the Court. In the later period the greatest of the nobles employed heralds and pursuivants to take their most important mail. Registers of the Black Prince and John of Gaunt contain much official correspondence, but otherwise little survives from medieval magnates.[60]

The rolls of the Earl of Lancaster in 1319 and 1320 are presented under fourteen headings of which four concern messengers, the purchase of horses and journeys on business. The accounts of Edward Mortimer, Earl of March, in 1413 and 1414 show entries for messengers' expenses: for example 28s 6d for delivery of a box, 13s 4d for a messenger taking a breve (a writ) to Parliament, and 6s 8d for a letter sent *sigillo privati*, that is under the private seal.[61]

The entries show that a great variety of men took letters and that rewards for taking them varied according to their status. Each great household had additionally a few permanent messengers for regular deliveries. The Black Book of the Household of Edward IV estimates that a duke would have 240 servants, a marquis 200, an earl 140 and a baron 40.[62]

In 1421 the Countess of Warwick travelled with fifty-seven horses. When the Duke of Bedford arrived that year near to Warwick he brought his chancellor, treasurer, twenty-four esquires and forty-two other persons. In the fifteenth century most nobles became less peripatetic, allowing regular services to develop around their main houses, a change discussed in Chapter 7.

On the road

Routine journeys by mounted messengers were normally taken at a leisurely pace. The horse had to be cared for and the rider could travel no quicker than the page or groom who usually accompanied him. His speed would be 3 or 4 miles an hour, with 25 or possibly 30 miles in a day. The *cursor* on foot could travel faster than the *nuntius* on horseback providing the latter kept to the one horse, but the *cursor* only carried a very limited amount of mail. For urgent messages a *nuntius* could ride post, that is he could commandeer horses on behalf of the king, in which case he would usually ride alone. The royal right of purveyance enabled him to take over horses and so, in effect, the king could send rapid messages throughout the kingdom at a traditional price of a penny a mile, far cheaper than setting up a relay of horses and riders, known as a standing post.

Probably from before the Conquest there had been inns along the Dover road with horses available for hire. There was a continuous demand for horses and carts by royal and private travellers, a demand that was increased after Thomas a Becket was canonised in 1173 and pilgrims began to flock to his tomb in Canterbury. Messengers wishing to hire horses were well served by innkeepers whose horses took the traveller from one stage to the next, each horse being prominently branded to minimise the risk of theft. A patent issued in 1396 is evidence that before then there had been organised stages along the road, because the hackneymen complained to the king that riders had seized their horses, often paying them nothing in return. The royal patent decreed:

> there shall be taken for the hire of a hakenei from Suthwerk to Roucester 12d, from Roucester to Canterbury 12d, and from Canterbury to Dover 6d, and from town to town according to the rate of 12d and the number of miles; that the petitioners be in nonwise compelled to let their horses for hire unless paid promptly; and that for the better security of the horses a branding iron be kept in each of those towns by an approved person for branding, without payment, horses on hire.[63]

The journey of Jack Faukes from Westminster to Avignon is the most detailed account of a royal messenger's journey that we have from the fourteenth century.[64] In 1343 he went with a *cursor*, Robin of Arden, to the Papal Court taking letters collected from the Wardrobe which it had received from Chancery. His advance of £10 proved inadequate as the final cost was £13 14s 10d. The two men went from Westminster to London by boat and on by stages to Dover, the cost of the three stages being 8d, 10d and 1s, from which we can calculate that riding post would at least double a messenger's costs. While he was abroad he was at times escorted by a French sergeant whom he had to pay for the privilege. His detailed accounts, including costs for meals and drinks, provide an important insight into life in those days. Another use of messengers by Henry, Earl of Derby, who travelled to Russia and separately to Jerusalem in the years 1390–1393 is also well documented. He sent messengers ahead at all stages to arrange for safe conduct and accommodation.[65]

As with journeys to Dover and York, should post horses not be easily available, the king would order that they should be provided. Edward I wrote to the justice at Chester to demand that 'speedy and safe passage' be provided for his messenger, William Clerk, on his way to Ireland, 'at the courier's own cost'. Accounts as early as 1297 refer to messengers travelling at night and such journeys must have involved changing horses. There are records of a number of very fast journeys in the fifteenth century, including one of 440 miles in 1437 from Perth to London bringing news of the death of James I of Scotland in seven days, and one in 1450 from Dover to Leicester reporting the murder of William, Duke of Suffolk, in four days.[66] It is obvious that those messengers changed horses on the way.

The messenger, like the modern court official, could have difficulty in delivering his letter. Those who expected a summons or demand for payment might not be found or might even arrange for the messenger to be waylaid. In Henry III's reign a writ to John Balliol describes the seizure of the King's mail in Sherwood.[67] Nevertheless, such cases were rare and those who bore the royal arms were normally safe from any attack.

There were increasing problems for a royal messenger who paid only a penny a mile for the hire of a horse on the Dover road. On 18 June 1372 instructions were sent by Edward III to the bailiffs at Rochester and Canterbury:

> To the bailiffs of the city of Canterbury. Strict order, as they would have themselves harmless, to cause any of the king's messengers, of whose coming to the king and council with letters or otherwise with reports from over the sea they shall have knowledge hereafter, upon warning received to have with all speed for reasonable payment hackneys to ride from the city to the city of Rochester, so that the king's business be not hindered by their default.[68]

It would seem that the bailiffs took no decisive action, as similar instructions were sent to Dover, Canterbury, Rochester and Southwark on 28 May 1373.

In the later Middle Ages there were so many cases of people impersonating royal messengers and carrying forged warrants that a Statute was enacted under Richard II to deal with the nuisance:

> Foreasmuch as the Commons have made complaint, that many great Mischiefs, Extortions and Oppressions have been done by divers people of evil Condition, which of their own authority take and cause to be taken royally Horses and other things, and Beasts out of the Wains, Carts and Houses, saying that they be to ride on hasty Messages and Business, where of truth they be in no wise privy to any Business or Message, but only in Deceit and Subtilty to any Colour and Device to take Horses and the said Horses too hastily to ride and evil intreat, having no manner of Conscience or Compassion in this behalf, so that the said Horses become all spoiled and foundered, paying no manner of thing nor penny for the same... Our Lord the King willing, for the Quietness and Ease of his people, to provide remedy thereof, will and hath ordained that none shall from henceforth take any such Horse or Beast in such manner against the Consent of them to whom they may be; and if any that do, and have no sufficient Warrant nor Authority of the King, he shall be taken and imprisoned till he hath made due Agreement to the Party.[69]

One practical difficulty that faced the constable was in locating horses for messengers as in times of crisis owners of horses would have them removed.

The Calendar of Close Rolls has an entry relating to the case of Henry Draper who had evaded providing horses. The entry reads:

> To the mayor of Norhampton [sic]. Order to Cause Henry Draper of N. to be taken and kept in custody in prison until further order; as the king is informed that certain messengers coming through the town with news which concerned him, and lacking horses, on the king's behalf the mayor ordered the said Henry, who had horses for hire, to cause them to have horses for their money, and he took no heed to obey, but withdrew himself and his horses, delaying the king's business in contempt of the king.[70]

Such was liable to be the case as long as the royal price remained at one penny.

Conflicts arose from the practice of selling commissions under royal patents to enable persons other than royal representatives to seize horses. That King Henry VI had to give way is shown in an Act of 1447:

> Whereas divers Hostlers, Brewers and other Victuallers, keeping Hostelries and other Houses of retailing of Victuals in divers places in this Realm, have purchased the King's Letters Patents some of them for term of life, and some of them to others jointly for term of their lives, to take Horses and Carts for the carriage of the King and Queen, more for their own private and singular lucre, than for any faithful service to the King and Queen ...All such Patents shall be void and of none effect; and if any such Grant shall be made to any such person or persons from henceforth, then all such Patents granted shall be null and void.[71]

The legislation reveals the conflict between king and Parliament, as it declares such patents illegal though still allowing the right of purveyance by royal representatives.

Throughout this period the court was often ignorant of important events taking place elsewhere in the country and in France, despite sending for news, and this was specially significant during the French wars and the Wars of the Roses. During Buckingham's rebellion in October 1483 Edward Plumpton wrote: 'Messengers come daily from the King's grace and the duke...'. Information received was not necessarily correct, for Edward IV's death was commemorated by a requiem two days before he died in April 1483. To confirm the accuracy of their information messengers often carried tokens, the news of the Battle of Barnet being conveyed to the Queen together with one of the king's gauntlets.[72] In 1513 Queen Catherine sent a piece of the king of Scotland's coat to Henry VIII after the victory at Flodden Field.[73]

An example of using a standing post in time of war is referred to in 1484 in the last *Continuation of the Chronicle of The Abbey of Croyland*:

> He [Richard III] observed the new method, introduced by King Edward [IV] at the time of the last war with Scotland, of allocating one mounted courier to every twenty miles; riding with the utmost skill and not crossing their bounds, these men carried messages two hundred miles within two days without fail by letters passed from hand to hand.[74]

By the end of the Middle Ages there were four Court messengers. A.L. Myres has edited the Black Book of the Household of Edward IV, written about 1472, and this confirms this number of *nuntii* at Court 'obeying the commandments of the Chamberlain for the messages concerning the King or secretary or usher of the chamber', but he states that the total number of all the messengers was twelve, which would include those royal messengers at the Chancery and the Exchequer.[75]

They were paid wages, each man having 3d a day, or 6d a day when sent out, with a mark (13s 4d) annually for clothes, plus 3s 4d (a quarter of a mark) for shoes. Earlier, in 1376, the wage had been 4½d a day, as shown in an extract from the Patent Rolls for that year:

> Oct 4 Westminster. Grant to John Nousley, the King's messenger, of 4½d a day at the Exchequer for his wages as long as he be in the office of a messenger not labouring at the king's wages among the King's messengers. The like to John Cok, John Elyot, William Hardyng.[76]

This could be taken to indicate the separation of four Exchequer messengers from those at Court. This was definitely the case during the reign of Richard II (1377–99), as is made clear in the Patent Rolls of 1410 where there is an entry:

> July 21. Grant for life to the king's servant John Sewale that he be one of the four messengers of the Exchequer in the place of Thomas Monk, deceased, receiving 4½d a daily at the Exchequer as the said Thomas had by grant of Richard II and the King's confirmation.[77]

It is likely that the Chancery messengers had also separated from those from those at court at this time.

The *nuntii* were treated with respect; an indication of this is shown in the *Book of Nurture*, written in 1452 by John Russell, the usher and marshal of Duke Humphrey of Gloucester:

> If the King send a messenger receive him as one degree higher than his rank.
> The King's groom may dine with a Knight or Marshall.[78]

The instruction is that the king's representative is always an important person, to be regarded as of higher rank than the corresponding servants of other men.

The heralds and pursuivants were more generously rewarded than the messengers, having a higher status. In addition to a wage they had a considerable range of perquisites related to their ceremonial functions. In 1376 Norroy Herald received 7½d a day. In the next century a King of Arms typically had an annuity of £40. They could also expect gifts such as those provided in a Privy Seal warrant of 1460 which gives payment to heralds of sums of £10 for Christmas and New Year, of £5 or 10 marks at Twelfth Tide and Easter, and 10 marks on St George's Day, Whitsuntide and Allhallows. The kings of the heralds received double payments and the pursuivants half that of a herald. They could also expect considerable rewards from the recipients of royal letters and messages.[79]

Conditions of service

Members of the king's household had the right to be fed but the messengers, frequently absent on journeys, had to be treated differently from their colleagues. When Prince Edward's courier arrived at Court in July 1303 he received 2d a day because he was staying away from his lord. Though the more important members of the household had a right to be lodged each night, the messengers attending the Court usually had to find their own accommodation. The provision of a horse was their responsibility; for a replacement they depended upon the king's generosity. An example of such a gift occurs in the Liberate Rolls of Henry III, 'To Geoffrey Gacelin, who is going as the king's messenger, 20 marks to buy himself a palfrey of the king's gift.'[80]

The messenger could expect the royal grooms to attend to his horse and one of them might travel with him if he left on an urgent or foreign journey. A senior messenger expected to have a page, a younger man who would hope for promotion after serving his apprenticeship.

On entering royal service the messenger took an oath of loyalty. Examples survive in the *Red Book* and the *Black Book of the Exchequer.* The former reads:

> You shall swear that you shall well and truly behave yourself in the Office or Place of a messenger of this Court of Exchequer and that you shall faithful-

> ly and truly deliver all such Processes, Summons of the Pipe and Green Wax [the Exchequer used green wax] and of other Writs and warrants that shall be delivered unto you by the said Court and do all other duties whatsoever that appertaineth to a Messenger of the Exchequer so long as you shall continue in the same place. So help you God.[81]

The other oath also refers to keeping 'the secrets of the king and the Court'. There do not seem to be any surviving oaths for Chancery messengers.

Wages were distinct from the allowances paid while travelling. On a given day the messenger would receive one or the other. During the reign of Edward I wages were as low as ½d a day but they increased to 3d in 1303–04 and later, as we have seen, to 4½d.[82]

A special clerk dealt with payments until, under Edward II, messengers were given warrants to be presented at the Exchequer. Messengers could now hope for a more reliable source of payment, but if they were with the Court they had the problem of getting to the Exchequer in London. They might ask a Chamber official to give cash in exchange for a warrant, though this depended on that person charging a commission and also having ready money. The system of issuing such warrants continued throughout the period covered by this book. On his return he would submit a claim for any additional expenses.

From the reign of King John, or perhaps even earlier, the royal *nuntii* received clothing. Instructions were given by Chancery to one of the sheriffs to provide a tunic and supertunic of either blue or russet colour. When the Wardrobe took over responsibility for the messengers, the Great Wardrobe was set up to buy cloth in bulk. *The Wardrobe Accounts* of 1285–6 name ten *nuntii* who each received a robe at a total cost of £6 13s 4d.[83]

At the beginning of Henry III's reign messengers were given a tunic and supertunic in blue or russet. By the end of the century fashions had changed and men were supplied with a suit, jacket and trousers. Colours are not mentioned as a rule but usually were striped and patterned or striped and blue. At times cloth was supplied instead of made-up garments. In 1326 cloth was normally being given, six pieces of worsted being delivered to John de Waltham, the king's messenger.[84]

The queen and royal princes had their own messengers, who also were provided with clothes of differing colours. Often provision of clothing was an obligation put on a sheriff who would have the costs deducted when he presented his half-yearly accounts, those messengers who were abroad at the time of distribution receiving a credit. The Wardrobe and later accounts show that shoes were also provided. Occasionally the *cursores* are shown as being given clothing but they were usually not included in the allocations. The frequency of the clothing allowance depended upon the state of the royal finances; it was normally paid six monthly though sometimes only once a year. There are even examples of messengers being years in arrears.

A drawing of a messenger in the year 1360 (Fig. 2.5) shows him wearing a buttoned tunic, with a cape and hood topped with a feather.[85] He is mounted, wears elongated spurs, and is accompanied by a groom. At his side is a pouch bearing the king's arms, which was his badge of office. The spurs, pouch, and bag for letters and documents were provided. In many cases he would need a case or a basket to contain larger quantities of documents. Smaller bags, perhaps one for each sheriff, were used for separate writs within a pouch. The National Archives retain some medieval leather pouches with drawstrings at the top. (Fig. 2.1) Similar pouches were used also in Chancery and Exchequer to contain writs. A king or queen might reward a messenger by providing a particularly fine pouch, as the Black Prince did when he gave a silver-gilt box enamelled with his arms to his favourite messenger in 1355.[86] Such pouches were intended for ceremonial occasions.

A *nuntius* could expect a gift when he arrived at his destination. In the account of the Wardrobe and Household expenses of Edmund Mortimer, Earl of March, from September 1414 there are two accounts relating to the arrival of royal messengers. They read: 'Item solutum nuncio domini regis portanti domino breve de prorogacione parliamenti xiii die Januarii. xiiis iiiid' and 'Item ....nuncio regis portanti unam commissionem. xiiis iiiid'. These are substantial gifts of a mark, or 13s 4d for each visit.[87] The gift related to the importance of the recipient.

One expedient used in times of financial difficulty was to pay wages by the grant of a pension payable from some feudal source. The Close Rolls of Henry III contain several instructions to sheriffs and to the Exchequer to pay regular sums to king's messengers.

Other sources of income were the perquisites whereby members of the household could expect a gift at the New Year and on special occasions such as a royal wedding. As previously mentioned, if messengers were fortunate enough to bring particularly welcome news they might receive the gift of a garment or of money. Permission is recorded in the Close Rolls in 1233 for the daughter of Willemo le Engleis, *nuntius*, under the feudal right of wardship exercised by Henry III, to marry the son of Jocelin de Maworthin. The matter was considered sufficiently important for the sheriff to be instructed to pledge the wife on the king's behalf.[88] Both were messengers or of messenger families and the action indicates their social background as small feudal

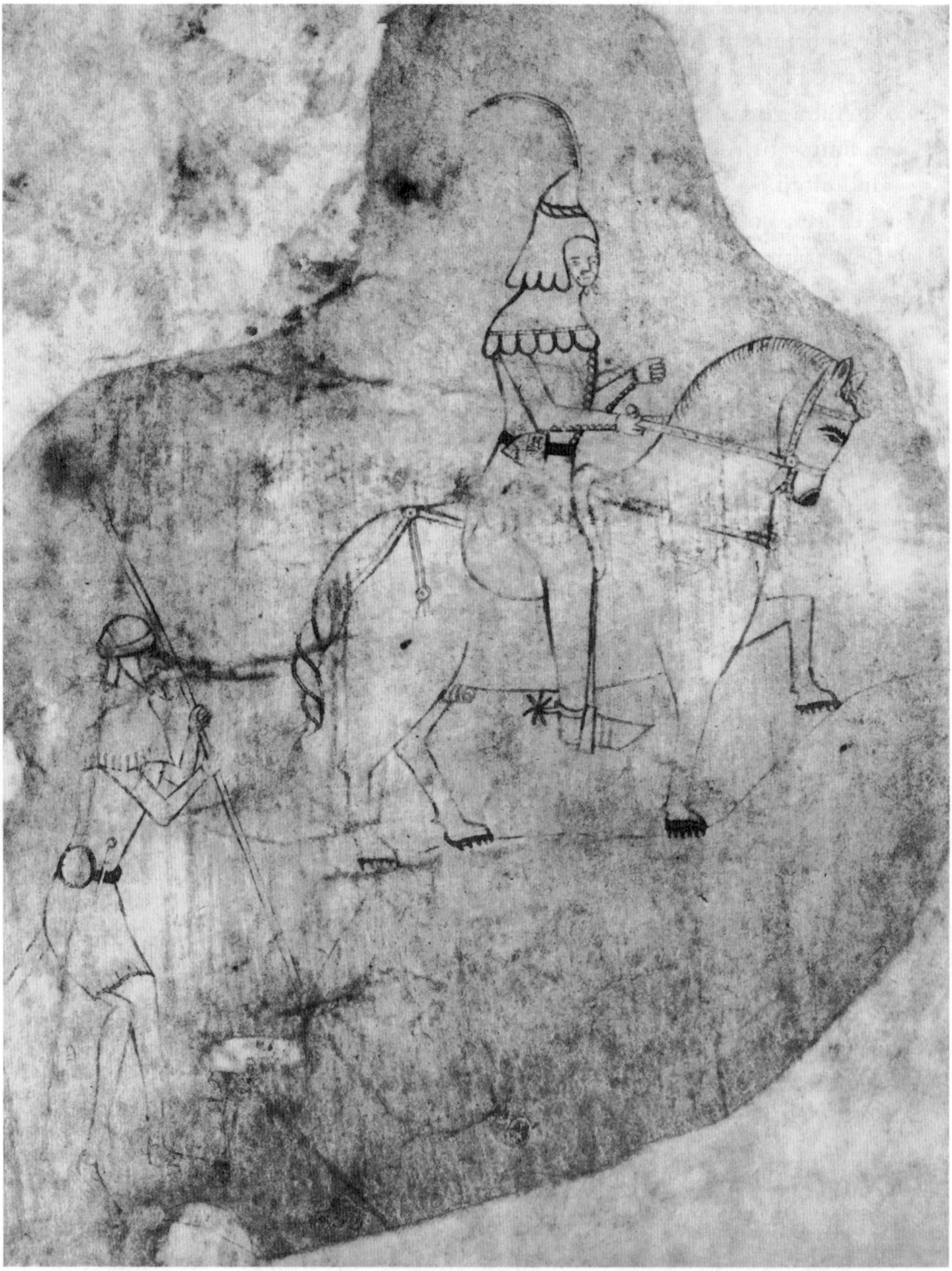

2.5 Fourteenth-century royal medieval messenger with groom. (National Archives E101/309/11)

tenants or freeholders, the sheriff being concerned because the action involved the holding of land.

Discipline within the royal household was very strict, a messenger not being allowed to leave the Court, Exchequer or Chancery except by permission of a senior member. The tradition grew up of the messengers appointing from amongst themselves one who would speak for them and often receive money and clothing on their behalf. No doubt a long-serving messenger would acquire a certain status and be known to the sovereign himself. The senior men carried the confidential letters, often bringing back important messages by word of mouth, so they would sometimes speak to the king and be respected members of the Court. In a letter from the Earl of March, the future Edward IV, and his brother to their father they thank him for 'the knowledge that it pleased your noblesse to let us have of the same, by relation of Sir Walter Devreux' and they wrote further, 'We have charged your servant, William Smith, bearer of these, for to declare unto your noblesse certain things in our behalf…'[89]

By tradition, the medieval king treated his household as members of an extended family. He cared for them in times of illness, helped them when bereaved, supported them in old age, and assisted with their funeral expenses. The continuous travelling of the household and the hard life on the roads took its toll, so there are records of messengers being granted sick pay or of being left behind in care at a royal manor when the court moved on. When Edward I was in Gascony in September 1287 one of his messengers, Adam of Bayworth, fell ill and was unfit to work until March 1288 during which time he stayed at Bordeaux on a sick allowance of 3d a day.[90]

The messenger who was taken ill while travelling would have to find a suitable substitute and he could expect to recover the costs he had incurred. If he were waylaid he could expect the king to take drastic action. Such an incident is recorded in 1385 when on 20 May a commission was sent to the sheriff of Devon, and John Orewell, a royal sergeant at arms, went to arrest one Simon Carselac and others to bring them before the king and his council to answer for a robbery of 400 marks (£266 13s 4d) in coins from three messengers, the robbery having been committed at Simon's inn at Honyngton.[91]

When the messenger became too old to work, he could expect to receive a retirement pension. Pensions are recorded from early in the twelfth century and this later entry for 24 April 1362 is typical:

> To the sheriff of Kent for the time being. Order to pay thenceforward to John Taylfer, one of the king's messengers, fourpence halfpenny a day, taking his

> acquittance for every payment; as the king of his favour and for John's good service hath granted him by letters patent fourpence halfpenny a day of the issues of that county for life or until order be taken for his estate.[92]

The sheriffs had sums to use as alms for pensioners or as gifts to religious houses, so as one regular recipient died another could take his place. It was always open to the king to provide a temporary pension or to give a permanent sinecure like that of porter at a royal castle. Royal revenues were augmented in many ways, for example by the seizure of properties, by wardships and by lands that were taken over through forfeiture or legal process, and so these might be used to provide for royal retainers. They could also be helped by gifts of houses or wood to build them, and there are cases of hospitals and monasteries being required to house and feed elderly former royal servants, a practice known as a corrody. In 1332 Richard Taxford, a royal messenger, was sent to the keeper of St Leonard's Hospital, York, 'for his good service' to be kept there,[93] and by another order in 1357:

> John atte Broke is sent to the abbot and convent of Kirkestall to receive such maintenance in the house for life as Adam Merlyn, late one of the king's messengers, had there for life at the king's request.[94]

Adam had replaced Cook Johan on 30 April 1354 following the latter's decease. Royal corrodies become rare after the fourteenth century.

An entry in the Charter Rolls for 1258 refers to the gift of a house:

> Gift to master John de Gloucestria, the king's mason, of the house in Bridport co. Dorset, which the king formerly granted to John Chubbe, sometime the king's messenger for his life, which is now the king's escheat because the said John Chubbe has taken the religious dress.[95]

By one means or another kings endeavoured to provide for the lifetime of their servants. Should a messenger die during his working life, the Wardrobe or Exchequer would pay for the burial, and the sums could be generous. In such cases grants are recorded as being made to the wife and family of the deceased and there are occasional instances recorded of widows receiving a pension. It is a tribute to the medieval monarchs that they tried to meet these traditional obligations. For his part, the messenger was bound by his oath of loyalty to his king which was respected until he became too sick or old to serve.

3

MEDIEVAL ROADS, MESSENGERS AND TRAVELLERS

The routes along which the letter carriers travelled were based on the surviving Roman roads, the older ridgeways, and the tracks which for centuries had linked local communities. Apart from a few references in the Anglo Saxon Chronicle, such as that to the route from Northampton to Southampton via Oxford, there is little documentary evidence about highways in the six centuries following the Roman departure. New road construction in the Middle Ages was rare except for improvements leading to the new towns founded in the twelfth and thirteenth centuries. A mid-thirteenth-century map by Matthew Paris (colour plate 3) provides some information, including an itinerary from Dover to Newcastle running through Canterbury, Rochester, London, St Albans, Dunstable, Northampton, Leicester, Belvoir, Newark, Blyth, Doncaster, Pontefract, Boroughbridge, Northallerton and Durham. There are four versions of the map, on which the order of the towns is not always the same. In all 250 names are given and although there is a displacement of the south of England, the points of the compass are shown with the north at the top. This is a remarkable map for the time, and on one of the versions there is an attempt at a scale. It is difficult to reconstruct an accurate medieval roadmap for which only two main sources exist, the fourteenth-century Gough Map (Fig. 3.1), named after Richard Gough who gave it to the Bodleian library, and a manuscript written about 1400 which describes routes leading to the Premonstratensian Abbey of Titchfield in Hampshire.[1] These will be discussed later.

The itineraries of medieval kings and bishops, court cases involving carriers, and fifteenth-century brokage books enable us to build up a picture of journeys taken on roads that were, after the Conquest, in a better state than most of those in the sixteenth and seventeenth centuries.

Once the Roman legions and their auxiliaries had departed there was no central government to oversee the maintenance of bridges, highways and embankments. It was not until the tenth century that kings were claiming

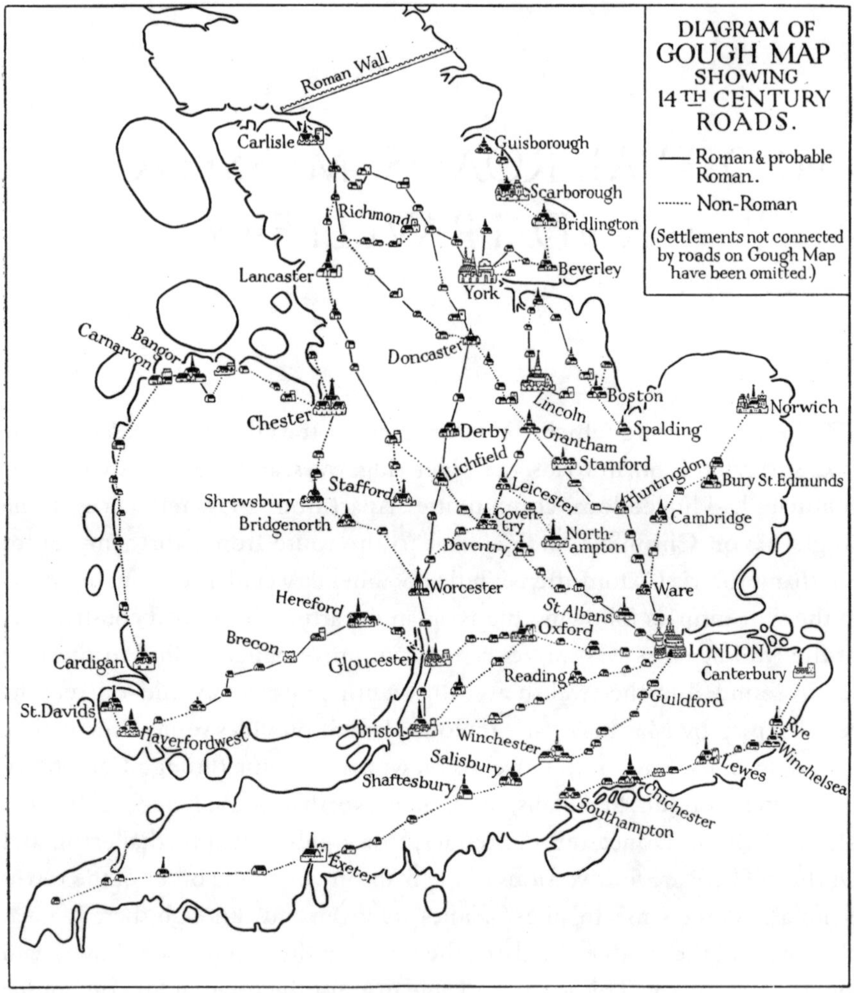

3.1 The fourteenth-century Gough map with routes. (Cambridge University Press from Darby, *Historical Geography of England to 1600*)

to have authority throughout what we now regard as England. After King Edgar had been crowned in 973, Aelfric, abbot of Eynsham, records that all the eight kings in Britain acknowledged his supremacy, though his control must have been tenuous over many parts. The Danish invasions in the early eleventh century ended with a settlement in 1016 which divided the country but eventually King Cnut restored a general authority and his successors were building on that in the years before the Conquest of 1066. The roads from the north must have remained in a reasonable state for they allowed King Harold in 1066 to travel quickly after the Battle of Stamford Bridge in Yorkshire to London and then down to Pevensey to fight the Battle of Hastings. In 1173 the messengers of the Scottish King William the Lion rode from Scotland to the Channel by the great metalled roads, 'par les granz chemins ferrez', showing that one of the principal Roman roads was still surfaced.[2] The Roman road pattern had largely survived. It made possible a centralisation of Norman government which was unique in medieval Europe.

By the time of Edward the Confessor the legal concept of the protection assured by the king had evolved. It applied to everyone at the seasons of Christmas, Easter and Pentecost and to all travellers on main roads and rivers, a most important development for the safety of all who carried letters and documents. It related to those using the four main medieval roads – Watling Street, which ran from Dover through Canterbury, London, St Albans and Wroxeter to Chester; Ermine Street, which originally led from Colchester to Lincoln and York but later linked to London in the south and to Hadrian's Wall in the north; the Fosse Way, from Axminster via Cirencester, and Leicester to Lincoln; and the Icknield Way, a series of pre-Roman routes crossing England from Cornwall to Norfolk. The concept of the Peace relating to major highways, rivers and ports was soon extended to those who travelled to fairs and markets. Legislation in the reign of Edward I obliged all those between the ages of sixteen and sixty to swear on oath to keep the Peace. When Henry I granted a charter in 1121–22 to the Archbishop of York as Lord of Beverley, it gave him an extension of a fair held at the feast of St John the Baptist, and all those visiting the fair were to enjoy the King's Peace.[3] Legislation led later to the formation of Peace Guilds in London.[4]

Under the terms of the laws of William I, severe penalties were listed for those who broke the King's Peace. An assault was punishable by a fine of 100s.[5] One section refers to the keepers of the roads and to a guardreeve who was to be their supervisor. There appears to have been a general obligation laid on all landowners to give time to road maintenance, and land charters issued before the Conquest frequently refer to a requirement to maintain bridges and to care for sections of road. Eventually the idea of the King's Highway was applied to all principal roads and rivers, and kings are known to have ordered landowners and boroughs to improve the roads. In 1260 the master of the hospital at Eastbridge, between Canterbury and Whitstable, was commanded to pull down a chapel and use the stone to fill in the highway.[6]

The Norman Conquest imposed the first firm control over England since Roman times. As we have seen, royal writs went at least monthly to the sheriffs who collected the royal revenues in the shires. There is a celebrated passage in Richard Fitz Neal's twelfth-century *Dialogus de Scaccario* regarding the system of Norman finance in which William I is described as bringing the whole country under the rule of written law. At least it depicts the intention if not

3.2 Agricultural fifteenth-century cart. (British Library Luttrell Psalter add mss 42130)

the result. To achieve this required a regular delivery of documents carried by royal messengers.

The picture we gain of the highways at the time of the Conquest is of rights of way, later called easements, for travellers over other people's land. They could pass along the highway but could not use it for any other purpose. Should the way be impassable then the traveller could deviate from it. Local inhabitants regarded the highways as strips of land used by travellers in return for undisturbed possession of the adjacent fields. Their breadth was considerable, allowing travellers to pick their way on the firmer parts. Where roads met a river or stream there was usually an obligation on a landowner to maintain a bridge or ford. The banks of major rivers were to be maintained by the local community. Sometimes bridges were looked after by a hermit. In Lynn, for example, a hermit received an annuity of 13s to keep the town bridge in order, and at Eccles another hermit kept the bridge there.[7]

The word road does not appear until the late sixteenth century, and previously various terms were used to describe them. The Anglo-Saxons used the word way, taken from the Latin *via*, and medieval statutes refer to common ways, byways, or highways, those leading to market towns or ports often being called portways. A holloway occurred where men and horses had worn down the original track so that it was below the fields alongside. Rainwater

3.3 Ladies in a fifteenth-century wagon. (British Library Luttrell Psalter add mss 42130)

would further assist the erosion. Occasionally, the holloways were raised by paving them with flagstones and then they were known as causeys or causeways. Double lines of flagstones might be laid on highways, such as those leading to Ely where the way was liable to be waterlogged, and they too were known as causeways. The sixteenth-century Leland describes leaving Oxford by the south gate where he 'travelled by a long causey' which took him over marshy ground to Hinksey. The Scandinavian settlers had used the word gate, which is still retained in street names in cities such as York. It needs to be distinguished from the English word gate, which describes a barrier. Another word found from the thirteenth century is lane, used to describe a narrow way.

The rapid growth of towns in the twelfth century resulted in many charters laying down obligations regarding highways, causeways, rivers and bridges. They became enforceable in the sheriffs' and common law courts. For example, in 1247 there is an entry in the Patent Rolls:

> Grant to the good men of Donecastre that to build the bridge of their town in stone they make take a custom of 1d on every carte with merchandise crossing the said bridge from Easter for three years.[8]

Another example is given in Gregory's *The Story of the Road*, where the Guild of the Holy Cross in Birmingham, founded in the reign of Richard II, kept 'two greate stone bridges, and divers foule and dangerous high wayes'. Rymer's *Foedera* cites a grant made in 1410 to the mayor and bailiffs of Cambridge of certain tolls for three years for the repair of ways and paving in the town. A further source of revenue for bridge maintenance could be from rents arising from buildings erected on it. Twice a year the sheriff was required to hold a tourn or court in every hundred or wapentake, the local administrative area, and one of his duties there was to enquire about the condition of bridges and causeways. When the system of eyre was established, under which travelling royal justices visited each shire, they too were charged with enquiring as to whether the law had been observed regarding highways, bridges and causeways. In 1235 the sheriffs of twenty-two counties were ordered to build or repair bridges so that the king might pass over them. Edward I sent commissioners to every hundred with a series of questions, and Article 13 of their instructions required them to report encroachments on every way. By such means the medieval kings endeavoured to maintain freedom of travel throughout the land.[9]

The problems of maintaining an important medieval bridge can be illustrated by records from Rochester.[10] The construction of a new bridge with an adjacent chantry chapel was started about 1387 and the accounts for 100 years from December 1398 have survived. The older bridge was made of wood resting on stone piers and over it went Chaucer's Canterbury pilgrims, soldiers going to the French wars, supporters of the Peasants' Revolt, together with a regular stream of carriers and travellers. The cost of maintaining the nine piers of the bridge was divided between fifty-three places in Kent, mostly parishes along the Medway and its tributaries. Achieving their co-operation in repairs was often difficult and, by 1382, despite a royal levy at the fairs of Rochester and Strood, the bridge was in such a state of ruin as to be impassable. Repairs enabled passage to resume but a new bridge was needed.

Rescue came from Sir Robert Knolles, who had commanded Edward III's army in France, and Sir John de Cobham, who together launched a joint project to finance a new structure. The king gave his support with the provision of lime from his kiln at Rochester and completion was achieved soon after 1392. There were eleven arches including a drawbridge. Wardens were appointed to maintain the bridge with its chapel, and land was provided to produce a regular income. About 2,000 acres were given and most of that was still in the hands of the bridge trustees in the twentieth century. Rentals were supplemented by frequent collections of alms and there was a box for gifts on the bridge. At one time the wardens employed a pardoner who sold pardons signed by a bishop's clerk, an example of the medieval practice of issuing indulgences in payment for money. In 1431 the wardens were granted a royal patent to charge for merchandise passing over the bridge for a period of seven years. On occasion London preachers were asked to solicit gifts. Fishing rights and produce from the estates were sold. By such varied means the wardens managed to maintain the bridge and rebuild sections as needed. It is a tribute to their success that this bridge lasted until its destruction in January 1857.

The repair of London bridges was a major and essential cost on the city and required special levies on all who used them. In 1344 a penny was being charged on every laden cart entering the city by Holebourne Bridge and a farthing for every laden horse for the repair of the bridge and the highway between it and the Bishop of Ely's tenement.[11]

Medieval wills often contained clauses leaving money for the repair of bridges, the most generous of which was the granting of £2,000 under the terms of Henry VII's will for the repair of bridges and highways from Windsor via Richmond, Southwark and Greenwich to Canterbury.[12]

Throughout the Middle Ages there was legislation regarding highway maintenance. In the reign of Edward I the first Statute of Westminster stated:

> That highways leading from one market town to another shall be enlarged, so that there be neither dyke, tree nor bush, whereby a man may lurk to do hurt, within 200 feet of the one side, and 200 feet on the other side of the way. [...] And if by default of the Lord that will not abate the dyke, underwood or bushes in the manner aforesaid, any robberies be done therein, the Lord shall be answerable for the felony, and if murder be done the Lord shall make a fine at the King's pleasure. And if the Lord be not able to fell the underwoods, the country shall aid him therein. And the King willeth, that in his demesne lands and woods within his forest and without, the ways shall be enlarged, as before is said.[13]

A commission was subsequently appointed to enquire 'upon the Statute of Westminster' to see that it had been implemented.[14]

In such ways medieval parliaments endeavoured to ensure the safety and good condition of the highways. Legislation could be supplemented by royal decree, as is shown for example in the Close Rolls of 1385 addressed 'To the sheriff of Oxford and Berkshire':

> To order men of towns whatsoever lying around Walyngford who have wains [carts] and by himself and others to stir them up as shall to him seem best [...] for repair of a certain way there which is rotten and dangerous, as the king has

> learned by credible report, whereby grievous hurt and peril has often happened to men, horses and wains...[15]

Within the towns the authorities assumed responsibility for the streets. These were typically so narrow that repairs were difficult. They had no crown and the lack of a foundation of large stones, such as the Romans had provided, meant that levels gradually rose and could become as much as 20ft higher than the surrounding ground. The street repairers were known as paviors, taken from the Latin *pavire*, to ram or beat, which describes their manner of working. Two men would use a heavy maul to hammer in stones onto a sand base.

London had street cleaners about 1280, when 'four reputable men', who became known as the 'scawageours', were appointed for each ward. In 1315–16 six men were appointed as paviors.[16] The mayor of London was able under the terms of its charter to issue instructions in February 1366:

> Appointing John Sonday, Stephen Baret, and William Prentys jointly and severally to collect and receive from citizens for the cleansing of the high road called le Westwater gate [...] for every cart carrying timber, charcoal, or water along the aforesaid road by the week one penny, and for every horse carrying packs along the said road by the week one halfpenny, and for every croudwayn [wheelbarrow] carrying entrails from St Nicholas's shambles along the same by the week one farthing, with power to distrain for the same on those unwilling to pay.[17]

An assembly of London masons had elected six paviors in 1315 who eventually grew in numbers to such an extent that they organised a craft or fellowship and had a set of ordinances approved in 1479. The Worshipful Company of Paviors of the City of London, as they were now called, has minute books surviving from 1565. Other towns followed their lead and during the fourteenth century most of them were employing paviors. Southampton's town pavior in 1482 was:

> ordained to dwell in a house of the town, price of xiijs iiijd rent free, and to have yearly a gown to this intent that he shall with a sergeant of the same towne do search the pavement of the said town, and also to pave in all places needful within the said town and do all things that belong to that office.[18]

The instructions are rather vague but the pavior was obviously a man with authority appointed to see that the streets were kept in a decent condition.

The cost of maintenance of that part of the street outside a house was usually put upon the owner though sometimes the occupier was charged.[19] The authorities were responsible for the area of the market, the stocks, the pillory, the town gates, the square, and the area around the guildhall. To assist with their costs they sought royal patents to enable them to levy tolls of pavage on outsiders who brought vehicles in to the town. Northampton gained Letters Patent from Edward I as early as 1284, enabling the borough to charge tolls for the next two years. Cambridge obtained seven patents for pavage during the fourteenth century. Town records show that carts with iron-rimmed wheels paid more than those with plain wooden felloes.

The generally good condition of medieval main highways away from remoter areas can be judged by the use they had. Medieval kings rarely spent more than a few days in any one place. They travelled through the land with the principal royal officials so that their households included both the government and the supreme legal authority, for the king was the source of all law. With him went his bodyguard, his wardrobe and crown, the marchalsea, responsible for his horses and carriages, his grooms and huntsmen, his portable chapel with a store of documents, his jewels and his bed. All this was carried on a procession of carts, protected by the royal bodyguard. Walter Map describes the mobile court of Henry II from first-hand experience in his book *De nugis curialum* ('Concerning the Trifles of the Court').[20] He compares it with an ancient legend of the spectral army, the Wild Hunt, that had been seen in the first year of the king's reign:

> They travelled as we do, with carts and sumpter horses, pack saddles and panniers, hawks and hounds, and a concourse of men and women. [...] They seem to have handed over their wanderings to us poor fools, those wanderings in which we wear out our clothes, waste whole kingdoms, break down our own bodies and those of our beasts, and have no time to seek medicine for our sick souls. No advantage comes to us unbought, no profit accrues if the losses be reckoned, we do nothing considered, nothing at leisure; with haste that is vain and wholly unfruitful to us we are borne on our mad course, and since our rulers only confer in secret in hidden places with the approaches locked and guarded, nothing is done by us in council. We rush on at a furious pace. [...] In this pitiable and care-ridden court I languish, renouncing my own pleasure to please others.

This large assemblage lived off the royal estates wherever they might be. The number of courtiers varied: King Stephen took 100 or more men and women with him, while early in the fourteenth century kings might be accompanied by as many as 500.[21] Even when food rents were exchanged for money payments the Court still travelled on its way, a means of ensuring control over the kingdom, using the resources of various places and enjoying the main royal pleasure of hunting. A convenient way of examining the continuous journeys of Edward I is in publications of the Index and List Society.[22] When royal itineraries are examined, it is clear that the kings made many of their journeys on cross-roads away from the main routes.

During his time as chancellor, Thomas a Becket travelled on an almost regal scale. Travelling to France in 1158 he took eight carts, each drawn by five horses with a driver and a man for each horse. Accompanying him were 200 knights, clerks and squires, twelve packhorses with their grooms plus men with watchdogs, greyhounds and hawks. On entry into a town without paved streets the wheels were bound with skins.[23]

Many royal itineraries survive which give a picture of restless energy. Walter Map described Henry II's travels in a further part of *De nugis curialum*:

> I saw the beginning of his reign and his subsequent life which in many respects was commendable. [...] He had skill of letters as far as was fitting or practically useful. He was always on the move, travelling in unbearably long stages, like a post, and in this respect merciless beyond measure to the household that accompanied him; a great connoisseur of hounds and hawks and greedy of that vain sport; perpetually awake and at work.[24]

One itinerary for King John shows that in the course of two months he traversed much of the north of England. An indication of the speed at which he moved is shown in 1200 when he was at Marlborough on 19 November and in Lincoln on the 23rd, 150 miles apart. Often he moved 35 or more miles in a day and in 1204-05 he is recorded as making 360 moves.[25] In the words of the contemporary Matthew Paris, 'he was faster than you would have believed possible'. He frequently descended on abbeys and monasteries including Waverley, Bath and Bury St Edmunds. Edward II's visit to Peterborough in 1310 was said to have cost the abbot £1,543 13s 4d.[26]

In times of war, the household became the command centre of a marching army that might swallow up the whole resources of the place where it stayed. During the fifteenth-century Wars of the Roses it could be accompanied by wheeled guns and a large baggage train. The constant royal travelling only ended with the more settled times which came with the Tudor monarchs. That it continued so long indicates that the main highways were maintained in a condition able to take the passage of the royal Court.

The Exchequer moved from London to York on six occasions during the thirteenth and fourteenth centuries.[27] Its journeys illustrate the way medieval transport depended upon the linking of roads with rivers. It was convenient to have the Treasury close to the king during the Scottish wars, but on one occasion in 1392 the reason was that the king had summoned the mayor and sheriffs of London to answer charges made against the city, and it was felt suitable to hold the enquiry outside the capital. The most fully documented of the moves is that of 1322 when the Exchequer with its rolls, tallies, memoranda and large sums of money went together with the rolls of the Common Bench. Sheriffs on the route had to provide an escort for the dignitaries, their servants and their twenty-three carts each drawn by five horses and accompanied by two men. With them went a considerable company, about fifty in all apart from the sheriff's escort. The documents and treasure were taken in wine casks, the chests and coffers being lined with waxed canvas.

The average distance covered each day on the move was 20 miles. They went via Cheshunt to Grantham for the Easter weekend, on to Lincoln and then to Torksey on the River Trent, where the carts were unloaded. From there they sailed to Burton upon Stather and, after being held up by a storm, they eventually reached York thirteen days after departure. The cost was £91 17s 10d. That national records could be moved by land and sea on several occasions is further evidence of a major highway that was suitable for the movement of a large company, a considerable procession of carts and the nightly accommodation required.

The great magnates, lords, abbots and bishops were frequently on tour visiting their manors and dioceses. They too took large escorts and lived off their manors as they progressed. Some had their own accommodation at each stage on the route to London. Until the consolidation of many great estates that took place in the fifteenth century, it was usual for magnates to have lands in various parts of the country and to travel with great numbers of retainers and their furniture in carts. Earls and magnates each maintained a household similar in style to that of the king. In the later Middle Ages the greatest of them employed heralds and pursuivants to take their most important mail. A very early letter from Hugh le Despenser written in 1319 gives orders for the defence of his castles, which he visited regularly.[28]

As mentioned in Chapter 2, it was expected that that a duke would have 240 servants, a marquis 200, an earl 140 and a baron 40, all of whom proceeded in great style. The Countess of Warwick travelled in 1421 with fifty-seven horses, and when the Duke of Bedford arrived that year near to Warwick he brought his chancellor, treasurer, twenty-four esquires and forty-two other persons.

On the manorial estates the lord's bailiff or reeve kept records in the form of account rolls. A series for the manor of Petworth has survived from the mid-fourteenth century and shows the costs of transporting goods, sending letters and maintaining the rolls.[29]

The accounts of Robert atte Sole for twenty-seven weeks in 1347 give a total for expenses and deliveries as £102 15s 8d. They include fees for two grooms carrying the steward's letters from Petworth in Sussex to Warkworth in Northumberland and for a groom coming back carrying the lord's letter to Petworth, totalling 8s 6d. There are entries for deliveries of money and tallies. One charge is for parchment for the court rolls, 4d, and another for the clerk writing the rolls, 6s 8d. There are no precise charges for messengers other than those concerning the grooms and it is obvious that local messages could be sent to the lord together with the regular deliveries of foodstuffs taken to his house.

Other travellers from the twelfth century onwards were the king's justices in eyre, who went with their clerks to the assize towns until the reign of Henry III. A century later, students were making their way to Oxford, Cambridge and universities abroad, while drovers, chapmen and local traders were common sights on the roads. Fairs and pilgrimages attracted great companies of people. Warfare caused many to travel and so in the fourteenth and fifteenth centuries a considerable proportion of men went over to France to fight. Others travelled to the royal Court wherever it might be for a variety of purposes. One such visit is shown in the Liberate Rolls of Henry III where there is detailed an instruction to pay made at Fareham:

> To find the expenses of Constance Saunz Aver and four other nuns of the Abbey of St Edward at Shaftesbury who are coming by the king's command to talk with W. Archbishop of York, with a horsed vehicle for their journey both ways.[30]

A larger proportion of the population left their homes and travelled along the highways during the later Middle Ages, often with carts and carriages, than in any century before the twentieth.

Those foreign visitors who landed at Southampton and needed to hire horses or waggons often followed a route to Canterbury, via Winchester and Guildford, that became known as The Pilgrim's Way. Venetian records show an authorisation in 1402 by the Venetian Senate of Lorenzo Contarini, captain of the Flanders galleys, to land at Sandwich and visit the shrine in fulfilment of a vow. He was to go and return within a day, not being allowed to sleep out of his galley.[31]

The costs involved in maintaining a vehicle could be considerable. The accounts submitted by a royal carter in Pickering, Yorkshire, during the year

1325–26 for himself, an assistant, a cart and six horses show that their combined wages were 4½d a day, hay and grass ¾d daily for each horse, to which were added 136 quarters and 7 bushels of oats, litter, 194 shoes with nails, shoeing costs, headstalls, cloth for harness, collars, carpenter's wages, smiths' wages, traces, lynch-pins and large nails for repairs to the carts, four axles, 46 nails, ointment and tallow for greasing, leather for repairs to the harness and hemp rope for binding the cart. In all the cost was £35 10s 2d. The carter bought four stones of iron, some of which was used for felloes to strengthen the wheels.[32]

More elaborate was the fifteenth-century coach. When Edward I went to Scotland the ladies travelled in coaches but he preferred a litter. Later, in 1503, Princess Margaret also travelled to Scotland for her marriage to James IV, when her transport was described as 'a chair richly dressed, with six fair horses, led and conveyed by three men'.[33]

A chair, or chariot, was a four-wheeled waggon with the centre slung on chains. The Pomeranian coach which had recently been introduced from Germany was slung on leather braces. A letter from Queen Mary describes a sixteenth-century carriage:

> We will and command you forthwith upon the sight hereof you deliver or cause to be delivered to our trusty and welbeloved servant Edmond Standen, clerk of our stable, one Waggon of timber work for ladies and gentlewomen of our Privy Chamber with wheels and axeltrees, strakes, nails, clouts, and all manner of work thertoo appertaining; fine red cloths to cover and line the same waggon, fringed with red silk and lined with red buckram painted with red colours; collars, draughts of red leather, hamer cloths with our arms and badges of our colors; and all other things appertaining unto the same Waggon; and these our Letters shall be your sufficient warrant and discharge on this behalf at all times.[34]

Carts were in use throughout the year, indicating that surfaces of the main ways even in winter were usually firm. Tenancy agreements from before the twelfth century show that many villagers owned carts, which they had to provide for manorial services. Some of them were of an unusual design in that they had a large wooden bumper at the front which would act as a drag when the cart was going downhill. Iron-rimmed wheels, which did much damage to the roads, were uncommon until Tudor times. Surviving documents from Beverley show how the authorities there strove to limit them. In 1367 carts shod with iron were forbidden entry into the town, and a fine of 12d was chargeable on offenders.[35]

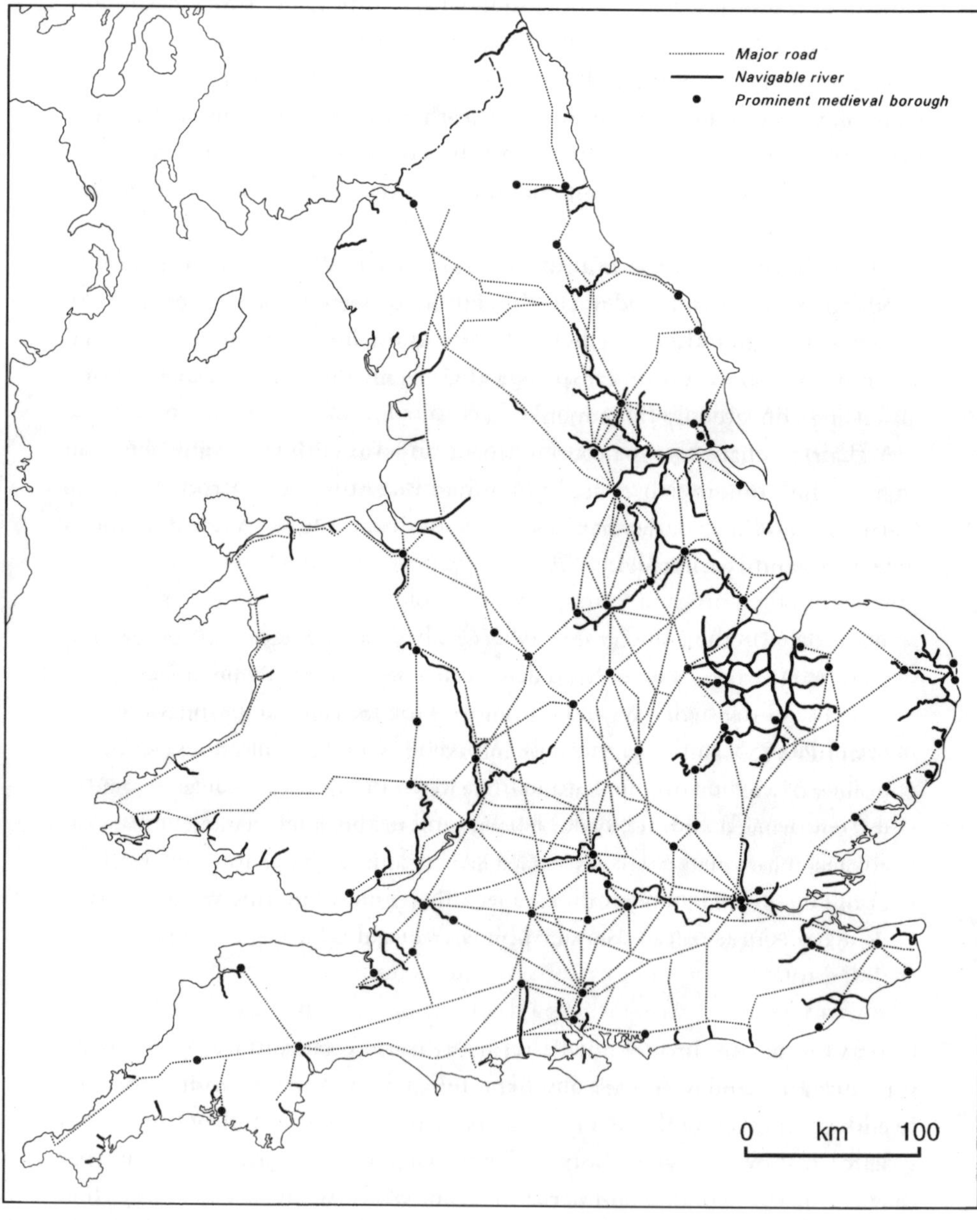

3.4 A map of medieval roads. (Paul Hindle, from *Roads and Tracks for Historians*)

In 1391 another order was made against such carts, though the fine was reduced to a penny. Southampton's town pavior had duties in 1482 which involved excluding carts with iron-shod wheels 'thought to be a great annoyance to the town in breaking the pavements of the same'.[36]

Carriers used carts along the main roads, with packhorses in the remoter and hillier parts of the country, and the regularity of their journeys is described Chapter 7, while their use of markets is further discussed in Chapter 5. Fairs drew people from all over the country. The greatest of these was Stourbridge, near Cambridge, whose control was a subject of dispute between town and university until it was settled in the town's favour in 1589.[37]

Other major fairs included Boston, Lynn, St Ives, Winchester, Smithfields and St Giles in London, together with Abingdon, the main cattle fair. Traders came from Genoa and Venice, bringing Oriental spices, Italian glass, velvets and silks. The Milanese brought the armour for which they were famous. Sugar came from Sicily, currants, raisins, figs and dates from the Mediterranean. From Flanders came the best quality linens. Spaniards brought wine and horses, Norwegians tar and pitch. Hanse traders came with furs and amber jewellery from Russia. The foreign traders needed to hire carts to carry their goods from the ports and to return with woolpacks, Cornish tin, salt, lead and iron and, later in the Middle Ages, with finished cloth. The fairs provided venues for letters to be collected and despatched to remoter destinations.

One use of the highways and byways was for the carriage of the stone used in the building of castles, town walls, cathedrals, abbeys, monasteries and parish churches. After the Conquest stone from Caen in France was brought for the construction of Battle Abbey at Hastings and of the White Tower in London. Materials were quarried as close to a site as possible but often involved the movement of vast quantities for 10 or more miles. The thirteenth-century building accounts of Vale Royal Abbey in Cheshire have survived and show that the stone was brought by carts 6–8 miles from the quarry even in winter. Many carters made two journeys a day, travelling a total of 25–30 miles.[38]

It is interesting to note that they worked in winter months, the slackest times being May, August and September. The great alabaster reredos of St George's Chapel, Windsor, was brought from Nottingham in 1367 in ten carts each drawn by eight horses. The journey of 120 miles took seventeen days.[39] Millstones often came great distances, the most favoured coming from the chert found in the vicinity of Paris.

During the fourteenth and fifteenth centuries wool merchants like the Celys travelled with trains of carts buying up the entire wool clip of areas in the Cotswolds, the sarplers or bales of wool they fetched being typically too large to be taken on horseback. As long as English kings claimed provinces in

France there was much regular traffic through the Channel ports and along the ways that led to them, for during the Hundred Years' War armies of up to 15,000 men were assembled in England together with their wheeled guns, supply carts and siege weapons.

Commenting on late fourteenth-century travel Thorold Rogers wrote:

> I am quite sure that the roads in England were in a far better state of repair in the time of Edward the third than they were in the times of George the third. I do not say that the ancient roads were level, macadamised, and well metalled; but they were infinitely better than the turnpike roads of which Matt. Bramble, in Smollett's novel *Humphrey Clinker* complains so bitterly.[40]

From the Gough map we can confirm many of the highways available to the royal household, soldiers, traders, pilgrims, students, pedlars, entertainers, carriers and others travelling throughout England and Wales. In the south it shows Rye, Winchelsea, Lewes, Chichester and Southampton linked by a road. Out of London ran five routes. The first led through Guildford, Winchester, Salisbury, Shaftesbury and Exeter into Cornwall. The second went through Reading to Bristol, and a third via Oxford to Gloucester. Leading north there was a fourth way to St Albans and Coventry and on to Lichfield, Lancaster and Carlisle. Coventry was an important junction, with roads to Worcester in one direction and Grantham in another. The last of the five was the way to Ware, Huntingdon, Stamford, Grantham, Doncaster, Richmond and Carlisle. A branch led from Ware to Cambridge, Bury St Edmunds and Norwich while another north of Doncaster led to York, Beverley, Bridlington, Scarborough and Guisborough. A circular route is also shown that led north from Gloucester to Chester via Bridgnorth and Shrewsbury and then round the Welsh coast through Bangor, Caernarfon, down to Cardigan and St David's, returning to Gloucester via Haverfordwest, Brecon and Hereford.

Gough's comprehensive pattern of direct main highways shows London linked to all parts of England except for a route to Northumberland, for that which existed to Durham, Newcastle on Tyne and Berwick is omitted, as are the roads from London to Dover and Rye, London to Ipswich and that from Winchester to Southampton. A further route is shown running from Lincoln northwards to the Humber and then south to Boston and Spalding. Several cross roads link towns in central England and we can see the strategic importance of Coventry as a major junction. Stafford is linked to the Lichfield–Lancaster section of the way to Carlisle; Daventry is on a cross road from Coventry to Worcester; and a further link runs south from Leicester to Northampton and south towards St Albans. While it was not the intention of the map to show the use of rivers, we know that the Thames, Lea, Stour, Wye, Severn, Avon, Humber, Trent, Witham and the Yorkshire Ouse were arteries of trade much used for heavier articles of trade. There is more emphasis on rivers in the Matthew Paris map than in Gough's.

It is notable that in the account of his journey through Wales with Archbishop Baldwin in 1188, Giraldus Cambriensis makes no references to the condition of the highways, so we may take it that they were in a reasonable state for an archbishop of Canterbury and his entourage to undertake such an extensive Welsh tour. During 1278 Roger Mortimer was appointed to enlarge and widen highways in readiness for the passage of troops and in 1283 Roger Lestrange and Bogo de Knovill were required to clear and widen the passes into Wales to a bowshot in width.[41]

The Titchfield manuscript is concerned with routes to and from the abbey near Southampton and consequently is selective in the ways it shows. No doubt it is primarily a map for pilgrims and the administrators of their estates but it adds to the knowledge we have from the Gough map. One way from Southampton to Exeter is as direct as possible and does not reach as far north as Winchester. Two routes are shown from London, one through Essex to Leiston, the other to Wendling via Newmarket. Further north there is a way leading directly north from Doncaster and then on to Alnwick, thus filling a gap in the Gough map. Doncaster is also the junction for travellers to Shap and Blanchland Abbeys. The Gough map gives mileages between the important centres and in his Creighton lecture on medieval roads Stenton compares the measurements with those given for a lengthy journey made by Robert of Nottingham in 1324–5 to arrange purchases of wheat for the king. The conclusion is that the Gough map represents carefully estimated and generally accurate mileages. We have no evidence that distances were measured but Stenton concludes that many of the total distances computed agree with those on Ogilvy's 1675 map in his *Britannia*: this is an interesting conclusion because, as we shall see in Chapter 10, different measurements for miles were being used in Tudor times.[42] A comparison with later maps indicates that the road system of the seventeenth century was in place three centuries earlier.

There was some decline in the overall condition of highways in the fifteenth century and the main causes are not difficult to identify. The Black Death and later pestilences had resulted in the loss of at least a third of the population; the monastic ideal had lost much of its appeal so the care of many ways suffered in consequence; and royal preoccupation with France was followed by the Wars of the Roses. The volumes of Public Works in Medieval Law give illustrations of that decline. It would be easy to quote from contemporary descriptions of flooding and attacks by highwaymen, but incidents such as the suspension of Parliament in 1339 because of the weather tend to be reported and may give a distorted impression of actual conditions. In January 1994 the city of Chichester was almost isolated by floodwater and that received extensive reporting in the press although the situation was exceptional. Surviving data, which tend to describe the unusual, can be given undue weight. Sweeping generalisations about poor medieval roads are not verified by the evidence of recorded journeys. In the fifteenth century the Southampton carriers took their loads by cart to much of the country, often in winter conditions, and their trade is described in Chapter 7. The country was generally well served by a road system which was sufficient for the volume and weight of traffic that used it, enabling trade to flow freely and allowing the king's messengers to keep him in regular touch with his sheriffs and mayors.

4
THE MEDIEVAL AND TUDOR CHURCH: EARLY LETTERS IN ENGLISH

Before the fifteenth century the writing of most legal writs, documents and letters, for both lay and Church employers, was undertaken by men in clerical orders who kept their control as long as records were in Latin. Literacy was almost a monopoly of the Church. It has been estimated that during the thirteenth century one in twelve adult males was in orders, a total of some 60,000 in a population of perhaps three million.[1] When we consider that the expectation of life was such that nearly half of the population consisted of children and adolescents, the percentage of men in orders was very high. Clerics were the administrators for both the government and the Church, their own estates being about a quarter of the land in England. Few people were far from one of the 800 or so religious houses. The control of their courts, manors, churches, hospitals, schools, almshouses, towns and other properties required much correspondence and a considerable messenger service. Over 9,000 parishes covered every part of the country and to them we can add the two universities of Oxford and Cambridge, which were also clerical institutions subject to the visitations of bishops.[2]

The Church touched the lives of individuals, from baptism to burial, far more closely than did the Crown. Everyone was in a parish; everyone paid tithes and other fees; all but the greatest nobles could be summoned to appear before a Church court.

The status of the bishops and heads of the leading monasteries was similar to that of the earls and lords who sat with them in Parliament as their peers. Most came from aristocratic families. Their households were often on a grand scale, comparable with those of the great nobles. Durham was a palatinate and at the height of its grandeur in the fourteenth century Bishop Anthony Bec received from the pope the title of Patriarch of Jerusalem and from Edward II the regal dignity of the Isle of Man. Describing him in *The History of Durham*, Surtees writes:

> Surrounded by his officers of state, or marching at the head of his troops, in peace or in war, he appeared as the military chief of a powerful and independent franchise. The court at Durham exhibited all the appendages of royalty; nobles addressed the palatine sovereign kneeling and, instead of menial servants, knights waited in the presence chamber and at his table, bareheaded and standing. [...] He regarded no expense, however enormous, when placed in competition with an object of pleasure or magnificence.[3]

In 1370 the bishop of Ely had ten castles, palaces and large manor houses from which to select his residence[4] while the bishop of Winchester had fifty manors at his disposal.[5] Pope Alexander III in the Third Lateran Council endeavoured in vain to limit the archbishops to retinues of forty or fifty horses and bishops to twenty or thirty.

Most abbots lived much as bishops did, constantly on the move from manor to manor. The travels of the thirteenth-century Abbot Samson of Bury were such that his monks complained they rarely saw him. Even the prior of Norwich kept a household of nine squires, six clerks and about thirty-five other men. The estates for which they were responsible were typically so extensive that an able monk was likely to spend much time in administrative work. The Cistercian Abbey of Meaux in East Yorkshire owned no less than 19,600 acres and the Abbey of Bury St Edmonds had 170 manors.[6]

The Wardrobe and Household accounts of Bogo de Clare for the years 1284–6 have survived and give a picture of the extensive business affairs and correspondence of an aristocrat who held a great number of ecclesiastical appointments. He was the son of the earl of Gloucester and Hereford. His account book shows the expenses of messengers, called *nuntii*, listing the letters they carried. It is related that when an emissary from the archbishop of Canterbury arrived to serve a citation on Bogo, he was made to eat the letter and its seals, then imprisoned and beaten. Bogo was fined about £1,000 for contempt of king and Church, with an additional payment of £20 to the victim. He was later pardoned by the King's Bench which discharged him of the fact of knowing about the event.[7]

The legal powers of the Church were wideranging. Their courts dealt with wills, intestacy and probate, the disposal of goods, matrimonial cases, debt, ecclesiastical disputes, heresy and defamations. They supervised the morality of the common people considering reported fornication and adultery. The Statute *De heretico comburendo* of 1401 empowered bishops to deal with heretics. Heresy was considered as a most serious offence, seen as threatening the stability of both Church and State, and those who relapsed after abjuring their heresy could be handed over to the sheriff and burned at the stake. All those concerns which related to the clergy came before ecclesiastical courts as men in orders were then exempt from common law actions through the traditional benefit of clergy. By this exemption they could not be brought to trial in the king's courts except for matters of high treason and some petty misdemeanours. At first they had merely to show their tonsure to qualify but in the later Middle Ages the test became one of ability to read. Medieval Church courts might therefore deal with cases of murder by clerics. The Church had its own prisons and could sentence like the temporal courts. The Canon Law administered was normally in the hands of professional travelling judges who, like the royal itinerant justices, took their own staff of clerks and porters, but bishops and abbots could reserve cases for their personal attention.

In practice the cases that came before ecclesiastical courts would surprise a modern reader, for they included illicit Sunday trading, non-attendance at church, fortune-telling and sorcery, and one heard at Canterbury involved divining the future from the croaking of frogs. In the thirteenth century the bishop of Worcester had a group of men, accused of molesting clergy in Little Comberton, arrested and publicly beaten by the rural deans in five neighbouring towns. The archbishop of Canterbury ordered a wealthy layman, Sir Osbert Giffard, to be seized and flogged in public at Wilton, at Salisbury and Shaftesbury, the floggings at the last two places being repeated three times.[8] When the archbishop of Canterbury heard in 1413 that barber shops in London had been open on Sundays he wrote to the mayor and aldermen requiring them to be closed.[9]

The gradual change from the dominance of the clergy in national administration began as early as 1340 when Sir Robert Bouchier was appointed the first lay chancellor. In the same year Sir Robert Parvyng was treasurer and after 1420 there was a succession of laymen as lord treasurers, for by that time lay appointments of administrators were becoming frequent both in government and in noble households.[10]

In the thirteenth century Archbishop Peckham had issued instructions to limit monks leaving their monasteries and this had begun the appointment of laymen as estate managers. The growth of the legal profession, the appointment of sheriffs' bailiffs and reeves who had to present accounts, and the expansion of the merchant class were all factors in spreading lay literacy.

The relationship of the medieval English Church with the state and the papacy had been laid down by an ordinance and a letter of William I, both composed about 1076. His letter to Pope Gregory VII, declining to accept papal supremacy, reads:

> To Gregory, the most noble Shepherd of the Holy Church, William by the grace of God renowned king of the English and Duke of the Normans, greeting with

> amity. Hubert, your legate, Holy Father, coming to me on your behalf, bade me to do fealty to you and your successors, and to think better of the money which my predecessors were wont to send to the Roman Church: the one point I agreed to, the other I did not agree to. I refused to do fealty, nor will I, because neither have I promised it, nor do I find that my predecessors did it to your predecessors.[11]

A document which survives in the archives of St Paul's gives the outline of the legal position.[12] Canon law was introduced, causing the separation of the ecclesiastical and temporal courts. Even the Reformation had little effect except to end appeals to the papacy by an Act of 1533, transferring them to Chancery. However, the influence of the Church was greatly reduced by the loss of much of its land when Henry VIII and subsequently the Protectors of Edward VI obtained Parliamentary authority to seize the estates of monasteries and chantries.

Medieval Church courts, which were responsible for a considerable part of its writs and correspondence, consisted of four tiers. Most cases were heard in the archdeacons' courts, superior to which were the bishops' and the archbishops' consistory courts. From these there were two provincial courts of appeal known as Courts of the Provinces; that for Canterbury became known as the Court of the Arches. Appeals from these could be made to Rome, though cases were not normally heard there but by a panel of bishops appointed by the pope. In addition there was a range of monastic courts controlled by the abbots and also others known as peculiars, courts belonging to foundations which had exemptions from the authority of bishops. There were many of these. At the time of the Dissolution there were fifty-two within the diocese of York, most of which then became obsolete.[13]

Each ecclesiastical court developed its own messenger service. The men who carried the courts' writs and mandates together with much of the correspondence of senior clergy were called apparitors, or sometimes summoners.[14]

The more important men were appointed by bishops or abbots, the others by archdeacons. In many ways they were roving inspectors for the senior clergy. The first reference in the Canterbury diocese to an *apparitor generalis* is 1397, when Robert Oates held the post and directed the diocese's team of apparitors.[15]

He was in charge of all summonses to those attending court and supervised the despatch of citations and letters. He probably controlled the apparitors attached to the deaneries. At times their duties involved the seizure of property and the sequestration of goods, but mainly they were on the road carrying the mail. Theirs could be a dangerous task, for there are cases concerning the setting of ambushes and assaults on members of the courts. They could be unpopular if we accept the friar's criticism in Chaucer's *Canterbury Tales* 'that of a sumnour may no good be sayd'.

Typically they received a penny a mile for journeys and combined their work with other positions. One Byrchet earned 38s 4d in 1482 in citing 115 persons to the Canterbury consistory court. Woodcock gives a detailed picture of such work which can serve as an example of ecclesiastical courts throughout the country. The diocese covered the eastern part of Kent and was one of the smaller dioceses, very different in size from Lincoln, the largest, which embraced several counties. The Canterbury team in 1482 consisted of an apparitor general and a team of sixteen apparitors who travelled around the local deaneries. Messages within Canterbury were carried by any of them who happened to be free. Their wages were based on a notional one penny a mile for travel. They went on foot and there is an instruction from Archbishop Statford that they should not use horses. However, there must have been times when a packhorse was needed to carry parcels of writs. They must have been a common sight on the roads carrying the post around the diocese. Those employed specifically by bishops and abbots wore badges to show whom they served.

Ritchie's study of York courts at the time of Queen Elizabeth I shows them dealing with similar cases to those heard some centuries earlier. Here the apparitors were usually known as mandatories. The apparitor general was nominated by the senior judge and received his commission from the archbishop. Not only did he supervise the despatch of writs and other documents but he handled much of the income of the courts. The dean was a peculiar not subject to the archbishop's jurisdiction so had his own court and appointed his own apparitor, who combined his court work with that of being in charge of the cathedral close. The consistory court in particular was kept busy. For example, it dealt with 243 cases between 10 October 1585 and 13 January 1586. Writs were taken either to the local clergy for them to deal with or else directly to named persons. It is likely that each apparitor had a deanery to which he would take documents. A payment of 4d seems to have been a typical charge for a 6-mile journey. A citation to appear at court would be delivered personally but, if the recipient was known to be violent, was fastened to his house door. Should an address not be known, the citation might be fastened to the gate of the parish church. Apparitors were popularly perceived as informers, always unwelcome, susceptible to bribery, yet whose employment was vital to the work of the courts.

Evidence of the hazards that apparitors faced are mentioned in various places in John Chandler's register. He was dean of Salisbury and during visits to churches under his jurisdiction, cases involved one William, who threatened to assault any apparitor who cited him; John Cokeswell, who stated that he would cut off the horse's tail of anyone who cited him; and Edith Smyth, who had to be warned that she would be excommunicated if she abused the apparitor again.[17]

Apart from the work of the courts, other kinds of business dealt with by the archbishops, bishops and abbots can be seen from their registers or letter books of which a great many survive, most dating from the end of the thirteenth century. W.A. Pantin has listed the registers of thirty medieval monasteries.[18] These registers usually list only the letters which bear the abbot's seal and so only relate to a small portion of the actual volume of letters emanating from the abbey. The Glastonbury register differs from most in that it contains some warrants sent to bailiffs and reeves, amounting to eighty documents in one year.

By the mid-thirteenth century important ecclesiastical letters and documents required by the bishops and abbots were being written by men known as notaries public, who had first been appointed by popes and emperors on the Continent. The earliest surviving Statutes of Chichester Cathedral required the chancellor to employ a notary for his secretarial staff in 1232.[19] They came to England early in the century but never achieved the status they had abroad. Although they had no professional organisation at that time, their training suited them to composing letters such as those to the pope, important marriage treaties and complex legal documents.[20] Their skills commended them to some lay employers.

One considerable episcopal correspondence that has survived is that of John Peckham, archbishop of Canterbury. His register between 1279 and 1284 contains 720 letters on a great range of business, ecclesiastical and secular.[21] In the fourteenth century Richard de Bury made a collection of 1,500 letters and documents, some sent to Rome and received from correspondents there. Another similarly large collection is that of the letter books of the monastery of Christ Church, Canterbury, many of which are about business concerns.[22] They include all writings that have survived, and so range from invitations to meals to letters concerning the excommunication of an archbishop. Unexpectedly they also include an affectionate love letter signed 'ye know me well' and part of the reply from the recipient, Margaret.[23]

The prior of Christ Church ruled in great style with his retainers clad in livery. Those enjoying corrodies could be housed in the abbey or in mansions owned by it. The prior's letters were carried by whomever was judged most suitable. For instance, Sir Thomas Gosebeck, one of the prior's clerks, carried a letter to the Bishop of Norwich. Other references show that clerks acted as messengers to important dignitaries. A journey with the expectation of entertainment and a reward would be an attractive prospect. The monastery maintained an agent in Paris, principally to deal with its wine sales and purchases there, so their letter carriers regularly crossed the Channel. Messengers of any rank were called *nuntii* and the same word is used of great persons who came as emissaries. During the exile of Archbishop Winchelsey in 1306 the pope endeavoured to seize his temporalities and those involved are also called *nuntii*. The same word is used for those who mediated between Edward I and his queen. They carried letters of introduction and had the authority to conduct negotiations.

The registers of Roger Martival, bishop of Salisbury from 1315-30, show that he had a staff of a chancellor, a registrar and various clerks.[24] When he travelled round his diocese, visiting his clergy, a large part of his current archives went with him. He spent little time in Salisbury, where problems of jurisdiction could arise with the dean. He stayed at various manors held by the see in Berkshire, Dorset and Wiltshire, at his family home and in London where there was an episcopal inn. A surviving itinerary for 1315 shows him continuously travelling with his staff. They had an office at each of the places he regularly used. A fragment of another roll of expenses, that for Bishop Swinfield of Hereford in 1289–90, shows that he moved house eighty-one times within 296 days. The forty men in his household were almost all liable to take his letters but he had one full-time messenger for routine deliveries. Messengers were sent ahead at every stage of his travels with his instructions. They wore a livery of striped cloth.[25]

Walter Moynton, Abbot of Glastonbury, was the originator of a large surviving collection of letters, including some to the archbishop of Dublin and the prince of Wales, composed between 1351 and 1366.[26]

The register of Bishop Langley of Durham kept between 1406 and 1437 also concerns matters both ecclesiastical and temporal, dealing not only with such legal matters as grants of land and charters, but with pastoral letters, synodial decrees, varied administrative tasks and financial accounts. Langley had two chanceries, the one temporal, the other spiritual. As a former lord chancellor and keeper of the privy seal, his records resemble the royal ones in many respects.[27]

Such registers provide much information about the delivery of the royal mail to the Church.[28] Those from Worcester between 1302 and 1307 and from Rochester between 1323 and 1331 record copies of royal writs and letters from the Exchequer and Chancery, giving the dates on the documents and of receipt, mostly from Westminster though a few are from York. Many of the letters to Rochester were handed directly to the bishop's officer in London. An analysis of the information in the registers has been made with the proviso that the dates shown on the documents may well be those of the original instruction, which means that the time elapsed between their composition and their delivery may be less than it appears. The dates show that when it was necessary to be prompt, in cases such as the summons of Parliament or the raising of troops, the average interval was sixteen days. Chancery writs took about three weeks and those from the Exchequer slightly longer. Documents could leave within a day or two of composition but when there was no urgency they could wait for three or even more months. In some cases they awaited a messenger from the person who had initiated the writ.

The survival of a collection of fifteenth-century letters from the English abbots to their chapter at Cîteaux shows that the abbots made fairly regular journeys across to France.[29] The editor of these letters describes their make-up in some detail. Most of them have been folded into twelve divisions, on one of which is written the address. On another wax is used to seal a further piece of paper that has been wrapped around the letter. In other cases letters are folded into nine divisions, a thread being passed through a centre hole and secured on the outside with sealing wax. Occasionally, two seals were applied when two officials were involved. Twenty different types of paper were used, being identified by different watermarks. A feature of the correspondence is the paucity of important information; hints within many of the letters indicate that such news was entrusted to the bearer to be related by word of mouth. We can deduce that messengers were not ordinary monks but persons of some seniority. The letters are a small part of what must have been a vast correspondence between the chapter and its dependent houses.

The employees of bishops and abbots before the fifteenth century were often closely linked to the royal service, for many bishops served as royal officials, envoys, and even as judges, so that their clerks frequently moved with them. Frequently, royal medieval documents before about 1400 were written by the secretariats of those bishops or abbots who were situated near to the court when the king passed by. Each bishop had his chancery headed by a secretary or chancellor, though that word appears rarely before the thirteenth century. By then many dioceses were developing both secular and diocesan chapters each with its own chancellor and clerks.[30]

Episcopal clerks, like those employed in royal and noble households, were typically trained at one of the two universities. From the early thirteenth century, Oxford offered qualifications in business studies involving the art of letter writing, the drafting of official documents and the keeping of accounts. Such non-degree courses were available until late in the fifteenth century when they appear to have ended, perhaps because the Inns of Court were providing a more efficient alternative in London.[31]

Clerks needed a working knowledge of Latin, Norman French and, later, English, with the skill to read and copy from each language. They had to be able to keep accounts, read back after dictation and maintain the diocesan rolls. Not every literate person in those times had the ability to read aloud as was required, for example, by the clerks in Parliament, who had the task of reading the bills to members. Pollard writes, 'The medieval Parliament was an affair of voice and ear, not of script and the eye.'[32] That observation applied to all deliberative bodies, church and secular, at the time. Reading aloud in public was a common practice and had continued to be since classical times. At the end of the preface to his *Ecclesiastical History* Bede addresses his 'hearers and readers', in that order.

Cheney considers the style of letter-writing used in the early twelfth century, which was so varied that he deduces a variety of officials wrote the letters.[33] Different sizes of parchment were employed. By the end of the century consistency has been introduced and this indicates the employment of regular scribes for the task. After the introduction of model letters, the registers of letters often needed only to contain abbreviated records. Before the reign of Richard I a variety of dating methods are found, but then the normal pattern of day, month and year appears, the day being according to the Roman calendar, occasionally the ecclesiastical one, the year being that taken from the bishop's pontifical year, which began on the day of his appointment, the same principle as was used when the regnal year appears on royal documents.

The twelfth century is acknowledged to be the great period of medieval letter-writing, and one of its most distinguished exponents was Peter de Bois, archdeacon of Bath. His letters are full of intricate similes, biblical references and elaborate language. Among his patrons was Henry II. After his death he served Henry's widow, Eleanor of Aquitaine, as her secretary. His style can be illustrated from a letter she wrote to the pope when her son, King Richard I, was imprisoned in Austria on his way back from a crusade:

> O holiest Pope, a cursed distance between us prevents me from speaking to you in person, but I must give vent to my grief a little and who shall assist me with my words? I am all anxiety, both within and without and as a result my words are full of suffering. There are fears which can be seen, but hidden are the disputes, and I cannot take one breath free from the persecution of my troubles and the grief caused by my afflictions, which beyond measure have found me out. I have completely wasted away with torment and with my flesh devoured, my bones have clung to my skin. My years have passed away full of groans and I wish they would pass away altogether. [...] As some comfort I have two sons, who are alive today, but only to punish me, wretched and condemned. King Richard is condemned in chains; his brother is killing the people of the prisoner's kingdom with the sword, he is ravaging the land with fires.[34]

The indignation is the queen's; the style Peter's. We can imagine her dictating her thoughts, he taking them down and recasting them in this ornate language.

John of Salisbury was one of the most distinguished twelfth-century scholars and theologians. He supported Thomas a Becket during his disputes with Henry II. On one occasion he travelled to France to enlist support for Thomas where he wrote a delightful, lengthy letter about his travels. It begins:

> Ever since I have been on this side of the water, I seem to have been breathing an entirely different atmosphere; and the country around is so rich, and the inhabitants so happy, that it is quite a change to me after my late troubles.[35]

Such personal, friendly letters are those least likely to have survived.

By the thirteenth century the religious centres had developed formularies or model letters and typically a medieval letter sent to person of some importance would have five parts.:

> After the salutation – as to which the medieval scribe was very exacting, each class in society having its own terms of address and reply – came the exordium, consisting of some commonplace generality, a proverb, or a scriptural quotation, and designed to put the reader in the proper frame of mind for granting the request to follow. Then came the statement of the particular purpose of the letter (the narration), ending in a petition which commonly has the form of a deduction from the major and minor premises laid down in the exordium and narration, and finally the phrases of the conclusion.[36]

Teaching the skills required to compose such a letter was known as the *ars dictaminis* and its great exponents were Thomas Merks and Thomas Sampson of Oxford, whose work can be dated to about 1355.[37]

A branch of the *dictamen*, the *ars notaria*, comprised those skills needed by a notary. Models, first intended for letters composed in Latin, influenced the early letters written in English. The earliest recorded in English, though not sent through the post, are those written by Troilus and Cressida in Chaucer's poem of that name composed in the 1380s. A Durham cartulary contains letters from the earl of March to the prior and are reckoned to have been sent in the 1390s.[38] Two other letters written from Florence by Sir John Hawkwood dated 8 November 1392 and 20 February 1393, thought to be the first surviving letters in English, may predate those in the cartulary. They introduce John Sampson, his 'welbiloved squyer', who is empowered to deal with matters concerned with his will and brings the letters.

A little later but of far more interest is a letter of 25 July 1399 written by Joan Pelham to her husband from Pevensey Castle.[39] It has some of the features of the ecclesiastical model described above: a salutation – 'My dear Lord, I recommend me to your high Lordship with heart and body and all my poor might'; an exordium – 'with all this I thank you, as my dear Lord, dearest of all earthly Lords'; and then the statement, or rather understatement:

> And my dear Lord, if it like you know of my fare, I am belayed in manner of a siege, with the county of Sussex, Surrey and a great parcel of Kent, so that I may not [go] out, nor none victuals get me, but with much hardship.

This is followed by the petition:

> Wherefore, my dear, if it like you by the advice of your wise counsel for to set remedy of the salvation of your castle and withstand the malice of the shires foresaid [...] soon send me good tidings of you.

The conclusion reads 'written at Pevensey in the castle, on Saint Jacob Day last past' by your poor J Pelham'. Her husband was John Pelham, constable of the castle, who was then in Yorkshire supporting the Lancastrian cause. No doubt she would have a clerk with knowledge of the *dictamen*, who would write the letter after she had expressed her thoughts to him. A very early letter written about 1400, Brackley 66A, is in the archives of Magdalen College, Oxford. Some early letters from Elizabeth, Lady Zouche, written between 1402 and 1403, are filed under 'Ancient Correspondence' in the National Archives.

Royal letters and writs which went directly to bishops and heads of religious houses concerned such matters as requests for prayers, the payment of subsidies and loans in time of war, the affairs of towns under their jurisdiction, and more minor matters such as the provision of horses for transport when the household was passing nearby. In the 1370 Issue Rolls an entry reads:

> To divers Messengers and Couriers sent to all parts of England with letters of Privy Seal on the 17th day of July past directed to the bishops, abbots and priors to pray for peace and [the] estate of the Kingdom of England.[40]

The same entry refers to messengers sent to bishops to contract for sums of money to be raised on behalf of the King of Navarre. On occasion Richard II required the abbots of Waverley and Tame to provide horses.[41]

There could be an unwelcome requirement for a great abbey to accommodate the royal household. It was the practice of abbeys and monasteries to keep cartularies which were primarily listings of their properties and privileges and consequently included correspondence.[42] A few are entitled 'Histories'. They provide a valuable source for the historian for among them we can find copies of royal letters and documents whose originals have now perished, though amongst them there are some notorious forgeries.

Those major abbeys that had liberties dealt directly with the king's Exchequer. Glastonbury was one such, and the Charter Rolls contain an entry which, after confirming earlier charters, continues:

> March 1327 in favour of the abbot and convent of Glastonbury [...] the king has now granted to them that they shall have return of the summons of the Exchequer and all precepts and mandates of the king and his heirs.[43]

In such cases all royal correspondence went to the abbey, so letters and other documents would be brought directly to the abbey by royal messenger.

The two universities were ecclesiastical establishments and their students were regular travellers. Carriers usually took the young men to and from their colleges and they were a recognised part of the university scene. A fifteenth-century indenture between the university and city of Oxford describes the following classes of person as enjoying the privileges of the university:

> All common carriers, bringers of scholars to the University, or their money, letters, or any especial message to any scholar or clerk from the University for the time of fetching, or bringing or abiding in the university for that intent.[44]

The congregations of the universities corresponded with kings, popes, bishops and nobles. Letters concerning Oxford University in the fourteenth century survive in the style of formularies, in Richard de Bury's collection and in other places.[45] They deal with disputes between the Dominicans and the university authorities, the privileges of the university, legal matters concerning the chancellor's court and the concerns of students. Letters to students from monks have been edited by Pantin.[46]

Much more Oxford correspondence survives from the next century, including some to the king and the pope, though often providing very little information. The bearer is introduced and the recipient is asked to listen to what is said. The messenger was chosen to be trustworthy, one suitable to the occasion, and frequently the chancellor would be asked to take a letter.[47]

Records show that bishops and abbots had some use of the king's messenger service in that the royal *nuntii* regularly brought letters and writs to their households. By entertaining them and paying the conventional reward, time would allow for replies to be prepared and mail taken on to other destinations. They also had their own messengers, as did the church courts. From Tudor times there are occasional instances of them using the town posts, but they had no unified messenger service such as that maintained by the king.

5
MEDIEVAL TOWNS, CORRESPONDENCE AND MESSENGERS

The twelfth and thirteenth centuries saw a steady expansion in the number, size and trade of towns, which were typically sited on ancient Roman settlements, around castles and abbeys, at the junctions of highways and at ports. The aim of their inhabitants became to free themselves from the authority of their lord, so that they could control the farm of the revenues, the *firma burgi*, which consisted principally of market tolls, the profits of the court and the rents from the burgages. They could then acquire their own corporate seal and issue their own documents. In most cases a town guild, having found from its lord the value of his rights, sought to pay him a yearly rent to acquire them.

The king, who was by far the largest landowner, saw the granting of charters as an important source of revenue, so towns became new places on which to levy taxes, often with the *firma burgi* fixed for a period of years and then renegotiated at a higher rate. Royal charters were in the form of letters, at first addressed to members of the county court and later to all the king's subjects. Henry I granted the fee farm to London and this was a landmark in the history of the English borough:

> Know that I have granted to my citizens of London that they shall hold Middlesex at farm for three hundred pounds [...] so that the citizens shall appoint as sheriff from themselves whomsoever they choose, and shall appoint from amongst themselves as justice whomsoever they choose to look after the pleas of my crown and the pleadings that arise from them. No other shall be justice over the same men of London.[1]

London soon lost this charter but it was the precedent which set a pattern for the future.

We can see from the 1283 Statute of Merchants, and its successor in 1285 of the same title, that towns had clerks keeping rolls on which were recorded letters and writs received from the king. The statute required that for greater security rolls were to be double, one part to be retained by the mayor, the other by the clerk. Debts had to be carefully recorded:

> Moreover the said clerk shall make with his own hand a bill obligatory whereto the seal of the debtor shall be put, with the king's seal, that shall be provided for the same purpose, the which seal shall remain in the keeping of the Mayor and clerk aforesaid.

The 1283 statute refers to the mayor of London, the chief warden of a city 'or other good town' together with their clerks. The 1285 Statute mentions the mayors of York and Bristol while the new Ordinances issued by Edward II in 1311 rehearse some of the previous legislation and extend the list of towns that must have clerks and enrolments. It refers to Newcastle on Tyne, York, Nottingham, Exeter, Bristol, Southampton, Lincoln, Northampton, London, Canterbury, Shrewsbury and Norwich, yet omits some important inland towns such as Coventry and Winchester. The legislation confirms that these towns already had a clerical staff responsible for enrolling correspondence, both their own and that which they received.[2]

The series of Charter Rolls contains the records of the new liberties granted by the king to boroughs. Here is a typical example, from 1253:

> Grant to the burgesses of Eschardeburg [Scarborough] of the following liberties. The burgesses and their heirs shall in future answer by their own lands yearly at the Exchequer of Michaelmas for the whole farm of the borough and all debts touching the burgesses; so that no sheriff or other bailiff saving themselves shall distrain the burgesses, or meddle with any attachment or ought else within the limits of the said borough, save in the cases of default of the said farm or debts of the said term.[3]

In Northampton the sheriff was not allowed to enter the borough without permission of the burgesses unless they had defaulted on a payment. That entry in the rolls reads:

> Grant to the burgesses of Northampton that they and their heirs shall have the return of all writs both of the summons of Exchequer and of others touching the said borough and the liberty thereof [...] so that no sheriff or bailiff shall in future enter the said borough [...] save in case of the default of the burgesses.[4]

Consequently the royal mail now went directly to such boroughs. Very few of their accounts survive before the fifteenth century but, for example, the Cambridge Treasurer's Rolls for 1346 have two entries:

> Item Johanni Tayllefer nuncio domini regis ijs. Item nuncio domini regis vebienti pro hominibus armatis xld.[5]

Behind these payments of 2s and 40d (3s 4d) to the royal messengers lies an interesting story as Cambridge had been asked earlier in the year to provide twenty armed men for service in France. It had pleaded poverty, claiming its population consisted mainly of privileged scholars and beggars. While the dispute continued, the battle of Crécy was fought in the August and when eventually in December they provided eight men they arrived too late to assist at Calais. A later reference to payment for the cost of sending letters is quoted in the Annals of Cambridge, where the proctor's accounts for 1458 show 'For one riding to the Bishop of Durham with letters in the matter of the heresy of Reginald Pecock 2s 8d.'[6]

The receipt of mail required rewarding visiting messengers while the despatch of their own mail obliged them to have their own messengers. The services of the town carrier would be sufficient for much private mail but not for communications with important persons.

A reference to royal mail in the records of the borough of Leicester mentioning payment of a shilling to the king's messenger in 1354–55 is an example of what had become a regular expense.[7] He would be entertained while a packet of letters or writs was got ready for him to deliver elsewhere. A pursuivant had to be rather more generously treated, as shown in the Cambridge Treasurer's Rolls:

> Unto the King's pursuivant when he brought down the acts of Parliament after halomas, at Mr Mayor's commandment 3s 4d.[8]

An interesting letter from the bishop of Coventry and Lichfield survives in the London Letter Books describing the defeat of the Scots at the battle of Falkirk in 1298. It is dated Sunday after the feast of St James (i.e. 25 July) and the entry concludes with 'the said messenger was given the sum of 26s'.[9] The generosity of rewards is often related to the interest and importance of the news.

Boroughs could be put under great pressure to support the king in times of civil strife as is shown in this letter sent by Edward II to the mayor of Newcastle upon Tyne and to other places dated 28 September 1326:

> Roger Mortimer together with their traitors and notorious enemies, and other aliens, have entered our realm and in the company of our wife, our son and our brother, the Earl of Kent etc, and our wife has written and still writes daily, divers letters to the archbishops, bishops, prelates etc, and to the commons and towns and to private persons, to draw to them the hearts and wills of our people, the better to accomplish their false encompassments etc. We command and charge you, upon the faith and allegiance that you owe to us, that if any letters come to you from our said wife, son or brother, or any of our enemies in their company, that without delay you seize the messengers and bearers together with the letters, and send them to us immediately without opening the letters.[10]

In such times the messengers of either side took great risks when they carried the mail and, no doubt, the royal mail service suffered interruptions.

It was usual for the King's Council to require sheriffs to receive local royal payments. The advantages were obvious in that some of the money received from such sources as rentals, feudal dues and customs duties did not need to be moved to Westminster. Now that towns owed fees to the king in return for their charters, the same principle was applied to them. Like the sheriffs they were obliged to support the local royal postal service and could be used as staging posts for the royal mail. The York Civic Records provide an example of how this was applied. On 16 April in the twelfth year of Henry VII (1497) came a letter missive from the Earl of Surrey to the Lord Mayor with a sealed box containing six letters of the privy seal.[11] These letters were handed to the sheriffs who found that they were charged with delivering them to the six addressees, some of whom did not reside in York. It seems reasonable to deduce from this chance survival that the incident refers to a more general practice.

Generalisations about the development of medieval towns are not easy to make. Within towns there could be liberties controlled by bishops, lords or religious houses, areas where the town authorities had no jurisdiction. Leicester was a town in the hands of a great lord. It had a mayor in 1251 but only obtained important rights from John of Gaunt in 1375. Later, with the accession of Henry IV, the borough became part of his Lancastrian inheritance and so eventually a royal borough. Norwich obtained its freedom more slowly than most, its first royal charter being obtained as late as 1404. Reading had once been part of the royal demesne but in 1125 it was granted to the abbey which Henry I had founded there. Many struggles took place between the abbot and burgesses so that the town only achieved a royal charter in 1542 after the dissolution of the abbey. Obviously in such towns some of the royal correspondence was directed to the lord rather than to a town mayor.

Those with royal charters made their own arrangements for payments of the farm to the Exchequer and for dealing with writs and summonses from the king's courts. Eventually, several boroughs were granted their own sheriffs. The charter of Bristol in 1373 provides the first example of a town granted county status with its own sheriff.[12]

Instead of its citizens attending the county court in Gloucester they were able to elect their own sheriff and hold their own courts. York followed their example in 1396, Norwich in 1404 and Southampton in 1447.[13]

While these developments extended the destinations of the royal messengers and opened up a far wider postal service, it has to be remembered that at the end of the Middle Ages, the great majority of people, perhaps 90 per cent, lived in the countryside. Estimates give London barely 50,000 inhabitants, Norwich over 10,000 and York, Bristol, Salisbury, Exeter, Colchester, Canterbury, Newcastle upon Tyne and Coventry perhaps 6,000, the county towns such as Lincoln, Cambridge, Oxford, Hereford and Worcester perhaps 4,000, ports like Southampton, Yarmouth, Plymouth, Lynn and Hull just over 2,000, and other towns between 2,000 and 500 persons. Altogether there were around forty towns with a population of over 2,000.[14]

Towns which had harbours were involved in much additional correspondence. Royal letters on a great variety of subjects went directly to the mayors and bailiffs or officials at the ports where royal comptrollers were overseers of the collection of customs duties. The first duties were imposed about 1150 on wines, and returns from thirty-five east and south-east ports are shown in the Pipe Rolls from 20 July 1203 to 29 November 1204. The tax of a fifteenth raised nearly £5,000.[15]

This duty was short lived and the efficient collection of customs taxes dates from the charges on wools, hides and fells imposed by Edward I in 1275. Duties were raised at a limited number of ports and by 1294 they had raised an annual total of £125,000.

These taxes were extended in 1303 to a range of imports, involving much correspondence and regular returns to the Exchequer. Geoffrey Chaucer, the poet, was appointed comptroller of customs and subsidies at the port of London in 1374, leading to an even more lucrative post of Comptroller of Petty Customs in 1382, entitling him to appoint a deputy who did the work. Collectors had to record the date of arrival and sailing of every ship, give its name together with those of the master and merchants, list the merchandise with its date and place of shipment, and detail the duty charged. Records were sent by messenger for audit and are summarised in the Exchequer Rolls from 1279 to 1547. Most towns had two comptrollers but London needed far more. In the reign of Richard II there were twelve collectors for cloth and petty customs, fifteen for tunnage and poundage plus fifteen others for the wool custom and subsidy.[16]

Their records provide a comprehensive summary of national trade until they were replaced by the system of Port Books in 1564, which were parchment books 'with Leaves nombred of record [...] in a Tynne Box'. Some of these books have survived and have been edited and published by the London Record Society.

Summonses to attend at the Exchequer in London could be of a peremptory nature. One dated 13 August 1433 was sent to various ports requiring their officers to appear before the lord treasurer and barons at the Exchequer at Westminster on the morrow of Michaelmas bringing with them all books, rolls, tallies, money and other things necessary for their charge and discharge in their accounts, and to make no payments in the meantime.[17]

Officials were regularly instructed to search persons and ships coming into port and to seize any letters they carried. Rymer's *Foedera* includes many such instructions of which this in 1324 is typical:

> Writ or letter to the Constable of Dover and Warden of the Cinque Ports, to the Mayor and Sheriffs of London, the Bailiffs of Bristol, Southampton and Portsmouth, and the Sheriffs of Hants, Somerset, Dorset, Devon and Cornwall, noticing that the previous orders de scrutinio faciendo had not been observed in consequence of which many letters prejudicial to the Crown were brought into the Kingdom. They are therefore commanded to make diligent scrutiny of all persons passing from parts beyond the seas to England, and to stop all letters concerning which sinister suspicions might arise, and their bearers, and to keep the bearers in custody until further directions, and to transmit the letters so intercepted to the King with the utmost speed.[18]

By letters patent in 1325 Nicholas Kyriel was appointed Admiral of the Fleet from the mouth of the Thames to the Cinque Ports, giving him:

> the power to search in all ports and places on the before mentioned shores all persons entering the Kingdom, whether they bear any letters prejudicial or suspicious to the King and his lieges, and to arrest the bearers, together with the letters and to keep them in prison, if the King should be in remote parts: all the King's Bailiffs are commended to assist the Admiral; but they are not, under pretext of such powers, to attack or oppress any merchants or others crossing the seas.[19]

Similar powers were regularly granted to individuals:

> to search for any bulls, letters, instruments, or processes, or other things prejudicial to the King or his subjects and to arrest as forfeitures all the above named articles with the ships, boats and persons bearing them, and to keep them until otherwise directed.[20]

Despite such searches, foreign correspondence undertaken by merchants seems to have passed freely. There are small surviving fourteenth-century correspondences from Italian merchants in London writing to Lucca and Florence. Those from the Riccardi of Lucca, perhaps the earliest surviving letters written on paper in England, tell us of the finances of Edward I, while those written by Florentines in the 1390s refer to the foreign policy of Richard II.[21]

Each merchant company had its own messengers, but the Italian companies often carried letters from other companies. From them we can find times for conveyance. When no special circumstances held up the messenger, letters to Lucca took about five weeks. One from London to Lucca dated 18 August arrived in Lucca on 22 September. Another sent on 24 February 1300 arrived on 5 April. Another early source for merchants' letters can be found in the accounts of Gilbert Maghfeld, dated between 1390 and 1395, which survive in the National Archives.[22]

As the towns gained their independence from the county sheriffs, a typical pattern of organisation emerged. Furley's study of Winchester records gives a picture of an important town in the late Middle Ages. It had an elected mayor, bailiffs, provosts, coroners, clerks or recorders to keep its records both legal and administrative, cofferers to deal with land registry, chamberlains to deal with finance, revenue collectors, aldermen (who at first each dealt with the policing of a particular ward), constables, sergeants and officials to look after the market and trade. The main towns required a clerical department similar to that previously described for a sheriff, and smaller places one which was suitable for a bailiff. In effect, the duties of the town mayor replaced those of the sheriff.

Winchester messengers are not referred to by name but there are entries in the town's Account Rolls which show they were employed. Most towns had a Memorandum or Remembrance Book into which went a note of payments for later use as precedents. Southampton had several Remembrance Books and York also had a Memorandum Book which contains a heterogeneous mass of information. Bristol had its Little Red Book dated about 1344, unusually written on paper, though the external pages are of vellum. The colour of the book typically referred to the original binding. The Chester Chamberlain's accounts for the year 1361–62 show that they were obliged to transmit royal documents:

> Costs of messengers. Various messengers carrying the prince's writs to the sheriffs of the counties of Chester and Flint and to the corners [coroners] and other of the Lord's officials in the aforesaid counties on various occasions. 4s 2½d.[23]

The York Memorandum Book mentions a letter from the King of Jerusalem received in 1393 but gives no indication of a reply nor how it would be despatched. Costs of messengers sent to London or more distant places are occasionally given. Hill mentions several fourteenth-century town messengers who are referred to by name; Adam and Ralph of York are referred to in 1317 and 1323–4 and another York courier, Thomas Hamond, in 1373. William of Bristol was a messenger in Chichester and William Sparewe a messenger at Lincoln.[24]

The records of Leicester mention payments to messengers in 1354–55 of 5s 6d and Southampton records give many others. Such random references are enough to show that towns had messengers in the fourteenth century, and some of the larger ones even before that. A few town letter books survive, which are haphazard collections like those transcribed in *Letters of the 15th and 16th Centuries*, edited by R.C. Anderson for the Southampton Record Society. Records sometimes refer to the post as meaning horses available for travellers and messengers.

The town of Dunwich was, before the encroachments of the sea, one of the most important of medieval ports and returned two members of Parliament. Only one of its medieval records has survived. The Bailiff's records of Dunwich between 1404 and 1430 consist of jottings on the town's finances.[25] He notes various expenses as an aide-mémoire. From them we can gain some insight into the use of messengers:

> To Philip Canon for writing an indenture for the first Parliament and for return of writ 6d. To the same Philip for carrying these documents to Beccles, Moreff's share of the payment 6d. Likewise his share of payment to Bernard the sheriff's clerk for carrying the writ to London 5d.

We see that Philip Canon was employed as a writer and was considered trustworthy enough to take a document to the sheriff's clerk together with a servant Moreff. The transmission of the papers to London was undertaken by the sheriff's clerk who was paid to add these to others from the sheriff, thus explaining the small sum of 5d. Another entry gives the cost of hire of a horse to London as 40d and, obviously, the bearer would take local letters sent in that direction. It was far cheaper to pay the clerk at Beccles to take letters to London with others than to send them directly. A year after the payment of

5d, the same clerk had to be paid 1s for the journey to London. We have seen earlier that the king's letters were sent to the county sheriff for onward transmission and the Dunwich records show that the towns could link their mail into that network.

It is possible to calculate the number of regular journeys made by late thirteenth-century royal messengers to the major towns. From the Issue Rolls for the year 1370 journeys can be extracted.[26]

There are, for example, forty-two to Southampton, twenty-five to Rye, twenty-one to Yarmouth and nine to Sandwich. It is obvious that the officials at the larger towns could rely on royal messengers arriving and being available to take letters back to Westminster. As in the case of Dunwich, they had the alternative of sending their mail to the nearest sheriff's office where there would probably be a weekly or fortnightly service back to London.

London has surviving court records from 1275 in a series known as the *Calendar of Letter Books of the City of London* with a further source of information in the *Calendar of Letters from the Mayor and Corporation of the City of London from 1350 to 1370.*[27] There were three courts of record, the Court of Husting, the Sheriffs' Court and the Mayor's Court, from which went writs and letters. The majority of letters in the last series are applications made by London to provincial towns to restore monies or goods taken from London citizens as customs or toll. Others demanded the surrender of runaway apprentices, and there are many letters to continental towns.

These records show that a petitioner or his attorney was usually the bearer of a letter received by the court and that he would normally take back the court's reply. A typical entry is:

> Adam Fraunceys, Mayor, and the Aldermen of the City of London to the mayor and Bailiffs of the town of Reading desiring them for love's sake to deliver up to Nicholas Ploket and John de Hardyngham, citizens or London, or to their attorney, the bearer of these letters, three sarplers and one pocket of wool belonging to them, which they had recently purchased from a merchant of Salisbury to carry to Redynge, where it had remained in the custody of Hugh Croft; that there might be no necessity to write again on the same subject. The Lord have them in his keeping. London 2nd February.[28]

A few other letters refer to a bearer who is not named but is evidently a person paid to carry mail. An example concerns John Else, imprisoned in the gaol of the abbot of St Albans, asking for his release and for a reply by the bearer.[29]

There is also a series of letters sent to the sheriffs and justices 'of the good towns of France in parts of Normandy'. The London records show that any

responsible employee might carry letters. For example, in July 1338 William de Iford, common sergeant, was despatched to the Abbot of Lesnes.[30]
Town officials and town courts needed letter carriers and many were employed at times by the government. The Issue Rolls for 1309–10 list twelve London couriers and in the next year nine are employed. During 1310 Richard le Mercer, courier of London, took royal letters to Berwick and there are many other examples in the next decade. The Rolls for 1370 record a payment:

> To divers messengers and couriers and other valets of the City of London hired and sent on the 29th day of June – to wit, John Typet, a messenger, Hugh Escote, Richard de Imworth and Thomas Durant to the Mayor and Bailiffs of Sandwich [...] 26s 8d.[31]

Another in the same year shows that the number of Westminster town messengers was considerable:

> To divers messengers and couriers and others, valets of the town of Westminster, hired and sent to all parts of England with letters of Privy Seal, directed to Archbishops, Earls, Barons and other Lords and Ladies of the realm of England and Wales, that they be ordered to be present at London at the exequies of Philippa, late Queen of England, and with letters of Privy Seal, directed to all mayors and bailiffs in all ports and other boroughs and towns of England, that they appear before the King's Council in eight days of St. Hilary, concerning urgent business of the said King, and for the benefit of the Kingdom of England; and also with letters from the Lord Treasurer, and divers writs and commissions of Great Seal, directed to the escheators in divers counties, to seize into the King's hands the lands of divers Lords who held of the King in capite. £8 1s 0d.[32]

A further source of information about London letter carriers in the late Middle Ages is in the surviving journals and repertories which summarise the administrative work of the city. They show that from 1482 to 1491 each of the two sheriffs had eighteen sergeants and as many valets. These were the men who took the letters and writs in addition to their other duties.
The office of Mayor of London dates back to at least 1193 and in a study of his household before 1600 it is estimated that by the fourteenth century he had four sergeants, two bailiffs and a town crier.[33] One entry for 1370 in the Issue Rolls is of particular interest:

> To divers messengers and couriers sent to all parts of England on the 3rd day of August, with writs from the Exchequer, directed to all Escheators and Sheriffs

> in England. to raise money for the King's use. In money to be delivered to John Bray for their wages, as appears by the particulars remaining in the hanaper of this term. £1 18s 4d.[34]

John Bray is not known as a royal messenger. It seems that in this case London men were being employed through an agent who received the total payment.

A patent of 1396 tells us of some of the difficulties incurred by messengers and other travellers in hiring horses. By far the busiest of the roads was that from London to Dover, and when Richard II was at King's Langley near York he received a petition from two hirers of horses on the road. The problems they raised were evidently familiar ones and a patent was issued on 3 April, reducing some charges but giving legal protection to the petitioners and others. Its instructions throw light on the practices at the time and the way in which responsibilities were put upon the towns, so they are quoted in full:

> Order to sheriffs, mayors etc. to publish in their bailiwicks - upon the petition of Reginald Shrowsbury and Thomas Athekoe, hackneymen, that they and other hackneymen of Southwark, Deptford, Rochester, and towns between London and Dover having heretofore had for the hire of a hakenei between Southwark and Rochester 16d and from Rochester to Canterbury 16d, divers men passing through these parts take the horses of petitioners and their partners and ride them against their will, paying little or nothing for the work or hire of the horses, so that they are often lost or sold or taken quite away, leading to their great scarcity – that there shall be taken for the hire of a hakenei from Southwark to Rochester 12d, from Rochester to Canterbury 12d, and from Canterbury to Dover 6d, and from town to town according to that rate of 12d and the number of miles; that the petitioners be in nonwise compelled to let their horses for hire unless paid promptly therefor; and that for the better security of the horses a branding iron be kept in each of those towns by an approved person for branding, without payment, horses on hire, and that no one buy or sell or remove a branded horse or dock its ears or tail or kill it, under heavy penalties; the petitioners and their partners to be at liberty, by view of the bailiffs or constables of the place, to seize and remove any such horse; provided always that should horses so hired fail by their own inability or weakness to complete the journey, and not through the fault of their riders, such sum to be returned to the hirers as they can show to have been reasonably paid by them to complete the journey.[35]

These practices so concerned the Parliament of the same year that the seizure of horses was the subject of legislation:

> Foreasmuch as the Commons have made complaint, that many great Mischiefs, Extortions and Oppressions have been done by divers people of evil condition which, of their own authority take and cause to be taken royally Horses and other things, and beasts out of the Wains, carts and houses, saying and devising that they be to ride on hasty Messages and Business, where of truth they be in no wise privy to any Business or Message, but only in Deceit and Subtlety by any Colour and Device to take horses and the said horses too hastily do ride and evil intreat, having no Manner of Conscience or Compassion in this Behalf so that the said horses become all spoiled and foundered, paying no manner of thing nor penny for the same.[36]

The act then prescribes 'for the Quietness and Ease of his people' that anyone responsible 'shall be taken and imprisoned till he hath made due agreement to the Party'. As we saw in Chapter 3, an Act of 1447 revoked all royal patents that had allowed innkeepers and brewers to seize horses and carts in the king's name.

By the fourteenth century there had developed a considerable demand for letter writing in towns by the civic authorities, the guilds and leading citizens. The volume of letter writing in London led to shops being used for the purpose. The *London Letter Books* refer to writers of court-letter and to tixtwriters (*sic*) both of whom were enrolled as crafts, then called mysteries. The first reference to them is on 20 May 1357 when the mayor and aldermen of London, by a curious juxtaposition, ordered that the writers of the court and text letter, together with the limners and barbers dwelling in the city, should not in future be summoned on judicial investigations or inquests. The writers of the court letter, the original scriveners, used the formal and professional style of writing required for legal and other documents that differed from the cursive handwriting used by amateurs. They differed from the text writers who used the style then required for books. The limners were those who illustrated books and manuscripts. It is particularly interesting to see these categories of men accepted in the city at this time, for it indicates that already there were professionals who were not clerics specialising in such work.

In 1364 the Mayor of London issued regulations for the government of all crafts within the city. Four or six men were to be chosen in each craft and sworn to see that the order was obeyed. Penalties were set and a scale of punishments ranging from fines to imprisonment was laid down for those who infringed them. Nine years later the writers of the court letter petitioned the mayor and aldermen that those who call themselves 'escryveys, undertaking wills, charters and all other things touching the said craft' might have a set of rules. They complained that 'foreigners' were bringing the craft into disrepute.

The ordinances that were granted on 26 September 1373 mark the foundation of the Scriveners' Company. No one was to practise the craft unless examined and found competent by their wardens. The writers of the text letter became separated and eventually they formed a distinct guild with the limners. They were the predecessors of the Worshipful Company of Stationers, who received a royal charter in 1403. The *London Letter Books* record in 1392:

> Came into the Chamber of the Guildhall good men of the art of writers of the Court-letter and presented to the Mayor and Aldermen Martin Seman and John Cossier, whom they had elected masters of their craft for the ensuing year, and the said Martin and John were sworn.[37]

There is another entry for January 1440 approving detailed articles for the craft, preventing a writer from opening more than one shop without permission and imposing a yearly fee of 12d.[38]

Except in London and a few major cities the text writers had no monopoly of their skills but the signature of a registered text writer on a document indicated that it had been professionally composed. Other letter writers included the clerks. The records of Nottingham, for example, mention the mayor's clerk in the middle of the fifteenth century. They also refer in 1481–82 to a chaplain employed to write letters for which he was claiming payment of 12d. A study of occupations in sixteenth-century Norwich shows five scriveners in 1525 and eighteen in 1569, an indication of the increase in the writing of letters and documents.[39]

Eventually the scriveners became known as writers, and the master, wardens and assistants of the Society of Writers of the City of London were incorporated by letters patent on 28 January 1618. The grant of arms made to them in 1634 describes them as otherwise known as the Worshipful Company of Scriveners.[40]

Apart from the statutory requirements that towns should have clerks there are many references to them in town records outside London. The importance of the boroughs was recognised by their incorporation into medieval parliaments. At the end of the fifteenth century 224 burgesses sat in the House of Commons, outnumbering the 74 knights of the shires. It has been calculated that there were 609 boroughs.[41] Much of the royal revenue came from customs duties raised in the ports which now equalled the revenue from all the royal estates.[42] Each important town had its carriers and its postmen who, as we have seen, could be asked to deliver royal mail. It was logical that when under Henry VIII an improvement in the distribution and collection of the royal mail took place it was based on the existing town posts. How this was done will be described in Chapter 8.

6
FIFTEENTH-CENTURY LETTERS

The fifteenth century is a turning point in the history of our language and of English letters. In Chapter 4 we noted the few surviving letters written in English before 1400 and just after that the group of letters from Lady Zouche in the National Archives.[1] A proclamation concerning the Provisions of Oxford had been circulated in 1258 in English, a Statute of 1362 had recited the reasons why English should be used in law courts and a few wills written in the vernacular are known before 1400, but all these examples of English usage are unusual. Kingsford analysed the proportion of French to English letters in the fifteenth century from those in the Proceedings and Ordinances of the Privy Council and concluded 'for the reign of Henry IV nearly all the letters are in French and only one in English; under Henry V the English letters are about equal to those in French; under Henry VI letters in French are the exception'.[2]

Latin was becoming limited to international correspondence, church liturgies and scholarly use by lawyers and churchmen. The use of French by the nobility began to decline. Despite Henry V's reconquest of Normandy, his early death and his son's minority had led to the French territories being lost by 1453, events which strengthened the sense of national identity and so promoted the use of English in the courts and Parliament. The poets Langland and Chaucer and the translators of the Wycliffite versions of the Bible had shown that the English language could be a medium for poetry and literature which was lively, humorous and dignified.

The availability of paper, cheaper than vellum or parchment, made letter writing possible for more of the population. Spectacles to rectify long sight had been exported from northern Italy since the end of the thirteenth century and so were extending the intellectual life of scholars. Those with short sight were not helped until a century and a half later. In the late fifteenth century many towns had their schools, often charitable foundations, and there were others at monasteries, nunneries and chantries. Collections of contemporary letters written in English began to appear, and they give us our earliest detailed insight into family relationships and conditions within the home. We meet our ancestors who write of the trivia of daily life, buying clothes and furniture, as well as sharing in the joy of a wedding or the anguish of a sudden death. William Harleston wrote from Denham in 1480 to console his nephew who had lost his wife, to describe arrangements he had made to provide him with 100 marks at The Sword in Fleet Street, to send suggestions for his garden, and to offer some personal advice:

> My Right reverend and worshipful nephew. I and my wife recommend us unto you with all our hearts. And I beseech almighty God to have mercy upon my lady your wife's soul, for verily she was a good woman and well disposed. [...] And of certain things I would desire and pray you in the name of God; that you will not over wish you, nor over-purchase you, nor over build you. For these three things will pluck a young man right low. Nor meddle not with no great matters in the law. For I trust to God to see you the worshipfullest of the Stonors that ever I saw or shall see my days.[3]

Suddenly, as we read such kindly letters, the fifteenth century comes alive and social historians have their first insight into the life and feelings of our ancestors. We are able to hear the voices of the past.

The most extensive collections of English medieval letters are those of the monarchy. Very few from the nobility survive, although their account books show they wrote many. Hundreds of medieval royal letters exist, considerable selections of which have been translated in the volumes of Ellis' *Original Letters* and Sir Harris Nicholas's *Proceedings and Ordinances of the Privy Council of England from 1386 to 1461*. Many of them are royal commands in letter form. They provide the authentic material of history, fresher and far more immediate than the pages of the chroniclers. Among them is an almost complete correspondence of Henry V to the mayors of London which contains detailed accounts of many major events in our history. It can be regarded as a newsletter of the type noted in Chapter 2. That Henry could write personal letters in his own hand is shown by a note on a state paper: 'For the secretness of this matter, I have written this instruction and sealed it with my signet of the eagle'.[4]

When Henry left for France on the first of his campaigns he sent his herald to King Charles with a letter. In accordance with the strict medieval rules for the conduct of war, he set out his claims to what he reckoned was his own territory. Its rejection would establish his right to use force. By this time heralds had become the proper carriers of such letters. The senior royal heralds had the title of Kings of Arms and wore a distinctive crown of lozenges with a royal coat of arms, appropriate to those speaking to sovereigns. During the Hundred Years' War they summoned towns to surrender, arranged ransoms, and could regulate behaviour even on the battlefield. At Agincourt the French and English heralds met at an agreed observation post and kept count of the dukes, counts, knights and squires who were killed.[5]

Before the battle for Harfleur Henry wrote to the city of London and described his plans, writing again later when he had accepted its surrender from the kneeling governor. Such letters describing his military triumphs provide a vivid picture of events. When he had concluded the Treaty of Troyes, which made him successor to the French king, he wrote to his brother, Humphrey, warden of England, telling him the news and giving instructions for the use of his new title and the amendments to be made on his seals.[6] Henry was our most important medieval royal letter writer, though his and other royal letters present problems. Rarely do they give the year, and often they omit both day and month.

The French wars are mainly remembered for the results of battles, but their effects on individuals are shown in petitions like this sent by a soldier to Henry VI in 1422:

> To the King our Sovereign Lord. Besecheth meekly your poor liegeman and humble Orator Thomas Hostell, that in consideration of his service done to your noble projenitors of full blessed memory King Henry IV and King Henry V, whose souls God assoil; being at the seige of Harfleu, where smitten with a springbolt through the head, losing his one eye and with his cheekbone broken; also at the Battle of Agincourt, and after at the Taking of the carricks on the Sea, there with a gad of iron his plates smitten asunder, and sore hurt, maimed and wounded; by means of whereof he being sore feeble and bruised, now fallen to great age and poverty; greatly indebted; and may not help himself; having not wherewith to be sustained nor relieved but by men's gracious alms; and being for his said service never yet recompensed nor rewarded, it please your high and Excellent Grace, the premises tenderly considered, and of your benign pity and grace, to relieve and refresh your said poor Orator.[7]

The variety of the royal letter carriers can be illustrated from contemporary rolls. Apart from the *nuntii*, the master of requests of the household was paid £66 for carrying messages and the royal almoner received £10 for a journey taking letters to Honeby Castle. One Gascon warrant dated 8 September 1436 shows how particular care was taken in choosing an appropriate person to take the mail. No ordinary servant or messenger was chosen, but someone who could discuss matters of state and bring back instructions:

allowed to the discreet and venerable person Master Jehan Levesque, master in theology, with a monk and a clerk in his company, to the King, our said Lord, to carry closed letters from my Lords Saint Pierre and from my Lords Scales and Fastolf, touching the affairs of the King my said Lord, the rebellion of the city of Paris, and the arrival of the enemies assembled at Granvelle, and to state to my saide Lords of England certain matters verbally, with which the said master Jehan has been entrusted.

His journey, which took in visits to the Lord Cardinal and the Duke of Gloucester, lasted fifty-one days and involved a cost of £77 18s 4d.[8]

The letters show that much diplomacy was left to the letter carrier who might be a nobleman or bishop. Among the letters from the reign of Henry VI is one from Henry to Charles VII of France, written in 1444:

These messengers, after we had received by them your gracious letters, which we saw with joy, have certified of your good state and health [...] and [how you] devoted yourself to deliberate and discuss the matter of the said peace.[9]

They were persons of rank who could speak freely to both kings about the negotiations.

The poignant tale of Joan of Arc is told in a long letter attributed to Henry VI and received by his uncle, the Duke of Burgundy, in 1431. After describing her trials he comes to her end:

And, because she was still obstinate in her trespasses and villainous offences, she was delivered to the secular power, the which condemned her to be burnt, and consumed in the fire. And when she saw that the fatal day of her obstinacy was come, she openly confessed that the spirits which to her often did appear were evil and false, and apparent liars; and that their promise, which they had made, to deliver her out of captivity, was false and untrue, affirming herself by those spirits to be often beguiled, blinded and mocked. And so, being in good mind, she was by the justices carried to the old market, within the city of Rouen, and there by the fire consumed to ashes, in sight of the people.[10]

For gruesome detail it would be hard to match a request sent to Henry VI in 1450 by 'your poor leiges, Thomas Canynges and William Hulyn, late sheriffs of your city of London'. After Jack Cade's revolt they had been ordered to deliver the quartered bodies of several traitors to various towns:

> And by another of your said writs to send and deliver the head of one Thomas Cheyny, feigning himself a hermit, cleped Bluebeard, attainted of high treason, to the mayor and Bailiffs of your city of Canterbury. And by another of your writs to set up a quarter of the said traitor cleped Bluebeard upon a gate of London, and to send and deliver another quarter of the said traitor to the Sheriffs of your City of Norwich, and to send and deliver two other quarters of the same traitor to the Wardens of the Cinque Ports or to their Lieutenants.[11]

There had been problems 'for and by cause that hardly any person durst nor would take upon the carriage of the said head and quarters for doubt of their lives'. The writers presumed to ask Henry for the farm of the City of London and the County of Middlesex as reward for their pains!

Royal letters give insights into the daily conduct of the king's household. There is one from Edward IV in 1473 to the earl of Rivers and the bishop of Rochester, who had been put in charge of the education of his son, Prince Edward, laying down very detailed rules for the pattern of each day and for the behaviour of his household.[12]

The day was to begin with mass followed by breakfast. Then came 'vertuous learning', including grammar and music, which took place before dinner-time, the dishes for which were to be carried by squires wearing the king's livery. During the meal noble stories were read 'as behoveth to a prince to understand and know'. He was to 'eschew idleness' and if not occupied with his learning was to be instructed in sports and exercises. After evensong there was supper and he was to be in bed by eight o'clock. He also had a sermon preached on holy days. Even the members of the household did not escape strict regulation. They heard Mass at six o'clock, had dinner at ten, and supper at four, except on fast days when dinner was at twelve. The opening and shutting of the gates by the porters was strictly regulated; between Michaelmas and May they were shut at nine and opened at six, the times being extended by an hour for the rest of the year. Present were three chaplains, a physician, a surgeon, treasurers, chamberlains, receivers, and a council governed by statutes and ordinances.

Nobles and towns faced crucial decisions concerning their allegiance during the civil wars. Richard III sent this command from Lincoln to the 'Mayor, aldermen, sheriffs and community of the city of York' in 1484:

> Trusty and right well-beloved, we greet you well. And let you to wit, that the Duke of Buckingham traitrously is turned upon us, contrary to the duty of his allegiance and intendeth the utter destruction of us, you, and all other of our true subjects who have taken our part; whose traitrous intent we, with God's

> grace intend briefly to resist and subdue. We desire and pray you in our hearty wise, that ye will send to us as many men, defensibly arrayed on horseback, as ye may godly make, to our town of Leicester the 21st day of this present month withouten fail; as ye will tender our honour and your own weal. And we shall so see you paid for your reward and charges, as ye shall hold ye well content; giving further credence to our trusty pursuivant, this bearer.[13]

Few documents can rival for interest and drama that despatched by Henry VII, the first of the Tudors, immediately after his victory at Bosworth in 1485:

> Henry, by the grace of God, King of England and France, Prince of Wales and Lord of Ireland, strictly chargeth and commandeth, upon pain of death, that no manner of man rob or spoil no manner of commons coming from the field; but suffer them to pass home to their countries and dwelling-places, with their horses and harness. And, moreover, that no manner of man take upon him to go to no gentleman's place, neither in the country, nor within cities nor boroughs, nor pick no quarrels for old or for new matters; but keep the King's peace, upon pain of hanging. And moreover, if there be any man offered to be robbed or spoiled of his goods, let him come to Master Richard Borrow, the king's sergeant here, and he shall have warrant for his body and his goods, unto the time of the king's pleasure be known. And moreover, the king ascertaineth you, that Richard, Duke of Gloucester, lately called King Richard, was lately slain at a place called Sandeford, within the shire of Leicester, and there was laid openly, that every man might see and look upon him. And there was also slain upon the same field, John, late Duke of Norfolk, John, late Earl of Lincoln, Thomas, late Earl of Surrey, Franceys Viscount Lovel, Sir Walter Deveres, Lord Ferrars, Richard Ratcliffe, knight, Robert Brackenbury, knight, with many other knights, squires, and gentlemen; on whose souls God have mercy![14]

The claims were somewhat exaggerated as several of those mentioned had not died.

Details of weapons of war can be found in writs such as this from Henry VII to the Lord Treasurer in 1489 concerning preparations against an expected rising:

> Whereas we be credibly informed that certain of our unnatural subjects in the north parties [parts] of late have assembled them, intending against the natural duty of their allegiance to make insurrection against us and to subvert the commonweal and policy of this our realm, whose seditious purpose we with God's might intend briefly to subdue in our person; we therefore will and charge

> you that without delay ye deliver and pay to the clerk of our ordnance, money competent as well for the carriage and conveying unto the said north parts of vi faulcons [light cannon] that come from beyond the sea, and vi other faulcons of brass with ii serpents [cannon] of brass, as for the purveyance and carriage of one whole last of gun-powder, mlccc bows with their strings, mcmlvii sheaf of arrows, and ml bills, ii barrels of caltrappes [balls with spikes to check cavalry], and cc pair of brigandines [body armour] with all their apparel etc. Given at the castle at Hertford.[15]

Few of the royal letters give us any personal insights but one written in 1497 by Henry VII to his mother Margaret concludes in a touching way:

> Madame, I have encumbered you now with this my long writing, but one thinks that I can do no less, considering that it is so seldom that I do write, wherefore I beseech you to pardon me, for verily, madame, my sight is nothing so perfect as it has been, and I know well it will appear daily, wherefore I trust you will not be displeased, though I write not so often with mine own hand, for on my faith I have been three days or I could make an end of this letter.[16]

Henry wrote in response to letters that had been brought by Margaret's confessor, who was John Fisher, Bishop of Rochester, later to be executed by Henry VIII.

Before the fifteenth century few personal letters have survived. However, by the middle of the century there are enough surviving letters to indicate that it had become customary among the lesser gentry and merchant classes to write to their families. They indicate that most of the gentry could write legibly in English. Their stewards were required to be literate and even some petty tradesmen who supplied them with goods could write clearly and produce accounts. A new social class had emerged of merchants owning town houses and country estates, able to afford the payment of messengers to carry their business and personal letters. Their style sometimes follow the style of the *Dictamen* but that probably depended upon whether they were written down by a skilful person trained in that manner. They are quite unlike those of Peter de Blois.

In the Paston Letters there is an account of the twenty witnesses called concerning Sir John Fastolf's will in 1466, which give an indication of literacy at the time.[17] They were described in the order they were called as a smith, a husbandman, a cook, a freeman, a gentleman, a husbandman, a clerk, a husbandman, a husbandman, a husbandman, a roper, a merchant, a husbandman, a tailor, a merchant, a mariner, a husbandman, a mariner, a freeman, not categorised, and a tailor. Of these twenty varied witnesses nineteen are described as either literate or illiterate. Eight are credited with the ability to read. One gentleman cannot read but two husbandmen can. In a letter from the same correspondence (probably Christmas Eve 1484) Margery Paston writes to her husband to say that the man he had left in charge of bread and ale cannot make up the weekly accounts though in other respects she finds him a wise man, the presumption being that even a person in so lowly a position should have been able to present written accounts.[18]

The Stonor letters contain six from apprentices to their masters and papers attached to the letters include accounts from tradespeople including a weaver and a shoemaker. We are left with the impression that a considerable proportion of the population could read and write by the end of the fifteenth century. So many could read that by 1489 it had been found necessary in establishing the legal benefit of clergy to distinguish between laymen who could read and those who were clerks. Many literate gentry employed scribes to write their letters; indeed, doing the writing themselves might be thought to be beneath their dignity.

Most letters have been preserved because of their legal importance. The Stonor correspondence was probably confiscated when Sir William Stonor was attainted in 1483; the correspondence was subsequently stored in the tower of London, but other evidence suggests that the letters, or parts of them, were preserved after a Chancery suit in 1512. The Shillingford letters concerned a long-standing legal dispute with the bishop of Exeter and were retained as evidence. The Cely papers also were a legal exhibit and some of the Paston ones may have been kept because of the legal disputes over the inheritance that came to them from Sir John Fastolf. However, the family had a practice, established over three centuries, of keeping their letters despite the warnings they contain about the dangers of preserving them. Eventually, many of them were sold in the eighteenth century to pay part of the debts of the second Lord Yarmouth, himself a Paston. Many of the collections of letters are gathered in the National Archives under the heading of Ancient Correspondence.

The backgrounds of the families are varied. Shillingford was the mayor of Exeter, employed to put the city's case in the London law courts. Marchall was a clerk in Chancery who never took holy orders and so was allowed to marry. Sir John Pelham was constable of Pevensey Castle and in 1399 was made a knight of the Bath. The Stonors were wealthy landowners whose family fortunes were founded by Sir John Stonor, a chief justice of the Common Pleas, who had died in 1354. Their estates extended over several southern counties.

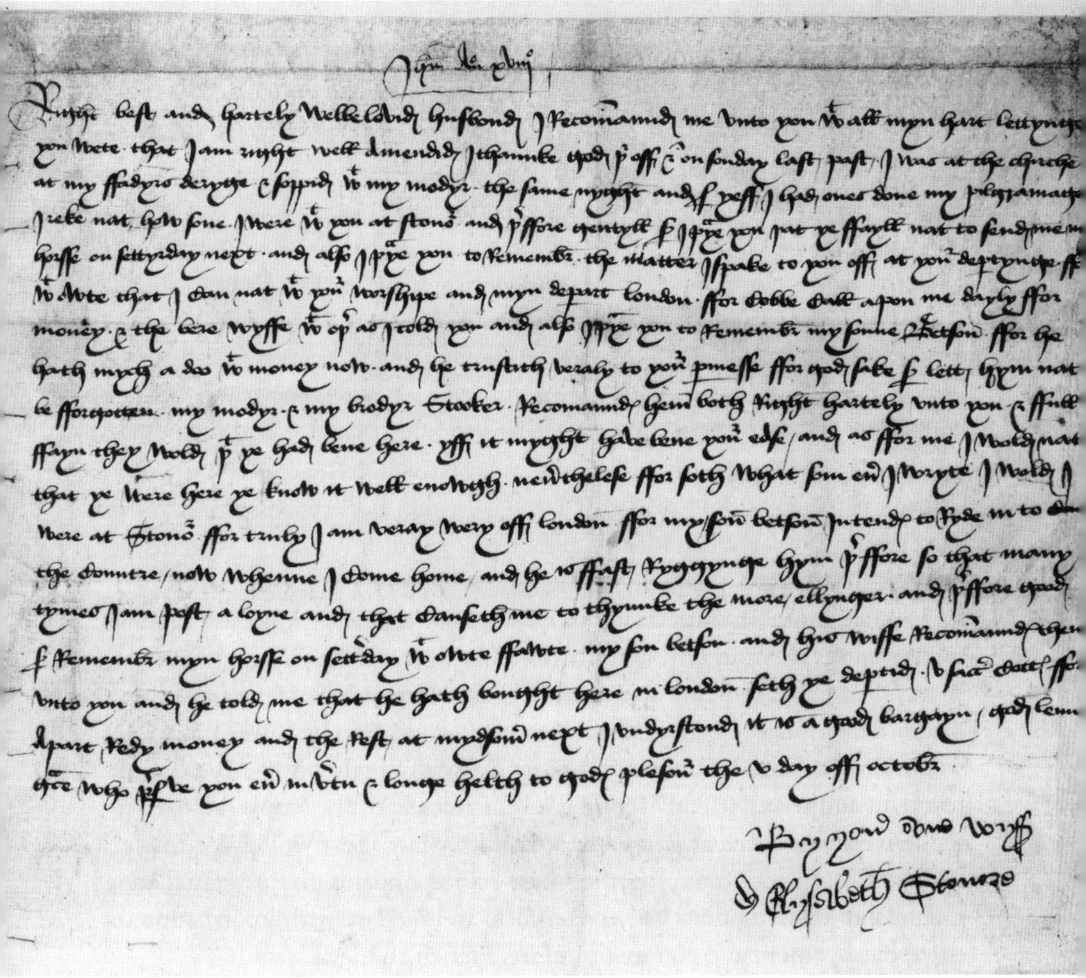

6.1 Letter from Elizabeth Stonor in 1478, headed 'Jhesu Ano xviij Right best and hartely well beloved husbond, I recommend me unto you with all myn hart, lettynge you wte that I am right wel amendid, I thannke God. (National Archives. SC 1/46 f190)

They were members of Parliament, justices of the peace and often sheriffs. The Plumptons were northern gentry, often in a penurious state, and the Pastons an important Norfolk family, much occupied with legal struggles to maintain their properties.

The Celys were merchants of the Staple, the principal trade association of later medieval England. From 1353 the only staple for exports was established at Calais and no wool, skins, worsteds, cheese, butter, lead, coal or grindstones could be exported to the continent except by this route. A century later, between 1475 and 1488, when the surviving letters were written, the Celys

6.2 Merchant's mark on a Stonor letter. (National Archives. SC 1/46/90)

had one or more of their family in Calais dealing mainly with the Flemish traders, and others at their London office. Those across the Channel frequently travelled to Bruges and the markets in Flanders, while those in London made their journeys mainly to Gloucestershire to purchase wool and fells. The address of a 1482 letter from Robert Eryke in London reads, 'To my right reverend and trusty friend George Cely, merchant of the Staple, be this letter delivered in Calais, at Bruges or at Barrow Mart'. Barrow was the English form of Bergen op Zoom. Together these correspondents give us a fascinating insight into contemporary society, business and the law, with information on estate management and comments on the French and civil wars.

The Shillingford letters date from 1447 to 1450 and concern the later stages of a long drawn out legal suit brought by the bishop, dean and chapter of Exeter against the mayor and citizens of the city. John Shillingford was the mayor and the correspondence shows the extraordinary lengths he went to in offering gifts to the lord chancellor and other dignitaries. While there is little postal information to be gleaned from the letters, we have contemporary evidence of the time taken in travel between Exeter and London:

> Memo that on Saturday the xii day of April [1448] Thomas Dowrissh and William Spere with him, rode out of Exeter to London wards, and came to London on Tuesday next following at iij at the bell afternoon.[19]

The distance was at least 170 miles. We also find note of payments made to messengers; 'payment to William Hampton for expenses taking le blak rolle et other writings to London xiijs iiijd [13s 4d]'. William was evidently a person of some status, for another London messenger is paid only 3s 4d while one who went to Tuverton (Tiverton) received 2s 7d.[20]

The five Pelham letters are fascinating. In 1399 John Pelham landed with Henry, Duke of Lancaster, and stayed with him until he was crowned king. His wife wrote to him from Pevensey Castle, a letter that was discussed in Chapter 4. Another from Sir John Cheyne is typical of many medieval letters in that the bearer is entrusted with the news: 'the bearer hereof shall declare it than by mouth more plainly than I can write at this time.' The other three letters come from France, where his son and son-in-law were with Henry V during a campaign and provide lively details of campaigning. The son-in-law, Sir John St Clair, sends his 'trusty servant William Bryton' to obtain £20 for him, and his son, Sir John Pelham, asks:

> that ye would purchase and send thereto, as touching another horse, and two garments for summer, and such things as you list yourself, for truly by your leave, there the time of worship for young men is now, and also by your leave, all that one side of Normandy is English, except Cherbourg and Harfleur.[21]

It is a moving request.

In contrast, the thirteen Marchall letters tell of the affairs of a small landowner and deal with rentals, building works and his chronic shortage of money to maintain his two estates. He becomes involved in the wool trade but lacks the capital to prosper. Of most interest are letters from John, a tenant who is a working smith, and Thomas Makyn, Marchall's agent. They describe the building of his 'chamber', a new room being constructed by two carpenters and two sawyers who worked by candle light to complete the task. The floors and parapets were of oak, the rafters of elm. Thomas wonders if a letter setting out the costs and taken by a parson of Gloucestershire who had claimed to know William Marchall had been received, as also that sent:

> by a carrier of Oxford to the which I pray you deliver twenty shillings without more and charge him to send it me in haste, and if you will buy one pound of pepper to carry money surely I will pay therefore, other else two pounds of rice for that makes great bulk. The carrier is at Inne in Friday Street, or at the Belle, other else at the Saracen Head as I suppose.[22]

The Cely letters dating from 1472 to 1488 number 247. Those written from London by Richard are to George at the wool staple in Calais. Like some other merchants' letters of the period they often have a personal device drawn on the outside, presumably to distinguish them from others in a bag. Such merchants' marks are of considerable antiquity, and were used over shop fronts or signs, on funerary inscriptions, to show ownership of a bale of merchandise or the origin of a document. In origin they were the signs of individuals or families, but later they were also used as the signs of merchant companies or guilds.[23]

In the later Middle Ages almost everyone used a mark, whether he was a trader or not. Letter 66 of the Cely papers describes an Essex cheese with the maker's mark on it. Most have an upright line with added initials or sign. It has been surmised that their origin goes back to the use of runes. Richard Cely used a quartered shield with a diagonal bar in the upper part and a circle in the lower. The Cely letters are usually headed with the year and conclude with the day and month. They are addressed most politely, such as to 'My loving friend' or to 'The worshipful master', followed by the name. Occasionally there is reference to an enclosure, being a letter to be forwarded to a friend.

It is obvious that the Celys had no public messenger service available to them even though the route from London to Calais was the most travelled of contemporary roads. We see, for example, in a letter of 28 November 1481 that they had sent a letter 'by the Fleming's man', another by Kay and a third by Benet Trotter. On occasion there were problems arising from the delivery of mail. This example sent from William to George Cely shows what could happen:

> Item Sir, I understand by your said letter that your masterships have received no writing from me since Addlynton was here whereof I marvel for I wrote ij letters to you while I was at Bruges specifying of divers matters of Flanders the one was sent from Calais by Jamys Jarfford mercer, the other by Peryman, packer of clyfte wullye. He is lodged at the Crosse Keye ...[24]

They allowed eight days for the transit of letters to Calais and rarely had a loss. These Cely letters are of great importance to the economic historian for they give an account of the current system of credit and of every part of the wool trade which was then the principal trade of England.

The extensive collection of Stonor papers, dating from 1290 to 1483, contains letters, estate and household accounts, inventories and bills from tradesmen. Twenty-seven letters date between 1377 and 1380, three in Latin, the others in French. The latter are a sample of correspondence between the gentry at that time. From the Stonor letters we can draw a wider range of information than from any other medieval family. We have descriptions of household furnishings in the manor house, of their clothing, litigation and marriage settlements, and of help given to Oxford students. Most of the letters are signed and show that the family and their principal servants were literate.

One letter dated on 'the Saturday after Ascension day last' (13 May 1480), written by Richard Germyn, an Exeter merchant and agent for Sir William Stonor, tells us much about the way in which letters travelled at the time:

> Right Worshipful and Honourable Master, I commend me unto you. And whereas you wrote unto me to deliver your letters unto the Gentleman that they be directed unto in Devonshire and Cornwall unto a trusty man, I shall so deliver them that your will and intent shall be fulfilled. [...] Moreover, I late wrote you a letter and send him by one John Symon, which gave you the oranges and marmalade at Exeter: which letter was delivered unto Lannos, skinner, inasmuch as you be not at London. I trust you have him. Also you wrote unto me, to have your plate, which is with Master John at Wille; at your letter's delivery he was not at home, but before Midsummer I shall bring it to London packed in the carrier's pack of Exeter: so by the grace of God I shall deliver you myself.[25]

The letters show us how respectful society was in those times and how strict was the obedience expected from the younger family members by their elders.

The Plumptons were a Yorkshire family, living near Knaresborough, whose surviving letters include news of marriage settlements, legal affairs and insurrections, together with information on the trials of Perkin Warbeck and the Earl of Warwick. The earliest letter, dated 19 February 1433, is from Lord Scrope of Masham; another from Henry VI is a command to bring troops to York to assist in dealing with the revolt of the earl of March. The correspondence shows that their messengers brought not only letters but a variety of gifts and animals. An undated letter (from the 1490s) from the earl of Northumberland asked for hounds:

> Right heartily beloved cousin, I commend me to you. And for as much as I am destitute of running hounds, I desire and pray you to send me a couple with my servant, this bringer. And of things like I have for your pleasure,. Written in my lodging at Spetell of the street [in Lincoln] the xxix day of October. Over this, Cousin, I pray you to send me your tame hart, for mine are deer or dead.[26]

Another from his cousin Ralfe Ryther asks that the bringer of the letter should return with 'two cople of conyes' for stocking his ground.[27]

One letter shows how a messenger might be sent into an area to find out what was taking place there. On the occasion of the Duke of Buckingham's rebellion against Richard III, Edward Plumpton writes to Sir Robart on 18 October 1483 giving news of the movements of various lords, 'Messengers come daily, both from the King's grace and the Duke, into this country'.[28]

The indications are that their letters were carried by relatives, family retainers or trusted persons travelling in the right direction. The Plumpton letters were normally sent by personal servants and rarely mention their remuneration. One from Ralph Aldburgh to his aunt mentions that he has paid the bearer 12d for taking the two letters he sends.[29]

A far more extensive collection of private letters is that of the Paston family and their correspondents. Gairdner's edition adds a number of letters from the records of Sir John Fastolf of Caister, and Fenn's edition gives some other contemporary documents. In all, over 1,000 of their fifteenth-century letters survive, providing a lively picture of the social and business concerns of a Norfolk county family and their friends. They were sheriffs, lawyers, soldiers and courtiers. There are descriptions of life at court, of legal battles, journeys abroad and travels on the roads, but their greatest value is the light they throw on social and family relationships at this time. Some documents are of historical importance like the two lengthy Yorkist accounts of the Battle of St Albans in 1455[30] and those which refer to Jack Cade's rebellion. A deeply moving unique copy letter has been preserved in the collection written to his son by the Duke of Suffolk just before his murder. It is an eloquent defence of his actions, which were far from being treasonable:

> Secondly, next him [i.e. God], above all earthly thing, to be true liege man in heart, in will, in thought, in deed, unto the Kyng our elder most high and dread sovereign Lord, to whom both you and I been so much bound to; charging you, as father can and may, rather to die than be to the contrary.[31]

It is evident that most Paston family members, in particular those who were lawyers, could read and write, their hands varying from excellent to moderate. The family was always concerned to educate its children. Many of the letters are drafts and it is obvious that some writers found composition difficult. Some apologise for the handwriting but most preferred to have the fair copy written by a scribe. For family correspondence copies were made and replies retained; many original letters are from correspondents of the Pastons. The important correspondents always had their letters composed by secretaries: they may add 'your faithefull cousin' or 'trusty friend' before their signature. Sir John Fastolf, who had as a secretary the distinguished contemporary writer, William of Worcester, did no more than sign his name. Few letters are dated but those from professional secretaries frequently give the regnal year, while clergy often give the year AD. The Pastons followed the usual contemporary practice when writing by referring to a Church festival such as Ash Wednesday, then called Pulver Wednesday, or Crouchmas Day, which was 3 May. In one case Agnes Paston dates a letter by reference to the collect used on the previous Sunday. There is a careful date at the end of a letter from Margaret Paston to her son Sir John Paston written on 7 August 1477 about various payments of money that had to be made, including his brother's 'boord and hys scole hyer':

> Written at Mawteby, the day after Saint Lauerons, the year and the reign of King E the iiijth the xvij year

This is exceptional, as it was unusual to give the year in personal correspondence.[32]

Despatching the letter was often difficult and many were written when it was realised that a messenger would be available. To send a personal servant was expensive, though sometimes necessary. Most of the bearers are named only once – 'a man of S. Michael's parish' or, even more vaguely, 'a man of Yarmouth'. The Pastons relied principally on local men. There were occasions when servants from nearby abbeys and priories were used. John Paston thanks his brother for a hat sent 'by John, the Abbot of St Bennet's man' and John Wykes writing in 1465 mentions 'I sent you an answer in a letter by a man of the Prior of Bronholm'. Otherwise a local carrier could be used and advantage taken of travellers to the great fairs such as Smithfields or St Bartholomew in London.

There are two references to 'runners' who took mail and documents to Rome. In 1473 Sir John Paston had contracted to marry Mistress Ann Hault but both parties eventually wished to be released from their obligations. Ann was perturbed about the moral consequences of withdrawal. John wrote to his brother about the matter, which was eventually settled after some years of negotiation:

> You prayed me also to send you tidings how I speed in my matters, and in chief of Mistress Anne Hault. I have answer again from Rome that there is a well of grace and salve sufficient for such a sore, and that I may be dispensed with; nevertheless my proctor there asks a M (1,000) ducats, as he deems. But Master Lacy, another Rome runner here, which knows my said proctor there, as he says, as weel as Bernard knew his sheeld, says that he means but an C (100) ducats or CC at the most...[33]

We can see from this comment that there were at least two local men who took correspondence to Rome.

It was possible for the county gentry to use the sheriff's post, which would involve sending a servant to his residence or the county castle and paying for the privilege. Margaret Paston was on occasion unable to obtain a messenger for over three weeks and writes:

> I could get no messenger to London, unless I would have sent by the Sheriff's men: but I knew neither their master nor them, nor whether they were well willing to you or not.[34]

The implication is that her use of the service would be not of right but by favour and she was not sure how well the sheriff was disposed to the recipient. Letters to the gentry were delivered by the sheriff's messengers; William Wayte, a servant of Judge Yelverton, wrote to John Paston about letters that had come by that means and by a lord's pursuivant, for great nobles had their own heralds and pursuivants:

> Sir, Like it you to know that my Lord Scalys sent his pursuivant unto my master on the twelfth day, that my master should meet with him at Wynche before my Lord of Oxenford on the Thursday next following. And when my master came thither, he delivered my master a letter from the Lord Chancellor, which my master will show you at Lenn. I should send you a copy thereof, but it is so long that I had no leisure to write it. My master rode to Walsingham on the Friday following, and there he met with the sheriff, and the sheriff delivered my master a letter from my Lord of Norffolk, which I send you a copy of. And at Walsinghan my master received a letter from Osberne your man.[35]

Important men could use both the royal *nuntii* and the sheriff's messengers in addition to their own.

The traveller had more difficulty in sending a letter because he lacked local contacts. John Paston's younger son went with the Duke of Norfolk to Newcastle, where he searched in vain for a messenger. He wrote to his brother: 'I sent no letter to my father, ever since I departed from you, for I could get no man to London.' A letter via London would be forwarded by a friend, relative, or innkeeper. Delivery could be a problem when the whereabouts of the recipient was not known and it was necessary to send mail to some forwarding agent. The major inns would send on letters knowing that the messenger would be well rewarded, so we have this direction on a letter:

> This bill to be delivered to Thomas Green, good man of the George by Paul's Wharf, or to his wife, to send to Sir John Paston, wheresoever he be, at Calais, London, or other places.[36]

Other people acted as agents and one letter is directed 'To Meye Barkere of Synt Clementys parys in Norwych to delyuer to my master John Paston in haste.'

Payment was normally made to the messenger before he set out and a further gift would be made on arrival. Elizabeth Stonor wrote to her husband in 1476 about the bargemen who maintained a regular delivery service for parcels and goods from London to Henley, 'for truly to my knowledge I had never thing carried by any of them but that I paid them truly before'.[37]

Only rarely do the Paston letters give us actual costs for taking letters. A royal *nuntius* would need at least a mark, that is 13s 4d. Others were far cheaper. Clement Paston writes, 'The man would not take my letter but I was fain to give him ijd before the bearing.' In contrast Robert Browne wrote to John Paston in 1469:

> Also my lord of York sends you a letter. [...] I took unto the bringer hereof xxs. That is sufficient as he will tell you; also the secretary vjs viijd'.[38]

The messenger sent on an urgent message could submit a substantial bill detailing costs of lodging, food, hire of horses and even the washing of clothes.

Writers were often concerned that the bearers might open a letter and took good care not to mention matters that could incriminate them in any way. When a personal matter was involved a trusted servant or relative would take the message by word of mouth. Sir John Paston wrote to his brother:

> I would not that [the] letter were seen [by] some folks. Wherefore I pray you take good heed how the letter comes to your hand, whole, or broken.[39]

Travelling time from Norwich to London depended upon the weather and the current state of the roads. The carriers went each week and, as the journey usually took five or six days, a reply by that service took at least a fortnight. A personal servant, however, would deliver a letter and return with a reply within a week. Letters were occasionally lost or misplaced but there are very few references in contemporary correspondence to such occurrences. A few letters are to foreign destinations and the Pastons could write to major Continental towns with confidence that they would find a means of delivery from Calais.

Some letters reveal strong human emotions. It would be difficult to exceed the violent invective of one from Joan Armburgh written about 1429 which, after a lengthy tirade, ends with these words:

> And therefore I give you my word that it shall not be long, though it cost me £40, but that I shall get me a judge to sit under commission on the franchise of Radwinter as I may and, if law will serve, with the grace of God you will be pulled out of the nest that you have gotten in your trust and laboured so sorely to destroy, and made to break your neck on a pair of gallows. I can say no more at this time, but I pray God send you what you have deserved, that is to say a rope and a ladder.[40]

Margaret Paston, however, reveals a depth of generosity and devotion when she writes to her sick husband in 1443:

> My mother bequested another image of wax of the weight of you to our Lady of Walsingham and she sent four nobles to the four Orders of Friars of Friars at Norwich and I have bequested to go on pilgrimage to Walsingham and to go to St Leonard's [Priory] for you.[41]

The fortunate survival of these fifteenth-century letters shows that husbands and wives of the gentry, nobility and merchant classes, separated by business, would correspond regularly and that communications between London and the provinces were well established. The amount of private and commercial correspondence must have been considerable, with messengers and carriers a common sight as they took bundles of letters and parcels along all the main routes in the land. They were the principal bringers of news and provided the inns with a regular clientele. Only severe weather, plague or civil war interrupted their efficient service.

7
THE CARRIERS FROM THE CONQUEST TO THE STUARTS

The early medieval village was a largely self-sufficient community but if it wished to obtain such goods as salt, fish, wine, millstones and metal implements it had to barter or find the money required for payment. As regular markets for food emerged in the towns and at fairs, so food exports from the villages were encouraged, thus involving an occupation of carters taking goods from place to place. A national pattern developed in which the 600 towns of England were typically supplied from an area reaching up to 8 miles outside their boundaries. A study of late medieval Colchester shows a catchment area for local foodstuffs of 7–8 miles.[1] The result was a local delivery service which could handle food, materials and messages from markets that were usually held weekly.

The thirteenth-century lawyer Henry de Bracton discusses the extent of a market in the context of whether a newly formed one could be a nuisance to one previously created. He declares that a market can be called neighbouring:

> if a new market has been raised within six miles and a half and a third part of a half … because every reasonable day's journey consists of twenty miles. The day's journey is divided into three parts, going to market, buying and selling, then returning.[2]

His definition of the proper range of a market is therefore of almost 7 miles in all directions. That is the area which we would expect to be covered by the local carters for the delivery of goods, parcels and documents. We can therefore picture the development of such delivery areas and of these being linked together by the town carriers. By 1300 about 10 per cent of the population was living in towns. London with perhaps 80,000 inhabitants and Bristol, Norwich and York being possibly 20,000 each were the largest.[3]

Then came the series of plagues known as the Black Death, which greatly reduced the population. The Poll Tax returns of 1377 suggest that those figures may have dropped by a half.

A similar pattern of local deliveries developed in the fifteenth century around the homes of the great nobles and bishops. Previously they had travelled extensively but now typically they stayed in two or three localities each year with a visit to London. The accounts of the great household of Humphrey, first duke of Buckingham, during the year 1452–53, show that he lived principally at Maxstoke Castle in Warwickshire and at Writtle Manor in Essex. Between 100 and 200 people accompanied him and a further number came for food. They were supplied from farms owned in the vicinity and so a service would operate in the area around his homes, which would be busier when he was in residence.[4]

The household book of the fifth earl of Northumberland in 1516 shows that he used three county seats and, having only furniture for one, took that around with him in a waggon and seventeen carts.[5]

The journals of two Norwich carters written in 1417 and 1418 have fortuitously survived and throw some light on the supply of food to the city. John Dernell and John Boys worked at the Lathes, a home farm for St Giles' Hospital, and were usually employed in fetching foodstuffs from the farm to the hospital for which they were paid wages of 14d a week, out of which they paid a penny to the clerk who kept their accounts. When they were not busy they were open to hire and so it was necessary for them to keep these accounts to separate their private from regular employment. Occasionally they took longer journeys: one to Ipswich, involving 45 miles each way, occupied four days, a speedy journey for a laden cart.[6]

The local pattern of trade created by the town markets was extended by the wider pattern provided by the fairs. The market provided for the daily and weekly needs of its users; the fairs provided for those purchases which would last far longer. In origin many arose as religious assemblies of pilgrims drawn to some holy place where traders could be assured not only of great numbers of people gathered together but of the protection of the Church. The annual gathering at the feast of St Cuthbert at Durham precedes the Conquest. The fair at St Ives in Huntingdonshire, founded in 1100, arose from the discovery of the saint's bones, which attracted pilgrims.

A statute of Henry VII in 1487 was passed to support small traders who wished to send goods to fairs and to prevent the Corporation of London from restraining them. Fairs cited included Salisbury, Bristol, Oxford, Ely, Coventry, Nottingham and Cambridge:

> There be many fairs for the common weal of your people [...] to buy and purvey many things that be good and profitable, as ornaments of Holy Church, chalices, books, vestments, [...] and also for household, as victuals for the time

> of Lent and other stuff as linen cloth, woollen cloth, brass, pewter, bedding, iron implements, flax and wax and many other necessary things.[7]

Tin came from Cornwall, salt from Worcestershire, lead from Derbyshire, iron from Sussex, in addition to the cloth and woollens that were sought above all by the foreign buyers. The carriers brought them all.

Fairs generated revenue for their owners, the traders and carriers. They drew people from a wide area. St Giles at Winchester became a centre for trade between England and France, Bartholomew fair at Smithfield became the chief cloth market of the country and Stourbridge, founded by King John, became the greatest of them all. Ely, Lincoln, Westminster, Bristol and Northampton were others of importance but most large towns held one. While the market was usually a regular weekly affair, the fairs were generally annual. However, Nottingham and Eton had two fairs, Bristol and Cardiff three and Wells four. Most lasted for a week. There was a gradual decline in the importance of the fair at the end of the Middle Ages, although they were still a vital commercial institution in the seventeenth century.

The larger fairs drew traders from across Europe, as described in Chapter 3. The foreign produce on sale was brought by carriers who were hired at the ports, and home-produced goods were brought from every part of England and Wales. Those who wanted parcels and letters taken abroad or to remoter parts of the country could rely on finding traders to take them. Each trade had its own section of the fair and so should have been easy to locate. Writing to London in the late fifteenth century, when he had for long expected a letter, Sir John Paston complained that he had heard nothing:

> I marvel that you sent never writing to me since you departed. I heard never since that time any word out of Norfolk. You might at Bartholomew Fair have had messengers enough to London.[8]

The two universities drew students from all parts of the country and their needs were met by special carriers licensed by the authorities. In 1492 Oxford students from the north of England had a poor service and the university appointed John Bayly as carrier to the north, employed to make a termly journey.[9]

Parents must have been particularly concerned as fifteen was the usual age for enrolment and there would be many homesick youngsters awaiting the arrival of the carrier with their fees, letters and gifts. When in January 1473 Margaret Paston made arrangements for her son Walter to travel to Oxford, she sent him with her chaplain, Sir J. Gloys. He had instrutions to take the boy en route to Cambridge and look for a carrier there to travel on to Oxford. She was, however, uncertain whether they would find a carrier available as it was unusual to start college life at that time of the year.[10]

The university chancellors exercised jurisdiction over the academic community through their courts, and gradually their authority extended to those who supplied goods and services. Oxford had a charter from Edward I in 1290 defining such privileged persons. After much controversy the town and university authorities agreed in 1458 on an extended list which included carriers and those messengers in the employment of scholars. A few students at both universities came from the aristocracy, with the majority from the middle orders of society, and most were able to afford to have regular contact with their homes by messengers and carriers. John Holles, the father of one Cambridge student at Christ's College, had a poor opinion of the carriers, for he wrote in June 1616 'your carriers be the most careless of any I know'.[11]

From the late Middle Ages sons of the gentry had often been sent to the Inns of Court in London to study common law even if they did not intend to complete the courses. In many ways they provided an alternative to the universities and their students were similarly served by carriers. Another letter in the Holles correspondence written in 1622 from Nottinghamshire by father to son comments on the service provided:

> To my loving Son Mr John Holles at Francis Pierson house near Clements Inn. I have sent to you lately 2 letters the one by Auditor Neale, alias Tom Long the carrier, for though he received it a fortnight since, he is at Nottingham, or there he was very lately, the other letter comes by a Yorkshire carrier, one Ayre who had 2d for it, therewith is a letter to my Lady of Lennox, and another from Den to you, all enclosed in a letter from your mother: these also be of an old date, so dainty be such messengers as we would have.[12]

The next year, he gives some advice on the carriers: 'Be circumspect by whom you write, and fit your packet to the messenger.'[13]

We find occasional references to the long-distance carriers in early town records and household accounts, but within many towns a monopoly of the carrying business was established by porters. As early as 1196 the guild rolls of Leicester included porters, carters and ostlers.[14]

The Beverley town documents show them being regulated in 1367 when 'all the porters and creelmen, who exercised that craft' had the charges specified for each load on a horse from the beck to the various parts of the town.[15]

In 1377 'porters, creelmen and other common carriers' were obliged to carry their wares on horses not on sleds, subject to a penalty of 3s 4d. The number of London porters must have been considerable, for in 1339 when an Inquisition was held concerning the smuggling of wool at the Woolwharf, twelve porters were available to sit on the jury.[16]

In the larger towns they occasionally formed organisations resembling guilds. The York civic records have an entry for 19 November 1495 showing that there were sixteen licensed porters in the city, two of whom were overseers.[17]

In Beverley, as in London, their charges were laid down by the civic authorities. By 1528 in Newcastle the 'free porters' had claimed the exclusive privilege of porterage over all goods in the Tyne, their fellowship lasting until the nineteenth century.[18]

There do not seem to be references to porters as such in medieval Winchester, where the merchant guild was so strong that smaller guilds were insignificant, but there are references to five carters and drovers in the period 1300–9 and to various properties owned by carriers, carters, drovers and sumpters.[19]

The carrier brought his goods to the town where they were transported to their destinations by the town porters. The procedure in fifteenth-century Southampton has been described:

> Carriers arrived in Southampton bringing the bulging wool sarplers from the Cotswold towns and handed them over at the Wool Beam to the local agents of the Italian purchasers. In the square stone Wool House, now a grain store at the end of Bugle Street, the shining fleeces were graded and packed by the local guild of women woolpackers, weighed at the King's Wool Beam, and finally carried by members of the town porters' gild to the West Gate for shipment in the galleys.[20]

Payment had been made directly to the Cotswold woolmen, the carriers taking documents confirming their loads, the merchants in turn sending bills of lading and letters to the recipients in Genoa and Venice.

As early as the thirteenth century the City of London, with the largest population and port in the country, had developed a trade of brokers. They are referred to in the Statute of the City of London of 1285: 'And there shall be no Broker in the City, except those who are admitted and sworn before the Warden or Mayor and Aldermen.'[21] They dealt with the carriers, arranging the transfer of goods from one to another. A case of cheating is recorded in the mayor's court rolls for 26 April 1300. John de Kirkton, John Bolychromp and two other brokers of carts were charged with meeting foreign (i.e. not London) carters outside the city and falsely advising them that if they entered the city their goods would be seized by the king's officials. They hired the carts for 'a mark or sixteen shillings' and then let them out 'for two marks or

30 shillings'. For this they were fined 100s. One of them who had admitted the offence was released but the other three were committed to prison.[22]

Individual carriers could travel long distances. The Merton College accounts refer to carriers from Oxford taking goods to and from Newcastle and Winchester in 1394. One Thomas Cursor of Cat Street, Oxford, is known by name.[23]

The Exeter carriers went directly to London and, in a case heard in the Star Chamber, evidence was given by merchants and carriers from the city about their business. This concerned the liability of the Exeter carriers to pay tolls at London. One William Nayrow had carried goods from Exeter for the past thirty-five years and a merchant, John Guscote, had sent linen cloth since 1473.[24] Cases brought before the Winchester city court at the start of the fifteenth century mention journeys to Guildford, London, Andover, Newbury, Reading, Oxford, Southampton, Christchurch and Taunton.[25]

Such carriers provided a regular service between towns and cities, and they would make regular stops along the route where they could pick up parcels and letters. Their liability for goods carried was well established in common law and it is clear from contemporary letters that they provided a reliable and trustworthy service to the public.

Thorold Rogers has shown that charges for the carriage of goods were remarkably steady throughout the Middle Ages. The cost for the transport of a ton of corn from the twelfth century was usually a penny a mile while heavy goods were charged at twopence. Prices were maintained at these rates even after the devastating plagues of the fourteenth century, continuing until the debasement of the coinage under Henry VIII and the protectors of Edward VI. By 1542 the cost of carriage had doubled. Thorold Rogers quotes charges of just over 5d a mile in 1583 but of 8d by 1635.[26]

Small loads had always been a matter for negotiation with the carrier, who could usually find the space needed. In 1588 Lord Pembroke had a parcel weighing 28lb sent from London to Huddersfield at a cost of 4s 8d,[27] and in 1616 sugar loaves sent from London to Cambridge, weighing about 10lb a loaf, were charged 6d each.[28] Bundles of candles went at the same rate. Packages sent on horseback went more cheaply than by cart. Sir Ralph Sadler noted in 1584 various items needed by the Queen of Scots, then in his custody:

> which may be brought down on horseback by the carriers of Derby and of this town for less than 1d a lib. And so may the plate be brought in a trunk, well mailed in canvas, much better cheap than by cart.[29]

Carriers took coins at rates which seem to have been the result of individual negotiations. The Bailiff of Middleton in Kent paid in 1284 a penny per pound for the carriage of 328lb from Pevensey to Bradmeld. A longer journey from Middleton to Marlborough required the payment of 1¾d per pound. In 1480 Merton College paid 8d in the pound for the carriage of money from Northumberland to Oxford and the Treasury paid 30s for the carriage of £1,000 from Portsmouth to London in 1562.[30]

The Paston letters show that small sums were often secreted amongst clothes and boxes, probably as an economy. John Paston wrote about one carrier:

> and with him might some money come trussed in some fardel, not knowing to the carrier that it is no money, but some other cloth or vestment of silk, or thing of charge.[31]

In the Marchall correspondence Thomas Makyn writes to William Marchall about 1465 requesting that he should send 40s by the Oxford carrier, secreting it in a pound of powdered pepper and two pounds of rice.[32]

Later in 1582 when Alderman Martin, Master of the Mint at the Tower of London, wrote about the arrangements for sending money from Bristol to Ireland he comments:

> If it be to Burghley's good liking a sum of money may be delivered into the charge of a carrier, but packed up in such a manner, amongst other things, as he shall suppose it to be merchandises for that place as are usually carried hence.

Bills of exchange are known from as early as 1311 in London, when a record survives of a cordwainer, who owed money to a draper, passing him a bond for £10 received from another person. Promissory notes given by London merchants were sealed with the common seal of the city but these were facilities for the few before the sixteenth century.[34]

There does not seem to have been any system of insurance available to the carrier, although he had some protection under the common law. The Statute of Westminster had laid down that in the event of theft, and the culprit not being found, the onus for restitution was to be put upon the hundred within which the theft took place. When a fire occurred while the carrier stayed overnight at an inn, the innkeeper was responsible for any loss. Apart from theft and fire, the carrier's liability had always been accepted. Southcote's case in 1601 established that a carrier could not evade his responsibility for loss of goods entrusted to him by attempting to pass on that liability. Southcote had entrusted goods to one Bennett from whom they were stolen by one of Bennett's servants. Nevertheless, Bennett was held to be liable.[35]

Where medieval customs records survive we can obtain an indication of the volume of goods that were taken by the carriers. The published accounts for Hull show that in the late fourteenth century between sixty-five and eighty-five ships arrived each year, a total that declined slightly to between sixty-one and sixty-five annually in the 1460s.[36]

However, the most detailed references to the carriers are to be found in medieval brokage books, which record the actual charges imposed by towns on packhorses and carts. The Southampton records are by far the most complete, providing listings of the sources of goods brought into the port and also their intended destinations. Brokage was originally a toll paid by all except the local burgesses and other exempt persons. In Southampton it included a penny pontage charge for using the bridge, the total charge relating to the distance of the destination. In time the brokers took a commission for arranging the services of carters and carriers.

The books for 1443–44 show that there was little use of packhorses except to the south west of England, almost all goods being taken in two-wheeled carts. They have the obvious advantage over the packhorse that they do not need to be loaded and unloaded each day. Occasionally, there are references to four-wheeled wains. Examples of charges are 9d for a full cart bound for Westchester (Chester), 7d to Farnham, 5d to Salisbury and a penny or more to Winchester. From each payment a penny was taken for pontage. In effect bands of charges were applied according to distance. Much of the traffic was local to Salisbury or Winchester, which had 367 recorded journeys, but there is a total of eighty-four different destinations. Fifty-four carts are recorded for Oxford, thirty-nine for Newbury, twenty-six for both Abingdon and Reading, with eleven for Henley on Thames. Carts regularly left for London, Kendal, Manchester, Gloucester, Yeovil and Sandwich. Coventry was the centre of exchange in the Midlands, being at the junction of various roads. In 1439–40 a total of 1,637 carts left the port with only seventeen packhorses. The figures for 1444–45 are 2,081 carts, with ninety packhorses.[37]

From these figures we can conclude that there were weekly journeys from Southampton to Winchester and Salisbury, with almost as frequent a service to London and Romsey. Carriers went regularly to many other places and, for example, Stephen Bateman carried cloth from Kendal to Southampton twice yearly between 1492 and 1546. His journeys were in May and September. In all, eighty destinations are recorded for 1448.

An analysis of the journeys made in 1448–9 shows an unexpected distribution through the year. The totals are: January 187, February 223, March 185, April 84, May 59, June 82, July 101, August 94, September 94, October 110, November 119 and December 67. The busiest month is February. This relates to arrival times of the mainly Genoese trading vessels and also to an increased seasonal demand for fish in Lent, but it is indicative of the good state of the roads and contradicts the view that road traffic was limited by their bad condition in the winter.[38]

A comment relating to the state of the roads to an East Anglian port was made during a case that came before the court of King's Bench in 1378. It was stated that 'All the counties of England except the county of Suffolk can have good and easy passage with horses and carts to the town of Yarmouth'.[39]

The evidence from Southampton and elsewhere demolishes the myths of wretched medieval roads and of most carriage being on packhorses except in remoter areas. It went mainly by water or in carts.

Loads from Southampton consisted of a great variety of goods. Woad was one of the commonest, much of which went to Coventry for dyeing cloth. Wine from Gascony, fish and foodstuffs were other main items entering the port and there were silks, linens and millstones. Letters and parcels could be sent for small sums, the carrier providing the only means by which ordinary folk could send news to friends and relatives. The unique evidence from Southampton shows a reliable pattern of carrier services throughout southern and central England. It also shows that goods often came from Cornwall by sea rather than by road.

After about 1500 the size of London steadily increased and a century later it may well have grown fourfold. Nearly 80 per cent of national trade passed through the capital, which led to a great increase in carriage. Despite the deterioration of many roads Stow's *Annales* record that the first long waggons 'such as now come to London from Canterbury, Norwich, Ipswich, Gloucester etc with passengers and commodities' were seen in 1564.[40]

Many of the goods landed at London had previously been taken up the Thames as far as Henley and after about 1540 as far as Burcot, about a mile and a half from Dorchester, where they were landed and transferred to the waiting carriers.[41]

By then the main towns had introduced a system of licensing town carriers, men selected for their trustworthiness and status in the town. Ipswich had two licensed carriers in the reign of James I and they were limited to one journey each week. A scale of charges was imposed by the Great Court, each man being bound with sureties of a hundred marks. Three men provided the surety for Thomas Lucas, one of the town carriers.[42] The Government also took a hand in regulation, their main concern being to control the carrying of letters.

The legal definition of the area served by a medieval market given by Bracton had been based, as we have seen, on the user who walked, hence its range of about 7 miles. An estimate of the number of markets at the height of the Middle Ages has been given as 1,600 but by 1640 that number had probably been halved. Spacing between markets became much greater. Other factors are involved. England and Wales were, apart from some local tolls, a free-trade area so there was no tax limitation on travel. Chartres estimates that between 1500 and 1700 the road transport industry increased three or fourfold and probate inventories from the mid-sixteenth century show that a great expansion in carting and marketing facilities was taking place. The small cart was being supplemented by the larger waggon or wain, so carriers could operate over greater distances. There had also been a considerable growth of credit facilities, which had led to an increase in the number of firms of carriers. Consequently, we see a steady expansion of the areas over which individual carriers took letters and parcels.[43]

Distinct from the common carriers was the even greater number of private carriers. It is likely that most men with carts acted to some extent as local carriers, ready to take parcels and loads whenever they had some free time. Others would take commissions for longer journeys on foot or horseback. They had the advantage of speed and of being ready to take a letter or parcel directly to the recipient. The lesser gentry used such men for making purchases in local towns and for carrying their letters. They could link with the long-distance carriers and so, by the fourteenth century, they were providing a means of sending letters and parcels between the main towns and cities. The accounts of Judge Shuttleworth, who lived 3 miles from Bolton in Lancashire, show him ordering hops and fish from Stourbridge fair in 1591 and having goods sent from London.[44] Thorold Rogers quotes examples of goods being ordered from the fair for transmission to destinations in all parts of the country.

While a novel does not provide factual information, it may give a reflection of contemporary life and we find a description of carriers in the Elizabethan writer Thomas Deloney's *The Pleasant History of Thomas of Reading*. In the first chapter King Henry I rides out from London to Wales and is held up by a procession of wains loaded with cloth bound for London. He is told that all is the property of Old Coles of Reading and he is obliged to wait in a narrow place for an hour while 200 vehicles pass by. Later he again held up by another line of wains from Suttons of Salisbury.

There seem to have been no proposals to co-ordinate the journeys taken by the carriers or to regulate them on a national scale until 1630, when the King's Council received a petition from Dame Anne Wigmore.[45] The preamble read: 'Many great abuses having resulted from dishonest and negligent carriers and footposts, by miscarriage of letters and other goods, as had been found in the practice of Stanley, West, and Waterhouse' so the petitioner prays for an incorporation of:

> carriers, footposts, hackney coachmen, badgers, kidders, laders, polterers, maltsters and drovers and that John Napper be Master, William Fors, senior warden, Miles Dodson, junior warden, and Robert Pepys and William Monk, clerks. Every member of the incorporation to be distinguished by a badge of silver with the King's arms on one side and his name and place of abode on the other. Such badges to be paid for at certain rates according to the number of horses driven by the wearer, and the payments for such badges to go to the petitioner for three years underwritten.

It was a promising initiative, for with organisation the carriers could have provided a far more efficient national service than existed. State Papers Domestic note that the lord privy seal and the lord chancellor both recommended that the plan be adopted and the king granted the petition at Hampton Court on 28 October 1630. Despite this, no action to implement the proposals took place and the carriers worked on without any kind of national timetable or direction.

At the end of the period covered by this book John Taylor published in 1637 a survey of the carriers, waggons, footposts and higglers who came to London, noting the inns, ordinaries, hostelries and other lodgings where they stayed. He listed in his *Carriers Cosmographie* the days on which they arrived and departed, giving directions as to how the public could contact them to send their letters and goods. To this he added a record of the ships, hoighs, barkes, tiltboats, barges and wherries that brought goods and carried them westward from London up the Thames. Taylor asks the reader for sympathy:

> The tedious Toil that I had in this Collection, and the harsh and unsavoury answers that I was fain to take patiently, from Hoftlers, Carriers, and Porters, may move any man that thinks himself mortal to pity me.[46]

He was suspected of collecting information for some new form of taxation or of being an official looking for a means of attacking the carriers' animals or persons. For such reasons he failed to complete the survey but it is nevertheless a most valuable document.

His introduction summarises the main routes along which letters were taken before 1637. The York carrier would deliver along his route and arrange for transmission to Berwick; the Lancaster carrier would send on to Kendal or Cockermouth; the Hereford man to St David's; from Worcester letters would be sent to Carmarthen; from Chester to Caernarfon; from Exeter to Plymouth and St Michael's Mount, passing Maxfield, Chippenham, Hungerford and Newbury on the way. The Bristol carrier delivered along his route and all places were served between London and Lincoln as also Boston, Yarmouth, Oxford, Cambridge, Walsingham, Dover, Rye or:

> Besides, if a man at Constantinople or some other remote part or Region shall chance to send a letter to his parents, master, or friends that dwell at Nottingham, Derby, Shrewsbury, Exeter or any other town in England then this book will give instructions where the Carriers do lodge that may convey the said letters.

Despite the lack of overall co-ordination, the means existed for goods and letters to be sent by carrier throughout the country.

Taylor's information has been analysed to show the regional share of London's trade. By multiplying the carrier services to a place with their frequency each week a table can be constructed showing that the Northern Home Counties achieved 71.5 journeys, the South and West 49.5, the East Midlands 45.0, the South East 32.0, the South West 19.0, the West Midlands 15.5, Lancashire and Cheshire 13.5, East Anglia 12.5 and Yorkshire and Lincolnshire 11.75. The far north had no direct trade and Wales had only 2.0.[47] As Taylor tells us his information is incomplete, some of these figures will need to be increased.

The carriers took most private letters during the period covered by this book and a letter sent by a merchant in 1556 may serve as indication of the trust given to them. It is addressed 'John horsmonden of gouders yn the shyr of Kynte be thys delivered with sped' with 'sythe smyth' added at the foot. The letter is folded to be 1½ by 1¾ inches:

> Goodman horsmondon I William hyll Recommend me unto you wishing to you prosperous health trusting in God that you are in health & so I pray God long to continue to the pleasure of God & to your welfare & profit Amen Sir the cause of my writing to you is that you shall receive of John Walter carrier xx li of good and lawful money of England the which xx li John Walter shall receive of William Wylkye clothier in London at the sign of the star more over if God willing at Michaelmas I will be there with you myself or before if I can moreover I marvel why you made my scythes so short this year whereby I have taken great loss for I have xvj dozen & odde stands upon my hand which I ought have sold if it had been good and long therefore if you send any more I pray you make them fully forty inches or more .... our scythes stand still before the feares [fears/fires?] came & harvest was so soye [soon?] and corn was so thin & no man would buy our scythes because they were so short therefore if you would wish that I should buy any more of you I pray you make them somewhat after way writing in the year of our Lord God 1556 & in the 3 & 2 of the year of

> the Reign of Philip and Mary by the grace of God King and Queen of England & Writing the xvj day of August by me William Hyll.[48]

The letter tells us that the carrier will collect the money from a clothier at an inn and is to take it to the scythe maker at Goudhurst in Kent. We can marvel at the writer's courtesy for he has every reason to feel aggrieved. There is a typical contemporary polite greeting and a careful dating at the end despite the fact that the regnal year should have been cited as '2 & 3' rather than '3 & 2'. The letter writer takes the trouble to pass on some news in addition to the business content. The 'good and lawful money of England' no doubt assures the recipient that he will not have any of the clipped money then circulating and that it will be good coin despite the devaluations of the currency under Henry VIII and the protectors of Edward VI. It is significant that the merchant and scythe maker are both literate men. The carrier takes letters, parcels, goods, money and the news.

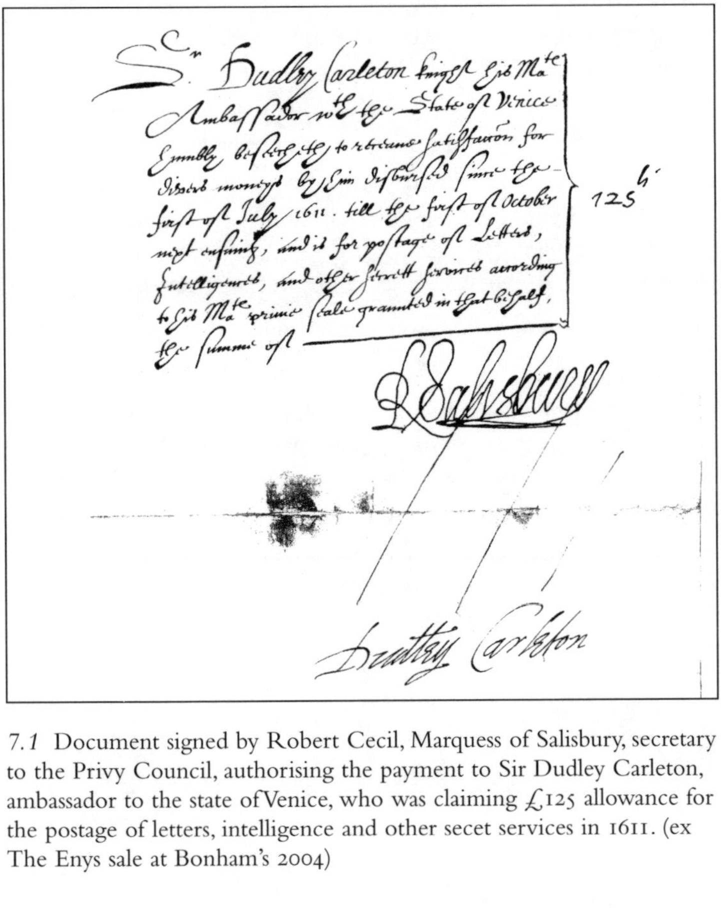

7.1 Document signed by Robert Cecil, Marquess of Salisbury, secretary to the Privy Council, authorising the payment to Sir Dudley Carleton, ambassador to the state of Venice, who was claiming £125 allowance for the postage of letters, intelligence and other secet services in 1611. (ex The Enys sale at Bonham's 2004)

8
THE ORGANISATION OF THE TUDOR POST AT HOME AND ABROAD

The victory of Henry VII at Bosworth in 1485 has often been referred to as a decisive event in our country's history and has been seen as a convenient date to mark the end of medieval times. In practice the new Tudor dynasty continued administrative changes that had already begun, steadily increasing its influence over an aristocracy weakened by the Wars of the Roses and over a Church whose allegiance to Rome was seen as a threat to the national identity. The medieval concepts that all land was held from the king and all jurisdictions derived from him were used to justify the seizure of monastic lands and the incorporation of ecclesiastical law within the king's law. It was the practice to grant many of the highest offices of state to men, often from humble backgrounds, selected for their ability rather than for their birth or connections. In the reign of Henry VIII the postal system was developed to serve the state, with a master of the posts who was also treasurer of the King's Chamber, a department that had been growing since the time of Edward IV at the expense of the Exchequer, thereby increasing the king's personal control over national finance and communications.

That the years following Henry VII's accession still presented dangers and difficulties to the royal messengers is shown by this grant:

> 25 May 1486. For as much as our well beloved servant, Richard Pudsey, sergeant of our selor, of late by our commandement was in our message, in the northern parts, and there by our rebels and traitors was robbed and spoiled of his horses and divers other things, to his great hurt and hindrance. We, having tender respect, as well thereunto as to his great costs and charges by him sustained and born in this our long progress and journey, have given and granted unto him, in recompense thereof, the sum of twenty marks sterling.[1]

Another messenger, John Thorp, was paid 40s on 27 December in the same year for a potentially hazardous mission:

> to certain mayors, bailiffs, customers and other officers of the King in the ports of London and Lenne, and in all other ports lying along the coast between London and Lenne; to take and arrest certain ships belonging to the dominion of Britain.[2]

This is an indication of the considerable responsibilities which could be put upon the messengers.

Lists of payments in the Issues of the Exchequer in Henry VII's reign show that while the permanent messenger service of the Court, Chancery and Exchequer continued to carry routine letters and commissions, a considerable part of the royal mail was being taken by other men. In 1488, for example, the royal messengers went as usual with commissions of Oyer and Terminer to twenty-three destinations, taking commissions for gaol delivery to fifty-one places, and to others such as one 'to examine how many archers each is bound to find for the King's army, and to take the musters of those archers preparatory to the expedition for the relief of Brittany'.[3]

However, many personal letters and those to influential people were being carried by members of the Court. A letter to the Duchess of York went with Richard Wylson, sergeant at arms, who was paid in total 24s at a rate of 4s a day; another went by a Court almoner, and the messenger referred to previously as being awarded compensation was a Court sergeant. Sheriffs' messengers were used to take mail back to the area they came from and there is record of a messenger from the Earl of Northumberland, returning in 1485 'with divers letters to persons in the north for the King's advantage'. He was paid the considerable sum of 53s 4d. Royal messengers' daily wages, apart from extra expenses when out of Court, were 4d. Letters and documents were normally written by Chancery clerks but there were times when they were unable to manage, as in 1487 when Robert Flemmyng, scryvener, is shown in the Issues being paid 20s on two occasions, as settlements for writing 240 letters.

The account of the arrangements for Henry VII's coronation provides some interesting information concerning travel and costs for carriage. Coffers were carried from Nottingham and Guildford in two carts at a cost of 2d a mile and watch had to be made over them each night:

> In expenses in keeping of the same stuff, and for watchmen to wait upon the same stuff by night, and their costs by the space of two nights, one night at Kingston, another night at Guildford 23d. To 3 men to help the stuff to be uncharged and brought in to the wardrobe 3d. To divers botemen and carters to drink 8d.[4]

In 1486 the cost of a journey to transfer royal monies from London to Winchester is given as 6s 8d. Charges were similar nearly forty years later when treasure for paying the army in Scotland was moved from London to Newcastle. Five carts were needed at 2d a mile for each cart, the total being £8 14s 2d.[5]

The messenger role of the heralds and pursuivants began to decline in the reign of Henry VII and continued to do so under Henry VIII, though he actually created a new herald, Somerset. There were then six heralds and seven pursuivants. The loss of the French territories had greatly diminished their status while the appointment of permanent ambassadors and agents abroad brought an end to their ambassadorial role. They still continued as masters of ceremonies and pageants and in controlling grants of arms but their role as letter carriers became more limited. State Papers record that the Calais pursuivant was paid £6 13s 4d in 1509 for taking letters to the emperor, the prince of Spain and Lady Margaret and that a pursuivant received in 1510 £4 for taking a letter to the king of Scots. Three years later the Somerset herald received £20 for carrying a letter to the king of Spain, but these are only occasional entries.[6]

An account written by Glover, the Somerset herald, describes their plight at the time of Edward VI.[7] He claimed that the king, being informed of their impoverishment through the discontinuing of their embassies, proposed to increase the wage of the king of arms from £20 to a 100 marks, that of a herald from 20 marks to £40, and for a pursuivant an increase from £10 to £20. However, Glover maintained, the king's death prevented the implementation of the awards. As heralds and pursuivants were answerable to the earl marshal they were not under the control of the master of posts but, when the Royal Council met, one or more of them would be in attendance at Court so that they could be despatched with letters if the Council decided that to be appropriate.

The masters of the posts

Henry VII's reign had seen no developments in the postal service but in his son's reign an improved system for the carrying of royal mail was introduced. Brian Tuke, treasurer of the King's Chamber and secretary to Cardinal Wolsey, was additionally made master of posts, the first recorded use of this title. He had been a clerk of the Spicery in 1506 and two years later had been made both a clerk of the Signet and bailiff and verger of Sandwich. In the list of the royal household present at Henry VII's funeral he is shown as one of the five clerks of the Signet and one of the thirteen squires for the Body, the royal bodyguard. Royal grants were made to him in 1511 and 1513 allowing him with others to export kerseys and woollen cloths. The actual date of his appointment as master of the posts is not known, for no entry was made on the Patent Rolls. The first reference we have to him in that office is of a payment made in February 1512 at Westminster which reads, 'Brian Tuke, for Master of Posts, 100L' (£100).[8]

The wording could indicate that he was paid the money as treasurer on behalf of another person who was master of the posts but there is a letter of later that year, showing no day or month, written by Wolsey to the king on the occasion of the outbreak of war with France, which makes reference to Tuke holding the position:

8.1 Sir Brian Tuke. Master of the posts by Holbein. The skull and hour glass are typical emblems of the time. (By courtesy of the Post Office. P4351)

> Watches on the coast must be duly kept, and beacons ready to be fired. Will devise with Brian Tuke, master of the posts, to know whether the posts laid in those parts can help to give you news from the sea coasts.[9]

Another letter from ambassador Spinelly dated 8 August 1512 refers to the master of the posts in England.[10] Tuke was a suitable person for he had been appointed as clerk to the Council at Calais, a position which gave him contact with the organisation of the posts by the count of Taxis throughout the Empire and those employed by the French king. Almost all the Continental mail to England passed through Calais which, for ease of communication, was far closer to the Court than were many of the midland and northern towns. When Henry crossed the Channel in 1513 for the invasion of France Tuke travelled with him, accompanied by fourteen messengers.[11] Three years later he was knighted. In 1533 he was sheriff of Essex. In the parliament of 16 June 1536 he acted as one of the two clerks.

After his death in 1545 Tuke was succeeded by two men, Sir (later Lord) William Paget and John Mason, their joint patent, granted 'in consideration of their good services', being dated 12 November. Paget was a privy councillor, controller of the household and, as principal secretary to the king, was senior to Mason, the royal French secretary and clerk to the Council. Tuke had carried out his control of the post from his own home and Mason probably did the same, for there is a letter sent to Paget in October 1546 addressed, 'At Mr Mason's, Master of the posts at Powlles' (St Paul's).[12]

By the terms of the warrant appointing them, Paget and Mason were paid yearly £66 13s 4d, which is 100 marks, the perquisites of the office adding considerably to that.[13] Another warrant was issued to the treasurer of the King's Chamber:

> to deliver to John Mason such money every month aforehand as he shall think meet for the contentment of her Highness' posts and messengers, and to take his account and make his discharge twice a year.

Mason became a member of Parliament, the master of requests, treasurer of the Chamber, clerk of Parliament and chancellor of Oxford University, in addition to travelling to France as ambassador in 1550–1 and then as ambassador to the Imperial Court between 1553 and 1556.

Paget, a Roman Catholic and lord privy seal in 1556 under Queen Mary, lived in retirement after her death and died in 1563. Mason lived a further four years. Their successor, Thomas Randolph, was appointed by a patent dated 4 May 1567, which gave him the title of:

> Master of the messengers and runners, commonly called the Queen's posts, as well within the kingdom of England as in parts beyond the seas in the Queen's dominions.[14]

His deputy was Robert Parminter, who assumed increasing responsibility as Randolph was sent on various diplomatic missions. When Randolph died on 8 June 1590, he was succeeded on the 20th by John Stanhope, treasurer of the Queen's Chamber. The patent appointing him, which is in Latin, describes his post as 'Master of the Messengers and Runners', though other documents describe him as master of the posts. His wage of £66 13s 4d, the same as paid to his predecessors, was payable for life.[15]

One of Tuke's tasks had been to sort and read letters sent to the king. In a letter to Wolsey written in 1528 he describes how he read them aloud after having sorted them 'by markings on the backs'. He subsequently directed them to the appropriate officials.[16] It was a task that eventually became attached to the position of the sovereign's principal secretary.

Under Tuke's direction all towns in England were commanded to hold post horses and provide guides in readiness for the arrival of royal messengers or those who carried authorisation from the Council, thus enabling them to travel with fresh mounts to the next post town. In times of emergency special post houses were set up temporarily and paid for by the government. As we have seen, such actions had earlier precedents; what was novel was the comprehensive nature of Tuke's instructions. The cost of providing the horses was in most cases to be met by the town rather than by the government. Those who carried commissions from the Council had to pay at rates which it prescribed. The authorisation, or placard as it was often described, was signed by Privy Council members and one such, dated 1541, reads:

> Forasmuch as the King's Majesty sendeth this bearer James, one of his Majesty's pursuivants into those parts in post upon certain of His Majesty's affairs, his pleasure and high command is that you shall see him furnished of post horses from place to place both outward and homeward upon reasonable prices as ye shall tender His Majesty's pleasure and as ye will answer for the contrary at your peril. From York the xvij of September. To all Mayors, sheriffs, bailiffs, constables, and all other the King's officers, ministers and subjects to whom in this case it shall appertain, and to every of them. T Norfolk. Charles Suffolk. W Southampton. Robert Sussex. Antone Browne.[17]

It was not difficult for the Council to put the cost of providing services onto the towns, either by direct order or by deductions from sums due to the

Exchequer. For example, when Henry VII had appointed by Letters Patent Maister Stephen Frion to be his 'secretary in French tongue' in 1486, the annual stipend of £60 was to be met out of the customs and subsidies of the city of Bristol.[18]

Town mayors and bailiffs in boroughs were bound by solemn oaths to obey the sovereign and these from the Dormont Book of the Corporation of Carlisle, recorded early in Elizabeth's reign, may be taken as typical. The Mayor's oath begins with:

> 1. You shall truly serve the Queen's Majesty her heirs and successors as Mayor of this her city and 2. Ye shall truly obey and serve all manner of processes writs and commandments sent from her highness or others in authority under her grace and thereof true return make.

The Carlisle mace which was the symbol of authority bore not the arms of the city but those of the sovereign.[19]

Privy Councillors regarded the mayors as, in effect, royal servants to whom instructions could be sent. The mayors were sheriffs under another name and so could be told to deliver letters; indeed, as we have seen, some of the larger boroughs had acquired the status of a shire with their own sheriffs.

From an early period the posts handled money in addition to letters and parcels. A letter from Lord Grey at Berwick to Uvedale, the Northern treasurer, dated 19 June 1548, tells him to send money by the post.[20] Other examples are quoted later in this chapter.

The town postmen were known as ordinary posts and any hired in emergencies were called special posts. The two royal messengers employed to carry mail between London and the Court, which was usually situated at Windsor or Nonesuch, were known as Court posts, being additional to the Chamber, Chancery and Exchequer messengers who continued to take most routine mail to the sheriffs, mayors, customs officers and nobles. In 1565 Robert Gascoigne was appointed as senior Court messenger to supervise those posts who were paid wages by the master of the posts and to organise postal arrangements for the royal progresses. Those letters and writs which were carried from the Chancery or the Exchequer to the Court were often taken by clerks for whom payment warrants were signed by the lord chancellor, the lord treasurer or their deputies.

Tuke wrote to Thomas Cromwell on 17 August 1533, at a time when Cromwell was a privy councillor and in the process of ousting Gardiner, the king's principal secretary.[21] The letter tells us much about the postal system instituted by that date:

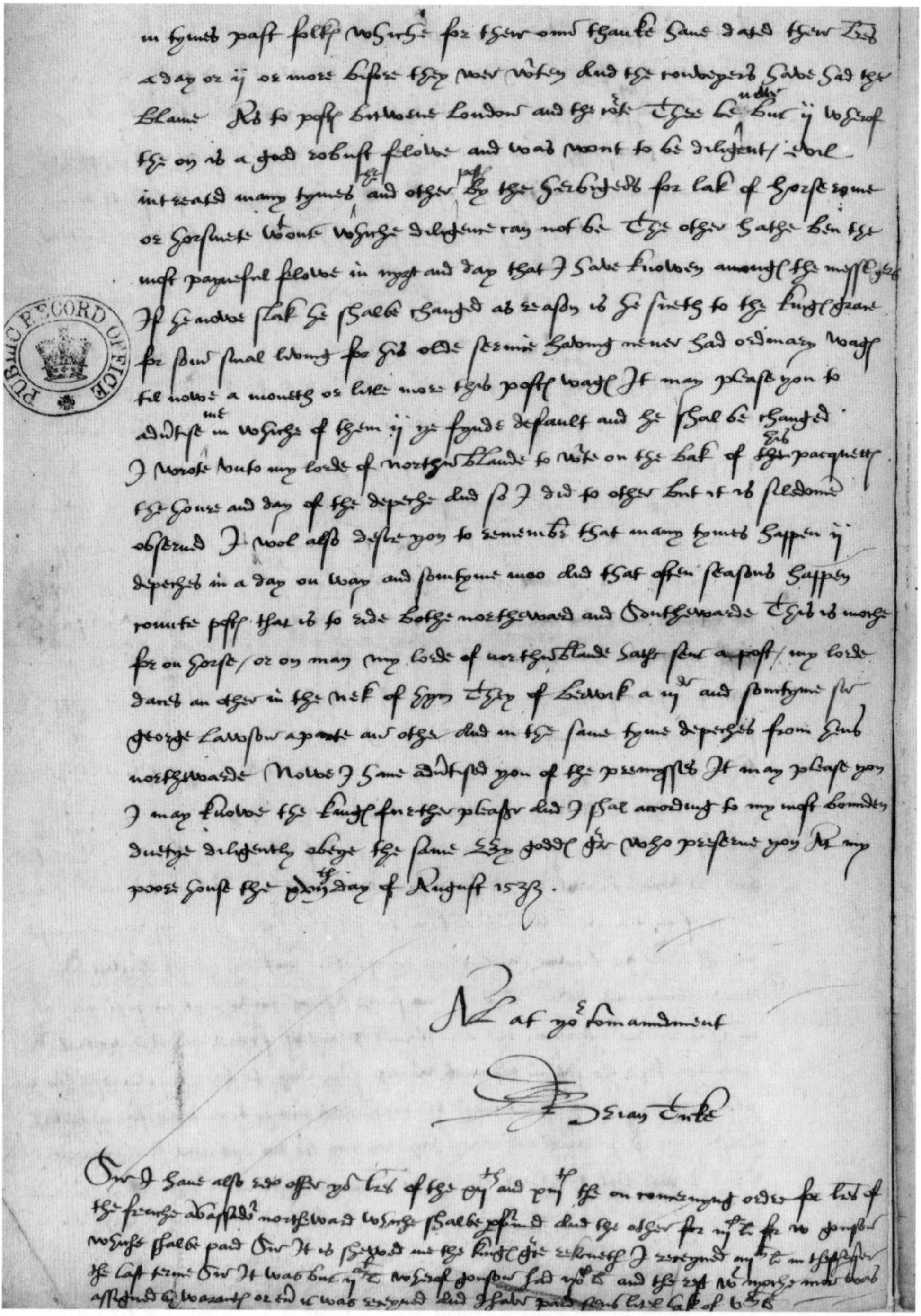

8.2 Above and opposite: Sir Brian Tuke's letter to Thomas Cromwell concerning the posts. This is transcribed in Appendix 2. (National Archives. SP 1/78 f128)

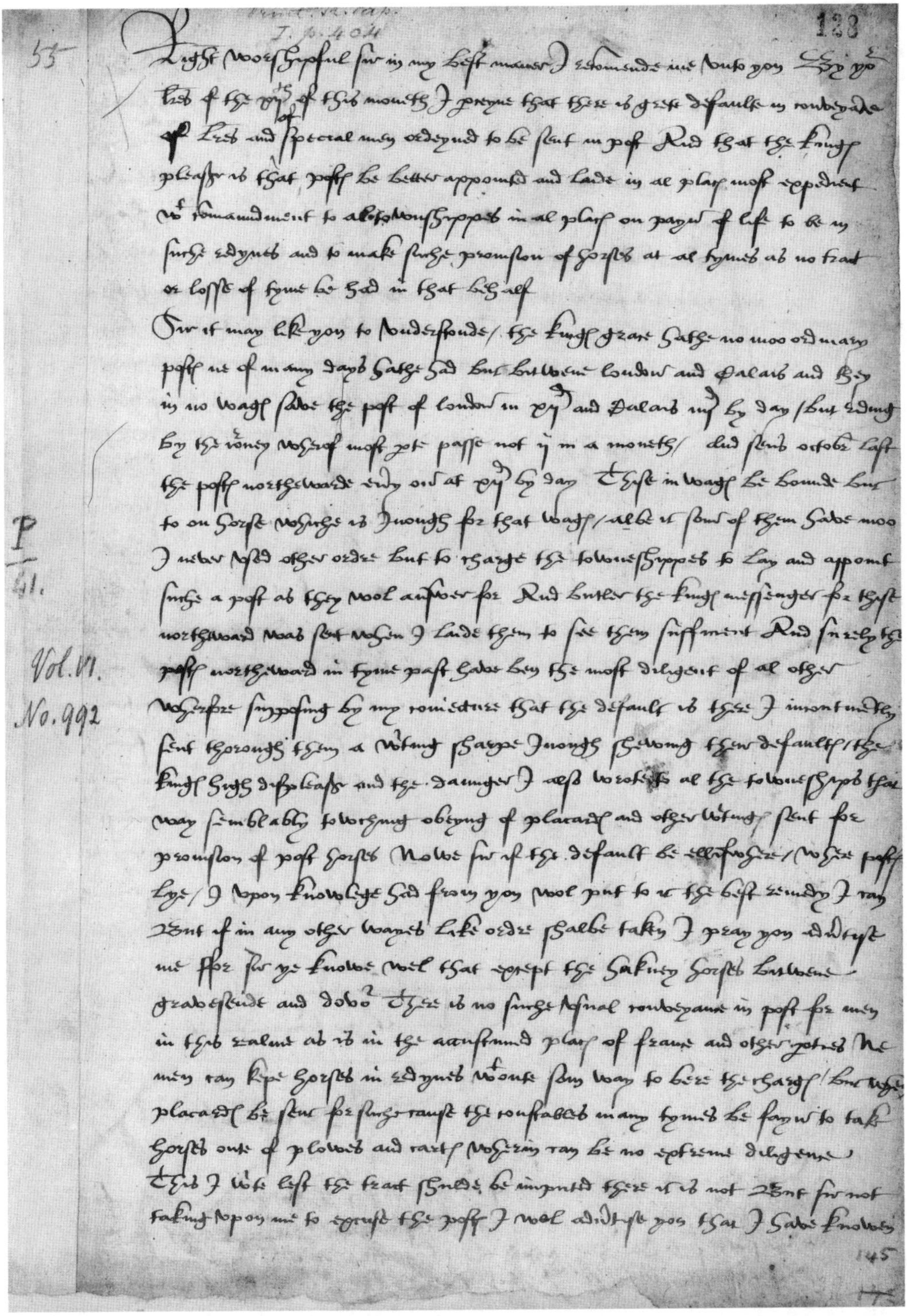
133

55 Right worshipful sir in my best maner I commende me unto you. By yo[ur]
lres of the xvth of this month I perceive that there is grete default in conveyance
of lres and special may ordeyned to be sent in post And that the kinges
pleasur is that posts be better appointed and laide in al places most expedient
wt commaundment to al townshippes in al places on payne of life to be in
suche redynes and to make suche provision of horses at al tymes as no tract
or losse of tyme be had in that behalf
Sir it may like you to understande that the kinges grace hath no moo ordinary
postes ne of many days hath had but betwene London and Calais and they
in no wages sithe the post of London in xij d and Calais iiij d by day / but ridinge
by the iorney wherof most yet passe not ij in a month / And sithe octobre last
the postes northwarde every oon at xij d by day Theise in wages be bounde but
P to oon horse which is inough for that wages / albeit som of them have moo
I never used other ordre but to charge the townshippes to lay and appoint
41. suche a post as they wol answer for And Butler the kinges messenger for the first
northwarde was sent when I laide them to see them sufficient And surely the
Vol. VI. postes northwarde in tyme past have ben the most diligent of al other
No. 992 wherfore supposing by my conjecture that the default is there I incontinently
sent thorough them a writing sharpe inough shewing their defaultes / the
kinges highe displeasure and the daunger I also wrote to al the townshippes that
way semblably touching conveyng of placardes and other writinges sent for
provision of post horses Nowe sir if the default be elleswhere / where postes
lye / I upon knowlege had from you wol put to it the best remedy I can
But if in any other wayes like ordre shalbe taken I pray you advertise
me ffor sir ye knowe wel that except the hakeney horses betwene
Gravesende and Dovor there is no suche usual conveyaunce in post for men
in this realme as is in the accustumed places of fraunce and other parties ne
men can kepe horses in redynes withoute som way to bere the charges / but when
placardes be sent for suche cause the constables many tymes be fayn to take
horses out of plowes and cartes wherin can be no extreme diligence
This I write lest the tract shulde be imputed there as it is not / But for not
taking upon me to excuse the post I wol advertise you that I have knowen
145

> the king's pleasure is, that posts be better appointed, and laid in all places most expedient; with the commandment to all townships in all places, on pain of life, to be in such readiness, and to make such provision of horses at all times, as no tract or loss of time be had in that behalf. (Fig. 8.2)

The intention was to have post horses available at distances of 10 or 12 miles with guides available to show the way and to bring back the traveller's horse. Each town was expected to provide the means by which royal documents could be forwarded to nearby towns and for their delivery to the person named on the letter. Royal messengers taking express letters were to be provided with horses, for which they would make payment, at any town. A minute of the Privy Council in 1541 shows that Tuke was expected to have an official at the Court with money available to hand to messengers before they set off so as to prevent any delay. Pursuivants and court officials who took letters expected to be given a prest, or advance, and to make a formal claim later for the balance of their expenses. Arrangements for royal messengers differed and are described in detail later.

The Plymouth Corporation records for 1490–1500 show a reward of 3s 4d given to a pursuivant who brought letters from the king, followed by the cost of forwarding two of them to Lord Broke, one at Exeter costing 3s 4d and another at Sherborne at 5s.[22]

Tuke was following the earlier precedent of requiring towns to forward royal letters and writs. In Chapter 5 we saw letters sent to York for delivery during Henry VII's reign. An instruction is preserved in Southampton's records regarding eight letters received by the mayor in September 1550. The covering letter from the Privy Council reads:

> We shall require you on the King's Majesty's behalf to see the letters enclosed conveyed to Jersey and Guernsey according to their several directions by the next convenient messenger which from that town shall repair thither.[23]

Another instruction from the Privy Council of 21 December 1557 shows a similar procedure applied to a sheriff:

> A letter to the Sheriff of Nottingham with nine letters from the Queen's Majesty to sundry gentlemen of that County, which he is willed to deliver according to the directions and to signify hither when and how he shall receive and deliver the same.[24]

A commission sent to Sir Ralph Sadler in 1569 is addressed to the post of Ware with 'see this letter delivered'. Sadler lived at Standon, about 3 miles away. A further example is preserved in the Salisbury manuscripts, where instructions are given in 1594 on a letter to the post at Rochester addressed to Lord Cobham, 'Mr Bowls, I pray you cause this letter to be sent to his Lordship. It concerneth his Lordship's special affairs'. In this case Cobham was 5 miles distant.[25]

The master of the posts' accounts show that additional payments were made during Elizabeth's reign to those town posts who received government wages if they had to make regular deliveries of this kind.

The procedures outlined above were continued by Tuke's successors. The next chapters will show how they were put into effect. Despite the assured style of their orders concerning the posts, they presided over a system which operated with very varying efficiency.

The post in London

The earliest reference to the London post in the Repertories, which record the administrative history of London, mentions a committee set up about 1528 in response to the receipt of a royal warrant, to view a place beside Lombard Street where the post might be located.[26] It was decided to instruct the innholders of the city to have four horses in the Old Jewry always ready 'to serve the king's post' and a number of inhabitants of Hackney were given a similar instruction.[27]

The wardens of the innkeepers were further required to make provision for additional horses should they be needed. By 1539 more than eight horses were being required and there were complaints from the hackneymen that their other horses were being seized for the king's post. Responsibility for providing post horses was then given to Gabriel Abraham and arrangements were made for payment by the innkeepers and hackneymen.[28]

Oaths taken by 'the King's Hackneymen' of London and Rochester were strict undertakings as shown in the Index to the Repertories and the Custumale:

> You shall swear that you shall be obedient to the Mayor of this City for the time being, and to his successor Mayors; and you shall be at all times ready, both early and late at the calling of the Mayor etc, to serve the King's Grace with able Hackney-horses within the said City, for the King's service and business, by his officers, messengers, and servants to be done at all times when they, or any of them, will ride on the King's message with the King's letters, or his other

> commandments. And also if any Hackney-men within the same City, purloin or hide any of their able Hackney horses in any privy places, whereby the King's service may be hindered, prolonged, or undone, that then the said Hackneyman shall show the Mayor or constable thereof.[29]

Henry VIII's attitude towards the London post can be illustrated by a letter, unfortunately without the year shown, that he sent concerning the provision of horses for his use. A request from his surveyor had not been dealt with promptly:

> Wherefore we advertise you of the same, willing and commanding you that whensoever any of our Surveyors either for wines or other stuff, shall resort unto you in our name for provision of carriage of the same hither or elsewhere where it shall fortune us to be, you shall effectually endeavour yourself for the quick expedition thereof, without any failing as you intend to please us.[30]

Horses and carts were to be provided for the sovereign whenever required, the expense to be met by the city authorities or at a figure agreed with the purveyor.

At this time the Mayor of London had eight valets or yeomen available to take his mail in addition to their other duties. His full secretariat is recorded in 1571 when his remembrancer, Dr Giles Fletcher, has the title of secretary and is described as being responsible for writing and engrossing the mayor's letters. The London Chamber Accounts include a few fragmentary paper accounts from the sixteenth century, the rest having perished in the great fire in 1666, but from them we learn a little about the secretariat needed by the Chamberlain of London who dealt with its accounts.[31]

Partial records of those accounts exist for 1585–86 and show that there were yeomen of the channel, yeomen of the market, yeomen of the chamber, yeomen of the sheriff, yeomen of the waterside and yeomen of the woodwharves. In 1584 William Seger, horner, was granted an annuity of £4 'to continue until he shall otherwise be advanced by this city or Christ's Hospital, provided he be always attendant upon the court days to engross all letters which shall be sent from this court or the Lord Mayor'. His occupation of horner refers to his original training of making the horn covers for books and registers.

A late entry in the Elizabethan period refers to the sheriffs of London employing as many yeomen as they may require. The total number of men who were carrying messages must have been considerable for they included employees of the Courts, the staff of the sheriffs, of the mayor, and others from the households of the recorder and the chamberlain, the two principal officers of the city.

The masters of the post appointed those postmasters who received wages from government and took from them various perquisites, while also claiming a right of consultation in all appointments of town posts. A trial of strength took place between the sheriffs of London and Randolph, when he was master of the posts. They had appointed John Clerke but in 1573 Randolph claimed the right of appointment and named Roger Robinson, who showed his warrant to the court of aldermen. The court grudgingly gave way, warning Robinson not to take horses from freemen or interfere with those using the markets.[32] When a new appointment was made in 1582 John Bradley and Roger Saunders were named by the city apparently without opposition from the master of the posts.[33]

The Privy Council could order the post of London, as their postmaster was called, to deliver its letters whenever needed and we have seen in an earlier chapter that London and Westminster messengers were employed by the Council. There are records of payments in 1584 to London messengers, such as one to Robert Hide for riding to the court with letters, for which he was paid 6s 8d. This would be a longer journey than one covered by routine trips within the city area, as the accounts show that yeomen were paid quarterly wages with additional payments for special commissions. One William Goffe evidently got into trouble for false claims. He is referred to as 'ordinary post of London' and submitted a demand for £4 for horsemeat, horse hire and guides which was later found to be untrue.[34] Evidently he had no legal immunity when carrying letters. A note in State Papers Domestic for March 1590 states:

> William Gough, her Majesty's post of London, received a packet from Sir John Foster to the Secretary at 6am on March 7th and was on his way to Court when arrested at the suit of Dr Harmer.[35]

In September 1591 the London post was Mr Gale and a contemporary letter refers to his address: 'Captain Selby is lodging with Mr Gale, the post of London, in Little Wood Street.'[36] We can presume that this was the address of the post office.

The local service could be surprisingly slow. In 1594 a letter was sent by Cecil to Windebank, then acting as private secretary to the queen, which went from the Strand to Hampton Court. It took ten hours to deliver and Windebank wrote 'such a fault could only arise from the great negligence of the post of London'.[37]

By then there was a limited postal delivery service in London, as shown in a letter from the king's secretary Davidson to the ambassador of Scotland, which is addressed: '18 October 1586. Post of London, see this letter delivered to my Lord Ambassador at his house in Lime Street.' On 27 August 1593 a letter to Cecil includes the comment: 'I have received your letter dated the 11 August which was delivered to my house in Seething Lane the 16th by the Postmaster's man.'[38]

There is further evidence for London postal deliveries in 1594, when the servant of Stephen White says he 'has fetched some letters from the Post that came from Antwerp, but they were generally brought'.[39] However, it is not clear whether the latter was by London post or a merchant delivery service.

The right to provide horses and have a monopoly of their provision on the London to Dover route became so lucrative that payment might be offered for the privilege. The position had the additional advantages of exemption from jury and military service. Late in the century an undated entry in the Repertories refers to the payment of £20 to the city chamberlain by three men, including a glazier and a wiredrawer, who were to provide four post horses.[40]

Most of the post horses and hackneys for hire were kept by innkeepers, but when a conflict arose in London over the supply of horses to Sir Thomas Eagles it transpired that some of the hackney horses used were kept by the coiners in the Mint. They claimed exemption from seizure and their claim was referred to the Privy Council in 1591 which ruled:

> whether they be coiners as they pretend or others, if they keep horses for hire, not to refuse or resist the post in the taking up of horses by virtue of his commission.[41]

The London constables were ordered to imprison those who resisted a warrant. Innkeepers sought to escape seizure of horses in their stables under the royal right of purveyance by making gifts to the postmasters and probably escaped seizure in that way.

Town posts

Times of crisis meant special instructions to the towns. The Pilgrimage of Grace in 1536 was a rebellion and it was not until December that Henry VIII could feel safe. An order by Tuke dated 6 October of that year had instructed the mayors of Waltham Cross, Ware, Royston, Huntingdon, Stilton, Stamford, Sleaford and Lincoln:

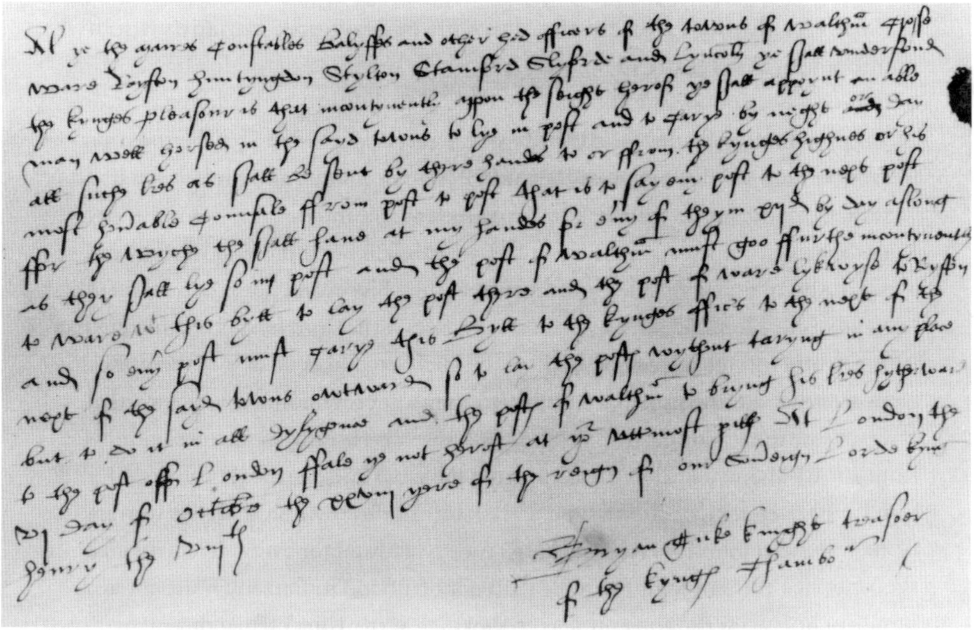

8.3 Sir Brian Tuke orders various towns to provide horses during the Pilgrimage of Grace in 1536. 'All ye the marres constables balyffes and other good officers of the towns of Waltham Crosse Ware Royston Huntyngdon Stylton Stamford Slyford and Lyncoln ye shall understand the kynges pleasour is that incontynently upon the seight herof ye shall appoynt an able man well horsed in the sayd towns to lye in post and to carye by night or day such letters as shall be sent by there handes to or from the kynges highness or his most venerable consale from post to post. Fale ye not herof at your uttermost peril – the xxviith yere of our Sovereign Lord kyng Henry the VIIIth. Brian Tuke Knyght treasorer of the kynges chambour.' (By courtesy of the Post Office. P3966_)

> you shall appoint an able man well horsed in the said towns to lie in post and to carry by night or day such letters as shall be sent by their hands to or from the king's highness of his most venerable council. (Fig. 8.3)

Lincoln responded by ordering every man with a horse to hold it in readiness to serve the king. Earlier than this, Lincoln had appointed a post as there is a payment of 6s recorded on 28 May 1523 to John Jakson for the time when he had been king's post.[42]

The attitude of towns to the king is shown after the Pilgrimage had failed. During Henry's subsequent progress, representatives met him with gifts, Stamford with £20, Lincoln £40, Boston £50, York, Newcastle and Hull each £100, apart from other entertainment.[43]

The major towns took care to provide horses for both the king's messengers and any travellers who carried authorisation from the Council. Guildford's records reveal how carefully the borough endeavoured to satisfy them. A memorandum of 1544 reads:

> That John Parvyshe the elder last Mayor has received at this day of the town xls [40s] sterling for the which xls the said John binds himself and his heirs to find sufficient post horses for the king's majesty's affairs and business from this day unto this day two years to be complete which shall be in the year of our Lord 1546. Also if it be demanded and taken, that then his second horse or gelding to be in readiness at one hour's warning. And in case the third horse be demanded before the receipt or coming back of the said two horses or one of them then that one of the townsmen according to their order shall find a horse for that course or time. Also if the said John Parvyshe mistrust the messenger with his horse that then he shall find a lad to fetch the same horse at the journey's end at his proper cost. Note also that the Constables of this town shall always warrant unto the said John Parvyshe the king's money allowed for every mile. Provided always that the said John Parvyshe shall not be bound to find any horse for any purveyor nor for the King's bakers to Wokinge at the King's being there.[44]

Evidently purveyors for the court's food together with the baker had in the past claimed a right to take horses and that right was disputed by the town.

The city of Leicester made payments in 1551 for keeping post horses and there is an entry in its records for Seth Berrage and Mr Jenkynson who received £6 13s 4d for keeping four horses. The rate paid for each animal fluctuated in subsequent years, being £1 6s 8d in 1569.

It was obviously convenient to have a post house with horses available both for the benefit of the town corporation and the merchants as well as for the sovereign. Their archives include this record for 9 April 17, the seventeenth year of Elizabeth's reign:

> Further at the same Common Hall it was for divers causes thought good and meet for the service of the Prince [the king] to have at the charges of the Town certain post horses kept, whereupon there was appointed four to be kept which these persons underwritten have undertaken to keep, and to serve from time to time so often as shall require......For the which there is allowed unto them of the town for every horse thirty-three shillings and four pence.[16]

The cost was to be paid for by the Mayor and his brethren, any shortfall to be found by a levy on the inhabitants. By 1597 the city was providing six horses 'to serve the Queen's majesty when required'. The costs fell on 'the mayor and his brethren' who finally in 1594 had the number reduced to four and an arrangement made by which the cost, then £5 6s 8d, was spread amongst seventy-two persons, twenty-four paying 1s 4d and forty-eight others 8d each.

The Southampton horse hirers were controlled by a town order issued in 1558 regulating the hire of horses. The hirers are named and are ordered to have horses or geldings available at all times for the post. The charges are mandatory, being 8d for the first day and 6d for subsequent days; the time allowed for journeys to London and Bristol is laid down.[47]

The costs of maintaining post and post horses could be considerable. For example the Ipswich chamberlain's records show in 1563 an entry 'Paid to Anthony Amis for the pursuivant who tired his horse 5s 20d' and in 1582 'for seeking out a post horse that went missing 4s'.[48]

Newcastle upon Tyne's accounts for 1566 have three entries of 4s for the safe keeping of post horses and another of 5s for carrying the Queen's treasure to Berwick.[49] Later, in 1572, a charge is shown for the conveyance by Sir John Forster of the Earl of Northumberland from Alnwick to York, where he was executed, as being £154 11s 4d for the post horses, an expense that was eventually paid by the Queen's Council.[50]

On one occasion the town paid the costs of six post horses needed by a Scottish nobleman. It seems that they prided themselves on their hospitality, for when the archbishop of York arrived in 1595 he was given sack, sugar, Rhenish wine, pears, caraway biscuits and sugar bread, the mayor being later reimbursed with 12s 4d.[51]

The Norwich records for 1567 show that an important factor in agreeing to provide horses was the disturbance that had been caused by royal messengers seizing them or requiring the constables and bailiffs to obtain them for their use:

> For the charge of keeping 12 horses it is very chargeable to the Postmaster and a great ease and quietness to the citizens and such as shall be troubled with the taking up of the same post horses, it is agreed that there shall be three postmasters who shall have lent to them out of the Treasury £20, to every one of them £6 13s 4d. for a year, putting in good security for the same. And also to have yearly delivered unto them by the Sheriff the sum of £12, to every one of them £4, which £12 shall be levied by the Sheriff, that is to say by the innkeepers and tipplers £6, and of the other citizens the other £6.[52]

An entry in 1568 rehearses the arrangements of the previous year adding that these had been agreed between the Duke of Norfolk and the mayor. Further details are given as follows:[53]

> no man was to take up any post horses in the city unless he was licensed by warrant from the Queen's Majesty, the Duke of Norfolk, the Privy Council, or the Mayor, nor to use any one horse above 12 or 14 miles together; for which he was to pay 2d each mile outward, and 6d to his guide, to go out and carry back the horses, and the said horses were not to carry any cloak-bag etc of above ten pounds of weight.

For other travellers wanting horses they made this provision:

> The hire of the hackney horses in the city was also now settled, at 12d the first day and 8d each day after till their redelivery, for which horses all strangers were to give security for their return, and if the horse held not out on his journey, the owner to pay all charges of such default, but journeys to London were excepted, for which everyone was to agree as he could.

The previous orders referred to in the preamble had limited the weight to be carried on each horse and authorised the imprisonment of a rider who abused a horse or took one without permission. It was much in the interest of the citizens of Norwich that they should maintain their own postal system, additional to that provided by the carriers, for their trade in finished cloth provided great wealth and could require speedy communication with London.

Ipswich took steps to support those innkeepers who kept post horses for the queen's use by instructing the bailiffs not to interfere with the tipplers frequenting their houses[54] and in 1584 St Albans limited the responsibility for providing post horses to one person:

> John Comport was to procure financial assistance to the mayor towards the keeping of eight geldings, mares or horses for the service of Her Majesty, for post horses and for carriage of poultry to Her Majesty so that strangers shall not have their horses taken for the service at any time.[55]

The same records mention that the Ipswich postman carried the town's letters and delivered the royal ones.[56]

The chamberlain's accounts for 1554 contain entries such as 'Paid for my costs and charges to London and from thence, to carry up the letters that were found in Sharplyn's Shop viijs iijd' and 'Paid to Smythe of St Clements for his Cote hire to go down to the Two Hoyes, and for carriage of a letter to the Capitain named Mr Cromwell vs'. The post took the duke of Norfolk's letters and in 1562 a man and horse went to Stratford 'for the priest that is in jail 16d'.[57]

Despite the attempts of the Council to provide for post horses in all towns, it was possible to obtain exemptions. Oxford University was charged with refusing post horses in a case that was heard by the Privy Council on 12 May 1575 but it was able to show Letters Patent granted in 1523 which freed the chancellor, all students and servants of the university from the obligation.

Soon after the 1588 Armada, when messages from the Continent were urgently awaited, a very clear instruction was given to Henry Gaymer of Rye in 1589 by Thomas Randolph, the master of the posts:

> Her Majesty's pleasure is that for the better expedition of each letter as comes to Her Majesty's self or Her Highness's Council out of France, post horses should be laid from your town to London in places most convenient, and to that effect hath given me express commandment to see performed with all speed. Whereof I pray you Mr Mayor of Rye to make choice in your town of the most sufficient man that either keepeth an inn or commonly serveth such horses as ordinarily arrive out of France, and in H.M. name to require him to furnish himself of three sufficient and able post horses at the least to carry H.M. letters or such as come to her Council, so oft as either Her Majesty herself or either of them please to serve. And for that they shall know that this their service shall not be unconsidered Her Highness is content to allow unto either of them 20 pence per diem from the day of their placings during their service, to be received quarterly at my hands as so soon as I can have warrant for the same without fail, and to the intent that they shall be the better able to do H.M. service, they shall be allowed for every man that rideth in post 2d the mile for each horse that he rideth with and 4d for the guide.[58]

This instruction contains all the elements needed for an efficient postal service which would additionally provide mounts for travellers. It could well have been extended to the carriage of private mail and might thereby have been self-financing. By granting a monopoly of providing horses to one person in each town, under the immediate direction of the mayor, the Council would have achieved its main aims of being able to control all foreign travellers and of censoring their mail. Alas, this was not to be. The Rye scheme was temporary, lasting only eight months at a cost of £75 10s 4d. With the exception of the Cinque Ports, no leagues of towns were established in England and so each town had to make its own postal provision. Despite the clear advantages that would accrue from organising a fee-paying postal system along the main routes in the country, none was proposed until the next century. Post horses were at times often unavailable and proclamations requiring them to be provided show how ineffectual the commands could be.

The Calais post

Apart from that to the Court, the only postal route mentioned by Tuke in 1533 paid for from state funds was the road from London to Dover and on to Calais, part of the royal domain until its loss in January 1558. At that time the London postman was paid 12d and the Calais postman 4d, those towns along the route being required to provide horses. Lord Lisle was the lord deputy at Calais and Tuke corresponded with him on the postal arrangements. Lisle received almost all the letters from the Continent destined for England, including those of the ambassador in Paris, Sir John Wallop. He forwarded Wallop's mail, which was addressed to the king, to Tuke and requested payment for the messenger's journey. Tuke's reply of 4 August 1535 explains the rules under which he worked:

> I suppose Sir John Wallop, when he desired John Broke to be sent with it, did not know that wherever the King is, posts are laid from London to His Grace, and there are always ordinary posts between London and Dover. So that John Broke's coming has been a double cost to the King from which neither Mr Wallop's writings nor any man's can discharge me if I pay it. I never object to special messengers unless asked to pay for them when I am not privy to their journeys. Nevertheless on your letter I have paid John Broke's journey to London and back.[59]

Later that year a similar incident occurred and on 6 January 1536 Tuke had again to write to Lord Lisle:

> I have received lately a letter from you with a bill of certain passages made by Sir John Wallop's servants and of some other messengers sent to England and Flanders from Calais from May to December last, which bill your Lordship has subscribed and desires me to pay. I have no warrant to pay it as Treasurer of the King's Chamber, and it has nothing to do with my charge as Master of the Posts. It is true I have paid passage money for the King's ordinary posts but not for special men without special warrant.

Lisle was evidently not satisfied with the reply because he considered that other deputies had sent such accounts to Tuke and this obliged Tuke to write on 20 January 1536:

> It is not true that other Deputies have acted as you suppose; but when ambassadors send letters by post or special men to Calais and write to the Deputy to send them on by the ordinary post between Dover and Court, I as Master of

> the posts pay for them. For it is the post's reckoning and there is no double payment. In such cases I take for my better discharge the testimony of the Deputy and the Mayor of Dover. But now that letters go by special men, I do not pay them as Master of the Posts, but as Treasurer of the Chamber.

From this we can see that Tuke was authorised to pay the costs for the transmission of royal letters by the posts along the road from London to Calais. He could normally forward letters to the court wherever it was without cost as there were two men employed to carry them there. Payment for letters carried by other means needed to be authorised by a warrant from the Council or to be met by the sender.

One other problem arose concerning the letters to Calais, that of who should pay the fishermen who provided the boats used by the messengers. Ordinarily costs would be charged by the posts but again there was the possibility that the king could be paying double for the service. Tuke wrote to Lisle on 17 February 1536:

> I have received yours of the 8th by John Broke and perceive Sir Francis Bryan has promised to get you a warrant for the money demanded by the fishermen for carriage of Ambassadors' servants and letters. Some of their demands are not just; for many of Wallop's servants and others have paid them at times for their passage.

On 25 April he wrote again:

> But now I trust your Lordship of your great wisdom perceiveth what I may do, and where the remedy is, which as I wrote to your Lordship is with Sir John Wallop, if he will confess unto me that in the reckonings of such post money as he receiveth of me, he doth not put nor reckon for the passage of his servants and messengers that he sendeth hither and that he will subscribe a bill of as much of it as concerneth him. Of which matter I hear nothing of him, whereof I marvel. I think if your Lordship write unto him he will make answer.

Such were Tuke's difficulties in dealing with a man who outranked him. Tuke's interpretation was eventually supported by Lisle's London agent, John Hussey, who wrote to Lisle on 6 February 1538:

> But it shall be best hereafter that when any letters come of that sort [to the lord privy seal] that Tuchet have the conveyance of them, and then he be to come, or send them by Broke, and so he be conveyed by the King's ordinary posts,

> and they to convey them as it hath been accustomed; for if your Lordship use to send any of your own folks at your charge you shall thereby be no gainer but rather lose such money as you shall defray for the charges.

This was agreed, for on 15 March Hussey wrote:

> Pleaseth it your Lordship to be advertised that I received by this bearer your sundry letters and writings, and delivered unto my Lord Privy Seal his letter with the packet that came from the Bishop of Winchester; and from henceforth all such letters as shall come from any of the King's agents or ambassadors, it shall be requisite that your Lordship deliver them unto Broke or Tuchet and they to convey them by the ordinary post at the King's charges.

The Lisle correspondence survives because he fell under suspicion of aiding the escape from Calais of men later considered to be traitors. All his papers, including some 3,000 letters, were seized in case a charge should be brought against him in court, and so they survive in the National Archives. His misfortune enables us to have this clarification of royal expenditure on the Tudor posts.

Royal couriers abroad

The introduction by the Tudors of ambassadors and representatives abroad required a more regular courier service to supplement the use of the heralds and pursuivants who still took the most important personal letters to sovereigns and nobles. During the Tudor period appointments were made in eighteen places as far away as Constantinople and Russia, the most important being at the Courts of the emperor and the king of France.[60]

Costs could be considerable: when William Thomas brought letters from the emperor's Court in June 1553 the expense was £13 6s 8d.[61] At the same time agents were paid to provide news from wherever interested the Council. The volumes of State Papers Domestic and Foreign reveal the vast correspondence that took place. Always short of money, the Council communicated with its ambassadors and agents through couriers but also used any means judged to be reliable. For their part the ambassadors usually employed their personal servants to take letters to England.

Four men frequently mentioned in State Papers who worked for Queen Elizabeth and the Council were Francisco Thomaso, Francis Picher, John Wells and John Spritewell, the Dover post.[62] Like the royal messengers in England they could be called upon for various duties, buying a jewel for the

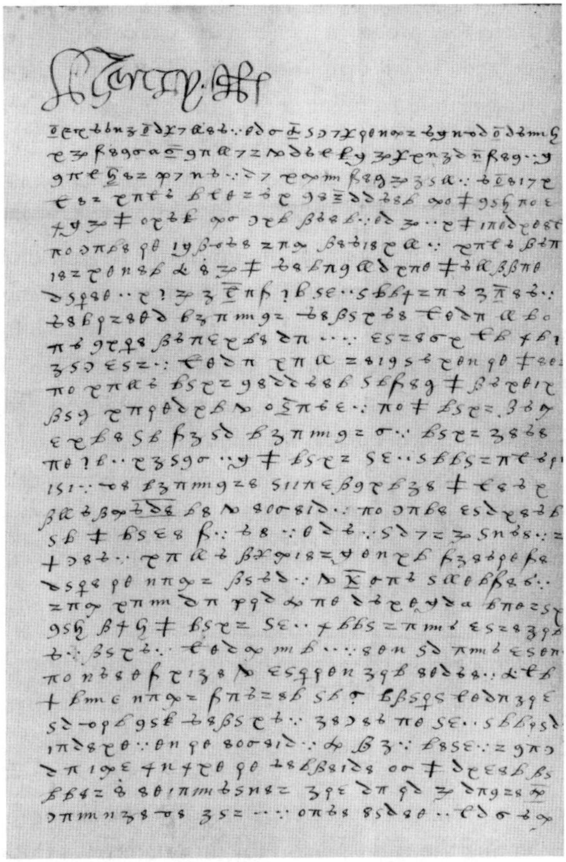

8.4 Letter from Henry VIII to the ambassadors at Ratisbon 1541, in cipher. (By courtesy York Merchant Adventurers. Royal Misc no.1 1541)

Henry VIII's letter

Henry r
Right reverent father in god, ryght trusty and welbyloved, and trusty and ryght welbyloved we grete you wel, and have receyved your sundry lettres of the last of may and the fyrst of thys present; and by the contynue of those in cyphre doo perceyve your procedynges with granvelle and the resolutyon theruppon taken by the emperor, and how the emperor's ambassador here resident should repayre unto us for lyke promyse to be made by us as the emperor hath made unto you, declaryng in the end of your sayd lettres as wel by us as the emperor hath made unto you, declaryng in the end of your sayd lettres as wel the pryncypal yointys and forme of the sayd promyse as what should be sayd here on the emperor's byhalf by the sayd ambassadour, in cace he shoulde accomplyshe the very purpose and effecte of those matyers as the same were entreated and agreed upon

> there. Your procedyngys wherein we take to be in good parte, and for aunswere doo you to wit that on trynty sonday last past the sayd ambassadour made his repayre unto us, beeng at our manor of grenwyche, and making his entree with us upon such good wordes as the regent spake unto him at his last repayre hether on ambassiate, coteyneng in effecte that, where he seamed loth to com agayn in respect of the tymes passed, granvelle encouraged him to it and tolde thoughe he had before eaten but broune breade he should nowe eate white breade and have the swete with the sower. And afterwardes the sayd ambassadour, declaring his oun good inclynatyon to thys amytye with the sodayn joye which he conceyved to see it frame to so good towardnes which with the labours he toke presently in the dysciphering of his lettres had sumwhat troubled him in his health, whereby he was enforsed sumwhat the lengre to forbeare his accesse to our presence, he descended to a repetytyon of the poyntys touched on in the regent's memoryal and of the emperor's promise upon thesame, which he touched as fully as you wrots them unto us, saving in twoo pointis. [this is about a fifth of the whole letter.]
>
> Henry VIII to his ambassadors at the Diet of Ratisbon 17 June 1541. Deciphered and edited by Christine Black and C.E. Challis. Ben Johnson & Co. Ltd. York.

queen, escorting prisoners, purchasing books or making a confidential report. Selecting the right person for more complex duties would depend upon the nature of the task. At times of crisis abroad, when a confidential assessment was needed, a skilled, well-educated man would be required. A letter from the queen in 1559 to Sir Nicholas Throckmorton, ambassador to the French Court, concerning conveying the earl of Arran to England, began:

> There needeth small writing where there is so good a messenger, and therefore I do make to you but a brief memorial of words rather than of matters.[63]

This was deleted and instead she wrote, 'the bearer will show you the state of things in Scotland'. Even then Cecil decided the letter needed to be ciphered. The role of courier on such occasions was so delicate and important that it is not surprising that some of them rose to high appointments. Sir Edward Stafford, who became ambassador to the French Court in 1583, had been employed as a courier on important business in his younger days.

John Wells was educated at Cambridge and was a servant of the Cecils. In the 1570s he travelled to France and Spain from where he sent reports on the political scene. When the duke of Anjou came to woo Elizabeth,

Wells had to find 100 horses and seventeen carts to be ready for the duke's arrival at Dover. In 1589 he was imprisoned at Rouen and accused of being a spy. His ransom was put at 500 crowns with a further 200 to the gaoler. Attempts were made to exchange him for four Papist priests held in England and eventually they were replaced by the nephew of the bishop of Ross. He had been imprisoned for a year and fourteen weeks, threatened with torture, the galleys and the rack. On his return the Council authorised him to claim the possessions of various Frenchmen by way of compensation.[64] The widely accepted inviolability of a royal courier certainly did not always apply in times of war or tension.

The courier used post stations that existed throughout Europe which, except in times of war or sickness, were usually in a more organised state than those in Tudor England. He would need a local passport and often a guide. In times of plague he required a health certificate, without which he might be confined in a pest house for forty days. Using an express messenger, who would be expected to travel by night if possible, was more expensive than using a courier. A courier's journey to and from Blois, when the French Court was there, was rated at about £15 and to the Low Countries about £5, of which the courier might take between a third and a half in profit. This was in contrast to the cost of a letter sent through the town or merchants' posts which could cost as little as a shilling, or of a tip paid to a reputable traveller going in the right direction who was usually given 6s 8d.

Even ambassadors might use the cheapest means to send routine news. When Challenor was the English representative in the Low Countries he wrote in 1559 with news of the death of Pope Pius IV:

> which being of no great moment I thought not meet to make other cost upon by express post and sent by the ordinary post of the English merchants.[65]

By contrast, the expense of a diplomatic mission could be very considerable. Sir Edward Stafford's bill 'for his transportations, post horses, passage and carriage of letters' while employed in France between 22 June and 11 August 1580 totalled £516 8s. Travel costs were £220 12s, food £153, transport £67 16s and the despatch of letters £75. Before he left he had been advanced £100, so he had to meet the rest from his own purse until his claim was paid, as was normal practice.[66]

In times of peace and absence of plague postal deliveries across Europe in the sixteenth century were generally reliable. Christopher Mundt, who was the queen's agent in Germany, wrote to Cecil in 1560:

> This letter will reach Antwerp by January 6th, and the Court four days after; the deliberation and answer will take up four days more; the answer will arrive at Antwerp on the 18th and will reach him on the 25th. It will take him nine days to get to Naumberg, which will make it the 4th February.[67]

The correspondence took one more day than predicted.

There was a regular fortnightly post from Constantinople, where an Elizabethan merchant, William Harborne, acted as correspondent, being given royal credentials in 1584. In Venice John Shers acted as English correspondent and a payment to him of £5 15s 3d for nearly a year suggests that he wrote weekly at a cost of about 2s a letter.[68]

Communications with France could be difficult when relations were at a low ebb and the ambassador, Sir Henry Killegrew, had the utmost difficulty in December 1559 in sending a letter to the Council. On the arrival of his despatch from Blois, the recipients sent it by express to Cecil, the royal secretary, quoting his words:

> There has been no negligence in them for they cannot cause their letters to be conveyed speedily nor certainly but by through posts; specially the Court remaining where it does, out of all trade towards England, the times being also so suspicious that no one may pass beyond Dieppe without let. Have essayed all possible by express messengers, French couriers, and extraordinary ways, and by sending to Paris and so thence by the bankers, yet all without success.[69]

There were times when ambassadors had to take any opportunity that presented itself, as is shown in one letter from Stafford to Walsingham about a meeting between the kings of France and Navarre dated 29 September 1584. The address is given as 'out of an alehouse on the river of Loire'.[70]

Spain was sometimes a difficult destination and the English ambassador, Sir Thomas Challenor, wrote in 1562 that he had had to wait for two months before he could find a courier to take letters to the Low Countries.[71] It was by no means certain that paying the considerable cost of a courier or express messenger would ensure a quicker or more certain delivery than by using other postal services.

Ambassadors were often inadequately paid for their expenses but diplomacy was seen as the path to preferment and they could expect to be rewarded with valuable sinecures. The courier could also hope for advancement and his role was a most important one for without him the ambassador had no instructions. Together with the agents he provided the Council with its main source of foreign information.

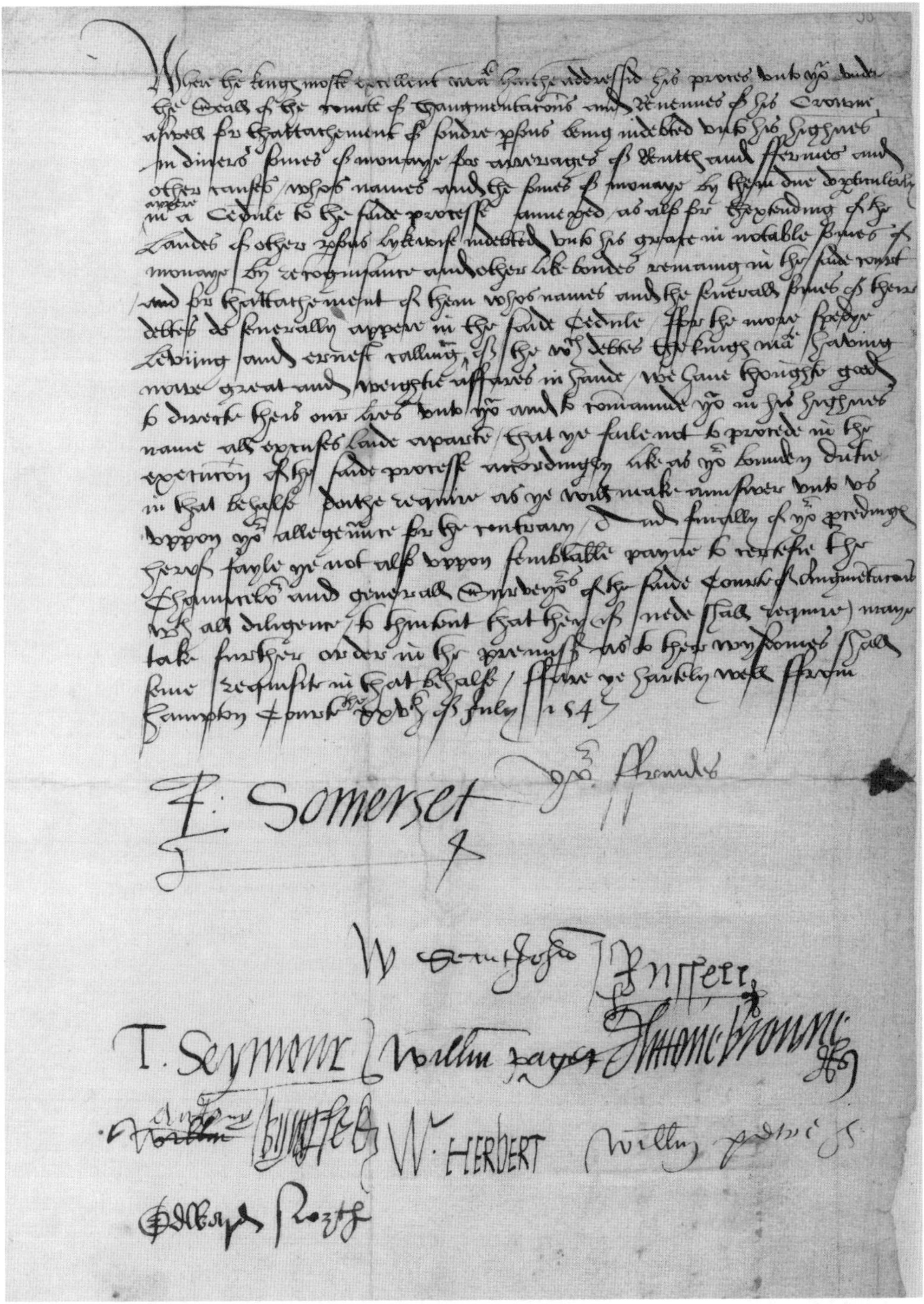
E. Somerset

T. Seymour

W. HERBERT

8.5 The Lord Protector and the Privy Council write to the Barons of the Exchequer, 1547. (Private collection)

9

CARRYING THE TUDOR ROYAL AND MERCHANT MAIL

The carriage of the royal mail by the town posts depended upon the provision of suitable horses and of riders being available at short notice by day and night. Speed was important and security required that packets were delivered unopened. Most letters from merchants and the public were handled by other means. This chapter looks at the problems which arose in providing the available services.

Those who carried warrants authorising them to be provided with horses might be travelling for a great variety of reasons. Apart from the royal messengers they could be such persons as ambassadors, officials taking up duties, foreign dignitaries, or officers with equipment going to the wars. A commission was issued on 10 May 1552 for Sir G. Dethyk to take the Order of the Garter to the earl of Westmorland, and he was authorised to take five post horses for himself, his servants and guides. In June that year Thomas Gower, the Surveyor of Berwick, who required help with its fortifications, was authorised to press and take up anywhere in England masons, smiths, labourers and others with such posting horses as he needed.[1]

In 1557 Stamford complained about the unfairness of the obligations put upon them to provide horses and a petition sent by Stamford in 1578 puts that town's case eloquently:

> So many riders and commissions granted for post horses for a penny the mile run so fast that our poor town and the towns adjoining are not able to serve them so well or so speedily as they would. So it is our poor officers are eftsoones put in jeopardy of their horses, threatened and very much abused to their great discouraging, our husbandmen from the plough and carriages, their horses already overlaboured are fetched away to some post and thereby spoiled to how great hindrance and want we know not; our townsmen now ready to set forth towards their markets have their horses forced from them, so missing oft their markets and livelihood: their horses oftime

> return hurt, maimed and utterly spoiled. [...] From St Luke's Day last past but one until St Luke's Day last we have set forth 4 hundred 3 score and 13 post horses together with the names of the riders and the granters of their commission, beside the number which the standing post of the town hath set forth, and also from St Luke's Day last past until this present day which we have set forth in writing and are ready to send if you command. We pray you to augment the wages, which we suppose would cause not so many to ride post.[2]

A letter from Newark on Trent to Secretary Cecil in 1570 complains that the royal messengers would not pay the 2d a mile asked for post horses.[3] Again in 1582 Grantham appealed for an increase in the rate paid for hire as the trade of the town was being ruined for want of horses.[4]

The Privy Council's problem was that it could not find the money to pay a proper rate for post horses. In 1568 the queen through the Council had written to Randolph saying that he was to discharge all the posts – that is those postmasters subsidised by the state – unless they would serve for half of their present wages.[5]

The Council did, however, help the principal towns by extending the area from which horses could be commandeered. In 1590 Newark, which had had 400 of its horses requisitioned for service in Scotland, was limited to ten post horses and any further needs were to be met from the surrounding area.[6]

Between 1599 and 1601 Staines, Maidenhead, Reading, Hounslow, Andover, Kingston and Guildford were given similar treatment. Those towns on the roads to France were helped in 1596 when it was ordered by a warrant for Kent 'that the horses should be drawn out of the towns and countries adjoining to the relief of the posts in Kent whose ordinary furniture at this time doth not suffice'.[7]

These posts were further protected by limiting the use of a post horse to only one stage. During the Irish campaign in 1601 towns on the routes to Ireland were overwhelmed with warrants to provide post horses and similar relief was granted.

The post road to Exeter was also under strain, as shown in a letter from Sir Thomas Gorges to Burghley on 16 July 1595:

> Coming on Friday night last to Exeter, I sent to the mayor for some post horses, but it was nine o'clock the next day before I could have any and then only such as carry wood up and down the town and very unfit if haste were required. Pray summon the Mayor to answer for such contempt and then leave it to my discre-

> tion. It will be a great terror to the mayor and cause those who come after me to be better regarded.[8]

It was not surprising that in times of emergency, when it was obvious that the demand for horses would increase, owners placed every obstacle they could in the way of those who demanded them. It was for that reason that Sir Thomas Randolph, master of the posts, had been obliged to double the price in 1569 during the rebellion in the north. The 2d rate was again paid in 1574 but when that emergency was over messengers were again paying only a penny a mile. In 1582 there had been so many complaints about the difficulties of obtaining horses on the roads to Ireland, Plymouth and West Country that instructions were issued to pay 2d mile as well as 4d to the guide. However, by 1583 payments had reverted to the penny for there is a letter from the Master of the Posts to Walsingham claiming that the posts suffered greatly:

> Yea all men that will ride in post served by the hackneymen for 2d a mile, and they for her majesty's affairs ride for a penny a mile. How the country crieth out your Honour is not ignorant; how the posts are daily beaten and misused is almost daily seen.[9]

In the face of these complaints the Council issued several regulations limiting those who could use the post at the penny rate or 'as they can agree by discretion', imposing limits even on their own members. In 1591 the signatories were so defined:

> The Lord High Treasurer of England, Her Majesty's principal Secretary, any two of Her Majesty's privy council, the Lord President of the North or his deputy, the Lord Governor of Berwick or his deputy, any of the Lords Warden of the Northern Marches or their deputies, any Ambassador or Agent for Her Majesty in Scotland, or the Master of Her Highness' Posts.[10]

The Council's attempts to retain the penny a mile payment for the use of horses caused deep resentment, which had increased with the steady inflation that had followed the debasements of the coinage in the reigns of Henry VIII and Edward VI. Edwards and Palliser have calculated that the cost of grain fed to horses had almost quadrupled between 1547 and 1603, the price of animals having increased similarly.[11] It is surprising that Tudor England was able to feed its people and animals despite their rapid increase in numbers and several disastrous harvests.

Deliberate refusal to provide a horse against a Privy Council warrant was a serious matter. One case amongst several recorded was against John Howard who 'very lewdly being on his way did beat the guide and went away with the horses' which led to the chief justice ordering that Howard should be made to give satisfaction.[12] Refusal to supply a horse could lead to a summons before the Privy Council. This happened in October 1577 when the mayor of Marlborough was called for refusing to supply Captain Furbisher travelling in the Queen's service.[13]

Another case was heard on 18 September of that year when the Privy Council met to consider the refusal of the constable of Bruton to provide a horse for Nicholas Scott who was on his way to Ireland. They commissioned two knights to investigate and to send any persons thought to be culpable before them. Such was the importance given to the posts that the councillors were willing to give time to what might be thought matters hardly fit for their consideration.

The town of Nottingham had its problems. In 1573 Messrs Cocking and Whedlow were summonsed for calling the constables 'knaves and wellanttes [villains]' when they were required to provide horses.[14] In 1577 a local jury presented a petition to the mayor asking that post horses be kept and in 1579, after such an order had been issued, it was so unpopular that there was a further request that 'it may be observed'. Nottingham's accounts for post horses are known for 1541 and also 1586, but post horses were not always available at this important road junction.[15]

The problems arising from unwillingness to provide horses and accept the penny a mile that was offered were increased by the numbers of persons who presented false documents. On 3 May 1596 a proclamation was issued against counterfeit messengers:

> There have of late been divers dissolute and audacious persons that falsely take upon themselves to be messengers of her Majesty's Chamber, and for that purpose undutifully wear boxes or escutcheons of arms as messengers are wont to do. These men go up and down the country with warrants wherein are counterfeited the names of the Lords of the Council or of the Ecclesiastical Commissioners, and by colour thereof they warn gentlemen, ministers of the Church, women, yeomen and others to appear before the Council, and exact fees of them for their labour and travel. And although divers of these shameless, counterfeit persons have been apprehended and brought before the Star Chamber, where some have been condemned and set on the pillory, lost their ears, and some marked in the face, yet these notable abuses continue more and more. Proclamation is now made that if any person so warned shall have any suspicion of the messenger or of the warrant to be counterfeit, he may cause the

> constable or the officer of the peace to bring the supposed messenger before the next Justice of the Peace, where the warrant may be viewed and the party thoroughly examined.[16]

Such a case was referred to Lord Burghley by the Marquis of Winchester, who wrote on 20 May 1596:

> There was of late brought before me by the constables and bailiffs of Basingstoke one James Nott (a gentleman as he termeth himself) who by virtue of a warrant under your hand did require to have post horses for her Majesty's service.

The man claimed to be a servant of Burghley's and the so called warrant showed Burghley's name, Cecil, had been spelt as Sisell.[17]

Even royal messengers could face problems concerning signatures and the Salisbury manuscripts contain an investigation made concerning three dubious name stamps. Christopher Porter was examined by two justices of Middlesex concerning hand stamps that had been made of the signatures that were used on Exchequer bills. He explained that such stamps were used to check the authenticity of signatures and evidently this was accepted by the magistrates.[18]

Equally difficult decisions faced the town posts when a letter arrived from an important person whose signature might not be authorised for despatching an official packet. The correspondence of the Lord Lieutenant of Ireland was sent with misgiving by the mayor of Chester in 1599 and the post of Plymouth refused to accept a packet from Sir John Gilbert. He was obliged to write to Cecil, the queen's secretary, on 7 May 1601:

> humbly beseeches [him] to take order with the postmaster that my packets may be carried, because the Plymouth post refuses to do it, saying he has no order for it.[19]

The same problem arose in September that year when the mayor of Dartmouth wrote to Cecil:

> The postmaster of Ashburton scruples to receive letters directed to you from this town. If you give some command in that behalf, those letters will be the more speedily conveyed.[20]

In 1603 William Stallenge, Deputy to the Naval Victualler at Plymouth, had to pay £5 to get an express letter forwarded to Cecil.[21]

Another problem that faced the local posts was that riders who had been provided with an order from the Privy Council to ride post for one journey would try to use the order a second or even a third time. To remedy this an open instruction was issued on 17 March 1582:

> An open placard touching the disorders of such as use to ride posts to & from Plymouth and other parts of the West Country; some without commission and some with one commission 2 and 3 times for little or no money, whereby many poor men's horses are spoiled and made unable to serve her Majesty. For redress whereof her Majesty's pleasure is that no man hereafter ride in post without Commission which shall serve him for one time unless it be otherwise specified in his Commission, and that he pay for every horse twopence the mile and a groat to the Guide for every Post or Place where the horses are to be changed. And in case of refusal of any to pay the same before he depart, it shall be lawful for the post of that place to refuse to serve him.[22]

The constant problems concerning the provision of horses and their equipment are shown in yet another proclamation of 11 April 1596:

> All Mayors, Sheriffs and other officers are commanded at their uttermost peril to assist in the service of the posts, providing 10 or 20 able and sufficient horses with furniture convenient to be ready at the town or stage where the post abideth, the owners to have such rates as the post from time to time pays for his own horses.[23]

So little attention seems to have been given that it was necessary to issue another order later that month strictly requiring that their previous order be obeyed. It was followed by an order for the Dover road:

> An open warrant directed unto all Mayors, sheriffs, bailiffs, head-boroughs and other magistrates, officers and ministers of the Towns and stages in Kent where her Majesty's posts are established, and also to all Justices of the Peace, postmasters and other officers in the Counties adjoining.[24]

The Privy Council regretted that 'our letters have not been so regarded as the importance of the service requireth' and that those who did not supply horses should have their names sent to the Privy Council.

Evidently the problems were such that discretion was to be allowed to pay the local rate. Despite all the measures taken by the queen and her Council the overall picture is of instructions that were not always obeyed, particularly in the last years of her reign, and of an often unreliable service that worked under considerable financial constraints.

The problem of security

Throughout the century there were many complaints about the reliability of the post and a variety of methods was tried to improve the service. One device used was drawing the sign of a gallows alongside the address, often with the addition of the words 'For life, for life', thus threatening the bearer with severe punishment should he fail to make a speedy delivery. (Fig. 9.1) The sketch was presumably intended as a warning to an illiterate postman that he was handling a government packet. The result was not always as expected for in 1548, during the protectorate set up for the young Edward VI, John Uvedale, treasurer of the northern garrison, received a letter from the

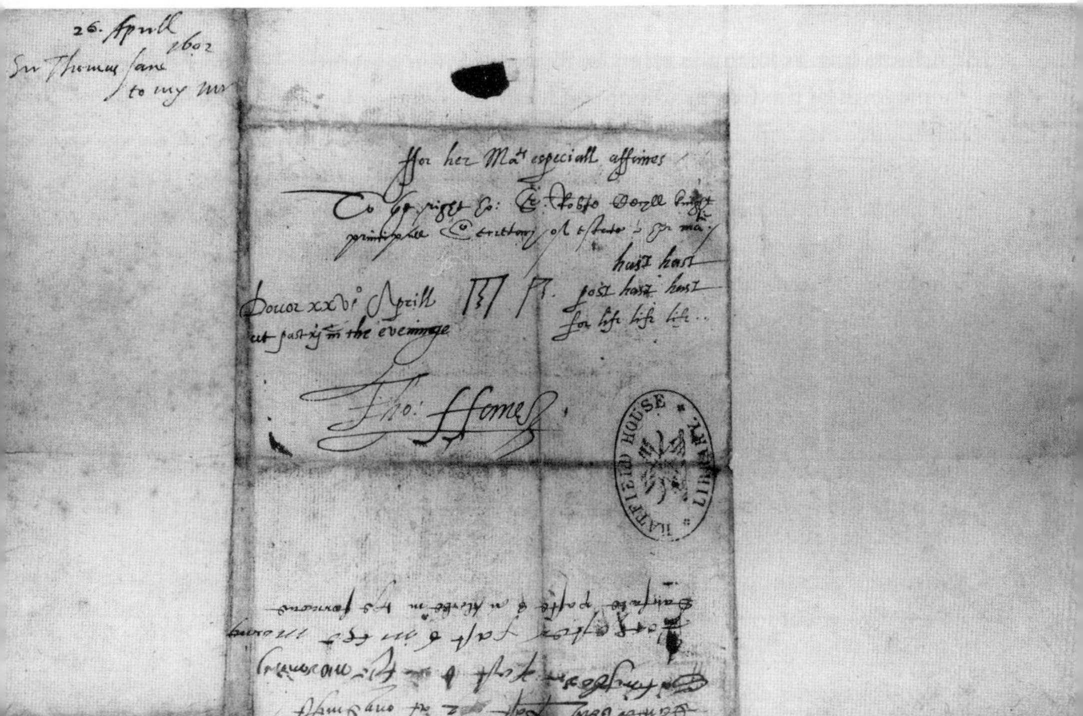

9.1 'Hast Hast Post' letter with gallows warning to the posts from Sir Thomas Fane to Sir Robert Cecil, 1602. The notes from the town posts read 'Dovor xxj Aprill at past xj in the eveninge. Canterbery past 2 at midnight. Sitingborn past 5 in the morning. Rochester past 6 in the morning. Dartforte past 8 aclocke in the forenoone.' (By courtesy the Marquess of Salisbury. Cecil Papers 92/162)

lord lieutenant which so incensed him that he wrote about it to the lord protector, Somerset:

> Riding towards York to fetch the treasure sent thither, the enclosed letter, signed with a pair of gallows, overtook me. What my Lord Lieutenant means to do with me I know not, or whether he meant it towards the posts, but it is a token meet for murderers and thieves, and not for so true a man and so old a servant as I. I must beseech you to write his Lordship to use me like a faithful officer and not thus openly through all the country from Post to Post in manner of a vile and worthy reproach to consign his letters addressed to me with a pair of gallows.[25]

That the dire inscriptions actually had little effect is shown from a letter of Lord Wharton to the lord protector from Carlisle dated 18 February of the same year: 'The Letters were nine days coming, notwithstanding the direction to the post twice, "For Life, For Life"'. Four or five days would have been normal.[26]

On 29 July 1556, in the reign of Philip and Mary, an order had been issued by the lords of the Council, then at Eltham, to require the posts on the northern route to record each letter they handled, adding the time of receipt:

> that the Post between this and the North should each of them keep a book, and make entry of every letter that he shall receive, the time of delivery thereof unto his hands, with the post's name that shall bring it unto him, whose hands he shall also take to his book, witnessing the same note to be true, which Order was also commanded to be given here at the Court and the Wardens of the Marches toward Scotland were required to do the like.[27]

Tuke's letter to Cromwell in 1533 had stated that he had tried to persuade the duke of Northumberland to enter the hour of despatch on each letter, but he lamented his lack of success. An example of the time being entered is on a letter from Archbishop Parker to Cecil dated 22 July 1566. Parker sent the letter from Croydon at four in the afternoon. It was endorsed:

> Waltham Cross about 9 at night, Ware at 12 o'clock, and Croxton between 7 and 8 of the clock in the morning.[28]

The journey was by town posts who in theory provided a service night and day, but delivery was slow for the letter took forty hours to travel 63 miles. One of the Postmasters' Books, that for Huntingdon in August 1585, has survived and has been summarised in *The Philatelist*. Details of the date and time received, together with the time of the original despatch and the names of sender and addressee, are given for packets on Her Majesty's service, but only dates with usually the name of the addressee are given for the letters. Packets, letters and batches were separately listed. On some days none were received though on one day nine packets and one letter were received. Times given show that the post operated through the day and night. A very detailed study has been published in the *Journal of Historical Geography* of the speed of the royal post, which uses the evidence of the Huntingdon record book.[29]

The instruction to enter times on letters had apparently not proved as reliable as intended and a replacement was used in the form of a label which is described in orders set down by commandment of the Queen's Majesty of 30 September 1582 as 'a label of parchment or paper wherein the packet may be wrapped'. On it was to be written the name of the post together with the day and time of receipt.[30] The requirement to keep a book in which to record the date and time of receipt of all packets was restated. A letter from Randolph to Walsingham in 1584 says:

> if packets are not brought with such speed as they ought to be [...] you would reserve the scroll or covering that thereby I might know the date and seek out the fault.[31]

The requirement was reiterated in a set of orders to the posts in 1602.[32]

An even more serious problem concerning the posts was the opening of letters en route. Occasional complaints came before the Privy Council. Lord Wharton wrote on 26 October 1547:

> I received your letters directed three times 'For the Life' and it seemed they had been opened, as sundry others have been. Some of the Posts cannot do their duty.[33]

In 1558 Mason was informed:

> signifying to him the usual slackness of the posts laid northwards in the conveyance of letters hither, the opening of them by the way, requiring of him to give order forthwith for their reformation .... or else to seek some new means to be served from time to time by a through post.[34]

A reply to Lord Evers, governor of Berwick, shows that the Council decided on a new security method:

> Whereas he writes that his letters appointed to be sent hither were opened by the way, his Lordship is willed to boult [find out] by whom the same was done and to cause such as he shall find faulty herein to be punished. And for the safer sending of letters unto him from hence it is signified they shall be henceforth pacqueted with thread and sealed with the Council's seal.[35]

Letters were far more likely to be opened when coming from abroad and the Privy Council arranged for many outgoing letters to be seized. Spinelly wrote to Wolsey in 1516 describing an arrangement by which for a total of 300 golden gyldins he could arrange for the French King's correspondence to Richard de la Pole to be opened.[36] In 1521 the Venetian ambassador wrote home:

> The letter I entrusted to the Royal Postmaster of England was, when opened, found to contain two blank sheets of paper only.[37]

Cardinal Wolsey intercepted mail to and from the Spanish ambassador and wrote in January 1525 at great length to Dr Richard Sampson, the English ambassador at the emperor's court, giving details of the seizure of various letters 'containing seditious and sinister reports to the emperor'.[38] At the same time English mail was being frequently intercepted on the Continent. Tuke wrote to Wolsey on 13 August 1529:

> A courier is come from Lyons with letters from Rome which have been opened at Florence, Genoa and Lyons. I have thought it good for every man's discharge to send them to the King. You will see that there will be no means of sending to Rome without the letters being read, unless they be written in cipher.[39]

A Privy Council minute of 25 July 1557 refers to the presence of official searchers at Gravesend. It provides some insight into the methods then used at ports for examining private letters:

> A letter to the Lord Cobham that the Lords have received his letters with such others as the Searchers of Gravesend have stayed. Which they have returned to him as they find no cause for suspicion in the same. He is also willed to charge the Searchers to have more consideration henceforth, so as they stay such letters only upon the perusing of the superscription may seem suspect to have come from the places that have been heretofore noted unto them.[40]

This shows that the practice of searching ships which we have seen taking place in earlier centuries was still operating and it is clear that the searchers had a list of those places from which all letters were to be examined. Mail addressed abroad was similarly examined.

In 1558 there was correspondence with the French ambassador who had objected to letters to the French king sent from Scotland being opened. Finally, on 14 February 1551 that matter was concluded by the Privy Council:

> When the French ambassador desired his packets of letters might at all times pass to and fro without impeachment it was agreed he should so have them. And that therefore order should be taken as well for post horses to serve the bearers of his said letters to and for their reasonable money as also that the Lord Warden of the marches should upon sight of the packets being either addressed to the King or to the said ambassador, suffer them to pass to and fro.[41]

Such undertakings meant little. In 1569 Lord Cobham wrote to Cecil to say that a packet had arrived from France which he had caused to be opened.[42]

The correspondence of John Shers' English agent in Venice, mentioned in the previous chapter, shows that for a bribe he was able to obtain copies of letters being sent by other agents and notables. A letter of 18 January 1561 encloses a copy of one from the abbot of St Salut to the duke of Savoy's ambassador; for 20 marks he had been able to read the ambassador's correspondence and that from the papal legate. Shers' yearly bill for bribes was £40.

Another incident is recorded in 1571, when Sir William Drury wrote to Burghley mentioning letters from a Monsieur Virac to the French king. He had apprehended a French boy who had them concealed in a staff or cudgel.[43] In the same year Lord Hunsdon wrote to the Privy Council about a messenger who was reported to be carrying letters to Edinburgh sewn in his buttons and the seams of his coat.[44] Even more dramatic were the letters inserted into the bung holes of barrels that incriminated Mary, Queen of Scots. Walsingham employed an expert cryptologist, Thomas Phelippes, to examine them and the other letters connected with the Babbington Plot.

Attempts were made at the end of the century to strengthen the control of incoming mail. On 29 January 1585 orders were published by Randolph, master of the posts, Cobham, the warden of the Cinque Ports, and Walsingham, the principal secretary, concerning the posts in Kent. They ensured the control of all strangers entering the country by requiring them to use only horses provided by the posts at 2s 6d a stage per horse. The ordinary through posts of the merchants of Flanders and of France were similarly restricted. Any other person supplying horses without the post's authority was to be imprisoned until he had given surety to observe the orders in the future.[45] In 1591 a proclamation set out strict regulations for mail received and sent by foreign merchants:

> In consideration of which inconveniences past, we do hereby straightly prohibit and forbid all persons whatsoever, directly or indirectly to gather up, receive, bring in, or carry out of this Realm, any letters or packets without the allowance or ordinary address and despatch of the said Masters and Comptrollers of the Posts. [...] And therefore our will and pleasure is, that you the Lord Treasurer of England, and the lord Warden of the Cinque Ports, together with our trusty and well beloved servant John Stanhope Esquire, Master and Comptroller of all our Posts cause public knowledge to be given unto all Merchants, both strangers and others of our city of London, and all others whom it may or ought to concern, that neither they nor any for them do hereafter take upon them, openly or underhand to employ any such disallowed person in the carrying of their letters, but to be such only as shall be found lawfully appointed for that service.[46]

The proclamation further authorised the searching of all messengers and suspected persons.

At the end the century English agents abroad were still being successful in intercepting letters. An entry in the Fugger Letters for March 1590 makes this comment:

> Monsieur van Aldegonde, who at the time of the fall of Antwerp was Mayor of the city, is said to be on a visit to the Queen of England in London, in order to decode for her some intercepted Spanish and Lorraine letters written in cipher and presumed to be from the King of Spain.[47]

In April 1594 Sir Edmund Uvedale wrote from Flushing to Cecil:

> That by means of Jacques Jelly he had been able to intercept and view all the letters brought by the post from Bruges, and to avoid suspicion and ensure safety for his own letters he had sent them by a female, Louise.[48]

English letters were still being intercepted and a letter from Sir Peter Hollins in 1594 describes how the Antwerp postmaster would seize any such correspondence he could and employed a man called Verstegan to translate them for him.[49] Actually Vestegan was receiving a pension from England for reporting on recusants there!

A letter in the Salisbury manuscripts describes the lengths to which Spain could go in punishing those involved in passing information to an enemy. The murder of over sixty men who had been detected on the Continent in giving intelligence to England is described in a letter from Anthony Paulet dated 15 July 1594:

> They were all beheaded, their bodies carried to Lisbon, and their heads carried with speed into Spain to the King. The cause given out there of this cruel murder was for that letters were intercepted, wherein they had intelligence with England.[50]

The trial of Louis Tinoco and Stephen Ferrara, the Portuguese conspirators with Dr Lopez in 1594, shows a reciprocal ferocity. They were accused of sending secret messages and intelligences to the King of Spain, their 'obscure words' relating to the poisoning of the queen. All were executed.[51]

Despite the dangers English agents continued to intercept mail, and a report from Thomas Honeyman to Cecil in May 1598 includes:

> Postmasters in Spain weigh out the letters to their servants and are easily corrupted for 28 ducats a month; the one at Madrid, Petro Martinez, let me have all of Cressold's and Englefield's letters, returning such as I did not care to keep.[52]

Honeyman's expenses for that year were £151 10s.

During the years 1597 to 1600 a young Silesian nobleman made a grand tour of Europe and his tutor, P. Hentzner, described their arrival at Rye where events followed those laid down:

> We arrived at Rye, a small English seaport. Here, as soon as we came on shore, we gave our names to the notary of that place, but not until he had demanded our business, and being answered that we had none but to see England, we were conducted to an inn where we were very well entertained, as generally in this country. We took post horses to London. It is surprising how swiftly they run; their bridles are very light, and their saddles little more than a span.[53]

Horses were changed at Flimwell and Chipstead. In London they used a coach. The return journey was not without its adventures. At Canterbury they changed horses and did not reach Dover until two or three o'clock in the morning, after having lost their guide. They saw horsemen whom they took to be thieves, though they had been warned that they might meet nocturnal spectres, who were frequently seen.

Attacks on messengers and lost letters

Sixteenth-century royal messengers appear to have been treated with respect and any assault on them was an unusual and serious matter. One such case that occurred in 1543 is described by Sir Ralph Salder in a letter, only a part of which has been preserved:

> the post was taken, as is aforesaid; I told them, that the man that hath taken him, whose name is Patrick Hume, hath not only put as many irons upon him as he is able to bear, as though he were a strong thief and murderer, but also hath threatened to hang him, with his letters around his neck.

In a letter dated 24 September of that year Sadler explains that the post was a soldier of Berwick who 'had previously harried and stolen the goods of Patrick Hume'. With that we hear no more of the incident but the area was a lawless one and Sadler, who was then negotiating with Scotland, says that his letters were opened and, even though some were in cipher, he suspects they were read.[54] Such cases were, however, considered important enough to warrant the attention of the Privy Council.

Another incident is recorded in January 1578 concerning letters to the Council in Wales being carried by Anthony Powell, gentleman, near to Worcester, which had been taken from him. It proved to be a complex matter for, as a result of the struggle over the letters, Powell and a friend were wounded and another died of his injuries. A charge of murder was brought. The Council ordered the sheriff and magistrates of Worcestershire to inform them of proceedings.[55]

A year later we find the Privy Council writing to Roger Lyon Esq. on 17 May concerning an assault on David Jenkins, a Chamber messenger. They understood from his letter that he had ordered those responsible to appear before their lordships and they asked for them to be sent forthwith. On 11 June they decided that Christopher Bancroft, gentleman, had received sufficient punishment for his involvement in the matter and ordered him to be released. The matter dragged on and in December their lordships heard several other persons and agreed to discharge them.[56]

References in State Papers to mail being lost are exceptional and the Council took prompt action where royal letters were concerned. Their records mention a case in January 1577:

> These letters sent to Lord Scrope, Mr Bradell, and Mr Carmichael upon advertisement, that the previous letters were lost by the spoiling of the post.[57]

Yet another case was considered by the Privy Council in 1599, when they examined Robert Crockett who had been asked by Hugh Rathbone, the Nantwich postmaster, to take his letters to Stoke. Evidently they had been left lying on a table and were never delivered.[58]

Other such incidents can be read in State Papers Domestic and in the Acts of the Privy Council. Under the Tudors a Court of Star Chamber, being the

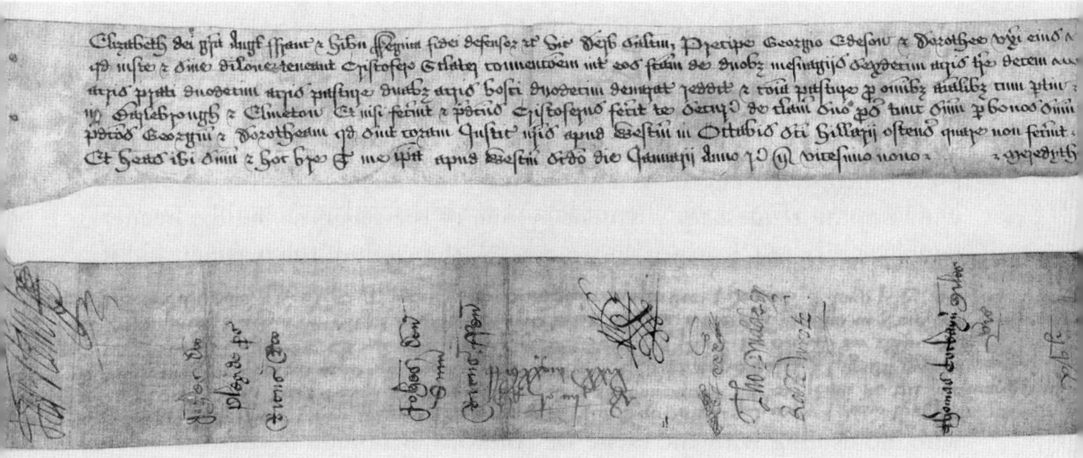

9.2 Tudor legal writ concerning an agreement between George Edeson and his wife Dorothy with Christopher Sclater concerning lands, rents and pasture in Barlborough and Elmeton in Derbyshire to be effective on 2 January in the 29th regnal year of Queen Elizabeth (1587). The address side is signed under the flap by Sir Edward Stanhope, Master in Chancery, by T.D. (Thomas Duddeley) and Robert Wrote, deputies in the Alienations Office. There are the names of witnesses and a scrivener's sign. The sheriff of Derbyshire's name, Thomas Cockayne, is at the foot. (Private collection)

Council sitting judicially, had been established with wide powers, and the knowledge that cases could be referred to it was sufficient to ensure the normal security of the mail and its carriers.

Despatching letters

The cost to the state of sending letters varied according to the method used. Some were passed onwards from stage to stage along routes to places where postmasters were being paid by the government. Between other towns, where they were not paid by the Crown, letters were forwarded without cost to the sovereign. However, if an Exchequer, Chancery, Chamber or other royal messenger used a town's post horses, he paid for each stage and would submit an account on his return. The practice of taking a single horse for a lengthy journey, as was generally done in previous centuries, seems to have been exceptional.

A number of the original submissions for payment made by Chamber, Chancery or Exchequer messengers and officials have survived and they show the claimant's name and usually the names, titles and addresses of those to whom the letters, commissions and writs were sent. Sometimes four messengers with similar tasks were paid by one warrant. Letters to the Court and to Privy Council members might be taken by senior clerks at Chancery and a few such claims exist. A few payment warrants from the reign of James I relating to messages on the king's behalf are made out to grooms of the Chamber. In the early Elizabethan period the daily rate of 2s 8d is usually mentioned, but this is not shown on later documents. A claim begins with a polite request for payment by one of the tellers at the Exchequer or, in the case of Chancery documents, by the clerk of the hanaper, and it may be quite detailed; but sometimes, as with some of those signed by Lord Chancellor Hatton, there is merely an instruction to pay a messenger a specified sum for a stated duty. Often the reason for the journey is set out, as with the one illustrated, where the messenger takes letters to the Commissioners who are dealing with the estate of 'Anthony Babbington, late attainted'. Babbington had been the leader of the plot to assassinate Queen Elizabeth. The involvement of Mary, Queen of Scots, in the plot led to her execution in 1587.

The Exchequer paid its own messengers and those from the Chamber. After the reorganisation of the Exchequer in 1554 it had resumed control of most of the Crown's finances that had been taken away from it by Henry VIII's Chamber. It was in two parts: a treasury with a pay office known as the Exchequer of Receipt, and a court of audit known as the Exchequer of Account. Only the chancellor of the Exchequer was involved in both sections. The royal messengers took most letters and documents addressed to nobles, sheriffs, lords lieutenant, bishops and others of similar status but other men were used in emergencies. For example, the account for payments to messengers riding to Plymouth during the Armada year in 1588 records fifteen men listed as messengers, grooms and others. Once a claim had been written out by an Exchequer clerk, it went to be verified by a senior official such as the remembrancer or auditor of the Court of Exchequer, who checked the cost and signed that he had done so. Then the claim went to the treasurer or, in his absence, to the chancellor of the Exchequer, who was his deputy. Normally the signatory approved the full claim but there are examples of his adjusting it. At this stage a tally was struck to record the payment and the details were written on the Pell Rolls, as they were then known, for the Issue Rolls had been discontinued until their revival late in the Elizabethan period.[59]

The Chancery, like the Exchequer and the Chamber, had four principal messengers and others of less importance. Their claims were verified by the controller of the hanaper in a similar way to those presented at the Exchequer, and the Lord Chancellor authorised the clerk of the hanaper to pay the approved amount. The hanaper, derived from a word that means either a basket for holding documents or a chest used for storing coins, was the department that received fees for the enrolment and sealing of documents. From its receipts the clerk paid the Chancery staff and had a sum available for the Chancellor's secretaries and assistants. Out of this he drew the messengers' payments.[60]

The Master of the Posts does not seem to have been involved in the process of authorising the payments for these messengers, but in his capacity as treasurer of the King's Chamber he dealt with payments to the senior messenger and the two court posts who mainly carried documents between the court and Westminster. His paymaster received the wages of those town and other posts subsidised by government and the accounts survive for the years of Elizabeth's reign. It is a tribute to the painstaking efficiency of the lord treasurer, the chancellor of the Exchequer and the lord chancellor that one of them personally examined and signed the principal messengers' warrants. That they did so is an indication of the importance they attached to the carriage of the royal mail. The signatures are clear and not hastily written. Sometimes the warrants are torn across the signature. In later centuries such warrants may be certified as having been paid by a large tick which ran from the top to the foot of the page.

The Elizabethan Chancery staff wrote those writs required by the central courts of Exchequer, King's Bench, Common Pleas, and Chancery. Professor Jones has made some calculations of the numbers of documents involved. The six Chancery clerks, each of whom had a large staff, dealt with all that required the great seal together with those writs required by the Chancery's own court. A Subpoena Office was created in 1575 and sent out between 8,000 and 9,000 writs each year in the 1590s on behalf of the central courts. Twenty-four clerks, called the cursitors, together with their underclerks wrote what were known as writs of course, the routine writs sent out by the four courts apart from Chancery. In 1593 they sent out 35,000. The central courts had a national jurisdiction though there were royal courts of the Council of the North and the Marches of Wales which dealt with justice in those remoter parts. Consequently, the 35,000 writs had to be taken to a wide range of destinations. Many went to sheriffs for onward transmission by their staff of messengers.

An account of the royal household that was made early in the seventeenth century shows that there were by then other royal messengers apart from those already mentioned.[61]

The Duchy of Lancaster, the Court of First Fruits and Tenths, the Council of the North and the Court of Wards and Liveries each had a paid messenger. Star Chamber and the Court of Requests are shown as using the messengers of the Fleet Prison. At that time there were six heralds, four pursuivants and sixteen

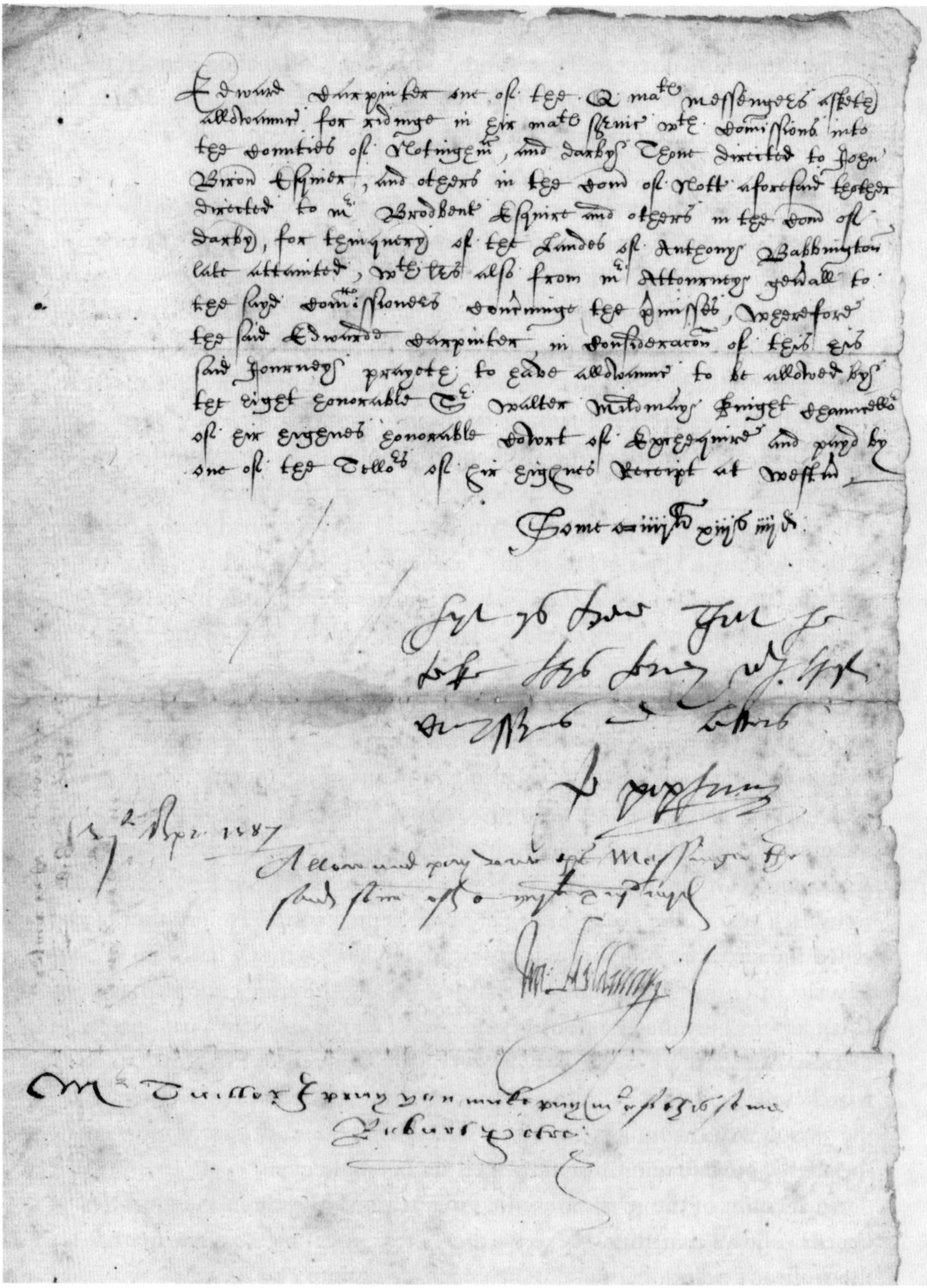
Edward Carpinter one of the Q. mates messengers asketh allowance for ridinge in hir mates service wth Commissions into the counties of Notingham, and Darbye, them directed to John Biron Esquier, and others in the Com of Nott aforesaid, thother directed to Mr Brodbent Esquire and others in the Com of Darby, for thenquery of the Landes of Anthony Babbington late attainted, wth thes also from Mr Attorneys generall to the sayd Commissioners concerninge the premisses, wherefore the said Edwarde Carpinter in consideracon of this his said Jorneys prayeth to have allowance to be allowed by the right honorable Sr Walter Mildmay knight chauncellor of hir highnes honorable Court of Exchequer and payd by one of the Tellers of hir highnes Receipt at Westm.

9.3 Messenger's warrant concerning the Babbington estates. (Private collection)
Opposite: Transcript of the above.

Edward Carpinter one of the Q[ueen's] ma[jes]t[i]es messengers asketh allowance for ridinge in hir ma[jes]t[i]es service with Commissions into the Counties of Notingham, and darby Thene directed to John Biron Esquier, and others in the Com[itatus] of Nott. aforesaid thother directed to mr Brodbent Esquier and others in the Com[itatus] of Darby, for thinquery of the Landes of Anthony Babbington* late attainted, with l[ette]rs also from mr Attourneye generall to the sayd Commissioners Concerninge the premisses, Wherefore the said Edwarde Carpinter, in Consideracioun of this his said Journey prayeth to have allowannce to be allowed by the right honorable Sr Walter Mildmay Knight Chauncellor of hir highnes honorable Cowrt of Exchequire and payd by one of the Tellers of hir highnes Receipt at Westm[inster]

Some o=iiij^{lb} xiij^{s} iiij^{d}

Hyt is trew that he
toke thys Jorney wth these
Comyssyons and Letters

J Popham**

vit$^{\text{[h] Apr 1587}}$
Allow and pay unto the Messenger the
said some of o - iiij^{lb} xiij^{s} iiij^{d}

W. Mildmay

Mr Taillor I pray you make paym[en]t of this some

Robart Petre

*Anthony Babbington was the leader of the Babbington Plot to assassinate Queen Elizabeth I and put Mary, Queen of Scots, on the throne. The plot was detected by Walsingham, one of the two Secretaries of State. Babbington was attainted of treason and put to death. Mary was executed.

** Sir John Popham was the Attorney General. Sir Walter Mildmay was Chancellor of the Exchequer and a Commissioner who sat in judgment of Queen Mary at her trial. Robert Taylor was one of the four Tellers at the Exchequer. Robart Petre was Clerk of the Receipt.

sergeants at arms. Even the king's harbinger, the two gentlemen harbingers and the four yeomen harbingers, whose task it was to arrange accommodation ahead of the king's arrival, carried letters relating to their work. As we have seen, each messenger was suited to the message. Aylmer's *The King's Servants*, which describes the civil service of Charles I, gives an approximate total of forty Chamber messengers attending the court, where the Privy Council, the household and the central executive were. All those parts of government that were settled in Westminster had their own messengers, as did the branches of the Council in the north and on the Welsh borders.

Much of the mail was carried by footposts rather than by mounted men. Stanhope's patent of appointment had described him as master of the messengers and runners. We have seen that in earlier times letters were often carried by men on foot and there are references throughout the century to runners and footposts. Bristol had a footpost, Thomas Lyne, who carried letters to the lord treasurer in the 1530s, being paid 13s 4d, or sometimes 15s, for a journey of 240 miles.[62] The Bristol chamberlain's accounts have an entry for August 1580:

> Paid to Savage, the footpost, to go to Wellington with a letter to the Recorder touching the holding of the Sessions, and if not there to go to Wimborne Minster, where he has a house, where he found him, and returned with a letter; which post was six days upon that journey in very foul weather, and I paid him for his pains 13s 4d.[63]

A later reference is in 1615, when 12s was paid 'for cloth to make Packer, the footpost, a coat'. He was paid 3s 8d for a journey of 60 miles that year.[64]

In times of emergency a system could easily be arranged and Randolph arranged for footposts to bring news of sightings of the Spanish fleet at the time of the Armada. Sixpence a week was paid to men from each parish to run to the nearest post house. They enabled the Council to be closely informed of the progress of the battle.

In 1597 a letter to Cecil, secretary of state, from Thomas Fane, lieutenant at Dover Castle, refers to a man being sent from Dover:

> Having this 6th received your letters of the 5th concerning James Beard I have accordingly sent him up to you by the Foot Post of Dover to whom I have delivered 20s towards his and the said Beard's charges.[65]

This was an unusual duty for the postman. Another letter, this time from Cornwall in May 1599 from the sheriff, has the endorsement:

> To be conveyed by the running post from Plymouth to the Lords of the Court Post Haste for Her Majesty's special service.[66]

It took a little over 73 hours to complete the journey to London, comparable to that taken by post horses. The journey shows that runners were available at all the principal towns on that route, the service being reliable enough for the sheriff to entrust a packet to the Privy Council. Southampton also had a footpost in 1599, for in August the mayor, having heard that a fleet was being mustered in Brest, wrote to the Council and added that in view of the need for haste he sent this advertisement 'by the running post'.[67]

By then the method of passing packets of letters by the town posts had largely replaced that of sending expresses by special messengers, who would obviously take longer because they needed rest and sleep. An earlier express along the same route is recorded in 1591:

> A Warrant to Mr ViceChamberlain to pay unto Thomas Rottenbury sent in post from Sir Francis Drake and the Mayor of Plymouth the sum of six pounds xiijs iiijd for pains and expenses.[68]

This was a considerably greater cost than if taken by runners.

The post and the public

When sending a letter, the private individual would have a variety of possible messengers. The carriers were usually employed. They went with a train of vehicles and horses and it was the practice, as they neared their destination, for one of them to go ahead of the rest to deliver the letters. Few places were without a weekly carrier to London, as described in Chapter 7. Apart from their services there would be the town posts, who might take a bundle of letters to London or to a nearby town from which they could be passed on from one postman to another. Otherwise there would be the occasional messenger or reliable traveller who might take mail to his next destination for a reward. Even a royal or sheriff's messenger would take letters, though he would no doubt be selective with regard to whose mail he took. There is a letter from Lord Dacre to the Privy Council in 1514 referring to one that he has sent by a royal messenger 'as the matter touches on himself he will pay the post for the occasion and has written to Bryan Tuke accordingly',[69] but Dacre was a great border lord to whom the royal messengers came frequently.

During Henry VIII's reign the merchant Richard Johnson mentions in a letter from London that he has sent it 'by the King's post in the night, when the merchants who had lain there for four nights refused to go'.[70] His preference was for the carrier rather than the royal post.

As mentioned previously, the proclamations of 1583 and 1584 refer to the delivery of private letters being made after those from the sovereign. However, in 1602 it was found necessary to order that 'The Posts for the Queen's immediate service', the royal messengers, not the ordinary posts, should only carry state despatches.[71]

The carriers' services described in Chapter 7 were reliable. Much of the extensive Johnson correspondence, which started in 1534 and is described later, went between London and a great variety of places including Glapthorn, Towcester, Newington, Oxford, Deene, Fotheringhay and Melton Mowbray. To each there was a reliable carrier, ready to take letters, parcels, wine, cloth, clothes, bales of wool or, indeed, any type of goods. The carrier could arrange for the innkeeper where he stayed to send a man to deliver a letter or else he would leave it with the town post who could rely on a payment for delivery.

The Corsini merchant letters, discussed later in Chapter 11, that were written in England usually have a simple address to one of the brothers in London, but a few bear a further instruction written in different handwriting such as one from Sudeley Castle which has the addition 'in St Clement Lane' while two others from Hatfield Palace add directions to the Corsini home 'in gras street' and 'in St Clement Lane next to Mr Pevine at London'.[72]

These amendments suggest either that a clerk has put a direction after a letter has been signed and sealed, or that it has been handed in at a central point where a note has been added for the benefit of a newly appointed postman who was not familiar with the streets.

Several of the letters written in this country and sent to the Corsinis in London give postal rates. All of them emanate from ports from which their agents write about cargoes and transport costs. Consequently the letters could have come either by land or sea. The usual cost is 4d, possibly a ship letter charge, though there is little evidence of coastal letter services at that time. Such letters started in 1571 from Dover – 'Payd a groate' (4d) – and one from Exeter in 1591 is at the same rate. After that there are several letters from Plymouth charged 6d or 1s. The 1s suggests that either the post was paid double for a large letter or that it is for a packet containing two or more letters. Probably there were two postal services from Plymouth, by carrier or by the town post. The merchant, James Bagg, refers to 'his messenger' but we cannot deduce with any certainty from this that he ran his own postal service. He may be referring to the town's postman whom he would know or that his messenger is the London carrier whom he used, or that he was sending a personal messenger. A letter from Tilbury in 1586 says 'pay the bringer iid', a very short journey and presumably carried by a private arrangement. Letters with such instructions or 'p the post' suggest that the sender is not using his usual messenger and in order to ensure certain delivery asks the recipient to pay. The evidence of the Johnson correspondence is that there was an efficient postal service at the time available throughout the country, with innkeepers and carriers being ready to arrange for local deliveries.

Another source of merchants' correspondence is from the Merchant Adventurers of England, whose society probably began as a fellowship of mercers in the fourteenth century.[73] The Old French word *mercer* means merchant and the Mercers' Company received its first charter in 1394. They had a royal charter in 1407 as merchants trading in Holland, Brabant, Zealand and Flanders. English merchants probably had a factory in Antwerp as early as 1296 and eventually bought a fine house in Antwerp in 1558.[74]

Other merchants in towns such as Bristol, York and Newcastle were associated with them. Their rivals in the woollen and cloth trade were the Merchants of the Staple, who had a monopoly of the shipment of raw wool. When that trade declined and the wool was shipped as cloth, the Staplers steadily declined. The Adventurers, who shipped most of the cloth, grew in wealth and influence. It has been estimated that the cloth trade was worth £1 million annually in the time of Queen Elizabeth. By making substantial loans to the Tudor sovereigns through their master, Sir Thomas Gresham, who had previous experience as royal factor, or agent, in handling royal loans at Antwerp, they were able to secure the ousting of their other rivals, namely the Hanse, the fellowship of Hanseatic traders, which had held privileged trading rights in England since the mid-fifteenth century.

The Adventurers developed their own postal agents who had their own postmen, using continental town posts and any persons they considered reliable. Within England there are payments recorded to carriers and to individuals. The York Adventurers, whose origins have been traced to a religious guild in 1357, have correspondence surviving from the late fifteenth century.[75]

We know that a century later they retained William Paige as their post in London and the accounts for 1560 show him being paid 20s a year to supervise their letter deliveries. A letter that he wrote in November 1567 to 'Mr Watson, the Governor, the assistants and generality in York' gives details of that service:

> Right worshipful sir and sirs, my humble duty considered unto your worships, your continual servant and orator, William Paige, your worships' post. Having of your worship xxs given for the fast conveyance of your letters from London unto your city of York, not having had any great benefit or profit other ways,

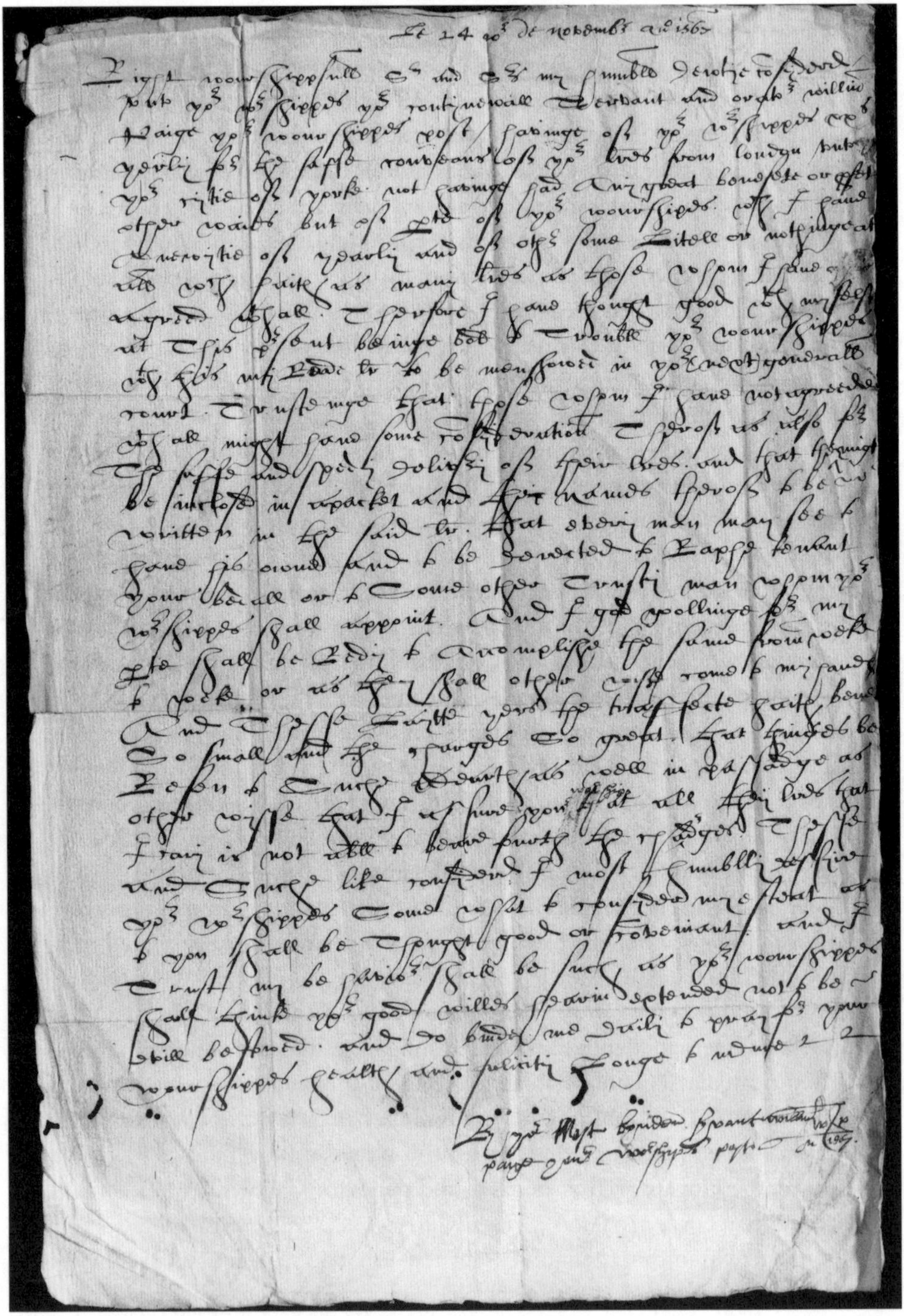

9.4 Letter from William Paige, York Merchant Adventurers' postman, writing about his employment. A transcript is given within the chapter. (By courtesy York Merchant Adventurers. Trade Correspondence no.^9)

> but of part of your worships which I have annuity of yearly: and of other some little or nothing at all, which hath as many letters as those whom I have agreed withall. Therefore I have thought good with myself at this present being bold to trouble your worships with this my rude letter to be mentioned in your next general court. Trusting that those, whom I have not agreed with withall, might have some consideration thereof, as also for the safe and speedy deliverance of their letters, and that this might be enclosed in a packet and their names be written in the same letter, that every man maybe seen to have his own, and to be directed to Ralph Tenant, your beadle, or to some other trusty man, whom your worships shall appoint. And I, God willing, for my part shall be ready to accomplish the same from week to week, or as they shall otherwise come into my hands. And these late years the traffic has been so small, and the charges so great that things be risen to dearth as well in passage as otherwise, that I assure your worships that all the letters that I carry is not able to bear forth the charges.[76]

Paige supervised the weekly despatch of letters from London for the annual sum of £1, selecting the most appropriate person to take the packet which contained them. The beadle in York received the letters and delivered them, as is shown in a letter of the following year addressed 'to his loving friend, Rauffe Tenent, bedal, unto the worshipful merchants of the city of York, give these':

> In London the last of April anno 1568. After my hearty commendations unto you, trusting in God you be in good health as I am at the making hereof. desiring you to see these letters herein enclosed delivered with speed, and in so doing you shall command me to do the like, as the Lord God knoweth, who evermore preserve us in his blessed keeping. From London as above written by your William Paige, post.[77]

Important letters were sent individually and costs varied according to the status of the carrier. A letter 'that went to the Lorde of Camfere' near Middleburg, cost 6s 8d in 1433.[78] In 1434 John Dene took a letter from York 'direct to the mayor in London', for which he was paid 3s 4d.[79]

A century later as much as 5s was paid on one occasion while 16d a day and 3d a day are recorded to letter carriers. Carriage of a trunk with 'other supplications and extraordinary affairs' cost 2s 11d. In 1576 they sent mail to London by the carrier for 3s 4d.

In the next century the Bristol Merchant Adventurers probably had a similar arrangement and their chamberlain's accounts in 1627–28 show several payments to Roger Justice for messengers:

> Paid to Roger Justice xs which he paid to a footman that was sent with letters to London by the Mayor's order.

He paid rewards to messengers who came with letters and proclamations, sums that varied between 6s 8d and £1.[80]

The Merchant Adventurers in Newcastle on Tyne paid from 1509 a composition of £8 to the London Adventurers and their account books show various payments to messengers. These have no particular pattern and clearly the cost of bearing a message related to its importance and to that of the bearer. Correspondence with Antwerp was received by the steward there and in 1553 he was paid 10s for answering letters. Two 'writings' sent to London cost 2s, but Gilbert Middilton received 53s 4d for his journey to London;[81] in other cases as much as £5 could be spent. The reward for serving writs in Northumberland was 16s 8d. An indication of the cost of materials in 1556 is that a skin of parchment was 10d.

Mail arriving in London from or to the Continent was sent by the most appropriate postal service for onward transmission. There are no surviving original letters in the records held by the Mercers' Company in London but the Acts of Court have been preserved and they contain many copies.[82] These show that on those occasions when letters and documents were not carried by the mercers' own servants special arrangements for payments were made and approved by the Court. Surprisingly, the early Acts between 1453 and 1527 mention several times when they used royal pursuivants for journeys to the Low Countries. Presumably the pursuivant was travelling on royal business but was willing to carry their letters. The Adventurers paid a reward of 20s for each such journey. A letter to the governor in Antwerp dated 1527 mentions:

> We [...] intend to send over to you a sad discreet person with the said writings the which shall well instruct you. [...] Also that you please there [decide] a convenient reward for to give unto the said person.[83]

Such special messengers would be paid a reward suitable to their status, and this is always mentioned within the letter, thus explaining why there are no postal markings or charges on the address panels of the surviving York letters from the Continent. On the occasions that letters had to be taken to the King's Council when he was out of London it was usual to send a deputation whose costs would be reimbursed. It was always considered appropriate to suit the messenger to the dignity of the recipient.

The alien merchants living in London in the sixteenth century had developed their own postal service to the Continent, which became known as the

Strangers' Post. By the terms of the treaty of 1496 known as the *Intercursus Magnus*, Henry VII had granted them protection. In the next year the Milanese ambassador wrote to the Duke of Milan recommending:

> the Genoa letter bag will be of good use, but get more such Florentine merchants as are in your confidence, as their correspondence passes through France without impediment and is but little searched.[84]

Evidently their postal service had been established by that time and a few years later they had chosen a postmaster.

Tudor monarchs gave special terms for traders, mainly because they provided loans for the state and brought goods into England that could not be produced locally. Indeed, the English Merchant Adventurers could only hope for trading rights on the Continent if reciprocal rights were negotiated. Customs duties were an important part of the government's revenue – in the last year of Henry VII's reign they produced £42,000 – so monarchs did all they could to encourage trade. The aliens' share gradually declined and by the middle of the sixteenth century the Venetians and the German Hansa had lost most of their influence.

In 1519 the Thurn and Taxis posts which covered much of Europe had been opened to Continental merchants and to the public. At that time they had no couriers travelling through to London but State Papers give several references to England using their services from Calais. Henry VIII made use of these when he crossed the Channel in 1513. Among the records of the treasurer at Calais is the entry 'to Francis de Taxis for wages of six posts from Mechlin to Calais the whole year 324 florins', and a further payment of 324 florins was made to Baptiste de Taxis for mails to Brussels, both made in 1520.[85]

However, letters soon followed complaining that the treasurer at Calais would not give a proper reward to those couriers who brought letters from Vienna. On 1 January 1525 Baptiste wrote to Cardinal Wolsey stating that he had long solicited payments and that despite Wolsey's orders the treasurer had paid only two months' charges instead of the twenty-two claimed. In January 1526 he wrote a final letter to Wolsey terminating the service.[86]

After the death of the Strangers' postmaster, Christian Suffling, State Papers Domestic refer to a struggle that took place during 1568 between Godfrey Marshall, who had been elected by the Merchant Strangers as their postman, and Raphael Vanden Putte, who was proposed by Hieronymus Jerlitus, Minister of the Italian Church in London.[87] Windebank wrote to Cecil stating that the Italians wanted Marshall. Since the loss of Calais ten years previously their postal service had grown in importance and the Privy Council's approval

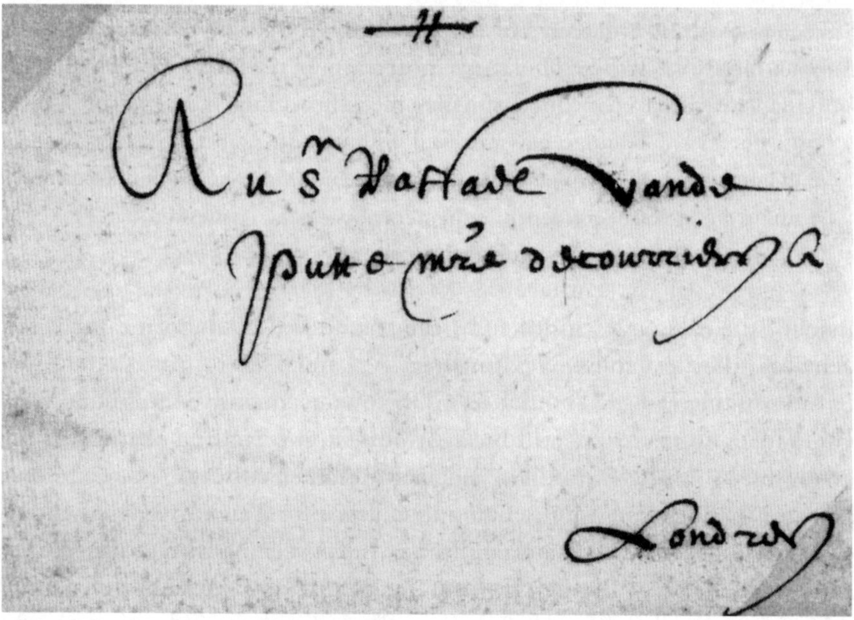

9.5 Letter from Spain to Raffale Vande Putte, master of the Strangers' Post. (By courtesy Mr B.C. Berkinshaw-Smith)

was needed for the appointment. Putte was eventually successful and probably held the position until early in the next century. He may have applied the postal charges that are multiples of ½d found on some letters. Evidence that their posts to the continent then linked with the Thurn and Taxis posts is shown in a letter from Charles de Tassy, postmaster of Antwerp, to Lord Cobham, a privy councillor, on 25 February 1595:

> As the ordinary couriers from London to Antwerp and hence to London can no longer pass by Calais by reason of the prohibition of all commodity and traffic with this country which is to the discommodity of the merchants of both places whose letters are delayed by sending them through Holland by which route the courier Gespard de Ferrard is now proceeding with the ordinary letters. He requests good offices of Her Majesty to move the Governor of Calais to allow letters to pass through that port, as well as for the merchants as for the poor couriers who have no other means to provide subsistence for their wives and families.[88]

The merchants were evidently obeying the terms of the proclamation of 1591 which had imposed strict controls on foreign mails.

A letter from Pickering, the English ambassador in Paris, written to Cecil in 1551 has a remarkable comment on one of the posts:

> The bearer hereof is the merchants' post and is a very knave withal. He would by no means carry these books under three crowns, which I gave him. He would have persuaded me that these were the only occasion of his going by the posts; when I knew him to have received his hire of these merchants before to be in London upon New Year's Eve. If he arrives not in time, hang him, according to the bargain made with me.[89]

Every significant sixteenth-century organisation had its postal agent who matched the messenger and thereby the cost to the letter. For example, the archives of Trinity House, Newcastle on Tyne, for 1541 record one letter to London costing 16d and another 4d.[90] The town records give the cost of three letters to London in 1591 as totalling 12d, but two to the Lord Warden in 1591 were 2s.[91] One taken by a special messenger cost 12d. In 1602 New College, Oxford, spent 3d in sending three letters to London.[92] Clearly, there was no nationally agreed charge and each sender made his own arrangements. Carriers often charged 2d.

A report by William Waad, Clerk to the Privy Council, made on 25 August 1595 described the arrest of a messenger called Casy charged with carrying treasonable letters and refers to the costs of carriage. Waad found that he had letters in addition to those he was authorised to carry by the Comptroller [or Master] of the Posts. Eleven were entered on a list which showed the name of the addressee and that of the sender with the amount paid in another column. The total cost for the eleven letters was 17s. They are charged at various rates of 3s, 2s and 1s.[93] None was a packet 'On Her Majesty's special affairs' but they were to people of some status who must have selected Casy as being a credible person and so were willing to pay him considerable sums for their letters.

Another letter in the Salisbury manuscripts, addressed to the lord high admiral concerning the capture of Spanish vessels, dated 8 November 1592, bears this interesting note:

> Received at Rochester of Mr Baker to be sent according to his direction, being for her Majesty's special affairs, though an extraordinary packet for which we are not allowed, but he had promised to see all the posts paid for it. Wherefore I pray you send it with all diligence. John Bowle Post.[94]

The letter had been accepted on the understanding that the posts would be reimbursed, implying that money could be passed along with letters so that each post could receive a sum.

An analysis has been made of the times taken for delivery of the Corsini letters despatched within this country.[95] Letters from Plymouth were usually written on Monday and Thursday with those from Exeter on Tuesday and Friday, which indicate use of the same service. The time taken from most places to London was based on an average of 35 miles each day. This seems to be a typical day's journey, though a Colchester letter travelled the 50 miles in a day and one from Sandwich managed 70 miles.

As we saw in Chapter 4 there were ecclesiastical messengers carrying letters from their courts and dioceses. The Paston letters showed that private individuals might use them. Records kept of the Communar's Accounts in the Diocese of Chichester for 1544 give illustrations of their letter carrying costs.[96]

A messenger to London was paid 2s, and one Richard Sommner 'riding to Portesmouth to the Dean on a common cause for an answer from Mr Gage' received 8d. A servant sent to warn tenants to attend the Canons' Court had merely 2d but when a letter was sent to the dean and chapter of Winchester at the time of the election there, it was taken by a prebendary who was paid 11s 4d, yet another illustration of the way in which the bearer was suited to the importance of the letter. Rewards were paid to those messengers who arrived with letters. Lord Wriothsley's porter had 4d for bringing a letter but another of his servants had 12d.

There is evidence from a letter in the Rutland manuscripts that the Church used the town posts. Dated March 1563, it reads:

> Dr Rokeby, having the subsidy for the clergy of this province [York] required to have the sum sent up by post, and I [Sir Thomas Gargrave] sent it up to Mr Secretary.[97]

This is further proof that money could be sent through the system.

Nobles had their own private messengers. The account books of Henry Percy, ninth earl of Northumberland (1564–1632) have largely survived and give us a picture of his expenses involved in the despatch and receipt of letters during this period.[98] From the incomplete list of servants that can be reconstructed, mention is made of four riders and a running boy, who would carry letters of no great importance. When the Earl was corresponding with King James in Scotland he used his son-in-law, the constable of Alnwick Castle. The accounts contain many riding charges, rewards for messengers such as the £2 given as a reward to the royal messenger who arrived with the writs for a Parliament in 1585–86, which appears in the cofferer's accounts, and payments such as 'cariage of letters vjs vjd' (6s 6d) in the 1597–98 general account. When he was living in London the earl used the Petworth carrier to convey goods to and from his House there and he took the post with him. The earl's riders were provided with a salary and with livery. One John Barnes received payment in 1610 at £10 per annum and 10s for livery. To carry most of their mail the nobility used their own servants, and it was a point of honour to provide them with a pouch and a distinctive livery. The German traveller, Hentzner, wrote in 1600:

> The English, like the Germans, are lovers of show, liking to be followed wherever they go by whole troops of servants who wear their master's arms in silver, fastened to their left arms.[99]

In conclusion, we have seen important developments in the sixteenth century towards the making of a national postal system. Two routes, those to Dover and Berwick, were maintained and in times of emergency postmasters at some towns and villages were subsidised by the state in order to provide for the speedier transmission of their packets by the shortest route. All towns throughout the country were required to provide stables with horses available to messengers authorised by the Council. The intention was that it should be possible to send letters, documents and money onwards from town to town, which would each be responsible for deliveries within the local area. By these means a national service for the royal mail was developed, supplementing the permanent royal messengers.

Those men still took the most important royal letters and documents such as a proclamation, a parliamentary summons, a judicial order or an instruction to attend at the Exchequer. A letter to an archbishop, duke, earl or Privy Council member would often be taken by a pursuivant. Royal messengers could still ask for horses to be seized but, because of the requirement to keep horses in readiness at each town, they could normally rely on mounts being ready. They paid the traditional, medieval, penny a mile but often paid double in times of crisis. Local innkeepers are known to have paid the town post a sum to avoid seizure of their animals, while the town authorities raised rates to subsidise their posts and ensure that horses were available for the royal post. The local postmasters' stables frequently acquired a monopoly of the provision of horses for private travellers, which brought them trade if they were innkeepers. Their owners were freed from jury and militia service; troops could not be quartered in their houses and thereby the Privy Council had some justification for retaining an uneconomic rate of payment. Such was the pattern that evolved. At times it broke down, whenever the Council failed to pay wages, granted too many commissions to riders, or sent more packets than was reasonable. The further from London, the less certain was the Council's authority. Although royal and town messengers took private letters,

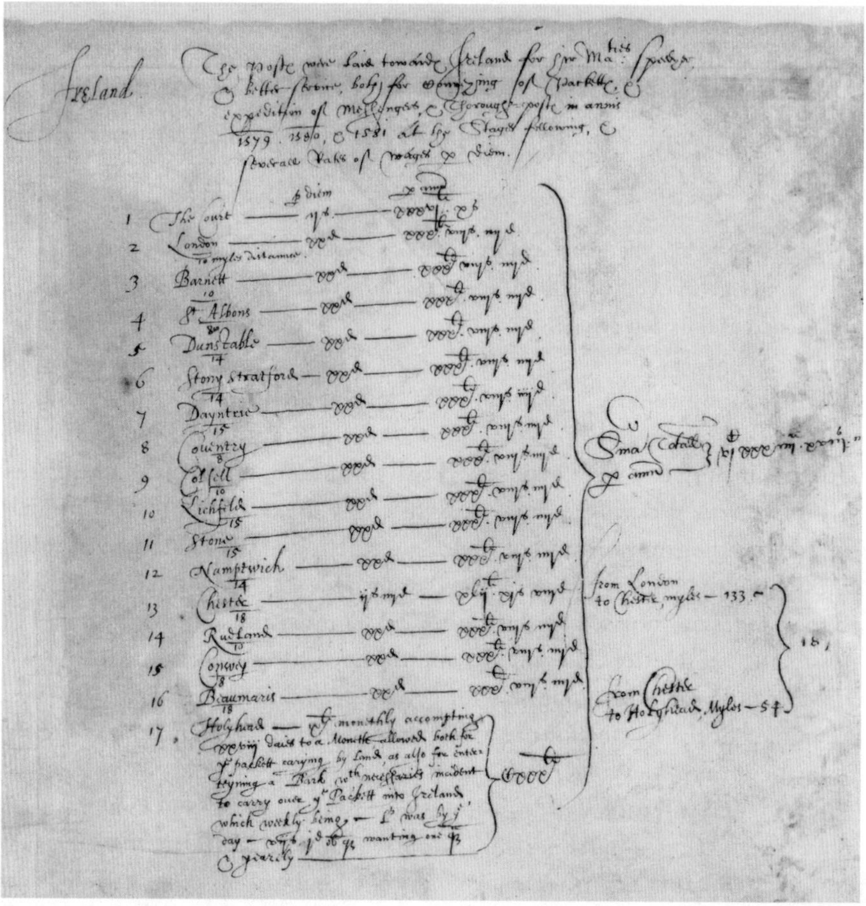
Ireland

1 The Court
2 London
3 Barnett
4 St Albons
5 Dunstable
6 Stony Stratford
7 Dayntree
8 Countrey
9 Colsell
10 Lichfeld
11 Stone
12 Namptwich
13 Chester
14 Rudland
15 Conwey
16 Beaumaris
17 Holyhead

from London to Chester myles — 133

from Chester to Holyhead Myles — 54

9.6 Notes made by Lord Burghley, Queen Elizabeth's chief minister, on the post road to Holyhead via Chester. The daily and yearly wages to the posts are costed and totalled for the years 1579, 1580 and 1581 together with those for a weekly packet boat to Ireland. The mileage to Chester is estimated to be 133 with a further 54 to Holyhead. (British Library. Royal 18D111 f 84v)

this was done without official approval. The precarious state of Elizabethan finances meant that subsidised routes were often closed at short notice and those postmasters who were due to receive wages from the state could not rely on being paid. The next chapter will show how the routes were organised and what financial arrangements were made for them.

The Privy Council took a close interest in the postal arrangements. Lord Burghley, Queen Elizabeth's chief minister, used a copy of Saxton's Atlas of 1579 to which was added a number of other maps.[100] In the margins and on some separate pages are the notes that he made including 'ways and distances from various cities and towns to London'. In his

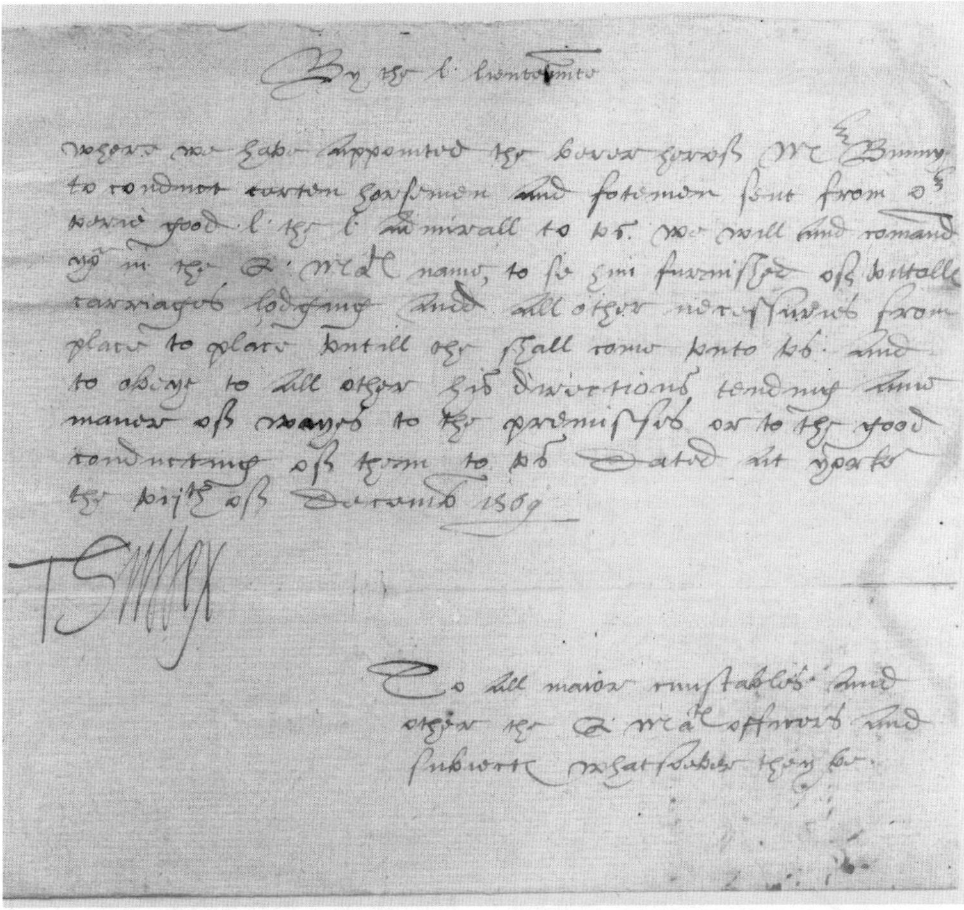
By the L. lieutenant

Where we have appointed the bearer hereof Mr Bunny to conduct certein horsemen and footemen sent from or verie good L. the L. Admirall to us. We will and command you in the Q. Mats name, to see him furnished of vittalls cariages lodging and all other necessaries from place to place untill he shall come unto us. and to obey to all other his directions tending any maner of wayes to the premisses or to the good conducting of them to us. Dated at Yorke the xith of Decemb 1569

T Sussex

To all maior constables and other the Q. Mats officers and subjects whatsoever they be.

9.7 Placard headed 'By the Lord Lieutenant' in 1569, signed by the Earl of Sussex, Lord President of the Council of the North, requiring all persons to assist Mr Bunny who was leading troops sent by the Lord Admiral at the time of the revolt in the north. (Private collection)

handwriting there are tables of the posts from London to Holyhead (Fig. 9.6), Tavistock, Bristol, Plymouth and Portsmouth, with his calculations of their annual costs. Together with the lists of musters of men for the militia required from the deputy lieutenants, the records of landholders made for tax calculations and the details of inns, taverns and alehouses supplied by the justices of the peace, the Council had a generally accurate picture of the population and the country's road system.

10.1 Map of main Tudor roads. (Cambridge University Press from Darby, *Historical Geography of England to 1600*)

10
TUDOR ROADS AND POSTAL ROUTES

Between 1534 and 1543 John Leland travelled widely throughout England, giving us the first detailed description of the English countryside.[1] His *Itinerary*, published posthumously, makes fascinating reading but was not intended to be a road book or to help the traveller. Apart from a comment on Stony Street, which ran from Lympne to Canterbury – 'It is the straightest road that I have ever seen, and towards the Canterbury end the paving survives continuously for four to five miles'– there is little on the state of the roads. He does, however, note the bridges he crosses and shows us how comprehensive was the pattern of cross roads linking the main highways. Perhaps we can take the general lack of comment to indicate that they were adequate for a man on horseback or the carrier with his cart. It was later, in 1569, that Grafton's *Chronicle, or History of England* briefly described 'the four highe waies of Briteyn' as 'Fosse from Totnes via Tutbury, Coventry, Leicester and Newark to Lincoln; Watling Street from Dover via London, St Albans, Atherstone and Stratton to Cardigan in Wales; Erming Street from St David's to Southampton [he gives no other details]; and Kykeneldes streete from Worcester via Birmingham, Lichfield, Derby, Chesterfield and York to Tynemouth.'

The earliest English road book intended for the traveller is Richard Rowlands' *The Post of the World*, published in 1576, which begins with 'A godly prayer very needefull to be used and sayde before any Iorney to be taken in hand', no doubt desirable before facing the hazards that could lie ahead. It describes seven roads which he calls 'Certaine used ways and passages in England', being roads recommended for the traveller. They are Dover to London, Rye to London, Oxford to London, Bristol to London, York to London, Berwick to York, and St David's in Wales to London via Hay, Hereford, Gloucester, Cirencester, Dorchester in Oxfordshire, and Maidenhead.

Holinshed and Harrison's *Chronicles of England, Scotland and Ireland*, printed in 1577, contains a section entitled 'Of oure Innes and Thorowfares', which lists twelve roads, including two alternative ways from London to Cambridge. They include ones from Walsingham to London, Caernarfon to Chester, Cockermouth to Lancaster, Yarmouth to Colchester, St Burien to London, and Canterbury to Oxford. Two years later, in 1579, Jean Bernard published in Paris his *Discours des plus Memorables faicts des Roys & grands Seigneurs d'Angleterre*, to which he added *Le Guide des Chemins D'Angleterre*. He describes nine roads – Dover to London, London to Berwick, London to Walsingham, Caernarfon to Chester and on to London, Cockermouth to Keswick and then to London, Yarmouth to London via Colchester, St Burien to Exeter to London via Shaftesbury, Bristol to London, and St David's to London. In the same year as Bernard's *Discours*, Christopher Saxton published his *Atlas of England and Wales*, which is useful for its depiction of county boundaries, rivers and towns but shows no roads.

The most important account of the roads for our purposes is a manuscript by William Smith, who became the royal pursuivant Rouge Dragon. He is also known for some county and continental maps that he drew. The title is *The Particuler Description of England with the Portraitures of Certaine of the Cheiffest Citties and Townes*. A few comments are included, such as 'Manor places belonging to the King', which indicate that it was completed in the reign of James I, but a date of 1588 on it shows that it was begun in Elizabethan times. Pursuivants took important letters and documents as part of their duties, so Smith's employment suggests that the account was based on the experience of royal messengers. The manuscript has a frontispiece showing the counties without roads. There is a list of fairs together with their dates, and then follows a detailed description of 'The High Wais from any Notable Towne in England to the Cittie of London and lykewise from one notable towne to another'. The roads correspond closely to those shown by Holinshed but with the important addition of cross roads and variations of routes. The volume ends with some attractive coloured illustrations of important towns.

The first road is from St Burien in Cornwall to Exeter and on to London in nineteen stages, alternative routes being shown at Honiton, one way going to Chard, the other to Burport. Other routes to Exeter are described from Totnes, Plymouth and Dartmouth. There is then a route from Exeter to Barnstaple and two to Bristol, one taking a road to Crediton, the other via Colompton. A coastal road from Southampton to Helford in Cornwall is in fourteen stages using five ferries and requires a guide from Salcombe to Plymouth. Roads from Southampton to Bristol and London are then listed. There are five roads from Bristol – to Barnstaple, to Oxford, to Shrewsbury with an alternative that leads on from there to Chester, to Cambridge, and one to London. The routes described from York are also five – to Berwick, to Nottingham, to Cambridge, to Chester and to Shrewsbury. Next are roads to London from Lincoln, from Boston, from St David's and from Worcester.

The road from Worcester to London via Evesham is in seven stages and that from Caernarfon via Chester to London is in seventeen. The route from Carlisle to Lancaster is continued as far as Coventry, from which there are roads to Oxford and London. Those from Shrewsbury, Cambridge, Oxford, Dover and Rye are shown as direct routes. Finally he gives the way from Yarmouth to Colchester and to London, with one from Walsingham and another from Yarmouth to London via Norwich. This comprehensive description with its lists of the halts on the way may have been used by the royal messengers.

In Tudor times distances were usually based on the measurement of about 1,500 paces, known as the old English mile. That was the calculation used by Richard Rowlands in *The Post of the World*. It was not until 1675, when John Ogilby published his *Britannia* with distances based on a mile of 1,760 yards that exact distances were calculated. The English yard had been fixed by Henry I in 1101[2] as the length of his arm, and a legal standard of 1,760 yards to the mile had been introduced by statute in 1593,[3] but that did not receive general acceptance until after Ogilby. His preface to *Britannia* explains that the mile is deduced from the length of three barleycorns which make an inch, 63,360 inches constituting a mile. For his maps he established the scale of one inch to a mile and instead of measuring by chains he used a foot wheel of half a pole in circumference. In his *Preface to The Traveller's Guide* published in 1699 Ogilby says that the calculations had been carried out at the express command of King Charles II, who had authorised the costs involved. The earlier road books gave generally consistent figures for the miles between main cities but the difference between them and Ogilby can be seen from this table:

	Rowands 1576	Ogilby 1675
London–Dover	56	71
London–Berwick	237	339
London–St David's	197	269

Another complication in data from before 1675 is the possibility of local differences in the measurement of a mile. In 1633 a case was referred to the Privy Council because the postmasters and hackneymen of Dover and Canterbury had measured the highway between those towns reaching the conclusion that it was 15¼ miles. Accordingly, they asked for a further 9d for every horse hire per stage, bringing the charge to 3s 9d. The mayor and jurats of Dover found them to be obdurate in increasing their charges, so Sir Edward Deering was appointed to inquire into the matter. He concluded that the measurement differed from that previously agreed because Kentish miles were longer than those in some other places. He recommended that while their Lordships considered the matter it would be suitable to put some of those who had complained into Dover Castle.[4] The deputy postmaster of Dover was brought before the Court of Star Chamber where he was pardoned on condition that he entered into a bond of £100 not to attempt another measurement.

The descriptions of the roads and the evidence of the extensive use of them by the carriers show that goods and people could travel freely in Tudor times. The government needed to communicate regularly with the sheriffs and lords lieutenant, who represented the sovereign in the shires, and with the mayors and bailiffs who had assumed a similar authority in the towns. They also needed to maintain a messenger service to members of the Council at their residences and with the sovereign's representatives in Ireland, on the Scottish and Welsh marches, at foreign courts, and with agents abroad. Their messengers distributed copies of proclamations and statutes, announced the arrival of judges, collected loans, benevolences, subsidies and customs duties, and often transported money and goods. They executed important processes arising from the national law courts and arrested malefactors. They also carried the writs summoning those who were to attend Parliament or the Council. When they took letters and documents directly to the recipients this was known as the through post. Even though the government's messengers might carry letters for private individuals, the Tudor state never considered providing a postal service for them, nor did it set up regular postal routes for the transmission of its routine documents except to Berwick and Dover.

Warrants authorising payments to royal messengers sometimes mention the places to which they went and show very varied routes. When in 1588 the queen's messenger, William Robinson, took letters together with copies of a proclamation concerning weights to the south of England, his claim for expenses describes a journey through Guildford, Lewes, Winchester, Southampton, Salisbury, Dorchester, Ilchester, Bristol, Exeter, to Lostwithiel. For this he was paid £5.[5]

Some indication of the relative importance of major towns of England at this time can be gained from a study of the tax yield from the Lay Subsidy authorised between 1523 and 1527. The largest totals are London £16,675, Norwich £1,704, Bristol £1,072, Coventry £974, Exeter £855, Salisbury £852, Ipswich £656, Lynn £575. York raised only £379.[6]

Before we look at those routes supported by the state it is interesting to note that many sections of them followed the lines of the Roman roads. In Elizabethan times London was still the hub of the road system and comparisons can be made with roads shown on the Ordnance Survey map of Roman Britain.[7]

For example, the road from London to Colchester via Chelmsford followed the Roman route and it was possible to follow it on to Harwich. Among other Roman roads still in use were London to Stamford via Royston and Huntingdon, Doncaster to Newcastle via Darlington and Durham, Newcastle to Carlisle, Morpeth to Berwick. The same comment applies to many sections of the road from London to Holyhead.

London to the Continent

The route to France had always been the principal road in England and we have seen legislation passed about it in the Middle Ages. In the early Tudor period its organisation was on a different basis than of the other roads. Posting inns at regular stages were well established and travellers from the Continent were required to use them. Royal messengers paid for the use of their horses stage by stage so it is unlikely that any government packets were handled by the towns and their posts until the time of Philip and Mary, when an ordinance regulating the posts to Dover was issued. It is likely that it was issued in response to the crisis that developed over Calais in 1557. The town was besieged by the French that year and captured in January 1558. Prior to this, the postman of Calais, who was paid a wage, sent or took government packets across to the Dover postman, who personally took them to London or arranged for them to be taken there.

The ordinance drafted by Mason dated 29 August but without the year shown is of particular interest because it provides details of local arrangements. (Fig. 10.2) It is entitled 'For the Order of the Posts and Hacquenymen betweene London and Dover' and requires ordinary posts to be laid at Dover, Canterbury, Sittingbourne, Rochester, Dartford and London, with an additional post at Gravesend 'where many couriers use to pass by the river', for most messengers began a journey to the Continent by a river sailing to Gravesend. Each post was to keep at least six horses, 'two for the pacquet and four for goers and comers by post'. No one was to ride without a guide, 'which guide shall ever in journey have his horn, which he shall blow at the Town's end, where the post is laid, and shall be bound to carry the Carrier's mail being of a reasonable weight'. Arrangements were very much to the hackneymen's advantage, for the ordinance specified that, 'No man shall deliver any horses to any Carrier or other riding in post but the ordinary post, or by his appointment, under pain of imprisonment and arbitrary fine.' Thus they had a monopoly for the provision of horses on the most-

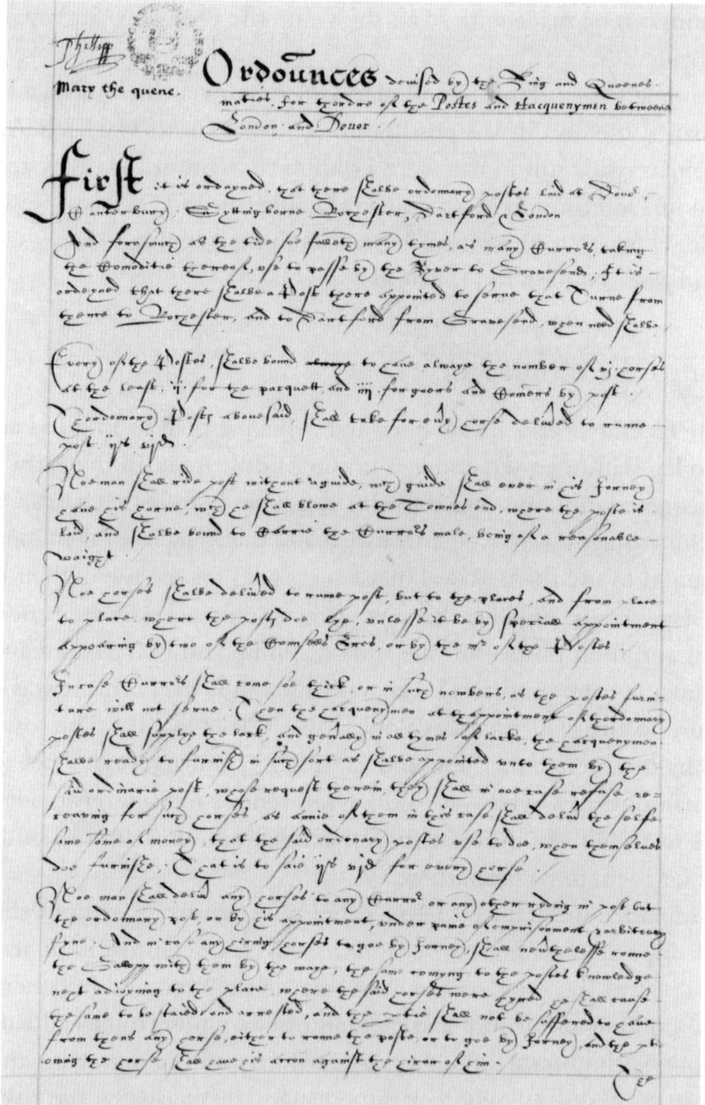

Phillip

Mary the quene.

Ordounces devised by the King and Queenes majesties for the ordre of the Postes and Hacquenymen betwene London and Dover

First it is ordeyned that there shalbe ordinary postes laid at Dover, Canterbury, Sittingborne, Rochester, Dartford and London

10.2 Above and opposite: The first known proclamation concerning the posts, 1557. (By courtesy of The Society of Antiquaries, London)

used route in the land. To ensure this, guides had to bring all riders to the door of the post which was to 'have a horn always hanging at their doors or some other painted sign declaring that to be the post house'.

With the publication of the ordinance a change took place and most government packets were passed along the Dover road from town to town, each town post being paid not by wages but by the number of packets he handled. Nevertheless, payments were irregular and complaints about the service were

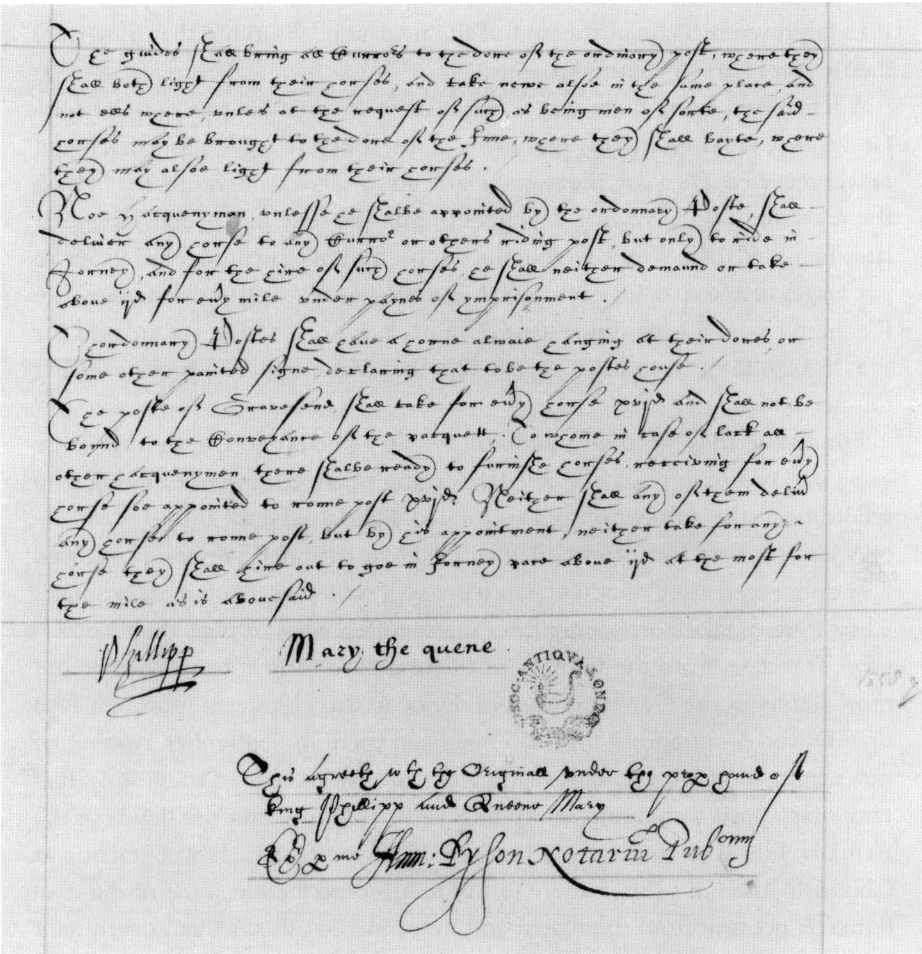

many. In 1566 Randolph, the master of the posts, wrote that 'every hackney-man taketh upon himself the Queen's standing post'.[8]

Later, in 1574, orders were issued to ensure that the stages along the road were to be inspected regularly, noting who was the post and whether he had sufficient horses. Nevertheless, the posts were often unpaid and Randolph wrote at length to Walsingham, the queen's secretary, in 1582 about the failure to pay them even though they were carrying more than double the number of packets that they had received three years previously:

> In respect of their poverty and inability to forbear the money due unto them & the daily use of their service I humbly crave that your Honour will be moved to pity them and to be a means to have them paid. Whereby they shall be most bound to pray for your honour during their lives.

Randolph wrote again at the end of the next year observing that they were then a year in arrears with payments.[9]

A return to paying them wages began in 1588 when the posts of Dartford, Gravesend, Rochester, Sittingbourne, Canterbury, Margate, Sandwich and Dover received 20d a day, the use of Dartford or Gravesend as the first halt on the way from London being dependent upon the state of the tide. Two years later many of their wages were reduced. By then it was thought cheaper to pay wages than to pay for each packet and the figures explain the change. The Rochester post was paid in 1564 for 79 packets, in 1576 for 135, in 1581 for 172, in 1586 for 275, and in 1589 for 392, the total number of packets during this period being 4,329.[10]

For a time they were termed extraordinary posts, but in 1594 they were known as ordinary posts and reverted to the previous system of being paid according to the number of packets carried. This lasted until 1603.

A set of orders issued on 29 January 1596, mentioned previously, showed how concerned the Council was to regulate travellers arriving in the country. They were to take horses only from the standing posts or with their knowledge. Travellers from the Continent often arrived at Rye from Dieppe and more letters in the Corsini correspondence in the 1580s came through Rye than Dover. A temporary post had been laid there in September 1562 when news from the Continent was expected, and we have seen previously that temporary posts were again set up to Rye in 1589 just after the defeat of the Armada. The Rye route was a branch road from that to Dover starting at Chipstead, though a direct route to London is described in some of the road books. A petition from the mayor and jurats in 1603 shows that government packets were being delivered and horses commandeered:

> Whereas in the past the packets have usually been sent to this town as the nearest place of recourse for the service of the State, until of late years they being sent other ways, the continuance thereof has drawn with it from the poor town the postage and recourse of merchants and others travelling the coast. [...] therefore we petition you to erect a postage here and recommend the bearer, James Appleton.[11]

Many letters sent along the Dover road in the 1590s to the Privy Council are found with endorsements showing arrival times at the post stations. One from the earl of Essex to Cecil in 1593 reads, 'For Her Majesty's especial affairs. Hast, Hast, Hast, Hast, Hast for Life. June 22 at Sandwich at seven of the clock in the afternoon. Canterbury past nine at night. Sittingbourne at past twelve at night. Rochester the 23 at one in the morning. Dartford at 23 four

10.3 Map of Tudor routes periodically subsidised by the state. Routes to Barnstaple, Southampton, Portsmouth, Rye, York and Harwich are shown by lighter lines. (Tempus Publishing)

in the morning.' It was unusual if a speed of 4 miles to the hour was achieved between any stages.

Another letter from the Earl of Essex sent from Deal in 1597 is timed Deal 8 p.m., Sandwich 11 p.m., Canterbury past 2, Sittingbourne past 5, Rochester 8 a.m. and Dartford 10.30 a.m. Obviously travel at night was slow. One from Thomas Fane at Dover Castle left at 1 p.m., was at Canterbury at 4, Sittingborne at 7, Rochester at 9, Dartford at midnight and London at 1 a.m. The distance of 56 Tudor miles, or 71 by our reckoning, was covered in twelve hours, averaging almost 6 miles an hour.[12]

According to Thomas Platter who made a tour of the country in 1599, the Dover postman was paying for the privilege of his office:

> After breakfast we took the post, for they would not let us hire hacks [hackney horses available for private hire to English persons], saying that we might not do this unless the postmaster, who has to pay an annual tax to the Queen so as to keep the posthouse, gave permission, so we rode the post horses [...] to Canterbury.[13]

As they were not suited to the small horses and were six in number, they then ordered a waggon pulled by five horses.

The temporary routes

When there were emergencies, routes to other parts of the country were required for the speedy transmission of news. Warfare or negotiation in Scotland and Ireland required chains of stables, financed by the state, to be set up whereby letters could be passed on from one rider to another. A direct route to Berwick via Newcastle was often needed during the many alarms and battles affecting the Scottish borders, and troubles in Ireland made it necessary to set up relays via Chester to Holyhead, or else to Bristol, the latter route being on occasion extended to Milford Haven via Cardiff and Swansea. Wars with Spain resulted in raids and armadas which necessitated speedy contact with the principal coastal ports of Portsmouth, Southampton, Exeter, Plymouth and Falmouth. Special arrangements were made in 1589 with Weymouth and Portsmouth to provide vessels to and from Cherbourg where Lord Willoughby headed an expedition to France. In 1601 when Spanish troops landed in Munster a link through the port of Padstow was arranged.

The temporary post roads might be used by the men who carried routine government letters but they were not established for that purpose. Messengers with letters to the county sheriffs and the lords lieutenant, the latter having taken over control of the armed musters in the shires during 1550–1, would not find most of them living on those routes. Although the temporary arrangements used some important roads, they also bypassed towns that would have lengthened the routes for the messengers. The early northern route bypassed York to the east, and Derby, Northampton, Leicester and Nottingham to the west. The shortest route to Plymouth bypassed Salisbury. The routes to Bristol and Chester provided no direct links with Gloucester, Warwick, Shrewsbury or Worcester. The one intention of the Council was to establish stables of post horses in order that urgent messages could pass along as quickly as possible. From this we can see that maps of temporary routes can be misleading if thought to show the usual roads used for carrying most letters. Had Tuke and his Tudor successors been able to finance a national pattern of postal routes for the transmission of government documents, their priorities would have been different. They would, for example, have needed to establish a permanent route to the East Anglian ports whose customs duties provided a most important source of revenue.

The northern route

We have seen that the first recorded subsidised postal route was to the north in the reign of Edward IV. During Tudor times there were many occasions requiring similar arrangements. In 1482 there was war with Scotland which led to the surrender of Berwick Castle and the establishment of a Royal Council to administer the north. Regular communications were frequently needed, for example when arranging the treaty of Ayton in 1497. Despite the marriage of Margaret, Henry VII's daughter, to James IV, there was continuous tension that led to the defeat of the Scots at Flodden Field in 1513. Ten years later Surrey again attacked the Scots and when the Duke of Albany at last left Scotland there followed a period of lengthy negotiation. In 1542 the Battles of Haddon Rig and Solway Moss took place, followed by the Battle of Pinkie in 1547. There was war again in 1557.

Throughout these periods of warfare and negotiations special arrangements to send urgent letters were made either by the master of the posts or such persons as the lords warden of the three Northern Marches, who submitted their expenses. The King's Book of Payments shows Lord Darcy, warden of the East and Middle Marches, paid £13 6s 8d in 1509 for messengers along the Berwick road.[14] William Pawne, who was master of the ordnance at Berwick, made claims for payments to posts set up on the north road during the wars in 1511 and 1513.[15] He received £11 6s 8d in 1511 and £172 2s 10d in 1513.

Lord Dacre, warden of the Scottish Marches, wrote from Naworth Castle on 8 September 1523 to the Earl of Surrey:

> I have laid three posts between myself and Starkey at Lancaster, Kendal and Penrith, the last of whom will have to ride to Lanercost. I have written to Starkey to lay posts into Cheshire.[16]

An undated letter to the Council, probably written at the time of the negotiations with Scotland in the next year, describes another such arrangement. He had sent his servant, Robert Rybton, to stay at the mayor's house in Newcastle to be available to travel to Durham, Darlington, Boroughbridge and Sisson House in Wetherby, a distance of 58 miles. At Wetherby another servant, Thomas Logan, would be waiting who could take letters to Newark and a further two servants were available to take letters to and from London.[17]

In July 1533 Tuke had ordered the posts to the north to be withdrawn as soon as peace had been concluded with the Scots, but Clyfford, the captain of Berwick, was constrained to write to the king:

> It may further like your Grace that, where Master Tuke wrote to me for the discharging of your posts in these parts at this time; yet, considering that the peace is not concluded but for twenty days, it is the advice of my Lord Warden and your Council here, that the posts shall remain in charge as yet.[18]

During the reign of Philip and Mary an attempt was made to make a permanent postal route to Berwick, each post being paid regular wages, and a post was established in July 1557 at York.[19]

An undated ordinance for the posts between London and the borders of Scotland was issued with similar instructions as those we have noted for the Dover road. The date is probably October 1557 as a Privy Council order of that month increased the wages that posts were receiving from the 16d a day settled in July to 20d, which is the figure mentioned in the ordinance.[20]

Each appointed place had to hold two horses in readiness for the packet (the government mail) and four others 'for goers and comers by post'. Those posts who had to deliver the packet to the surrounding area were paid more: London 3s, Ferrybridge, Darlington, Durham, Newcastle, Morpeth and Belford 2s, and Alnwick 2s 2d. Being a direct route to Berwick, it bypassed York. In all there were twenty-eight stables with on average a little over 10 Tudor miles between each one.

Wars were expensive in terms of messenger costs. During the period of war with Scotland in 1551 there were additional costs for messengers and an entry in 'The Kinges booke of Receyptes and Paymentes', dated midsummer, reads:

> To the Mr of the Posts for April, May and June, by estimation, by reason of the war, at ij Cli [£200] a month.[21]

The arrangements that had been made under Philip and Mary for the northern posts soon ran into difficulties as dissatisfaction with their performance grew. The Privy Council wrote in August 1558 to Mason:

> signifying to him the usual slackness of the Posts laid northward in the conveyance of letters hither, the opening of them by the way and therefore requiring of him to give order forthwith in that behalf, or else the Queen's Majesty must be enforced to discharge them everyone, and to seek some new means to be served from time to time with a through Post.[22]

Mary died in November 1558 and the Council of her successor, Queen Elizabeth, now had three methods of sending letters to the north. It could use the subsidised routes to Dover and the north; it could send messengers carrying letters who could choose their own routes and pay for the hire of horses supplied by any town post; or it could send packets to be passed from town to town which could be directed to be delivered to nearby places. To improve communications along the border a branch route from Newcastle to Carlisle was established in 1572.[23]

The need for the subsidised northern route was to continue throughout Elizabeth's reign. On her accession in 1558 Elizabeth had felt threatened by France, which had sent troops to Scotland where Mary of Guise was ruling as regent. Elizabeth successfully intervened to support those Scots who wished to drive out the French Catholics and a peace treaty was made at Edinburgh in 1560. Later, when Mary Stuart, Elizabeth's cousin, returned to Scotland following the death of her husband, the French king, there began a long period of tension with Scotland, continuing until the border raids that followed Mary's execution in England in 1587. Threats of war stopped near the end of Elizabeth's reign when the Protestant king James VI knew through his secret correspondence with Robert Cecil that he would succeed to the English throne. His accession in 1603 as king of England meant that as ruler of both countries he needed to maintain regular communication between them. Despite his unpopularity in England and his failure to achieve a political and constitutional union of the two countries, warfare between them had come to an end.

In February 1568 the Council considered that an economy could be made and as mentioned previously the posts' wages were halved, inevitably reducing the standard of the service. Gascoigne, the senior royal messenger, reported on the post stations on the north road in a letter to the secretary, Walsingham, dated 1 October 1582 stating that he had found the records of each place defective.[24]

He noted that few of the postmasters had any horses in their stables 'all at grass, and many ill horses'. Eminent men found the provision of horses along the northern route to be unreliable and State Papers include many complaints. A letter from Lord Huntley, who was warden of the East March, to Burghley in 1587, quoted in the Calendar of Border Papers, explains the reasons for some of the difficulties and the depression of the postmen:

> I have sought to understand the cause why the posts be so negligent. I am very credibly informed that whensoever Mr Randoll [sic] does put in a post, he keep his first year's wages to himself, so as the poor man serves a whole year for nothing! And besides he has a yearly pension of every one of them – of sum xls, 3li, 5li, and of some more, and I know that when he went unto Muscovya [the embassy to Moscow], he had of every post 20li so as I marvel how they are able to have and keep their horses.[25]

From this we can deduce that even when wages are recorded it does not follow that they were always being received by the posts. The accounts, which are not complete for all years, show that in 1558, 1568 and 1570 there were twenty-eight posts on the northern route paid for by the government.

In May 1574 Randolph drew up a set of orders to be observed by the posts, which extended many of the instructions that had been laid down in 1557 for the Dover posts to the northern route and the rest of the kingdom.[26] Posts were only to deliver horses to those who had a commission signed by authorised persons and they had to keep in a book a record of the names of those riding post. For the transport of the mail each post was to keep two leather bags, lined with good cotton or baize, 'to carry the letters in to the end that they might be kept clean and unbroken', and to carry nothing but letters or writings in the bag. The post's horn was to be sounded at least four times each mile. The horses were required to be kept at hand so as to be available for departure within a quarter of an hour of hearing the horn of the arriving post. Their speed was set at 7 miles an hour in the summer and 5 in the winter. The post was to allow no one to look in his bag and, should he be caught sleeping with it, his master was to pay 6s 8d into the local poor box – evidence that at this time it was a common practice to appoint a deputy. A new rate was set of 2d per mile for those on the queen's service with an extra halfpenny for others, but the former was only temporary. Apparently, riders other than the post used to blow horns to clear the way ahead and they were now forbidden to do so.

The siting of the post houses was covered by the instruction that they should be 'in such places in every town as he that rideth in post may have commodity both of lodging and of meat and drink if he is like to tarry'. So that the priority of the royal mail was protected, it was decreed that no postmaster should be liable for jury service. Finally, it was ordered that all posts to Berwick, like those to Dover, should be inspected within two months to see who was resident as post and that the horses required were available.

That wages were still not being paid regularly is shown by the account in a letter of 1578 to Burghley from Richard Swynshed, the post of Ware:

> Since Michaelmas he went to London to one Robert Parmenter deputy to Mr Randolph, Master of the Posts, thinking to have received his wages for three quarters of a year (which is a very long time for a poor man to forbear) but he was told he could not have any money, as the Treasurer of the Queen's Chamber had denied the payment thereof.[27]

The master of the posts was at that time also treasurer of the Queen's Chamber. Swynshed maintained that letters and packets came in numbers of at least thirty-four each month so that, without payment, he would be unable to maintain the service.

Further requirements for the post were set out in January 1583/84, the first in orders dated 14 January issued by the Privy Council, the second in instructions on the 22nd by Randolph.[28] Both related to the posts from London to Berwick. Many previous orders were repeated, ensuring that those riding with commissions were only to take horses from the ordinary posts. Should hackneymen, ostlers, tapsters or others take the packets without permission of the post, they were to be imprisoned until such time as they gave 'sufficient bond and surety to the post for the keeping and observing of these orders'. The payment by those with commissions was now fixed at threehalfpence a mile, others paying twopence. The books recording travellers were to be reported on each month. Posts were forbidden to appoint deputies. The practice of posts not stopping at the next posting house was to be prevented by a 10s fine.

The desired speed of the mail was reiterated with the conclusion that the journey from London to Berwick should be 42 hours in summer and 60 in winter. There was also an instruction that no private letters were to be delivered before the queen's packet was handed over, another confirmation of the increasing carriage of private mail which led to delays in handling the official packet. In 1583 Randolph had written to Walsingham, secretary of state, giving a list of those who 'charge the posts with their private letters and commissions at a penny the mile'.

Despite all these attempts at improving the service along the route to Berwick, the performance of the northern posts were often a cause for complaint, particularly in the last decade of the century when Elizabeth's authority was in decline. Those contemporary letters from the Cecil manuscripts which give times for arrival at the post houses show that in the 1590s letters travelled slowly across Northumberland and Durham, often only achieving on average a mile an hour. Further south speeds increased with 3 miles to the hour by Grantham and 4 on the stretch southwards to Huntingdon and London. According to a post label made out in 1589 the distance between Berwick and Huntingdon was accomplished in 91 hours. The distance was reckoned to be 203 miles, though it is 282 by our reckoning. The speed works out at 3 miles an hour.[29]

A letter dated 31 January 1603 from the Royston postmaster to Secretary Cecil in London covered part of the northern route and tells us about the delivery service.[30] He had received a packet for Cecil and rode to Cambridge from where he thought he could achieve the quickest delivery. He looked for a Dr Butler but he had left for London and so he left the letter with his apothecary who undertook to despatch it. The letter was taken to nearby Royston where it was endorsed '31 Jan at 10 before noon', Ware 'the last of January one in the afternoon', Waltham Cross 'at past three in the afternoon and sent away presently', and 'R. at London past six at night'. Given the time of year that seems a satisfactory performance, and quicker than the post would deliver a letter today.

Another account among the Hatfield Papers shows the cost of sending a personal messenger along the road from Berwick to London and back during the summer of 1603. Thomas Meade spent twenty-one days on the road, charging for the journey a bill for £7 8s. He spent eleven days travelling south and ten on the return journey.[31] In exceptional cases it was possible to travel very quickly. A journey, probably for a wager, was made by John Lepton who rode from London to York in fifteen hours.[32]

When Queen Elizabeth died in 1603 Robert Carey left the court at nine on a March morning carrying a letter from the Council to Edinburgh. He stopped at Scrooby that night for a few hours' rest, then rode on to Whittingham near Morpeth for a second break. The next day in the evening he was at Holyrood with his message. He had ridden over 400 miles in three days and two nights, achieving an average of about 7 miles per hour, demonstrating the effectiveness of the direct post road if properly maintained. It is likely, however, that the posts had been advised to expect him.

We know little about individual postmasters, but one of the postmasters on the northern route, William Brewster, achieved fame. After his education at Peterhouse, Cambridge, he had travelled to the Low Countries with William Davison, who was Queen Elizabeth's representative there. In 1586 Davison became a privy councillor and secretary of state. Through his influence Brewster was appointed postmaster of Scrooby, which lies between Doncaster and Tuxford, a place that his father had previously held. His Puritan convictions caused him to go to Amsterdam in 1608 and in 1620 he sailed in the *Mayflower* to become one of the founders of New Plymouth in the New World.

Routes to Ireland: Chester and Bristol

Subsidised routes to Ireland via Chester and to Bristol with their extensions to Holyhead and Haverfordwest were, like the northern one, the result of political necessity. Henry VII had inherited an area around Dublin known as 'the Pale' and a general claim to much of Ireland which was as unrealistic as his claims to parts of France. In 1494 he sent as his deputy, Sir Edward Poynings, who called a parliament which declared all Irish legislation to be under English control, and Henry VIII assumed the title of king of Ireland in 1540. Despite such actions, the Tudors were only able to maintain their show of authority because of the rivalries of the Irish chiefs. There was little liking for the English and the spiritual allegiance of most of the population was to Rome not to the new Anglican Church. During 1583 the estates of the Desmonds in Munster were declared forfeit to the Crown and settlements of English people were made there. Feelings came to a head in 1598 when the Irish tried to throw off English control. They received Spanish support, which in the end proved ineffective, as the Earl of Tyrone capitulated in March 1603. There was always a need for communications with Ireland and the last five years of Elizabeth's reign saw intense pressure on the posts.

Before 1560, when Elizabeth's first Irish parliament met, letters to Ireland had been taken by royal messengers. In the following year records show payments for a chain of posts to Holyhead. Wages of 20d a day were paid to eight stages until August 1562.[33] That they were temporarily revived soon afterwards is evident from Privy Council minutes, which contain a letter of 24 November 1565 from the Lord Deputy stating that the Irish post should be discharged again.[34] In 1573 the postal route was revived but the posts were discharged in 1574 and then revived later in that year before being discharged yet again. The service to Chester was revived in 1579 and the post there was instructed to send to the Court any letters that arrived from Ireland concerning the queen's affairs.[35]

During August 1580 a warrant was issued by the Privy Council to Robert Gascoigne, the senior royal messenger, to lay a post to Bristol and Holyhead where £10 a month was being paid for the use of a vessel at the port.[36] The post was ended in July 1582. In such manner the posts were erected and discharged until 1599, when warfare required them to be restored.[37]

The instruction to the master of the posts explains that since the last discharge the postmaster of Chester had been paid 2s a day with 5 marks (£3 6s 8d) for every journey he made to the Court with letters from Ireland. Additionally he received ten groats (3s 4d) for every day's stay at Court after the first two while awaiting an answer. The annual cost of the posts to Chester was predicted at £634 18s 4d yearly, plus the hire of a packet boat at £130. During times of war Chester and Bristol were known as Exchanges where the treasurer at war in Ireland, Sir George Carey, kept deputies. At the end of the decade there were sixteen postal stages from the Court to Holyhead. In 1602 new stages at Birmingham and Bewdley were added, reflecting their growing importance.

Speeds along the road could average 3–4 miles an hour but this depended upon whether the letter involved travelling at night. A letter from the mayor of Chester left the city at 1 p.m., reached Nantwich at 5, Stone at 10, Lichfield at 2 a.m., Coleshill 'after four', Coventry 'past six' and Daventry at 10 a.m. It eventually reached Barnet at 11 p.m.[38]

Accounts for the nine stages to Bristol start in 1579 and in the next year Gascoigne went with a warrant requiring 'Her Majesty's officers to be assisting him in this service'. He established a route that went through Hounslow, Maidenhead, Reading, Newbury, Marlborough, Chippenham, Marshfield and Bristol at the cost of £14 9s a month. The purpose was to have routes for supplies and messages because Italian and Spanish troops had been sent by Philip II to Ireland.[39]

The subsidies soon ended but they were revived in 1598 at an annual cost of £273 15s, the postmasters at the nine stages being paid either 10d or 20d a day. In 1600 the route was extended in seven stages to Haverfordwest.

Speeds along the Bristol road were, as would be expected from the terrain, quicker than along sections of the northern road far from London but comparable to those achieved along that road further south. A letter from the mayor of Bristol dated 18 June 1601 left the city at 10 a.m., was in Marshfield at 11.30, Calne at 1.30, Marlborough at 3 p.m., Newbury at 6, Reading at 9 and Maidenhead at 11.30.[40] The post ran throughout the night at a slower rate; a letter of the same year arriving at Marlborough at 3.30 a.m. reached Newbury three and a half hours later.

The Plymouth route

Similar arrangements were made for erecting and then discharging posts on the route from London to Devon with its branch roads to Portsmouth and Southampton. The main use had always been for sending messages to the London merchants informing them of the arrival of trading vessels as Plymouth was usually the first port of call in England, but political information also came along the same route. In January 1506 Archduke Philip of Burgundy and his wife had been forced by a storm to land in England at Weymouth and while they were being detained by Henry VII and their fleet was reassembled, riders kept the Council informed of developments. In April the same year a chain of stables was set up between Bagshot and Exeter. Another temporary arrangement was made in July 1574 when the Privy Council ordered post horses to be provided from the Court at Windsor to Exeter for packets for the queen's service. There are accounts for a post to Exeter and on to Crediton from August to November in 1579 which was set up in response to a renewed rebellion in Ireland led by James Fitzmaurice.[41]

The expected arrival of the Spanish Armada in 1588 caused Chamber messengers to be sent to Plymouth and this was followed in 1589 by appointing a person in each town or village on the route to assist riders, whose payments were increased to 2d a mile.[42]

The route was again temporarily revived in August 1595 after renewed fighting in Ireland. Posts were planned from Plymouth to Falmouth in August 1600 and implemented in December that year. The arrival of 3,000 Spanish troops in Munster led to the extension of the post road to Padstow in October 1601 with post boats requisitioned there and at Falmouth. A letter to Cecil in January 1602 from the Padstow postmaster, Robert Bellman, explains that a letter received at eleven at night was sent by ship to Ireland leaving at a quarter to eight in the morning and was expected to arrive in Munster that night or the following morning.[43]

The writer asked for authority to impress another vessel should the post bark be at sea. Padstow was still in use early in 1603. By the end of the year the war was over and the post route beyond Plymouth was closed.

Speeds along this road were varied. One letter sent by Sir William Bevill, High Sheriff of Cornwall, left his home at Killigarth on 4 May 1599 at 8 in the evening. It went by footpost from Plymouth at 2 p.m. the next day, reached Ashburton at 4, Exeter at 9, Honiton 'after midnight', Crewkerne at 6 a.m.,

Sherborne at 8 a.m., Shaftesbury 12 noon, Salisbury 4 p.m., Basingstoke 8 a.m. and Hartford Bridge at 9.30 a.m. The main delays occurred at night.[44] Another letter received by Bellman from Ireland arrived at 10 a.m. on 5 February 1602. It was at Ashburton two days later at 4 p.m. and at Exeter that evening at 9 p.m. From there it reached Honiton at 2 a.m. Andover at 11 a.m., Basingstoke at 4.30 and Hartford Bridge at 9 p.m.[45]

The Portsmouth and Southampton routes

Another route ran from London to Alton via Kingston, Guildford and Farnham. From there one branch went to Southampton through Twyford and another to Portsmouth through East Meon. Royal messengers frequently visited both places to gather intelligence from the Continent. During January 1558, at the time of the fall of Calais, posts were laid to Portsmouth;[46] there is a letter to Sir John Mason in 1558 about the posts laid from Bagshot to Portsmouth going by Guildford and, exceptionally, via Petersfield.[47] These were soon dismissed but Elizabeth restored them in September 1562.[48]

Later Southampton and Portsmouth were the bases for the expeditions to France led by Sir John Norreys and the Earl of Essex, both in support of Henry of Navarre. In 1596 an English fleet attacked Cadiz and Philip II of Spain assembled a second Armada. As a result temporary posts were set up briefly in February 1583 and for longer between 1593 and 1603. Speeds were good, for a letter from Portsmouth in 1597 left at 4 p.m. and arrived in Farnham at 9 p.m.[48]

At the end of Elizabeth's reign an undated proclamation, probably of 1602, summarised the arrangements made for the transmission of royal letters received from abroad. Those from Spain came via Falmouth, Truro, Plymouth and Portsmouth; from Ireland via Padstow, Barnstaple, Milford Haven, Chester, Bristol or Holyhead; from Flanders and France via Sandwich, Margate, Dover or Rochester; and from the North from the three Marches, Berwick and York.[50]

Mary, Queen of Scots

An exceptional postal need arose during the imprisonment of Mary, Queen of Scots and Dowager Queen of France, when she took refuge in England. She was the obvious focal point for any Roman Catholic-led insurrection. The arrangements for her captivity at Tutbury Castle were made by Sir Ralph Sadler and, as Tutbury was not on any post road, special posts had to set for communications with the Court. Sadler's secretary sets out the details in a letter addressed to the Lord Treasurer dated 25 January 1584:

> In answer to your Lordship's letter to me, Mr Chancellor has laid a post to this place to carry his packets to Loughborough, xv foul miles hence, and he to carry his charge to Witham, xv miles further, which is the post and highway between Grantham and Stamford, by which way he sent the last and first packet from hence in post. This is the nearest way to get to the ordinary post way. These two posts are paid xxd per diem a piece, whereof he of Loughbrough is not pleased but on a proff [offer] for a while; and he of Witham looks also for some consideration for breaking out of his accustomed way, which will cause him to keep one horse more, as Howlson says he did, and for allowance for that service during our being at Wingfield [her previous place of captivity] has made petition to Mr Secretary'.[51]

During a later stage of her imprisonment Mary was placed under the care of Sir Amias Poulet, who reported regularly to Sir Francis Walsingham, the queen's principal secretary. A letter from Poulet of 27 April 1585 describes the posts set up between Tutbury and Stamford enabling the two men to keep in touch at a cost of 3s 4d each day.[52] A year later he asks 'that the extraordinary posts be commanded to exercise more diligence and to that purpose to keep two horses at least in the house for the packets'.[53] The post at Stilton received an additional 12d for taking letters to Fotheringhay Castle when Mary was sent there prior to her execution.

The maintenance of roads and bridges

The upkeep of the roads and bridges followed medieval practice. The principle was that town corporations were accountable for those within their bounds while parishes and landowners were responsible in the countryside. In larger towns companies existed to oversee repairs. Within London the Worshipful Company of Paviors, referred to in Chapter 3, dealt with the repair of the streets under the direction of the city chamberlain. The company has a remarkable series of records, which are complete from 1565.

The repair of individual roads could be attempted by national legislation. One law included provision for paving the Strand in London.[54] It required owners of land adjoining the highway to pave it at a penalty of 6d for 'every yard square not sufficiently paved'. During Tudor times the same requirement was also applied to other named London streets and those in Cambridge and Chester. Mary's parliament in 1553 required the roads from Shaftesbury to

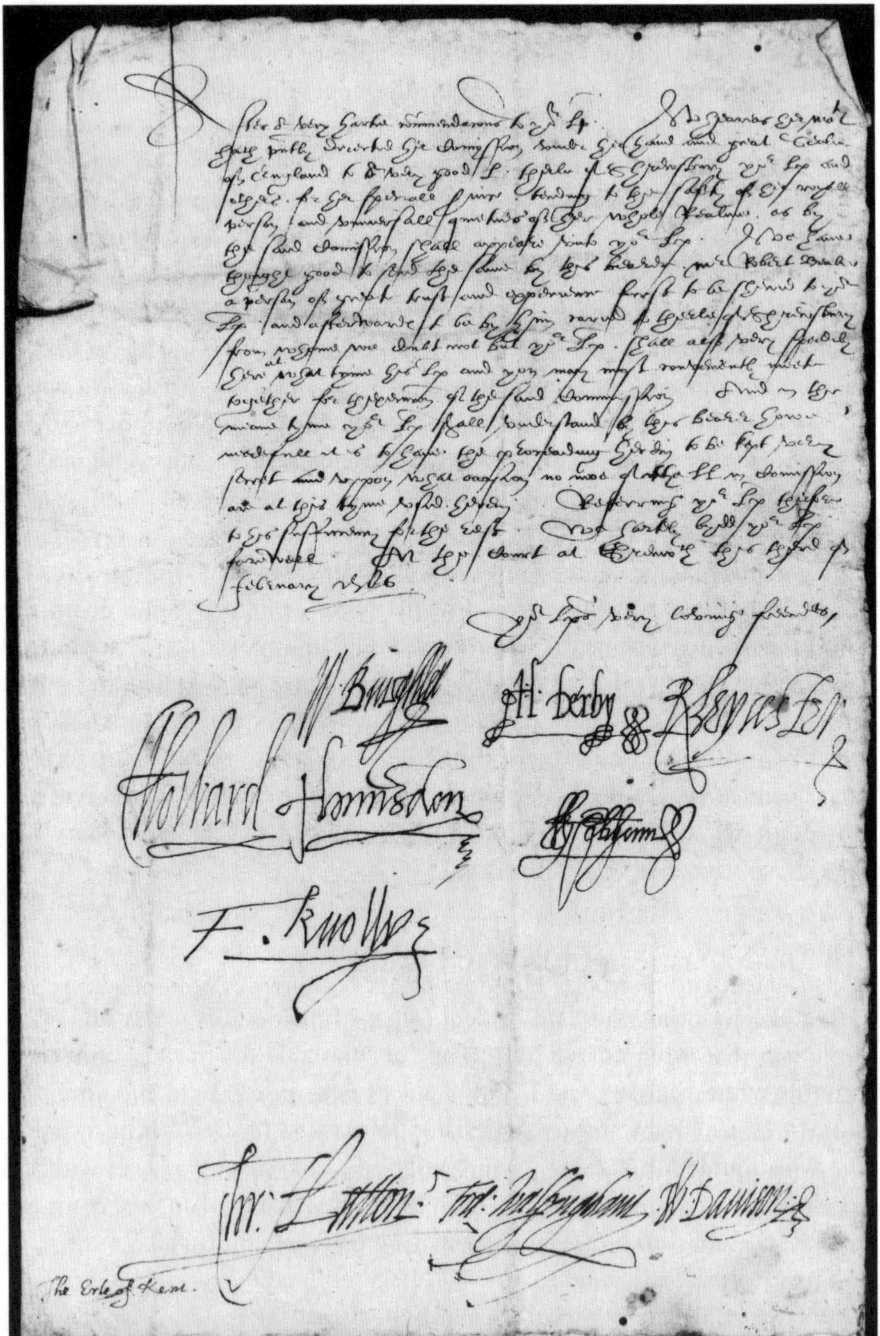

10.4 Privy Council letter to the Earl of Kent authorising the execution of Mary, Queen of Scots in 1587, taken with the warrant signed by Queen Elizabeth I. (By courtesy of Sotheby's)

Sherborne and from Gloucester to Bristol to be paved, and Elizabethan legislation ordered the paving of roads within 5 miles of Oxford. The arrival of the monarch on a progress was a reason for the upgrading of roads and bridges. By a proclamation of 1511 those laws concerning the highways in the time of Edward I were restated and enforced.[55]

A new elective parochial office was established in 1531, that of surveyor of the highways, whose holder had powers to levy services on everyone in the parish. Soon afterwards, in 1555, 'An Acte for thamendyng of Highe Wayes' indicated that there was great need of repairs throughout the land as it describes 'highways being now both very noisome and tedious to travel in, and dangerous to all passengers and carriages'.[56] It laid down that in each parish the constables and parish wardens should call the parishioners together on the Tuesday or Wednesday of Easter week and appoint from them two surveyors and orderers for one year, who were to supervise the repairing of the highways and bridges, requiring the parishioners to work for eight hours on four days and to provide all the carts and tools needed for the work. Parish officers now had the right to raise revenue and fines could be imposed on those who did not collaborate with the surveyor's instructions. That Act ran for seven years and in 1563 under Queen Elizabeth further legislation extended its terms for a further twenty years and increased the days for working to six.[57] It also allowed the surveyors to dig for such gravel, sand and cinder as they needed for their work. At Quarter Sessions the justices were empowered to punish any surveyors who had neglected their work.

The development of iron works and mines in Kent, Surrey and Sussex during the sixteenth century did much damage to the existing roads and was the subject of legislation in 1584.[58] Under this Act occupiers of iron mills and coal mines were required to lay specified quantities of stone and gravel for every ton of iron that they produced.

An altogether different approach to road construction had taken place in Kent during the reign of Henry VIII.[59] The Act is entitled 'For Altering the Highways in the Weald of Kent', and the first section provides for a new way to be built from Hempsted to Totenden, in compensation for which the provider was granted the right to enclose the old road. This principle is then applied to other new roads:

> And in consideration that many other common ways in the said weald of Kent be so deep and noyous, by wearing, and course of water, and other occasions, that people cannot have their carriages or passage of horses upon or by the same, but to their great pains, peril and jeopardy ...

the Act allows any person, having the agreement of two justices of the peace and twelve discreet men of the hundred, to build a new way and to 'be given the soil and ground of the old way'. Again, there is no direction as to the standards to be achieved.

Assuming responsibility for the perpetual repair of a bridge was an expensive obligation to be evaded if possible. For centuries the maintenance of embankments and bridges had been seen as special acts of mercy. An Act of 1531 empowered justices of the peace to deal with 'all manner of anoysances of bridges broken in the highways' even in those places exempt from the jurisdiction of the sheriff.[60]

Where no person or corporation could be found to be responsible, the justices were able to tax the inhabitants of the local town or parish. If a bridge lay outside such limits then the inhabitants of the whole shire could be made to contribute. By Queen Elizabeth's time legislation was needed for various important bridges that were still not being maintained; an Act in 1575–76 provided for particular bridges, including one for the perpetual maintenance of Rochester Bridge.[61]

Bridges at Chepstow, Newport, Caerleon, Wye, and over the Eden near Carlisle were specifically named in Acts. One of the first actions of James I was to order the replacement of the wooden bridge over the Tweed at Berwick with a stone one.

All this legislation caused some improvements but it was often not put into effect nor did it keep pace with the increasing flow of traffic. Great hooded waggons pulled along by teams of eight horses are mentioned in Stow's *A Survey of London* as early as 1564. Such vehicles with metal-shod wheels, often with protruding iron bolts, dug deep into the highways and town streets, but proclamations to limit the use of large carts and the damage they caused were not passed until 1618, 1622 and 1630. Despite the penalties imposed by the Tudors and Stuarts, these failed to restrict the vehicles. Moreover, no standards were set for the condition of roads or bridges that needed repair and there was no provision for records to be kept.

1 Reconstruction of the Roman site at Wall in Staffordshire showing in the foreground the mansio serving the postal service. (English Heritage by Ivan Lapper. J970011)

2 An English medieval scribe. The penknife held in the left hand was used to sharpen the pen, to erase errors and to hold the document firm when writing. (Bodleian Library Ms 602 f36r)

3 Map of England by Matthew Paris showing a route from Dover to the north. Mid-thirteenth century. (British Library. Cotton Claudius d. DV1 f12v)

4 *Above:* The perception of Britain about 1540 by an anonymous mapmaker. (British Library. Cotton Augustus I i 9)

5 *Right:* The Court of Chancery in the fifteenth century. Writs are on the table while a clerk rolls the Great Seal onto a document. (Middle Temple Library. Misc mss no.188)

6 *Left*: An English Herald receiving a letter from King Edward IV and delivering it on the continent. (Taken from the manuscript The Legend of St Ursula by courtesy of Stad Brugge Stedelijke Musea)

7 *Above*: Georg Gisze, London merchant, by Holbein. Letters hang in racks with a string holder, scales, crystal ball, seal, inkwell and quill pen. The Latin motto translates as 'No joy without sorrow'. The notice dated 1532 reads 'The picture you see here records the features of Georg. Such are his lively eyes, such is his face.' (Courtesy of Bildarchive Preußischer Kulturbesitz, Berlin)

8 The great seals of Henry I and Henry VIII, held by the Lord Chancellor to authenticate royal documents. (National Archives. SC13/H88 and E30/555)

9 Letter from Sir Walter Raleigh to Sir Robert Cecil. (By courtesy the Marquess of Salisbury. Cecil Papers 43/84)

For her majestyís speciall affaires / To the right honourable Sir / Robert Cecyll knight / principall secretary / to her majesty at the Court / from Sherborne the 13th of / post hast, hast post / August at 12 the night. / hast, with all spede / hast post hast hast / W. Ralegh / for life

[Notes added by the posts] Sarum paste 10 in the fore none beinge Thursdaye / Received at Andever at 4 of the clocke in the after nowne the same Thursday / Received at Basingestoke at 8 of the clocke at nite the same daye

11
SIXTEENTH-CENTURY LETTERS

Substantial collections of letters have survived from the sixteenth century. We can read Henry VIII's love letters to Ann Boleyn; Sir Thomas More on events that led to his execution; the business correspondence of the Johnson family; Sir Amyas Poulet describing his custodianship of Mary, Queen of Scots; Sir Thomas Gresham on the management of royal finance; and Queen Elizabeth teasing her courtiers. Bishops give their views on ecclesiastical controversies, courtiers share their scandals, ambassadors send news from abroad, and a seaman with Sir Richard Grenville writes from the *Revenge*. A few letters such as that transcribed in Chapter 7 to a tool maker survive from humble folk. The vast correspondence of the Cecils and the Privy Council letters preserved in State Papers provide a detailed insight into the business of Tudor government. At last it becomes possible to derive much of our political and social history from the correspondence of those who made it, for the country's business was carried out by writing letters.

Throughout the century there was a steady growth in literacy, defined as the ability to read. In his edition of the fifteenth-century Paston Letters Gairdner wrote, 'No person or any rank or station in society above mere labouring men seems to have been wholly illiterate. All could write letters; most persons could express themselves in writing with ease and fluency' and during Henry VIII's reign Thomas More gave the surprising total of those able to read the Scriptures as nearly six in ten of the population:

> All the people shall be able to read it when they have it, of which people far more than four parts of all the whole divided into ten could never read English yet, and many now too old to begin to go to school.

Perhaps More wrote only from his experience in London, for no doubt a larger proportion of people there were literate than in rural areas. While we have no statistical data concerning literacy rates, modern research does suggest that More's figure for reading skills was not unreasonable as long as it is not applied to understanding academic books. Guy concludes, 'it is entirely probable that spelling out the commandments from a version painted on the wall of a parish church, or extracting the gist of a printed ballad or broadsheet, was within the competence of half the population, as More thought.'[1] Henry VIII's 1543 Act 'for the advancement of true religion and the abolishment of the contrarie' attempted to forbid those below the rank of the gentry or substantial merchants from reading the Bible, hardly necessary unless many were literate.

From late medieval times it had been customary in grammar schools to hold additional classes for the 'petties', young children including girls who were taught the alphabet and how to read. Although the Dissolution of the monasteries, nunneries and chantries brought the closure of many schools, the dispersal of their inmates sent numbers of literate men and women into the villages and towns. Chantry priests, whose occupation had primarily consisted of saying masses for the dead, were now freed to provide education. A growing proportion of the population was interested in acquiring the skill of literacy, while the introduction of affordable printed books, some in the form of useful textbooks, gave a great impetus to acquiring reading skills. Ninety-one signs of London stationers, who were booksellers, have been traced before 1558.[2]

Most towns established schools providing a free education, some funded by legacies, others by the poor rates. In *A Description of Britain*, written about 1577, William Harrison has this to say:

> Besides the Universities, also there are great number of grammar schools throughout the realm, and those very liberally endowed, for the better relief of poor scholars, so that there are not many corporate towns under the Queen's dominion that have not one grammar school at the least, with a sufficient living for a master and usher appointed to the same.[3]

Such was the enthusiasm for education that many well-known schools were founded during the Tudor period. The impetus to found new schools continued under the Stuarts, and Davies estimates that as many new foundations were made in the first half of the seventeenth century as in the whole of the previous one.[4]

Many collections of contemporary letters are available in the National Archives and some have been made more easily accessible by having been printed in the publications of the Camden, Surtees, Thoresby, Roxburgh Club and other societies. Others have been transcribed by Sir Henry Ellis in the four series of letters he published, by Robert Steele in his *Kings' Letters* and also in the Rolls series published by the Historical Manuscripts Commission. Notable are the editions of the Lisle letters, those of Henry VIII edited by M. St Clare Byrne, and the correspondence of William Cecil, Lord Burghley, and his son Robert, Marquis of Salisbury. Other Tudor statesmen, like Thomas Cromwell and Sir Thomas More, have left substantial collections. Anne Crawford has edited letters from the Tudor queens. A selection will suggest to the reader what a fascinating historical treasury has survived.

The letters of Henry VIII reveal a remarkably talented and sensitive person. Some, like those to Anne Boleyn, are tender and affectionate, others show him dealing with matters of theological controversy or dictating foreign and domestic policy. His masterful style is shown in the letter he sent to his judges in June 1535.[5] After reminding them of the authority granted to him by Parliament and the Church, 'how the said title, style, and jurisdiction of supreme head appertaineth to us', he requires them to be:

> showing and declaring to the people at your said sessions the treasons traitrously committed against us and our laws by the late bishop of Rochester [John Fisher] and Sir Thomas More, knight, who thereby and by divers secret practices of their malicious minds against us, intended to disseminate, engender, and breed amongst our people and subjects a most mischievous and seditious opinion, not only to their own confusion but also of sundry others, who lately have condignly suffered execution according to their demerits.

Then follows the warning:

> if you should, contrary to your duties and our expectation and trust, neglect, be slack, or omit to do diligently your duties, in the performance and execution of our mind, pleasure and commandment as before, or would halt or stumble at any part or speciality of the same, be you assured that we, like a prince of justice, will so punish and correct the default and negligence therein, as it shall be an example to all others.

There is no notion of impartiality or the independence of the judiciary here!

During the fighting between English and Scots in 1542 Henry VIII's herald was murdered.[6] Accompanied by an English pursuivant and a Scottish herald, he had been negotiating the exchange of prisoners when he was set upon by two men who were later found to be English refugees trying to win favour with the Scots. The event is described by Henry VIII in a letter to the king of France:

> The Scots have, against all laws of arms and order used amongst Princes, to the most pernicious danger of all ministers, slain and wounded Somerset, one of our Heralds at arms, being sent with letters to the king of Scots from our Lieutenant for delivery of the said prisoners, as he was returning homewards, with their answer of refusal of the same.

Henry was obviously concerned to avoid the French becoming involved by supporting their Scottish ally. The usual carrier of a royal letter was a herald or ambassador and by tradition he was always guaranteed a safe conduct. To his credit, James V was disgusted with the affair and instigated a thorough enquiry which led to the seizure of the murderers and their eventual execution at Tyburn.

A letter of Thomas More's to Cardinal Wolsey describes a day's business at court.[7] He had received from Wolsey a number of letters, some personal to More, others including the return of one in the king's own hand and one comprising instructions for an expedition to Russia:

> which things with diligence I presented forthwith unto the King's Grace the same morning, and to the intent that his Grace should the more perfectly perceive what weighty things they were that your Grace had at that time sent unto him, and what diligence was requisite in the expedition of the same, I read unto his Grace the Letters which it liked your Grace to write to me.

Henry approved Wolsey's letter to the French king but delayed the rest until that evening when after dinner he signed one to the emperor and another concerning the Russian expedition. Others he left until the following morning, by when further letters had arrived. More sent the royal opinions on various matters to Wolsey for his consideration. It was in such ways that business was transacted. The king's views were paramount but More had to walk a tightrope in consulting Wolsey and Council members.

Henry's minister, Thomas Cromwell, suddenly lost his great office as principal secretary.[8] He was in the Council room when he was arrested, stripped of his decorations, and taken to the Tower, from where he wrote an abject letter to the king:

> Sir, I do knowledge myself to have been a most miserable and wretched sinner, and that I have not towards God and your Highness behaved myself as I ought and should have done; for the which mine offences to God, whiles I live, I shall continually call for mercy; and for mine offences to your Grace, which God knoweth were never malicious nor willful, and that I never thought treason

> to your Highness, your realm, or posterity, so God help me, either in word or deed. Nevertheless, prostrate at your Majesty's [feet] in what thing soever I have offended I appeal to your Highness for mercy, grace and pardon, in suchwise as shall be your pleasure. [...] Written with the quaking hand and most sorrowful heart of your most sorrowful subject and most humble servant and prisoner this Saturday at your [Tower] of London.

The decision of the king was supreme. Cromwell has lost the royal support; his years of loyal service mattered little. Within eighteen days he was beheaded. On the same day Henry married his fifth wife.

A personal letter of Princess Mary, the future queen, to her younger brother, King Edward VI, shows that she was a woman of ability who could write with moderation and skill about a matter that deeply concerned her.[9] By an order of Edward VI's Council her chaplains had been forbidden to say the Mass. She wrote:

> My duty humbly remembered unto your Majesty. It may please the same to be advertised that I have by my servants received your most honourable Letter, the contents wherof do not a little trouble me, and so much the more for that any of my servants should move or attempt me in matters touching my soul, which I think the meanest subject within your Realm could evil bear at their servant's hand; having for my part utterly refused heretofor to talk with them in such matters, and of all other persons least regarded them therein; to whom I have declared what I think as she which trusted that your Majesty would have suffered me your poor humble sister and beadeswoman to have used the accustomed Mass, which the King your father and mine with all his predecessors evermore used; wherein also I have been brought up from my youth, and thereunto my conscience does not only bind me, which by no means will suffer me to think one thing and do another, but also the promise made to the Emperor by your Majesty's Council was an assurance to me that in so doing I should not offend the Laws, although they seem now to qualify and deny the thing.

She had been carefully educated together with her sister, Elizabeth, mainly under the direction of Queen Catherine Parr, and while she may not have attained all the skills that her sister acquired, and which were so eloquently described by her tutor Roger Ascham in *The Schoolmaster*, she was obviously well able to express her feelings in a dignified way.

Edward had distressed his sister and Mary did the same when she sent Elizabeth to the Tower on suspicion of complicity in Wyatt's rebellion.[10] Elizabeth wrote:

> I most humbly beseech your Majesty [...] that I be not condemned without answer and due proof, which it seems that I now am; for without cause proved I am by your Council from you commanded to go to the Tower, a place more wanted for a false traitor than a true subject. [...] Therefore, once again, kneeling with humbleness of heart, because I am not suffered to bow the knees of my body, I humbly crave to speak to your highness, which I would not be so bold as to desire if I knew not myself most clear, as I know myself most true. And as for that traitor Wyatt, he might peradventure write me a letter, but on my faith I never received any from him.

The letter is in her own hand, the blank portion carefully crossed with lines to prevent additions and at the foot is 'I humbly crave but only one word of answer from your self'. She must have been greatly afraid, having no near relative apart from the queen, but yet she writes with a steady hand and in a calm manner. Her request for a reply or interview was not granted.

About a hundred holograph letters have survived in Queen Elizabeth's own hand, with a far larger number which were signed or passed by her. She chose to write letters when matters interested her and these would override any decisions of the Council. Her magnificent signature, sometimes several inches in length, usually appears at the head of documents. Henry VIII had authorised a dry hand-stamp copy of his signature, which could be inked in, but she did not follow that practice. The letters she wrote tell us much about her character. Chancellor Hatton commented on them: 'The cunning of her style of writing exceedeth all the eloquence of the world.'[11]

An example of her abruptness is in this letter to the Bishop of Ely, who had refused to hand over an estate belonging to the bishopric to Hatton:

> Proud Prelate, You know what you were before I made you what you are now. If you do not immediately comply with my request, I will unfrock you, by God. Elizabeth.[12]

Yet she could be kind in letters sent on bereavements. When Sir John Norris was killed on service in Ireland she wrote at length in her own hand to his mother:

> Mine own Crow [...] although we have deferred long to represent to you our grieved thoughts, because we liked full ill to yield to you the first reflection on misfortune, whom we have always sought to cherish and comfort [...] we resolved no longer to smother either our care for your sorrow, or the sympathy

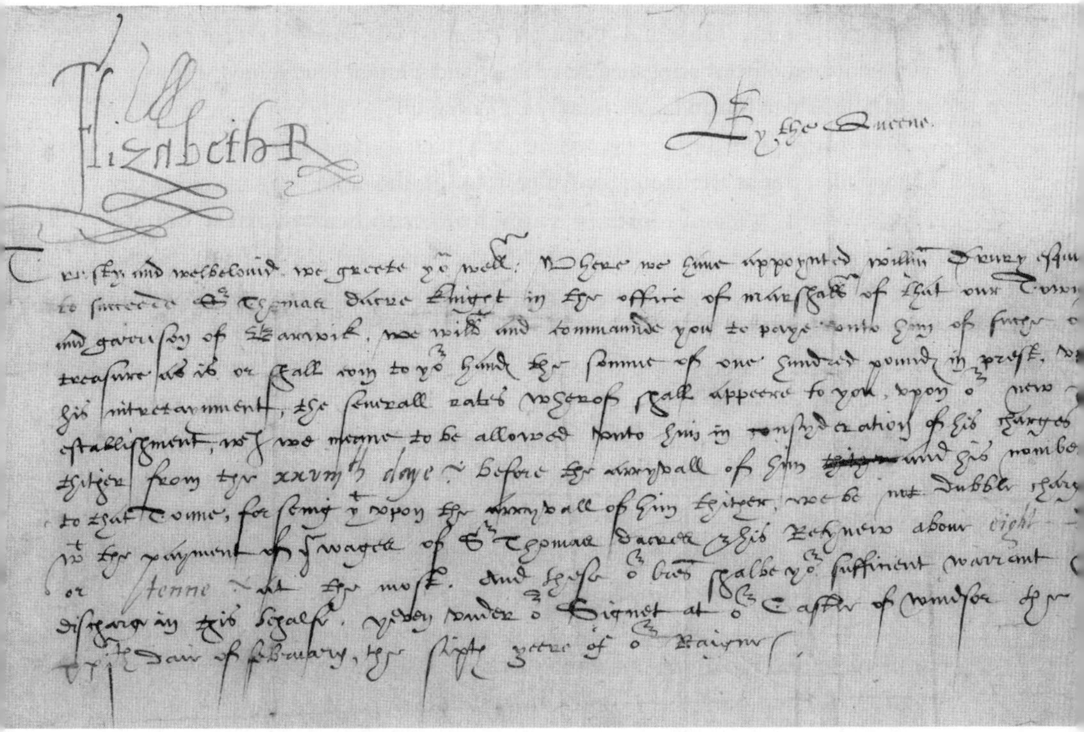
Elizabeth R

By the Queene.

Trusty and welbeloved we greete you well.

11.1 1564. Queen Elizabeth I writes to the treasurer of Berwick about her appointment of William Drury, a Protestant, as marshal of Berwick to replace the Catholic Sir Thomas Dacre, whom her sister, Queen Mary, had put there. The clerk has been required to leave spaces for the important details which she fills in personally. He writes in secretary hand while she writes in italic. The town of Berwick was the listening post for Scottish news, with the largest English garrison in the country. (Private collection)

> of our grief for his love, wherein, if it be true that society in sorrow works diminution, we do assure you, by this true messenger of our mind, that nature can have stirred no more dolorous affection in you as a mother for a dear son, than gratefulness and memory of his services past hath wrought in us, his sovereign, apprehension of our miss of so worthy a servant.[13]

Her correspondence concerning the imprisonment of Mary, Queen of Scots, shows her moods, her forthrightness and deviousness. To Mary she wrote:

> You have in various ways and manners attempted to take my life and to bring my kingdom to destruction by bloodshed. I have never proceeded so harshly against you, but have, on the contrary, protected and maintained you like myself. These treasons will be proved to you and all made manifest. Yet it is my will that you answer the nobles and peers of the kingdom as if I were myself present.

> I therefore require, charge, and command that you make answer for I have been well informed of your arrogance. Act plainly and without reserve, and you will sooner be able to obtain favour from me. Elizabeth.[14]

To Mary's keeper at the time, Sir Amyas Paulet, she used even stronger language: 'Let your wicked murdress know how, with hearty sorrow, her vile deserts compel these orders.'[15] Yet, after Mary's execution on a death warrant signed by herself, though whose actual despatch she did not authorise, she could write to Mary's son, James, king of Scotland:

> My own dear brother, I would you knew (though not felt) the extreme dolor that overwhelms my mind for that miserable accident, which (far contrary to my meaning) has befallen. I have now sent Sir Robert Carew, this Kinsman of mine, whom, ere now, it hath pleased you to favour, to instruct you truly of that which is too irksome for my pen to tell you. I beseech you, that as God, and many more, know how innocent I am in this case: for you will believe me, that if I had bid ought, I would have bid by it. I am not so base minded, that fear of any living creature, or prince, should make me afraid to do that were just; or done, to deny the same: I am not of so base a lineage, nor carry so vile a mind. But as not to disguise, fits most a King, so will I never dissemble my actions, but accuse them to show even as I meant them. Thus assuring your self of me, that as I know this was deserved; yet, if I meant it, I would never lay it on others shoulders; no more will I not damnify myself, that thought it not. The circumstance it may please you to learn from this bearer. And, for my part, think you have not in the world a more loving kinswoman, not a more dear friend, than myself, nor any that will watch more carefully to preserve you, and your estate. And who shall otherwise persuade you, judge them to be more partial to others than to you. And thus, in haste, I leave to trouble you, beseeching God to send you a long reigne. The 14th of February, 1586 [1587]. Your most assured loving Sister, and Cousin, Elizabeth.[16]

Often she conveniently passed her problems to Burghley:

> I am in such a labyrinth that I do not now how to answer the Queen of Scots after so long delay. Therefore find something good that I may put in Randolf's instructions and indicate your opinion to me.[17]

To her friends she could be flippant. When she heard that Leicester, a hearty eater, was to stay with the Earl and Countess of Shrewsbury she sent advice on the food to be supplied:

> allow him by the day for his meat two ounces of flesh, referring the quality to yourselves, so as you exceed not the quantity, and for his drink the twentieth part of a pint of wine to comfort his stomach, and as much of St Anne's sacred water as he listeth to drink. On festival days, as is meet for a man of his quality, we can be content you shall enlarge his diet by allowing unto him for his dinner the shoulder of a wren, and for his supper a leg of the same, besides his ordinary ounces.[18]

There are familiar letters to Leicester and one, written to him when he was her lieutenant-general in the Low Countries, begins:

> Rob, I am afraid you will suppose by my wandering writings that a midsummer moon hath taken large possession of my brains this month, but you must need take things as they come in my head, though order be left behind me. When I remember your request to have a discreet and honest man that may carry my mind and see how all goes there, I have chosen this bearer, whom you know and have made good trial of. I have fraught him full of my conceits of those country matters, and imparted what way I mind to take, and what is fit for you to use.[19]

After giving various instructions she ends:

> Now will I end that do imagine I talk still with you, and therefore loathly say farewell, O O, though ever I pray God bless you from all harm and save you from all foes, with my million and legion of thanks for all your pains and cares. As you know, ever the same. E.R.

The O Os represent two eyes, her nickname for him. It is through such personal letters that we can best come to an understanding of this remarkable woman, of her imperiousness and dignity, her learning, her deviousness, and her capacity to create devotion and respect.

Among the royal letters are some to unusual destinations. Queen Elizabeth wrote in 1595 to the Muslim emperor at the request of Sigismund, Vayrod of Transylvania, reminding him of the 'ancient union of friendship of his family towards us' and asking for protection for those Christians who have rejected 'the superstition of the Pope of Rome and the worship of images'. Another letter of 1597 'To the Most Invincible and Puissant King of the Abassens, the Mighty Emperor of Ethiopia, the Higher and the Lower' introduces a traveller, Laurence Aldersley. The collections of travels by Hakluyt, Purchas and Astley contain many early letters, including one from Elizabeth to the king of Achem in Sumatra, and his reply which refers to her as 'Sultana in the Kingdom of England, France, Ireland, Holland and Frizeland'. He sends the gift of 'a ring of gold, beautified with a ruby, richly placed in his seat, two vestures woven with gold, embroidered with gold, enclosed in a red box of Tzin' (China). It is dated 1011 in the Muslim calendar (1602).[20] There are also letters to the Emperors of India and China introducing John Newbery, a merchant.[21]

Perhaps the most interesting of her letter carriers was Francis Cherry, who was sent as a messenger to the tsar of Russia to explain Elizabeth's relationship with the pope. On his return in 1598 Cherry wrote a lengthy account of his adventures which is preserved in the Egerton Papers. He describes the elaborate protocol of the court, witnessing the tsar's coronation, and the thirteen carts of wines and foodstuffs sent to him after he had met the tsar. He was supplied with sixteen post horses at no cost for his return from Moscow to the border.[22]

Philip Gawdy was a young adventurous Elizabethan whose correspondence in the British Library totals eighteen volumes. It includes his time at Cliffords Inn, when he trained as a lawyer and relates the news from the court including a story of Mary, Queen of Scots, discovered hiding in a chimney, planning that eventually she might escape. His family relied on him to send not only the Court news but clothing and food. On one occasion the carriers took artichokes, canary wine and a lamprey pie. He was in the *Revenge* with Sir Richard Grenville in one of the most gallant episodes of English naval history, and there is a letter from prison in Lisbon where he and the other fifty-nine survivors were taken. Another letter describes the voyage of the *Defiance* in 1591, a long account of adventures at sea. To a letter from the *Revenge* is added a tribute from Grenville, testifying:

> no sickness, no danger, no fear....nor no extremities of weather, mutiny, hard [ship] or other peril or grief could provoke Philip [to return].[23]

Another letter to his mother tells how he dutifully obeys her wishes that each morning he should take 'the bricke and wormwood as a remedy against all pestilence and infection' and 'I have long since laid up your motherly good counsel that I do every day meditate upon as a medicine against all bad company and all other bad actions whatsoever.'[24] Philip was the second son of the first Sir Bassingbourne Gawdy, a leading Norfolk gentleman, and his letters trace the story of a young man who, knowing that he was not destined to succeed to the family estates, made his own career.

Another fascinating letter collection that survives is that of Sir Walter Raleigh. We can read, for example, of the division of spoils from a Portuguese carrack, the naval action at Cadiz, an account in great detail given to Prince Henry of the building of a ship, and the moving correspondence from Guiana to his wife, Bess. He tells her of the death of their son, Wat, who perished in the attack on São Tomé:

> I was loath to write because I knew not how to comfort you. [...] Comfort your heart dearest Bess I shall sorrow for us both. I shall sorrow the less because I have not long to sorrow, because not long to live. My brains are broken and tis a torment to me to write.[25]

He sensed the fate that awaited him when he returned after attacking the Spaniards without permission and lacking the treasure that might have placated the spendthrift King James.

Many accounts of dramatic events come from contemporary letters. One such from Thomas Randolph and the Earl of Bedford addressed to the Privy Council in March 1566 describes the murder of Rizzio at Holyrood Palace in great detail. Letters from ambassadors and agents abroad, such as those from Poulet during his embassy to France in 1577, recount major events.[26]

There are also large collections of correspondence from noble families, among which is that of the Cliffords, great northern landowners. In 1536 Lady Katherine Scrope was at Bolton Castle. She was about nineteen, mother of a baby son. Her husband, John, fearing capture by the leaders of the Pilgrimage of Grace, had left her. She wrote to her father, the Earl of Cumberland, on 14 October:

> My duty promised unto your Lordship in my most humblest manner; advertising this same that yesterday the commons of Richmondshire did meet at Richmond, where undoubtedly they divided them in three parts, whereof one company there was commanded to come this day for my Lord my bedfellow or his little son and mine, Sir John Metcalf or his son Christopher, and Richard Sigiswick, and to bring them with them or else to pull down their houses and spoil them of their goods. Another company goes for my Lord Latimer and his son, Mr Danby, and others in those quarters. And the third company goes to Barnard Castle to bring them to my cousin George Bowes and his two uncles. My Lord my bedfellow is this night at Helbeck Hall and will be with your Lordship at Skipton in as convenient speed as he can make, to take such part as your Lordship does. And I will come this morning towards Katelwell and tarry there off my bedfellow, and would come with him to Skipton, if you think it good. And this night I have sent my little boy with his nurse unto one poor man's house, to be kept privy there to [till] we know further. And what

> your Lordship's mind is in the premises I will heartily beseech you to send it to Catewell with this bearer. Thus the Holy Ghost preserve your good Lordship with my Lady my mother and all yours in comfort. At Bolton the Saturday before day, your humblest daughter Kateryn Scrope.[27]

Given the circumstances and her youth, this is a remarkably composed and sensible letter, which tells us about the methods used in the uprising. Katherine survived to marry again after her husband's death and the family correspondence contains a letter of hers written in 1583 when she was Lady Cholmeley.

Several collections of merchants' mail, including the Johnson, Gresham and Corsini letters and those of the Merchant Adventurers of York, survive from the sixteenth century, many others having presumably perished in the Great Fire of London in 1666. Of these the most comprehensive are the Johnson letters, now in the National Archives. They comprise about 1,000 documents. John Johnson filed every letter he received from his family, friends and business correspondents together with a copy of each letter he wrote. It has been calculated that this totalled 20,000 in all. When the firm went bankrupt in 1533 some of the correspondence was sent to the Privy Council as evidence. Barbara Winchester describes the Johnsons:

> They knew, as we do, love and laughter, sickness and sorrow, and the intimate details of their lives – the venison and green ginger that they ate, the red wine and potent ale they drank, the velvet gowns and ruffled shirts they wore, the carved furniture in their rooms, the conduct of their households in town and country, the occupation of their leisure hours, their comments on religion and trade and the affairs of state – all is revealed in what is surely the most magnificent collection of Tudor letters.[28]

The Johnsons wrote their own letters, often sending a copy by another messenger to be certain of its arrival, always keeping a further copy in their letter book. The large sheets of quarto or double quarto were fine ivory handmade papers purchased in Antwerp at 4s a ream. They were secured by a thread which was sealed with scarlet wax ensuring that the letter could not be read without breaking it. Each letter was dated, sometimes being marked A B C D or numbered 1 2 3 4 to indicate a series. Among the letters is an eye-witness description of the execution of Queen Catherine Howard. John's brother, Otwell, was there:

> I see the Queen and the Lady Rochford suffer within the Tower the day following, whose souls (I doubt it not) be with God, for they made the most godly

> and Christian's end that ever was to tell of (I think) since the world's creation, uttering their lively faith in the blood of Christ only, with wonderful patience and constancy to death.[29]

Another of his letters tells of the trials of Doctor Crome and others for heresy and of how Anne Aske was put on the rack even after her condemnation to death for not recanting her belief in transubstantiation, 'which is a strange thing to my understanding'.

The letters tell us of the plagues and 'the sweat' which brought sudden death to many households. The latter was a phenomenon of the times, thought to have been a virulent form of influenza, that struck down tens of thousands of people including Prince Arthur, elder brother of Henry VIII. There was no antidote. Sufferers were put to bed, deprived of fresh air, given as little to drink as possible and prevented from sleep which was considered certain to induce death. Most sufferers died within a few hours of showing symptoms. John heard the news of Otwell's death from his brother-in-law, Bartholomew Warner:

> With so sorrowful a heart did I never write as now I do unto you, good Mr Johnson, to signify to you the departure out of this life of your loving brother and mine, Otwell Johnson, this day in the morning about three of the clock, of the sweating sickness, which here reigneth wonderfully, God be merciful unto us. After hearing of the death of Harry Bostock, and many other of his very familiar acquaintance yesternight, coming from the Street at seven o'clock, he went to his bed; and suddenly was in so extreme pain that within four or five hours we could get no word of him, and so continued in pain until three o'clock.[30]

The firm never recovered from the loss of its key partner.

We are given a vivid picture of the economic situation at the end of the reign of Henry VIII and the years that followed. Henry's continental wars encouraged piracy and no cargoes were safe. English vessels plundered ships belonging to the French and the emperor. In retaliation the Johnsons and others lost vessels. During 1545 John wrote from Calais:

> This day, I thank God, I arrived here in safety, in Company with the Commissioners that come over for the Diet. The French galleys have roamed in the sea, for upon Thursday last, the weather being calm, they came bragging into Dover Road, being in number four, not far from the King's ships, who shot at them very much, but the galleys not at them.[31]

Such were the perils of the Channel crossing. The pirates on both sides paid little attention to negotiated peace treaties and when he was lord high admiral of England, Thomas Seymour provided capital for many of their ventures.

At the same time merchants had to contend with the financial chaos brought about by the debasements of the coinage. John's brother, Richard, wrote from Antwerp, 'Englishmen's credits are nothing esteemed.' They had no means to obtain gold coins to pay their debts, for 'there is no more gold to be had at any reasonable price'. On 12 June 1551 Otwell sent John a copy of a proclamation from the Council:

> First concerning gold and the course of the exchange, know that this day at our noon was published the enclosed proclamation for the stay, or rather abolishing of the said exchange [...] whereby merchants are brought to a wonderful perplexity of their trade.[32]

The Exchange was in Lombard Street, Gresham's Royal Exchange not yet having been built, an open place where all bills of exchange were presented and loans arranged. The shilling was devalued to ninepence and then to sixpence, the fourpenny groat to twopence. Creditors begged their debtors not to pay their bills and great sums were offered almost free of interest. This tragedy which ruined so many merchants can be followed in the Johnson letters.

Two years later the firm had collapsed and we read about the seizure of their goods by creditors, a haphazard practice allowed by the law at that time whereby those first on the scene could take what they wanted. John's manor was stripped and his merchandise taken. Only through letters like the one John wrote to Sir William Cecil are we able to realise the horrors that could be perpetrated:

> Truly, sir, I have the possession of nothing in the world, nor have not fraudulently conveyed my goods into other men's hands as it is reported, yet done anything else to the defrauding of my creditors, yet in all places my goods be spoiled and attached. [...] I hope there will be some good order taken that my goods may be distributed amongst my creditors, and not be spoiled as they be.[33]

However, Cecil's first aim was to recover a debt of £41 2s owed by the firm to his father.

An equally poignant letter from Sir Thomas More's wife to Henry VIII tells of harsh events. On the chancellor's imprisonment in the Tower all his goods, chattels and profits from his fees and lands were seized, only the moveable goods and revenues from his personal lands being left for his wife and her household. In her letter she tells that now even those are to be forfeit so that she and her son are 'likely to be utterly undone'.

Some of the Johnson letters tell us about the post. The firm used local carriers to take the family letters to their various homes and to carry their clothes, spices, wines and other luxuries. They could be located at their inns in London to which the Johnsons sent their goods and payment for the journey. Money was a problem for its weight was considerable and so was usually entrusted to a personal servant. The Johnsons were, like the Celys, merchants of the Staple and could use fellow members' servants. Letters for the Continent went by Calais and boats left London daily for Gravesend, where the bags could be sent overland via the royal posts. Letters could also be handed in and paid for at the London postmaster's house. Alternatives could be found by using the Merchant Adventurers' post – providing relations were amicable at the time – the Antwerp post, or the Merchant Strangers' men. The Calais postmen linked with the Dover post. A letter of 1551 describes the service to Spain: 'Sir, the ordinary post from Antwerp to Spain passeth now through England, and maketh London in its way.'[34]

Times for letters to further places are mentioned. Those from Seville took six weeks but one from Venice sent on 30 November arrived in the following April, presumably detained en route by accident or bad weather. The Johnsons were a small business yet they sent letters each day: tens of thousands of letters were being exchanged efficiently each year by a variety of competing postal services.

An interesting feature of merchants' correspondence is the reference to merchants' marks, which are often used to show the ownership of an item of merchandise. Their use was described in Chapter 6. Most are based on a central, upright stem, while a few are in the shape of shields until these were prohibited by the heralds in about 1605 as being too close to representations of armorial bearings. The Johnsons kept a record book with the marks of fellow traders. Marks may be monograms or occasionally in the form of a rebus, the representation of a name in a picture or diagram. N. Hudd's *Bristol Merchants' Marks* illustrates 483 marks from that city and acknowledges that there must have been many more. The Johnsons used their own 'fell mark' and the Staple at Calais had an elaborate device incorporating the outline of a sheep.

Another merchant correspondence, that of the Corsinis, was unknown to historians until the 1980s when it was sold by Christie's auction house in London. As the auctioneers divided the material into single lots or small groups of letters, it was distributed to large numbers of dealers and collectors worldwide and so is not available for study except through the photographic record made by the Getty Trust. For descriptions the researcher will need to look at the auction catalogues and the comments of Robson Lowe in *The Philatelist*. The decline of Venice and of the once great Hansa of Baltic merchants had made way for the return of other Italian merchant bankers and traders to England. Among these were the Corsinis who imported and exported a great variety of goods and had links with the leading continental trading houses. Their letters originating in England are mainly from the ports of Bristol, Colchester, Dover, Exeter, Gravesend, Hull, Ipswich, Norwich, Plymouth, Poole, Rye, Sandwich, Southampton and Yarmouth. The majority, however, came from Continental destinations. They were addressed to Philip Corsini or his younger brother Bartholomew between the 1560s and the end of the century. Bartholomew died in 1601, when the firm's papers went to Italy.

Some letters from the Continent show markings relating to the post which have been discussed in Chapter 9. We have seen that the Merchant Adventurers employed their own couriers to handle their mail as did the Merchant Strangers. They could link with the Thurn and Taxis postal system, covering most of western Europe and thus with each major European town's postmen. The picture we gain is of a merchant having a variety of means by which to send his letters, so it is difficult to attribute a particular endorsement to a particular postal service. The wealthy Fugger merchant house maintained correspondents through Europe and the mail seems to have got through in almost all circumstances. At the end of a despatch from Antwerp dated 31 May 1586, Fugger's Antwerp agent describes events at a turbulent time but ends: 'Letters from London arrive daily by post notwithstanding, and letters are being sent there from here without any hindrance.'[35]

Post from continental towns is sometimes marked to show that the cost has been paid or may have a direction to pay. Those which bear figures from ½ to 33 may be multiples of a ½d delivery charge, bundles of letters having the total charge applied to the top letter, though they could be payments to the courier or the handler of the bag. The preceding letter appears to be a G, presumably for a groat. The letters with 'pp', *posta pagata*, or a variant such as 'ptto' presumably indicate postage paid and 'pq', *per questa*, indicates postage to be paid, any numeral which follows being the cost in the local currency. The content of some letters suggests that merchants corresponded weekly. It was unusual to request the recipient to pay the post and we can presume that this would be done as a means of ensuring delivery by a messenger not well known to the writer. A reason for prepayment is mentioned in a letter from Calais in 1585:

> When your Honour sends me letters please be so kind as to pay the cost of the carriage otherwise they make me pay here whatever they wish.[36]

Comparatively few of the Corsini letters are written in English. Among these are four from Plymouth and neighbouring Kingswear, written by James Bagg and Richard Kelley, which refer to the Guinea trade and the sale of 253 tusks, 'olyvantes tethe'. They give us details and prices of trade in pilchards, ambergris, wheat, tin, lead, raisins, pepper, sugar and naval supplies. One remarkable letter from Exeter tells of the pirate, Clinton Atkinson, who stole a ship, wrecked it and was captured. Corsini's agent bribed the Admiralty judge and his registrar, thus securing a delay in the thief's hanging in order to have him further cross examined by Walsingham's agents, and this enabled him to escape. Unusual documents in the correspondence are insurance policies and passports for ships.[37]

The costs of furnishing vessels can be established. There are notes on porterage charges and bills of lading with valuations, together with information about costs of sending goods by carrier. Seven bags of pepper weighing over 16cwt were charged at the rate of 4s 2d a hundredweight for the journey from Exeter to London, with higher costs liable in the winter. Pepper was so desired that it was known as 'black gold' and frequently used in place of currency.

The Corsinis sold luxury goods to the queen and members of her court. One letter from Hatton, the lord chancellor, tells Philip:

> my desire is to have four pieces of the most excellent velvet, the softest and gentlest in hand that may be found. Whereof one piece to be wrought velvet, which would contain two or three and thirty yards because it is ordered [for] the making of two gowns. One other piece thereof to be shagged velvet which is called flushe satin, both in the gloss and softness of silk. And all these silkes to be black for mine own wearing, the purest that may be had, whatever the price may be, which shall be paid to you with great thanks. I pray you Signor, let these things be provided accordingly, and with expedition, wherein you shall make me beholding. And so I bid you very hearty farewell. From the Court at Oatlands the viiij of September 1587. Your very loving friend, Christopher Hatton, Chancellor.[38]

Hatton was called 'the Queen's dancing master' and clearly liked his elegant clothes.

An extensive correspondence survives from Sir Thomas Gresham, the royal factor and agent in Antwerp, who was also governor of the English Merchant Adventurers there. From it we gain a detailed understanding of how royal loans and finances were managed and how Gresham procured the armaments his country required. That was achieved by various devious means. One letter asks that Sir Jasper Schenz be sent a bribe of 500 crowns 'which he well deserves' so Queen Elizabeth sent a gold chain to that value.[39]

When letters from Schenz were forwarded they came with the request that 'as soon as the Queen had considered them, they might be burnt'. Schenz was referred to by a cipher. The goods that Gresham obtained were similarly described:

> In the last ships that went from hence, I sent you x pieces of velvet, viz. v pieces of dobbill, and v pieces of pill and halfe: and for that you write me you understand not what velvets should be, you should understand that every piece of double green velvet is one thousand lbs weight of corrin powder: and one piece of velvet of pill and a half is one thousand lbs weight of serpentyne powder.[40]

Corrin and serpentine are two types of gunpowder.

Gresham had to bribe the searchers of the port and wrote to the Privy Council about his concern that Dutchmen in London might discover what was happening: 'you must needs devise some ways whereby the things that be sent from hence may be secretly conveyed to the Tower'. In such manner were munitions obtained for the royal forces.

Mention has been made of the way in which posts were bribed to show letters to agents of foreign countries, and Gresham would be well aware of this. State Papers give an example of the unusual use of a merchant's letter from Bruges in 1574 when Richard Fox wrote to Burghley: 'The English post was gone, and as the Dutch post might intercept a letter to you, I enclose it in one to John Taylor, merchant.'[41] A letter to the queen's principal secretary was enclosed inside a merchant's letter.

The correspondence gives us details of the postal arrangements he used. At this time the weekly English post left Antwerp on Sunday nights or very early on Monday morning. The mail went in a trunk and travelled via Bruges, Nieuwpoort, Dunkirk and Calais, taking four days to reach London. Gresham often had communications from his agents elsewhere in Europe to enclose and he was used as agent by any English noblemen travelling in Germany or in the Low Countries. One letter refers to 'Princes and Dukes out of Germany' who sent him mail for forwarding. Gresham had his own agent in London, usually Richard Clough, and he in turn would forward correspondence from the Continent to his master.

These letters give us very little personal information but they throw some light on the tragic life of one of the three Grey sisters. After his final return to England, Gresham and his wife were obliged to act as reluctant warders of Lady Mary Grey. Her eldest sister, Lady Jane Grey, had been executed at the age of sixteen in 1554 as posing a threat to Mary's succession to the throne, and her other sister, Lady Catherine, was imprisoned for life in the Tower for the crime of contracting a marriage to the Earl of Hertford. The sisters may be considered to have had a better title to the throne than Queen Elizabeth, if it is conceded that Henry VIII's divorce from Catherine of Aragon was invalid. Consequently, the third sister was held under continuous surveillance. In 1565 she married Thomas Keys, a member of the queen's household. Keys was committed to the Fleet prison, where he died, and Mary was placed first under the care of William Hawtrey at Chequers, then of the Duchess of Suffolk and eventually of Sir Thomas and his wife. Many letters survive of their pleadings with the Council to be relieved of his charge. One is to Cecil:

> I have written to my Lord of Leicester to move the Queen's Majesty for the removing of my Lady Mary Grey, who hath been with me these fifteen months. I pray you to set your good helping hand for the removing of her; for that my wife would gladly ride into Norfolk for to see her old mother who is ninety years of age and a very weak woman, not like to live long.[42]

This ploy was to no avail; nor was another attempt when Gresham sent to Cecil in 1570 'four pillars of coloured marble with their furniture in good order' together with a further reminder of their unwelcome guest. After Keys had died in prison he wrote yet again but without success, even though the death removed the possibility of her bearing a legitimate heir. We can presume from the eventual end of letters on the subject that he was finally freed of the burden. Mary seems to have led a less restricted life for she was allowed to appear at Court before she died in 1578.

Such letters, which give us so vivid a picture of events, were often written in the heat of the moment, never composed for publication. They give us an authentic picture of a brilliant age where the lives of even the greatest were overshadowed by the fear of the plague and where a misjudgement could lead to the gibbet or the executioner's axe. To put your hand on a letter, to see its address panel and seal, to read the text and signature, is to come as close as you can to the essence of our history.

12.1 The first Lord Stanhope, master of the posts, whose plans led to the opening of the royal postal service to the public. (By courtesy of Lord Tollemache)

12
THE ORGANISATION OF A NATIONAL POSTAL SERVICE

The courtiers who hurried to pay their respects to King James in 1603 included Stanhope, the master of posts, and four years later he obtained the grant that he desired. On 26 July the newly ennobled Lord John Stanhope and his son, Charles, were jointly awarded the position of postmaster of England for life.[1]

There are warrants issued in May and June 1603 showing the annual costs of the posts at that time as £4,150.[2] Before James left Scotland a proclamation concerning the royal progress southwards and the despatch of government packets was issued by the Privy Council, addressed to all mayors, sheriffs, justices of the peace, postmasters, bailiffs, constables, heads of boroughs and others. Thomas Myles, paymaster of the posts, and Rowland White, postmaster at the court, were to oversee the arrangements. Shortly afterwards two other undated proclamations were issued. The first, 'Orders for the thorow Posts and Curriers', summarised the regulations that had previously existed including the monopoly of the royal posts, and was followed by 'Orders for the Posts of our Realms', which put clear obligations on all town posts to accept packets from the principal secretaries and the master of the posts. By these two instructions James re-enacted the regulations that had applied at the end of Elizabeth's reign.[3]

Should a postmaster be unable to supply horses required to meet a warrant, then the local magistrates were obliged to find them. Tighter rules were introduced for the signatories of those letters which were to be accepted by the posts without charge, and the payment made for hiring post horses by the warrant holders was increased to 2½d a mile in addition to the guide's 4d.

By this time a decision of the Scottish Privy Council dated 1 May 1603 had brought the route from Berwick to Edinburgh into the same system as existed south of the border. The Council 'thought it expedient to appoint postmasters in suitable towns between Edinburgh and Berwick, and grant them a standing fee for serving the packet day and night, according to that lovable custom observed in England for many years'.[4]

Regulations dated four days later settled postmasters at Cockburnspath, Haddington and the foot of the Canongate with fees for keeping horses for the service of the post by day and night.

The northern route was improved by providing additional paid postmasters, for in 1603 an extension to serve Tadcaster and York was introduced, with payments to their posts and in 1604 further wages are recorded for Catterick, Bowes, Brough and Penrith. Four years later Babraham and Thirlwall were added to the list. At the same time Haltwhistle was removed, bringing the total of posts being paid to thirty-five, increased by the addition of Newmarket, where James often stayed, in 1618.[5]

Despite the firm tone of the proclamations concerning the posts and the provision of horses, even the king was to have difficulty in obtaining them. The Salisbury manuscripts contain a letter of 2 April 1604 written at Royston by Sir Thomas Lake to Robert Cecil, the king's principal secretary:

> Yesternight his Majesty was resolved to have gone on and gave out Warrant for post horses. Wherein I cannot but note to your Lordship what disorder I find here, that there was no man about the King of authority to command horses to be ready or to give warrant for them, so as the King was fain to sign warrants with his own hand. And yet this morning the post brought in the warrants again and told me that no man would obey them, which is a strange contempt, and if the King had gone he could not well have done it for want of horses. Here is neither Councillor nor Postmaster nor his deputy nor the post of the Court, but only a boy. Whether this contempt grows for want of the ordinary officers, or of any other cause I know not, but I have concealed it from the King that his own warrants should be disobeyed in so vulgar a manner.[6]

Such problems continued throughout James's reign and that of his son Charles.

The integration of the Scottish posts with those in England continued.[7] In 1615 the Council in Scotland considered proposals put to it by Sir William Seton to establish post horses both for the transmission of urgent despatches and for the convenience of travellers. The following year he was appointed as master of the posts in Scotland. During 1617, when King James travelled to Scotland, extraordinary posts were laid along his route as was done for all royal progresses. The postman on each stage was granted 2s a day. For every royal progress during James's reign Stanhope received £50.

The English Privy Council was always concerned with the security of the posts and the reason is not difficult to understand. A change of sovereign and a return to Roman Catholicism, as had happened in the reign of Mary, would mean that members could lose their positions and possibly their lives. The Gunpowder Plot of 1605 attempted the destruction of Parliament and the overthrow of the monarchy, so leading to a general tightening of security with further regulations to control the carriage of the letters.

A proclamation was issued on 15 May 1609 forbidding any person to carry packets or letters to or from any city, or town, by foot or horseback, 'except only as shall be lawfully appointed for that service'.[8] It declared a state monopoly of the carriage of letters, though there is no evidence that this was imposed nationally or that it was applied to the carriers. The main intention was to ensure that the letters of all foreigners entered the official postal system. It was supplemented by orders within the county of Kent and to ensure that the proclamation and orders were obeyed they were widely distributed, including all mayors, searchers at the ports and justices of the peace.[9] The Council was concerned:

> to meet with the dangerous and secret intelligence of ill affected persons both at home and abroad, by the overgreat liberty taken both in writing and riding in post, specially in and through our County of Kent

and referred to:

> disorders offered by certain persons called hackneymen, tapsters, hostlers and others, in hiring out their horses to the hindrance of public service, danger to our state and wrong to our standing and settled Posts in their several stages.

It also provided for sanctions:

> But if it so fall out, that the obstinacy of any herein offending require further punishment than the ordinary power of the magistrate of the place can or may conveniently inflict, then we require our said Master and Comptroller of the Posts, upon notice thereof given to him, to send for the party or parties to answer their contempt before our Privy Council.

For reasons of security, careful watch was always kept on the movements of Lady Arabella Stuart, a possible claimant to the throne under Queen Elizabeth and James I. When she escaped from custody in 1611 her guardian, the Bishop of Durham, reported her arrival at Barnet to the Privy Council, stating that as the postmaster there refused to send an express he had used his own messenger.[10] The Earl of Dumfermline wrote to Cecil, secretary to the Privy Council, on 15 June thanking him for news of her capture.[11] He complained about the slowness of the packets which had taken six days when their journey should have been three or four.

Throughout the early seventeenth century those postmasters paid wages by the government often felt that they were unreasonably treated. The postal routes from London to Edinburgh and to Dover were the only ones open throughout every year of James' reign and use of the others was intermittent. When king of Scotland, James had never been at war with Spain so negotiations for a peace settlement began soon after his accession. The need for the posts on the western route was therefore reduced and in 1603 the services via Bristol, Barnstaple, Padstow and Milford were discharged as were those between Plymouth and Falmouth. When the posts on the western route as far as Padstow were closed down, Thomas Miles, who had succeeded Gascoigne as Court postmaster, wrote to the King's vice-chamberlain on 18 June 1604 about the plight of postmasters on the Western route and in particular the one who had supplied the packet boat at Padstow. It had been lost in the Irish wars and redress was needed not only for that but for the costs of seven voyages to Munster.[12]

Payments along the road to Padstow were resumed in 1608. An instruction of 21 March 1611 to the Exchequer closed the posts to Ireland and those to Plymouth together with its branches to Padstow and Portsmouth.[13] The Plymouth post was once again reinstated in October 1620, when relations with Spain had deteriorated, and for a third time in 1625 when a fleet was being assembled for the disastrous attack on Cadiz. In 1628 eight post stages were erected further west as far as Penryn. As three of the previous eight posts on the Portsmouth road were being paid in 1626 and 1627, an unrecorded reinstatement had taken place on that route. The chronic shortage of money that developed during James' reign had led to this summary treatment of the subsidised posts, but the routes were always in use for those who paid the rates asked by the postmasters.

Another temporary route was set up in September 1625 when the Earl of Warwick went to Landguard Point at Harwich to inspect the defences prepared against an attack by the Spanish force assembled at Dunkirk. The route ran from London but was soon disbanded when the decision was made to rely more on ships than land fortifications.[14]

That the postmasters could be treated with disdain by important men can be shown by two examples. In April 1612 the Daventry postmaster wrote to Lord Stanhope complaining that he had supplied two horses to a royal pursuivant, Lewis Harris, who had refused to pay for them and had been violent and abusive.[15]

Another incident arose at Dover. The requirement was that horses supplied to warrant holders were to be provided at a recognised post house and so, for example, those arriving at Rye, when it had no postmaster, would have to make their way to Dover. In 1626 Sir Walter Montague had landed almost a mile from the posthouse and ordered ten horses to be sent to him, which requirement had been refused. Montague asked the Council to reprimand the postmaster, who wrote to Conway, secretary of the Privy Council, reminding him that Sir Walter had disobeyed the orders that warrant holders should come to a posthouse.[16]

We can also sympathise with those posts who faced refusals to provide horses. The Waltham postmaster wrote to Conway in 1623 telling him that warrants had been refused by the high constable and that he needed help from the countryside around.[17] Stanhope wrote in 1624 to secretary Conway requesting that William Cole of Coleman Street and Thomas Derby of Finsbury, both hackneymen, should be imprisoned for refusing the posts' orders to provide horses, and later in the year he requested that men in Newcastle, including town officials and constables, who would not supply horses to the post, should be summoned.[18]

The posts often saw their monopoly of providing horses challenged. The Newmarket postmaster asked the Privy Council in 1622 to summon Frances Perkes and others to appear before them for denying his appointment 'by spitefully setting forth post horses, with horn and guide, contrary to his appointment as carrier of posts and packets'. Later, in 1632, the Canterbury postmaster complained that he needed to keep 'divers servants and 12 or 14 horses at any time' yet others were providing horses to strangers who entered the town.[19]

The cause of the inability to pay those posts who were subsidised did not lie with the master of the posts or with his deputy, the paymaster, for the government did not release the necessary money. Until 1615 payments to the posts had usually been regular but by 1617 difficulties had started and Thomas Hutchins, the postmaster of both Lichfield and Crewkerne, had taken the role of spokesman for most of the local postmasters. In State Papers he is referred to as their solicitor. That year he petitioned Lord Zouche of the Privy Council on behalf of the postmasters for payment of eighteen months' wages, stating that Lord Stanhope had promised the money at Easter.[20] The following year Hutchins sent yet another petition for payment of three years of arrears.[21] There is a Privy Council note that the king had decided to pay them out of customs revenue and this was done, though after some delay.

About this time Stanhope proposed radical changes in the postal service. A draft of 'Orders for a Letter Office for missives within the Land' is preserved in a series of State Papers that are gathered together and listed as being between 1620 and 1622.[22] Another hand has dated them as 1620. Many of its features were to be incorporated in a proposition dated 1634 and the proclamation of 1635 that opened the posts to the public. The figure of £4,125 given in the draft Orders as the annual cost of the posts is closer to costs around 1620 than to the figure of £3,400 mentioned in Privy Council minutes of 1628 or in the proposition of June 1635, and so supports a date of around 1620.

We know that Stanhope wanted to extend the postal system. During 1618 he ordered the justices of the peace in Southwark to aid the postmaster with deliveries within a six-mile radius[23] and in 1620 another local order has survived published by the earl of Bath, lord lieutenant of Devon, covering the county which required 'two or three fit men be appointed in every parish by the Constables to be footposts for conveyance of letters upon all occasions', thus considerably extending the reach of the post roads in that part of the country.[24] Stanhope's long experience as Master of the Posts and the continuous series of complaints he had received must have taught him that some dependable means of financing the postal service was essential. The draft begins with a preamble:

> Now both his Majesty's affairs of Government and Justice, and all Intercourse and trade of his subjects, either by express messengers at an excessive charge: or by footposts, and pack carriers, with so little speed, that addresses and returns may be made by packets from Italy or Spain in shorter time than from the remoter parts of his Majesty's Dominions. His Majesty out of his Royal Wisdom and care for the good of his Subjects (without restraining any man from means he liketh best), is graciously pleased to allow them the favour of sending despatches by his ordinary posts and letter boats [the later copy in State Papers Domestic explains that this means carriers] with far greater expedition and without increase of charges in the manner here set down.

It was proposed that there would be six principal roads with branches and a service linking them from every market town:

> and for every market town a footpost must be hired either by the magistrate of the town, or by the post master or letter boate carrier next adjoining in the said Road to perform the service.

The existing postmasters could be retained and they would receive letters from adjacent places together with the postage due upon them. Letters would be forwarded to London where they would be sorted for despatch. Payment for the posts was to be at the rate of 3d a mile and would be rendered quarterly. Express letters for the state were to be sent without waiting for the regular despatches of letters. Ordinary mail would be charged 2d for up to 80 miles, 4d for 150 miles and others 'within the borders' 6d. Those to Edinburgh or Leith would be 8d. Letters across the main roads would be charged at similar rates. The draft ends:

> By the establishment and performance of this proposition his Majesty's ordinary charge of Postmaster amounting to £4125 may be quite taken away and his charge of messengers from the Council table, for sending Proclamations, letters for musters or other public service; or from other Courts or Officers which may employ these posts and boats, may cease or at least be lessened by one half.

These Orders proposed opening the posts to the public, extending the service to all market towns, providing a system of recording all letters and the costs involved, so funding the service by fixed charges. If we can accept the date of 1620, then it was the first Lord Stanhope who laid the foundation of the present postal service which is based upon these principles.

In March 1621 Stanhope died, aged seventy-six. He had been in charge of the posts since 1590 and was a man of influence at the Court. Previously a member of the Council of the North, he had become treasurer of the chamber in 1596 and was vice-chamberlain at James's Court. No doubt those positions had helped in obtaining the funds he needed. However, the post of treasurer of the chamber passed to Sir Walter Uvedale in 1615 and Stanhope's previous authority must have begun to wane, partly explaining the difficulties in funding the service that began then. His son Charles, who succeeded him in 1621, lacked his father's prestige and during his tenure there developed a time of near chaos in the service, though not of his making. By 1621 the king was nearly £1 million in debt. The plans for Prince Charles to marry the Spanish infanta and acquire a large dowry had collapsed. Money was wanted to support an expedition to help the Dutch and then for an expedition against Cadiz.

The need for information about affairs on the Continent became more urgent, so the postal routes were expanded but without money being found to pay for them. Since 1590 wages had been paid to the postmasters more or less regularly and, with some delays, to about 1619, yet between 1621 to 1632 there was only one payment. The proposed Orders were not put into practice although in one respect they seem to have been carried out, for the posts began taking private letters quite freely as shown in the 1628 summary discussed below. No doubt they accepted any business that came their way.

Their plight had caused Hutchins to return in 1622 with a further petition which complained of the fees charged to the posts by the paymasters who

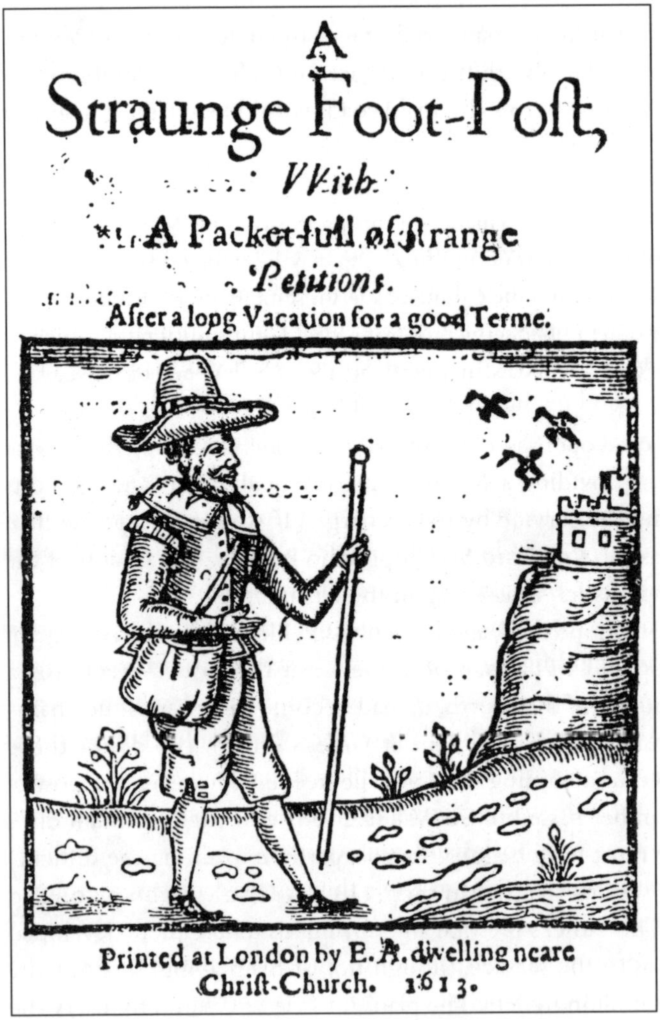
A
Straunge Foot-Poſt,
VVith
A Packet-full of ſtrange
Petitions.
Aſter a long Vacation for a good Terme.
Printed at London by E.A. dwelling neare
Chriſt-Church. 1613.

12.2 The Dover footpost in 1613. (By courtesy of the Post Office)

acted for the master of the posts. The Privy Council took it seriously enough to refer it to the comptroller of the King's Household, the master of the rolls and the chancellor of the Exchequer, or any two of them, who constituted a separate board of the Council.[25]

A report of January 1623 considered the charges put on the posts and concluded that the charge of 2s in the pound for poundage should be reduced by half while the charge of 40s for their Orders, the copies of postal regulations, should continue, as should the usual levy of 2s 6d a quarter. The master of the posts was to receive his customary 1s in the pound on wages and the paymaster was to be contented with his 5s a day.[26] On balance, the postmasters had made gains.

In May Hutchins was put into the Marshalsea prison for submitting yet another petition. The Council received from him an apology and plea for release:

> whereupon they have been pleased and accordingly ordered to release the said Hutchins of his imprisonment with this caution and admonition – that if he shall presume either to trouble His Majesty or this Board with any more Petitions about this business, he is to stand committed Ipso Facto without any further order from this Table.

During the same year the Privy Council twice considered charges against Hutchins and others who, it was said, were living away from their stages, while employing inefficient deputies, and were seeking exemption from control by the paymasters. Having gained remission of some fees, it was maintained they had become insolent and negligent. Later in December that year the Council heard further complaints from the paymasters who claimed that as a result of the reduction of their fees they were unable to perform the king's service.[27]

Stanhope meanwhile had put another man into Hutchins' position as postmaster of Crewkerne, which he held in addition to Lichfield, but when Hutchins petitioned the Council they ordered his reinstatement.

The following January the Council was again petitioned by the paymasters on various grounds including the need for the restoration of their fees and complaints of the lucrative positions being given to the posts, who often paid their deputies only a quarter of their allowances. No doubt their case was valid in some places, for in 1619 it had been alleged that Paul Axhall, postmaster of Bishopsgate Without, was receiving contributions from the innkeepers to avoid them providing post horses and consequently sent warrants for horses as far as Southwark, which lost John King, the postmaster there, as much as £200. Some postmasterships were profitable appointments.[28]

Grievances concerning lack of pay continued to be made to the Privy Council. One, undated but probably of 1623, declared the postmasters had been unpaid for two and a half years. The postmasters of Andover and Salisbury wrote in 1626 to the duke of Buckingham, King James's favourite, telling him that, as they had had no pay for six years, they were so indebted that 'they dare not show their heads'. They said that despite attending on the treasurer for a month they could not obtain a penny.[29]

In April in the same year Sir Henry Palmer wrote to Buckingham to report that no postmaster could be found at Portsmouth and that the mayor had told him that unless posts were paid at the stages he could not help.[30] The Council recommended a postmaster and in June they laid posts to Portsmouth when the fleet was there.[31]

The Council needed all the money it could find for the war against Spain and then for the outbreak of hostilities with France that started in 1627. Apart from the Dover route, which was always supported, the other posts to the

Channel ports were only reinstated in times of crisis. When those between Plymouth and Falmouth were erected in December 1625, the five posts were supposed to be paid 2s or 2s 6d daily. Posts to Southampton were laid in October 1627 and a warrant 'To all postmasters, constables, heads of boroughs and all others to whom it may concern' dated 30 May 1628 begins:

> Whereas there is daily occasion in these dangerous times to send packets by post from here to Plymouth, Portsmouth and other places for the King's service which will not admit of delay; these are in the King's name to will them to take special care that all packets as come signed by Sir Allen Apseley, surveyor general for the victualling of the King's navy & Fleet, to any of his Deputies, or back from them to him, may be speedily carried.[32]

Despite the increased demands put upon them, most posts remained unpaid. The royal secretary Conway had written to the lord treasurer on 22 August 1627 saying that the posts could not perform their service to the king because they were years in arrears. To make his point he sent the postmaster of Hartford Bridge, who was six or seven years without pay and had been obliged to sell his cattle and other goods, with the request that he should receive a year's pay.[33] The grievances led to a collective petition in June 1628 from all the postmasters on England 'being in number 99 poore men':

> Divers of them lie in prison, and many are daily threatened to be arrested for their great debts which they are in for want of their entertainment being unpaid even since November 1621, which now ariseth at £22,626 19s 3d. They pray for present supply and a certain course of payment hereafter.[34]

The posts were not paid, for in 1630 £25,525 10s 2d was due to them. In that year £4,737 1s 8d was made available but it was obviously quite insufficient. Examination of the accounts during this period shows that a few payments were made to selected postmasters who may have had influence at court. The London postmaster, Thomas Clerke, petitioned Lord Treasurer Weston in 1631:

> The Lord Treasurer having heretofore given order for such a proportion of the petitioner's wages as has kept him from starving, prays for such a payment in this hard time as will enable him to satisfy his creditors.[35]

Another solution to the crisis had been mooted in 1628 when the Council considered a summary of the stages of the posts payable by government on the roads to Berwick, Plymouth, Holyhead and Southampton; instructions were given by the Council to the Treasurer and Chancellor of the Exchequer to pay them 'from tyme to tyme'. Their minutes contain a description of the postal service that deserves printing in full. It is written in two hands, which may explain the difference in rates recommended for the posts:

> Not only the Secretaries make dispatches in the King's name but all the Lords of the Council & in effect every Lord and man of note subscribe the letters as being for his Majesty's service. And the Lord Stanhope sends pacquets every way & for all men as for the King's affairs. And all their letters they send in the King's name and entered in the postmaster's book and so the posts are oppressed & forced in the king's name to carry all men's letters, whereby they well deserve their daily allowance.
>
> The posts will be glad to quit all their daily wages so as they may receive certainly for all packets they really carry ijd of a mile.
>
> You may please to take notice. That till the 15th of September 1625 there was paid to all the posts of the Roads of England but £3404 3s 4d per annum. Then by occasion of wars with France and other Countries, there were new Stages settled the several fees whereof does amount to £720 17s 0½d annum which was so settled by the Lords of Council. With provision in the said Order to be continued till their Lordships should give further order therein. And for the same hath continued till this present time to the great prejudice of his Majesty not now useful.
>
> Whereas the £3,404 3s 4d anciently having been paid to several Posts upon the Roads to some ijs per diem to others ijs vjd, xxd and xijd per diem for which the said several Posts have from time to time freely carried his Majesty's packets being for his own services. Under colour wherof the poor men have been oppressed by carrying without pay several packets directed for his Majesty's special services by the Lord Stanhope and others. Which said packets in number have been at the least 3 or 4 a week in all Roads. For which they have been paid but 2½d a mile in the whole would have amounted to near as much as the whole fee from his Majesty's amounts unto which hath almost undone all his Majesty's poor Posts of the several Roads. The particular packets will appear in their books.
>
> Now it is conceived. That all the said Posts will rather be contented with half the Fee formerly paid them, and will be paid 2½d a mile for all his Majesty's packets and others as they shall hereafter carry. Provided always that the said Posts may receive their moneys certainly once in three Months without charges in the Exchequer or otherwise.[36]

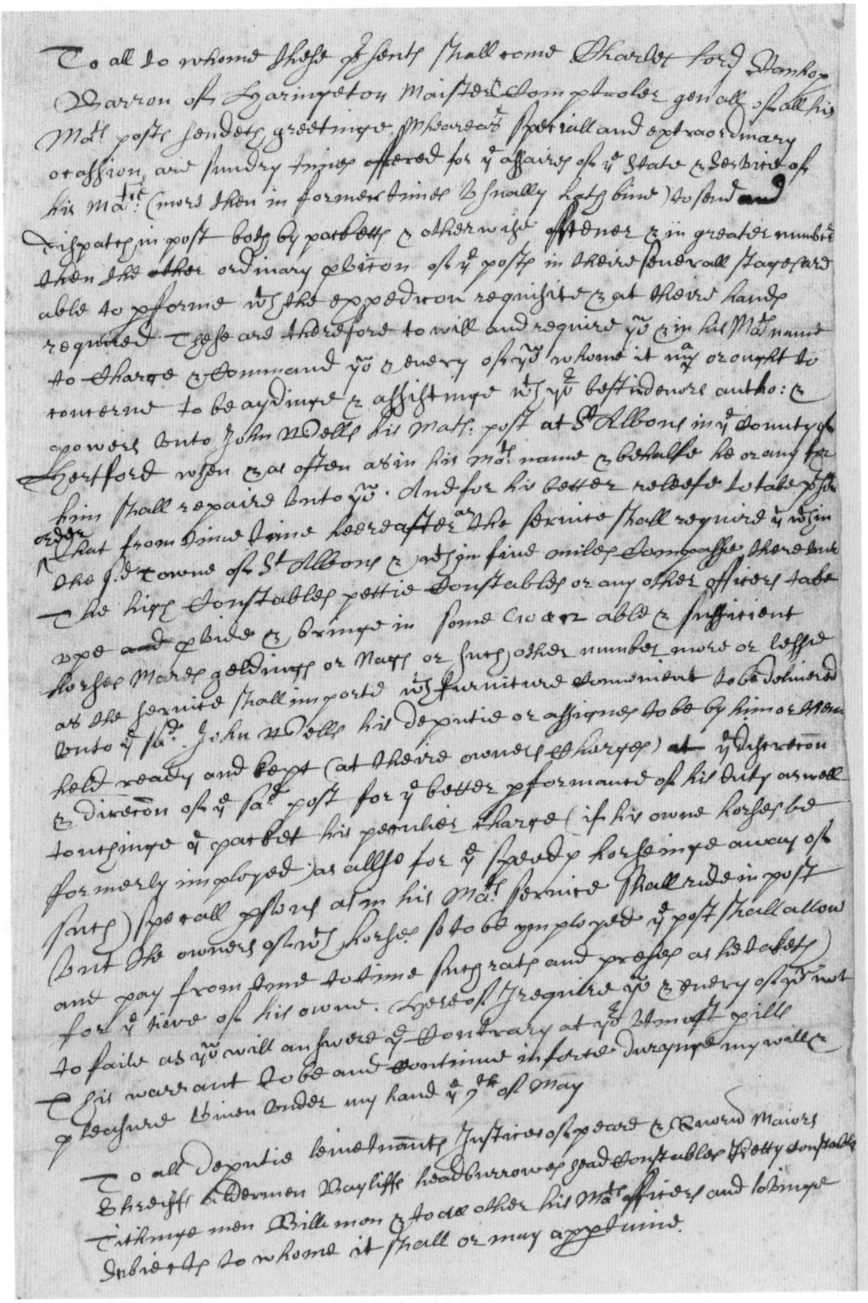
To all to whome theise p[re]sents shall come Charles Lord Stanhop
Barron of Harington Maister Comptroler gen[er]all of all his
Mats posts sendeth greetinge. Whereas the spetiall and extraordinary
occasion, are sundry times offered for the affaires of the State & service of
his Matie (more then in former times) to finally hath bine) to send and
dispatch in post both by packetts & otherwise ofttener & in greater numbre
then the other ordinary Station of the posts in theire severall stages are
able to p[er]forme wth the expedition requisite & at theire hands
required. These are therefore to will and require you & in his Mats name
to charge & command you & every of you whome it may or ought to
concerne to be ayding & assistinge wth yor best endevors autho: &
powers unto John Wells his Mats: post at St Albons in the County of
Hertford when & as often as in his Mas name & behalfe he or any for
him shall repaire unto you. And for his better releefe to take order
That from time to time hereafter as the service shall require & wthin
the s[ai]d towne of St Albons & wthin five miles compasse thereunto
the high Constables pettie Constables or any other officers take
upp and provide & bringe in some ten or twelve able & sufficient
horses Mares geldings or Naggs or such other number more or lesse
as the service shall importe wth furniture convenient to be delivered
unto the s[ai]d John Wells his deputie or assignes to be by him or them
held ready and kept (at theire owners charges) at the discretion
& direction of the said post for the better p[er]formance of his duty as well
touchinge the packet his peculiar charge (if his owne horses be
formerly imployed) as allso for the speedy horsinge away of
such) speciall officers as in his Mas service shall ride in post
But the owners of wch horses so to be employed the post shall allow
and pay from time to time such rates and prices as he taketh)
for the hire of his owne. Hereof I require you & every of you not
to faile as you will answere the Contrary at yor utmost perills
This warrant to be and continue in force during my will &
pleasure Given under my hand the 7th of May
To all deputie Lieutenants Justices of peace & severall Maiors
Sheriffs Aldermen Bayliffs headborrowes head Constables petty Constables
Tithinge men Bille men & to all other his Mas officers and lovinge
Subiects to whome it shall or may apperteine.

12.3 Lord Stanhope's orders to St Albans. The second Lord Stanhope, master of the posts, sends orders to the postmaster at St Albans in May 1633. All sheriffs, deputy lieutenants, mayors and other officials are required to supply ten to twelve horses and equipment as requested by the postmaster for those riding in his Majesty's service. (Private collection)

Privy Council minutes give a calculation of the amount owing to the posts to the end of 1625 as being £12,204 12s 6d plus an addition of £16,332 13s 1d to the end of September 1630. Stanhope received £3,001 leaving arrears of about £25,525. The post at Daventry was then asking for nearly £900, which represented six years of arrears. In 1630 Hutchins saw the newly appointed secretary Coke about the posts' arrears of wages. The next we hear of Hutchins is of him again petitioning the Privy Council in 1631 from Marshalsea prison where he was held on the indictment of Ranulph Church, the paymaster of the posts.[37] To the credit of the Council it ordered his release. Two years later he died, a tenacious individual whose death deprived the posts of their spokesman.

During 1630 and 1631 the Privy Council attempted to resolve the long-standing differences between the paymaster and the posts concerning fees. A minute of 2 March 1631 summarised these as follows:

> Until May 1620 the Master of the Posts and the Paymaster had each taken 12d per pound from the posts and 2s 6d on every acquittance. Subsequently the 12d was reduced to 6d and the acquittance reduced to 12d. However, the 12d was reinstated in 1625. The Paymaster had received no pay for the five years he had been in office but had nevertheless been required to pay the Exchequer and Auditor's fees. Now the posts strive to get their own monies upon their own acquittances because in that way they can receive more than is due to them.[38]

A later minute approved the 6d in the pound for Lord Stanhope and the deduction of 12d in the pound for each acquittance, together with 5s a day being the daily allowance paid to the paymaster. The years from 1632 to 1637 saw a small improvement in the payment of arrears to the posts. A total of £11,227 2s was released but this was still quite inadequate to make up the backlog.

In 1631 Secretary Coke had issued regulations 'for the transmission of portmantles along the principal roads of England':

> Two portmantles to go upon one horse to Uxbridge, and so from stage to stage to Oxford, the other of which goes to Gloucester and so to Bristol, the other to go to Worcester, Shrewsbury and so to the marches of Wales. One portmantle to go to Epping, Saffron Walden, Newmarket, Bury, Norwich and so to Yarmouth.
>
> Two portmantles for Westchester [Chester] to go to Stony Stratford to be carried upon one horse from stage to stage, the one to go northwards to Westchester and Ireland. The other to go to Northampton, Leicester, Nottingham, Manchester and so to Lancaster.[39]

This is probably the first official service not provided for military or diplomatic needs.

Among the problems facing the posts was an unusual situation that arose at Farnham in 1631, when two men riding on post horses had them seized. The Privy Council ordered an investigation and subsequently a Royal Chamber messenger was sent to arrest the main offender.[40]

In the same year they considered an incident in Grantham where the deputy postmaster had seized a horse and was then charged with felony. Another case referred to them in 1632 was presented against the St Albans postmaster who, it was maintained, had seized post horses on several occasions and then sought a bribe for their release.[41]

While the financial controversies were taking place a most important development had happened along the road to Plymouth. Agents for the London merchants brought news to them of ships from the Mediterranean, Spain, Africa and the far East which had made their first call at Plymouth. As early as 1626 a London trader, Samuel Jude, had offered a postal service to the commissioner of the Navy, the farmers of the customs, the East India Company and other merchants. For this he had gained a warrant of approval from the Borough of Plymouth. It was the first privately organised challenge to the posts who carried the packets along the post roads. The postmasters along the road to London responded to Jude's service by speeding up their own and extending it to places within 20 miles of each side of the road. An order in Council authorised them to carry all private letters 'upon the road and twenty miles out of the road if need shall require'.[42] A letter from the Privy Council to the Lord Mayor of London, the mayors of Salisbury, Exeter and Plymouth dated March 1629 describes the proposals:

> Whereas His Majesty's posts of the Western stage from London to Plymouth have propounded unto us that for the better despatch of His Majesty's service and the common good of all others, they would undertake the speedy despatch of all private letters weekly between London and Plymouth and from Plymouth to London besides the faithful delivery of all letters and despatch of other business on the road and twenty miles out of the road if need shall require, for single post pay for 2½d the mile without further charge except 4d to the guide for the return of the horse, which course for the reasons aforesaid we do very well approve. And therefore for their better encouragement and cheerful proceedings in the execution of this said undertaking we do heartily entreat the addressees not only to permit the posts and their agents to address themselves to the execution of this service, but to be assisting them as occasion shall require.[43]

The Privy Council approved the private carriage of the public's letters along with those from the king.

In 1630 the posts complained to the Privy Council that Jude had tried to obtain the letters of all the merchants using the route and had even arranged for their handbills to be pulled down. The Council ruled that Jude could carry packets for the merchants who employed him but that he was not to restrict the service operated by the posts in any way. This is still the case in English law as, despite the Post Office's monopoly, messengers may carry letters for their employers.[44]

The posts had responded by providing a service similar in many respects to that set out in the draft Orders of 1620. The challenge of Jude's competition had shown that a self-financing postal service, carrying both private and official letters, could be organised along an important route serving those who lived within 20 miles on either side of it.

The mayor and aldermen of Barnstaple were so convinced of the effectiveness of this service that in September 1633 they arranged that a footpost should be paid to take mail every Tuesday morning to Exeter to reach the postmaster's house there on Wednesday morning so that letters could be forwarded to London. The charge was 6d a single letter and 8d for a double. It was calculated that thereby those living in north Devon could write a letter to London and receive a reply within eleven days. The footpost would wait for the letters that came from London and pay for them. A footnote to the document that describes this arrangement gives a charge of 2d for a letter from Barnstaple to Exeter.[45]

Another efficient postal route not subsidised by the state was that operating in East Anglia by the energetic work of a carrier of Ipswich, Jason Grover. Unlike other carriers he became a postmaster. During the 1620s he became postmaster of Ipswich and other East Anglian towns and in 1631 the Corporation of Yarmouth asked him to become their postmaster and to extend the twice-weekly service that was running to London to their town. For this he was paid £1 a quarter.[46]

Although the London to Plymouth route, the East Anglia route and that to Dover were operating effectively, the other routes were not so. Even so important a man as Sir Francis Windebank, one of the two royal secretaries, was obliged to send a letter to Sir John Coke, the other secretary, along the northern route by a private messenger. Writing to Coke, who was in Edinburgh with the king, on 9 July 1633, he says:

> I send these letters by Davis again because of the slowness of the posts some of your letters being ten days upon the way, and never any packet dated at the stages as they ought to be.

The crisis in the inland postal service was mirrored by that which went abroad, so we need to examine the foreign service and the national demand for improved services before we see what solution was found in 1635.

The foreign post

Since the loss of Calais the royal post had never included an organised service to the Continent beyond Dover or Rye. Messengers took the Council's letters at considerable cost, as can be shown by these varied examples. A warrant of 22 May 1609 authorised payment of £300 each to John Barclay and Robert Ayton for expenses on their journeys 'to divers foreign countries'.[48] In 1623 the cost of carrying a royal letter from Spain was given as £15 4s 9½d and in 1624 Robert Wood was paid £60 for carrying six cormorants as a gift to the King of Poland.[49] A statement of costs submitted by Matthew de Quester in 1626 shows express letter costs to the Hague as £7, to Brussels or Paris £10 and to Vienna £60.[50] He was to demonstrate that, if private letters could be included with those from the state and passed from stage to stage, then royal mail could be taken at a fraction of these charges.

Mathew de Quester, a naturalised London merchant, had obtained a grant as one of the king's couriers in 1604. He and his son were employed by Stanhope as messengers and the father seems to have supervised the official mail sent abroad, submitting quarterly accounts. He petitioned the king that the inland and foreign post be separated and on 30 April 1616 James granted to him and his son by Letters Patent the office of 'Postmaster General for Foreign parts out of the King's Dominions'. No copy survives of the appointment but it is referred to in proclamations of 1623 and 1632.[51] That De Quester had been carrying private letters before 1619 is shown by one in the Holles' correspondence. John wrote to his son in Paris in April 1616:

> I wrote to you the last week by Jones, and enclosed in mine a letter from my Lord Burley, this Questor has in his care, who is a dear deliverer of letters for he made me pay 3s for the last packet he brought me, a strange extraction for no further than Paris. Henceforth I will acquaint myself with Burlomachi, that you may receive your money from his respondent whom you commend, and besides will serve for all other places, where you shall have cause to travel.

He wrote again at the end of the month to say that he had forwarded money by de Quester but that henceforth he would be using Burlomachi, another London merchant.[52]

In 1622 a new postal service from London had begun when the Thurn and Taxis posts, which covered much of Europe, appointed Pierre Ronson as their courier between Antwerp and London.[53] It appears that this arrangement was later withdrawn as the negotiations of 1633, to which I refer later, describe the reinstatement of their posts to London. Merchants made their own arrangements for their Continental mail and at this time Edward Quarles was postmaster to the Merchant Adventurers of London. De Quester's appointment was unpopular among them and Lord Stanhope challenged it by claiming that his own position included the foreign posts. Patents granted to the masters of the posts had included the words 'beyond the seas within the King's dominions', the issue being whether these words had been restricted to Calais. It was claimed that de Quester had 'treacherously obtained a patent for foreign parts on the false suggestion that there was no such office granted'. The Council took advice from the Attorney General and others on the legal position, which led to a proclamation of 19 December 1623 affirming de Quester's position and that of his son.[54]

By then Stanhope had begun a case against de Quester in King's Bench which eventually found in his favour in some respects but not in others.[55] Pending these decisions, the London merchants had been allowed to appoint Henry Billingsby to organise their posts following the death of Edward Quarles. Billingsby then published a notice that he had set a place for receiving letters:

> behind the Exchange, at one Widow Bayneham's, at the side of the George, a little beyond the Antwerp Tavern, at the other side of the way and that on the Saturday next, after midnight, he purposed to send away a post for Flushing, Holland and the Hanse towns and so every Saturday and thereafter, if God spared life and health, to other places.

The Council saw this as a direct challenge to de Quester's patent and summoned those concerned to appear before them, but their decision was that the Merchant Adventurers and other companies of merchants might convey their own letters and despatches to foreign parts.[56]

In 1627 Billingsby further extended his influence by obtaining an appointment from the governors of the Turkey Company and of the East India Company to convey their letters.[57] De Quester rightly reckoned this action was in contravention of his own authority and to the proclamation of 1609 which had declared the royal monopoly of the posts. Billingsby was arrested in March 1627 for having taken the title of public postmaster without authorisation and later that year the two secretaries of the Privy Council wrote to the Merchant Adventurers affirming that Billingsby had disobeyed their orders, warning them that they must not employ any other person who would not conform to their instructions. Coke expressed his opinion in a letter to Conway:

> I confess it troubles me to see the audacity of men in these times, & that Billingsby, a broker by trade, should dare to attempt thus often to question the King's service, and to derive that power of foreign letters unto merchants which in all States is a branch of regal authority: neither can any place in Christendom be named where merchants are allowed to send their letters by other body or posts than those only which are authorised by the state.[58]

An order of Council dated 24 October 1627 revoked the permission given earlier to all companies of merchants to send foreign letters by their messengers.[59] All companies except the Merchant Adventurers were to send their letters by de Quester. On 20 January 1628 even they were told to use only de Quester's service. A petition by Billingsby to the Privy Council secretary, Dorchester, begged that he should allow him to serve Stanhope, to whom belonged the right to send letters overseas, but this was to no avail.

De Quester retired in 1632 after the death of his son, having shown that a foreign service carrying both private and official letters could operate at a profit. His charges had shown considerable savings. Those presented in February 1628 listed twenty-eight despatches to ambassadors at 30s each and thirty-three others at 6s each.[60]

The costs were far cheaper than those incurred by express messengers and so it is obvious why the Council had been supporting him. He assigned his position to William Frizell and Thomas Witherings, both of whom had worked for him as couriers, and this was confirmed by a patent dated March 1632 and by a proclamation of 19 July.[61] Witherings had connections with the Court, having been harbinger to Queen Henrietta, a position that had involved finding accommodation for her when travelling. He came from Staffordshire and was a minor landowner, married to a wealthy woman.

A financial statement of that year shows that de Quester's staff included three couriers to France, six for the Netherlands, Germany and Italy, with four extraordinary posts for Paris and France.[62] After his retirement he submitted a final account for his last seventeen weeks which provides some interesting details concerning the office staff. He charges for three portmantles £1 12s, cord and cloth to cover the mails 2s 6d, packthread to bind them 9s 5d, pens ink and paper £1 1s. George Martin and George Ridge are each due pay for seventeen weeks of £2 11s. Two clerks who were paid at £60 a year needed

£39 4s 8d. Rent for the office and rooms was £10 and costs outstanding for candles, wax and thread were £5 4s.[63]

In 1632, Coke had written to Burlomachi, who was then a prominent London merchant stranger born in Sedan in France and naturalised by Act of Parliament, asking for his views on the posts in Germany, Holland and Belgium. He replied to Coke's secretary, who provided a summary:

> He imputed the fault merely to the posts who have heretofore bought their places. They more minding their own peddling traffic than the service of the State or the merchants. There was no regularity. Sometimes they stayed for the sending of their own commodities, many times by lying in tippling houses.[64]

Burlomachi supported the appointment of Witherings and Frizzel as de Quester's successors. Meanwhile Witherings had been busy on the continent and wrote to Coke in April 1633:

> I have found here, the Countess Taxis' secretary with the Postmaster of Ghent. They having settled Stages between Antwerp and Calais for the speedy conveyance of letters; they have placed a Postmaster at Dunkirk, having dismissed all their couriers. And seven days hence they intend to begin by way of Staphetto [Estafette] from Antwerp to London; their request is that we shall do the like. Which accordingly I have ordered my man to do.[65]

While at Dover he had arranged for a man to take the packet across the Channel whenever it arrived and to take nothing besides. Coke gave his approval and so the through messenger was replaced by the transfer of the packet from one stage to another. In January 1633 'Orders for the Foreign Postmasters and Foreign Posts', over eight pages in length, were issued:

> In consequence of complaints, it is thought fit to send no more letters by carriers who come and go at pleasure, but, in conformity with other nations, to erect staffette or packet posts at fit stages, to run day and night without ceasing. [...] The foreign postmaster to have an Office in London and to give notice at what time the public are to bring their letters. A register to be kept of the writers and bringers of all letters and the parties to whom they are sent. The letters to be put into a packet or budget, which is to be locked up and sealed with the postmaster's known seal. [...] Letters to Government or foreign ministers to be immediately delivered to them.[66]

These arrangements involved the dismissal of the former six couriers to the Low Countries, men who had purchased their positions, but there is no indication that they received any recompense.

On Witherings' return he was accused by Frizzell of trying to oust him from the joint control of the posts and the dispute went to the Privy Council, where Coke strongly supported Witherings. For a period King Charles restored de Quester to the office but this caused further confusion for Robert Kirkham claimed that King James had promised him the office after de Quester. John Hatt, an attorney, managed the foreign posts from September 1633 until the end of December as de Quester's deputy. Burlomachi wrote to Coke to tell him of the deterioration of the service and of an attempt to set up a private courier service to Paris. Witherings showed that the post who travelled to Rouen was smuggling gold and silver and, no doubt, these criticisms helped him to be confirmed as foreign postmaster.[67]

To achieve this he made cash payments to Frizzell and effectively mortgaged the profits of his position to the earl of Arundel. The role of the king in these disputes was equivocal because it was known that courtiers had been promised the patents of de Quester and Stanhope on their deaths. The conclusion of the long dispute was a clear separation between the inland and the foreign posts.

The mail to Paris usually went via Dunkirk but it was frequently interrupted by fights at sea between French and English seamen and on occasions it was lost. Witherings travelled several times to Paris to meet Denoveau, the French king's postmaster, and eventually a postal treaty was negotiated, the first in our national history. It was agreed that all post would go by Dover, Calais, Boulogne, Abbeville and Amiens and that no carriers except those authorised by Witherings and Denoveau could take letters between the two countries. A proclamation to this effect was issued in England on 11 February 1638, this part of the preamble giving its main justification:

> And his Majesty likewise in pursuance of the said Agreement and taking into his Princely consideration how much it imports the State, and the whole Realm, that the secrets therof be not disclosed to foreign Nations, which cannot be prevented, if a promiscuous use of transmitting or taking up of foreign Letters, by these private Posts and Carriers aforesaid, should be suffered, which will also be no small prejudice to His Merchants in their tradings. [... Therefore] His Majesty does hereby prohibit all the said messengers and French posts and all other posts and letter carriers whatsoever [...] except such as shall be appointed by the said Thomas Witherings.[68]

The demand for an improved service

Pressure to improve the postal service throughout the country came not just from the Council but from merchants and the public. The early seventeenth century was a time of steady population growth and of the rapid development of London's trade. London increased its population from about 250,000 in the early seventeenth century to 400,000 in 1650, leading to a great demand for foodstuffs, which were mainly carried by land transport.[69] Chartres' estimate is that the road transport industry grew three- or fourfold between 1500 and 1700.[70] A letter from Prestwick Eaton in 1633 shows that the London postmaster was using waggons to deliver the mail as the correspondent 'wishes letters to be sent by the wain of the postmaster of London'.[71]

Grants for new fairs during the sixteenth and seventeenth century reversed the decline in the number of fairs since the Black Death and the increased population meant that their transport needs grew. More trade involved more letters, documents and parcels.

One way of estimating the demand for the efficient carriage of letters was to calculate the number of letters required to pay the posts' wages. This was the basis of the decision made in 1635 to extend the royal posts to the public. If an annual cost to the Crown of £3,400 for the posts was to be met by a average charge of 3d a letter, it would require 272,000 letters to pay the costs. Should the service be extended to all market towns plus various cross posts and the new posts be paid, then a far larger total would be needed. This would not, of course, be a total of all letters carried, for it excluded those taken by carriers, by private messengers and from the state whose mail would be taken without charge.

The growth of the postal service and the population was not matched by any improvement in communications. The man on horseback could travel as quickly as in former times but carts and waggons probably went more slowly than in the previous century. Increased use of the roads by large waggons was harming them. The proclamations of 1618, 1622 and 1630 had endeavoured to forbid vehicles with iron-shod wheels and protruding bolts by limiting their loads to one ton without much effect. Putting a heavy load onto two wheels rather than four only further damaged the road surface. The attempts to prevent common carriers using any wain or cart having above two wheels or carrying more than 20cwt, or restricting the number of horses pulling a waggon had been ineffective. They provoked protests such as that from the justices of the peace in Surrey who sent a petition observing that such restraint would 'be greatly detrimental in fetching chalk from the downs'.

That the roads and bridges saw little if any overall betterment until after the Restoration was admitted in the preamble to the Act of 1662:

> Whereas the former Laws and Statutes for the mending and repairing of the Common and Public Highways of the Realm have not been found so effective as is desired by means whereof and the extraordinary burdens carried upon Waggons and other Carriages divers of the said Highways are become very dangerous and almost impassable.[72]

Legislation had failed to reverse the gradual worsening of the road surfaces since the fifteenth century.

A national postal service

By the year 1635 circumstances were ready for change. Sir John Coke as the king's principal secretary was keenly interested in the posts and he had an able servant in Thomas Witherings. Any reform needed direction at the level of the Privy Council and men with the drive to implement changes. We have seen that during Elizabeth's reign it had been demonstrated that letters could be sent throughout the land from stage to stage providing the posts were adequately and regularly paid, but it was not until Jude's service on the London to Plymouth road that it was shown that the post could be self-financing if it carried both royal and private letters. Witherings had then applied the same principle to mail sent to the Continent.

We have also seen that plans for a national service had been drawn up fifteen years previously, under which the posts would be opened to the public, and a copy of the same draft document exists in Coke's handwriting with various amendments. It is also undated but it is filed in State Papers among documents of 1635.[73] That year in June Witherings submitted to Coke a 'Proposition for settling a staffeto or packet post betwixt London and all parts of His Majesty's dominions for carrying and recarrying his subject's letters'.[74] He proposed an office in London from which portmanteaux would be sent out along the roads. They would hold sealed bags for each of the postmasters who could take out their own bags and add the ones they had prepared. Footposts would take letters from the post towns and they would charge 2d for a single letter, then the usual rate paid to a carrier. The post would go by day and night covering 120 miles in 24 hours. Mail brought along one road to London and addressed to a town on another road would be transferred at the London Office. A footpost would go to market towns within 6 to 10 miles from the post towns and a riding post to towns such as Hull far off the roads. He anticipated that the present charge to the Crown of £3,400 would be entirely covered by profits from private mail. Witherings was farsighted enough to argue that this 'will be a great furtherance to the Correspondence between London and Scotland and London and Ireland

and great help to Trade'. His estimate that the posts would travel 120 miles each twenty-four hours was to prove to be unrealistic.

Coke approved the proposals and on 31 July 1635 a royal proclamation was issued 'For settling of the letter Office of England and Scotland'.[75] (Figs 12.4) It gave postage rates of 2d per single letter for journeys of under 80 miles, of 4d for 80 to 140 miles and of 6d for journeys above that. Letters to or from Scotland were 8d. The same payments were to be applied to the road to Ireland. Routes to Bristol and Norwich were to be settled. An exception to the charges applied to the Plymouth road where Witherings was ordered 'to take the like as is now paid as neere as possible he can'. When a bundle of letters was handed in the charge would be according to its size. Witherings was to have a monopoly of the carriage of letters with the exception of those taken by the common carriers and those by friends or private servants. His men would pay the posts 2½d a mile for the use of a horse and if they used two horses they would pay 5d for a guide. The postmasters were not to hire out their horses on the days on which the post was expected.

The idea of providing bye posts connecting post offices on the main routes with other places had originated in the previous century when, as we have seen, certain postmasters paid extra for delivering letters to places some miles away, but these had been exceptional arrangements. Barnstaple had set up such a service to Exeter, 40 miles distant, timing the arrival of their footpost to meet a weekly delivery from London.[76] Witherings started such an arrangement along the Northern route with bye posts to Lincoln, Hull and other places, and by 1636 the reform was being applied to other routes.

Witherings set up his central post office at Bishopsgate in London. A letter of 19 March 1635 in the Coke correspondence has this instruction: 'Be pleased to secure the Secretary's hand to the enclosed and send it into Bishopsgate to the posthouse.'[77] Stanhope's office as Postmaster of England had to be reviewed for it was difficult to see how Witherings could organise a new system that was under Stanhope's ultimate control.

The circumstances concerning Stanhope's loss of office without compensation are complex. In March 1637 he petitioned for redress and put the valuation of his position as £5,000, claiming that his basic salary of £66 13s 4d had been unpaid for nineteen years and that there were other sums owing to him. He declared that he had resigned 'sore against his will'. There is evidence that he had become unpopular at the Court for he had been involved with the Parliamentary party. An address by the House of Commons to the king dated 27 July 1628 had supported Stanhope's case against de Quester and requested the freeing of Billingsby then in prison. This earlier assistance by the Parliamentary party would not have helped Stanhope's cause nor the fact that

K. Gt. Brit. & Ireland — 42
Charles I Kg
506 h. 12. (42)

By the King.

A Proclamation for the ſetling of the Letter Office of England and Scotland.

WHereas to this time there hath beene no certaine or conſtant entercourſe betweene the Kingdomes of England and Scotland, his Maieſty hath beene graciouſly pleaſed, to command his ſeruant Thomas Witherings Eſquire, his Maieſties Poſt-maſter of England for forraigne parts, to ſetle a running Poſt, or two, to run night and day betweene Edenburgh in Scotland, and the City of London; to goe thither, and come backe againe in ſixe dayes, and to take with them all ſuch Letters as ſhall be directed to any Poſt-towne, or any place neere any Poſt-towne in the ſaid Roade, which Letters to be left at the Poſt-houſe, or ſome other houſe, as the ſaid Thomas Witherings ſhall thinke conuenient: And By-Poſts to be placed at ſeuerall places out of the ſaid Roade, to run and bring in, and carry out of the ſaid Roades the Letters from Lincolne, Hull, and other places, as there ſhall be occaſion, and anſweres to be brought againe accordingly; And to pay Port for the carrying and recarrying of the ſaid Letters, Two pence the ſingle Letter, if vnder fourescore Miles; And betweene fourescore, and one hundred and fourty Miles, Foure pence; If aboue a hundred and fourty Miles, then ſixe pence; and vpon the borders of Scotland, and in Scotland, Eight pence: If there be two three, foure, or fiue Letters in one Packet, or more, Then to pay according to the bigneſſe of the ſaid Packet, after the rate as before; which money for Port as before, is to be paid vpon the receiuing and deliuery of the ſaid Letters here in London.

The like rule his Maieſty is pleaſed to order the ſaid Thomas Witherings to obſerue to Weſtcheſter, Holyhead, and from thence to Ireland, according to a prouiſion made by the Lord Deputie and Councill there; and to take Port betwixt the City of London and Holyhead, as before to the Northward; and to goe thither, and bring anſweres backe to the City of London, from all the places in that Roade in ſixe dayes, which is conſtantly hereafter to be obſerued; and to ſetle By-poſts in the ſaid Roade, as there ſhall be occaſion, for the benefit of all his Maieſties louing Subiects.

His Maieſty is pleaſed further to command the ſaid Thomas Witherings, to obſerue the like rule from the City of London to Plymouth; and to prouide ſufficient meſſengers to run night and day to Plymouth, and to returne within ſixe dayes to the City of London, and for carriage of the said Letters to Plymouth, Exeter, and other places in that Roade, his Maiestie doth Order the said Thomas Witherings to take the like Port that now is paid as neere as possibly he can.

And further, his Maiestie doth Command and Order the said Thomas Witherings, so soone as possibly may be, to settle the like conueyance for Letters from Oxon, Bristoll, and other places on that Roade, for the benefit of all his Subiects, And the like the said Thomas Witherings is to obserue with all conuenient speed to Colchester, and so to Norwich, and diuers other places in that Roade.

The three first conueyances from London to Edenburgh, from London to Westchester and Holyhead in Wales, and from London to Plymouth and Exeter, are to begin the first weeke after Michaelmas next.

Now for the better enabling the said Thomas Witherings to goe forward with this seruice, and for the aduancement of all his Maiesties Subiects in their Trade and correspondence; his Maiestie doth hereby Command and Order all his Post-Masters vpon all the Roades of England, To haue ready in their Stables one or two Horses, according as the said Thomas Witherings shall haue occasion to vse them, to carry such Messengers with their Portmantles, as shall be imployed in the said seruice, to such Stage or Place as his present occasions shall direct him to: If the said Messenger shall haue occasion but for one Horse, then to leaue him at the place where he shall take fresh Horse, paying for him Two pence halfe-peny for euery Mile; if two Horses, then to take a Guide and pay Fiue pence a Mile.

And that the said Post-Masters may be prouided for this seruice, his Maiestie doth hereby Order and Command, that such Horses as shall be prouided for the said seruice, shall not vpon that day the Messenger shall be expected, let, or send forth the said Horses so prouided, vpon any other occasion whatsoeuer.

And his Maiesties further will and Pleasure is, that from the beginning of this seruice or imployment, no other Messenger or Messengers, Foot-Post or Foot-Posts, shall take vp, carry, receiue, or deliuer any Letter or Letters whatsoeuer, other then the Messengers appointed by the said Thomas Witherings to any such place or places as the said Thomas Witherings shall settle the conueyances, as aforesaid. Except common knowen Carryers, or a particular Messenger, to be sent of purpose with a Letter by any man for his owne occasions, or a Letter by a friend. And if any Post, Messenger, or Letter-Carryer whatsoeuer, shall offend contrary to this his Maiesties Proclamation; his Maiestie vpon complaint thereof made, will cause a seuere exemplary punishment to be inflicted vpon such delinquents.

And his Maiestie doth hereby strictly require and Command all his louing Subiects whatsoeuer, duly to obserue and performe his Royall Pleasure herein declared, as they will answere the contrary at their perils.

And lastly, his Maiestie doth hereby charge and command all Iustices of Peace, Maiors, Sheriffes, Bailiffes, Constables, Headboroughs, and all other his Officers and Ministers whatsoeuer, to be aiding and assisting to the said Thomas Witherings, in the due accomplishment of this his Maiesties will and pleasure.

Giuen at Our Court at Bagshot, the last day of Iuly, in the eleuenth yeere of Our Reigne. 1635.

God saue the King.

¶ Imprinted at London by *Robert Barker*, Printer to the Kings most Excellent Maiestie: And by the Assignes of *Iohn Bill*. 1635.

Opposite and above: 12.4 The 1635 proclamation opening the royal posts to the public. (Courtesy of the Post Office. H1128/1 and 2) in 1629 he had visited Denzil Hollis and other prisoners in the Tower. Hollis had held the speaker of the House of Commons in his chair and thus given great offence to the king.[78]

Another criticism of Stanhope had been contained in the patent appointing Frizell and Witherings in 1632 which referred to de Quester's control of the foreign posts:

> the said Lord Stanhope and some others, pretending to be authorised under him [the king] had, as well by setting up of Bills and Writings in public places within the City of London as otherwise, endeavoured to interrupt His Majesty's said grant and letters patent made to the said Matthew de Quester the father and Mathew de Quester the son, in derogation of his said Majesty and to the hindrance, disturbance, and distraction of the service to be executed in foreign parts.[79]

This passage shows that Stanhope had lost the support of the Council. However, Stanhope unsuccessfully petitioned the House of Lords for redress in 1646, when he gave his description of what had happened:

> Thomas Witherings [...] prevailed to have your petitioner to attend the Council Table, and to bring hither his Patent, and then, before he was suffered to depart, to subscribe somewhat then penned upon the petitioner's patent by the Lord Keeper, Coventry, which whatever the same was, was then enforced by that power, and is since then endeavoured to be made use of, to destroy the petitioner's patent and right.[80]

In 1660 the allegation was repeated and it was recommended that Stanhope should be compensated for his loss of profits. This was achieved in a curious way for in 1662 a warrant was issued for the creation of a general office for sale of lands, tenements and merchandise by way of outcry, which was to be called the Office for Public Sales. It was described in the following terms:

> Statement of the King's pleasure to erect an office of outcry, or sale by the candle, after the manner of foreign countries, and grant thereof to a petitioner, not named, who was the first propounder: with reversion therof also, in consideration of his contriving the improvement of the Post Office, and his title to the profits thereof, during the life of Charles Lord Stanhope.[81]

After Stanhope's patent had been surrendered, the two secretaries of state, Coke and Windebank, acquired the monopoly of control of the inland posts in 1637. A letter in the Coke correspondence shows that they then appointed Witherings as their Deputy:

> Your letters come sometimes late. I hope that will, by Mr Witherings's posts, be amended. For we, the Postmasters General, have made him our Deputy, that he may better accommodate his letter office.[82]

Witherings was now postmaster for foreign parts and deputy postmaster for the inland posts. The establishment of the national postal service had involved a mixture of motives including a concern to raise revenue for the state, the self-interest of those who aimed to make money by acquiring a monopoly, and also a desire to improve communications.

A warrant of July 1637 shows the number of postmasters still paid wages by the state to be sixty-one. Witherings used his position to put in some new men who paid him considerable fees, and various petitions from those dispossessed have survived, of which one from Thomas Parks concerning the route from London to Barnet, can be taken as representative:

> Has executed that office about six years, which had stood him in £180, without any neglect, as Mr Railton can inform you, and has received but two years pay at the rate of 20d per diem. Notwithstanding his diligence, Mr Witherings endeavours to bring in another, and has already taken from petitioner the through posts place of Charing Cross, which cost the petitioner £66 6s.[83]

During the next two centuries a series of changes extended the practices laid down by the historic proclamation of 1635. The cumbersome method of exchanging all letters at London was eventually replaced by local sorting offices, bye roads were set up to link all towns to the main routes and the principle of delivering letters to every address was established. An efficient means of paying the postmasters out of receipts had to be agreed. It was not until 1840 that payment by number of letter sheets was replaced by weight or that calculations of payment based on distance were abolished, but the basic decision to take both official and private mail together from stage to stage and thereby make the postal system self-financing had been made. At the time this may not have appeared to be important, yet in retrospect we can recognise it as a significant event in our nation's history. The proclamation of 1635 began the withdrawal of the separate letter carrying services once provided by the monarchy, the Church, the towns, the carriers, the merchants, the nobility and the gentry. The consequence was to be a service that assisted the development of trade and industry and brought great social benefits to the country.

Appendix 1

Books and articles on the English post before 1635

Apart from Mary Hill's work *The King's Messengers* and Dr Stone's *Calendar of the Inland Posts*, to both of which I am indebted for many references, a number of other books have been written on the history of the English post, some for the serious reader, most of a popular nature. Of the former, three Post Office officials, William Lewins, Herbert Joyce and Wilson Hyde, composed sound and very readable accounts. Their starting points are late, for Lewins devotes only four pages to English posts before the reign of Henry VIII, Joyce begins in 1533, reaching 1609 after seven pages, and Hyde starts in the seventeenth century. Lewins provide occasional references to his sources but Joyce and Hyde give virtually none. Another Post Office employee, J.G. Hendy, wrote in 1903 a most useful unpublished manuscript, *The Early History of the English Post*, with references, but he too gives little about events before Henry VIII. Previous to these books there was the 1844 Report of the Secret Committee on the Post Office, presented to the House of Commons. This was the result of an inquiry set up by the House into the law regarding the detaining and opening of letters. The report included transcripts of various records, some medieval, relating to early posts. Those writers who knew of its existence used it as their starting point. I refer to it particularly because it contains many lengthy documents printed in full.

In the twentieth century two American historians, J.C. Hemmeon and Howard Robinson, wrote books with the same title, *History of the British Post Office*, the first published in 1912, the second in 1948. As would be expected, they are carefully written with references and lists of sources. However, like their predecessors, the authors limited themselves to writing on a service which they considered began with Tuke's organisation of the posts under Henry VIII. Covering five centuries, they give only modest treatment of the Tudor and Stuart periods. Neither refers to Hendy's work. There is a carefully researched article by J.F. Willard on the dating and delivery of fourteenth-century letters patents and writs from which I quote.

Short historical accounts by J.A.H. Housden, including *The Early Posts and The Masters of the Posts*, appeared in the *English Historical Review* in 1903 and in the Post Office's journal, *St Martin Le Grand*, between 1902 and 1906. They were followed by others from Sir Cyril Hurcomb, who made a study of Tudor posts. He wrote in *The Antiquary* in 1914 and in the *English Historical Review*. He was aware of Hendy's manuscript, to which he gave acknowledgement. He looked carefully at State Papers Domestic, always giving accurate references. I acknowledge my debt to him. Samuel Graveson continued Hurcomb's work by writing a series on Stuart posts in the Postal History Society's *Bulletin*. He was in the tradition of those like the Earl of Crawford, who in 1906 had composed notes on, and listings of, all proclamations concerning the post from the time of Philip and Mary. These had appeared in *The London Philatelist* in 1906 and 1907.

Denis Way wrote a series of well-researched articles for *Stamp Review* in 1937 and 1938, which drew on various Elizabethan and Stuart sources. Only occasionally does he reveal what these are but those I have checked I have found to be accurate. The same comment applies to George Walker's interesting and popular *Haste Post Haste*. Robson Lowe was responsible for various publications. As a director of Christie's, he dealt with the Corsini correspondence and other sales of historical letters. Articles concerning them, mainly under his name, have appeared in *The Philatelist*. His firm, Robson Lowe, published *The Inland Posts 1392–1672*, by J.W.M. Stone, a most valuable selection of extracts from State Papers and manuscript sources relating to the postal history of the sixteenth and seventeenth centuries. Despite the title, it reaches 1506 on the second page. I have found this an excellent reference book. Another most useful publication is J. Crofts' *Packhorse, Waggon and Post - Land carriage and communications under the Tudors and Stuarts*, which draws on a wide reading of contemporary literary sources. Kenneth Fowler worked on a PhD thesis entitled, *The strategic importance of the post roads in England and Wales and their management 1590–1635*. Sadly, illness prevented him from completing it. His largely finished text, which I have been privileged to read, is in the Post Office archives. It is a valuable study. A series of excellent articles by Mark Brayshay on Elizabethan postroads is listed in the bibliography. John Allen's *Post and Courier Service in the Diplomacy of Early Modern Europe* gives a thorough account of the Tudor English couriers, though it is mainly concerned with those employed by continental rulers. I also mention in the text articles that have appeared in *The Philatelist* by M. Scott Archer and J.W.M. Stone.

Appendix 2

Sir Brian Tuke's letter to Thomas Cromwell 1533

Sir Bryan Tuke to Thomas Crumwell [sic] 17 August 1533
Right Worshipful Sir,

In my best manner I recommend me unto you. By your letters of the 12th of this month, I perceive that there is great default in conveyance of letters, and of special men ordained to be sent in post; and that the King's pleasure is, that posts be better appointed, and laid in all places most expedient; with commandment to all townships in all places, on pain of life, to be in such readiness, and to make such provision of horses, at all times, as no tract or loss of time be had in that behalf. Sir, it may like you to understand, the King's grace hath no more ordinary posts, nor of many days hath had, but between London and Calais; and they in no wages, save the post of London in 12d and Calais 4d a day; but riding by the journey whereof, most part, pass not 2 in a month; and since October last, the posts northward, every one at 12d by day. Those in wages be bound but to one horse; which is enough for that wages, albeit some of them have more. I never used other order, but to charge the townships to lay and appoint such a post, as they will answer for. And Butler, the King's messenger, for these northward, was sent when I laid them, to see them sufficient; and surely the posts northward, in time past, have been the most diligent of all other. Wherefore, supposing by my conjecture that the fault is there, I incontinently sent, through them, a writing sharp enough, showing their defaults, the King's high displeasure, and the danger. I also wrote to all the townships that way, seemingly touching obeying of placards and other writings, sent for provision of post horses. Now, Sir, if the fault be elsewhere, where post lie, I, upon knowledge had from you, will put it to the best remedy I can; but if in any other ways like order shall be taken, I pray you advertise me. For, Sir, you know well, that except the hackney horses between Gravesend and Dover, there is no such usual conveyance for men in this realm as is in the accustomed places of France and other parties; no men can keep horses in readiness without some way to bear the charges: but when placards be sent for such cause, the constables be fain to take horses out of the ploughs and carts, wherein can be no extreme diligence. This I write, lest the tract should be imputed there it is not. But, Sir, not taking it upon me to excuse the posts, I would advertise you that I have known in times past folk which, for their own thank, have dated their letters a day or 2 more before they were written, and the conveyers have had the blame. As to posts between London and the Court, there be none but 2; whereof one is a good robust fellow, and was wont to be diligent, evil entreated many times, he and other posts, by the herbigeours [the royal harbingers], for lack of horse room, or horsemeat, without which diligence cannot be. The other hath been the most painful fellow, in night and day, which I have known amongst the messengers. If he now slack, he shall be changed, as reason is. He sueth the King for some small living for his old service, having never had ordinary wages, till now, a month or little more, this posts's wages. It may please you to advertise me, in which of them 2 you find default, and he shall be changed. I wrote unto my Lord of Northumberland, to write on the back of the packets the hour and day of the despatch, and so I did to other[s]; but it is seldom observed. I will also desire you to remember that many times happen 2 despatches in a day, one way, and sometimes more; and that often seasons happen contra posts, that is, to ride both northward and southward; this is much for one horse, or one man. My Lord of Northumberland hath sent a post, my Lord Dacre another in the neck of him; they of Berwick a 3rd, and sometimes Sir John Lawson apart, another; and, in the same time, despatches from hence northward. Now I have advertised you of the premises, it may please you I may know the King's further pleasure; and I shall, according to my bounden duty, diligently obey the same, by God's grace, who preserve you. At my poor house, the 17th day of August, 1533.

All at your commandment,

Bryan Tuke.

Sir; I have also received your other letters, of the 12th and 13th, the one concerning order for letters of the French ambassador, northward, which shall be performed; and the other for £300 for W Gonson, which shall be paid. Sir, it is showed me the King's grace reckons I received £4,000 in the Exchequer last Term. Sir, it was but £2,000, whereof Gonson had £900, and the rest, with much more, was assigned by warrants, or ever it was received; and I have paid little lack of £5,000.

Superscribed

To the Right Worshipful Mr Thomas Cromwell, Squire,
Counsellor to the King's Highness, and Master of his Jewels.
(See pages 146-147)

Appendix 3

Viscount Montague's secretariat, 1595

A detailed account of the household maintained by Viscount Montague in 1595 is entitled 'A Book of Orders and Rules' and is typical of an important Elizabethan establishment. From internal evidence its editor deduces that the instructions are based on earlier compositions. The most senior official was the steward, who dealt with the receipt and despatch of the viscount's letters and the ordering of his messengers. The passage relating to those duties reads:

> I will that if he have occasion to send in foreign message or errand any groom of my great chamber or wardrobe, or any groom of my stable, that he first acquaint the gentleman usher, or gentleman of my horse with it, to the end the place of them may be supplied. Muchmore I will that he give me fore-knowledge, and have my leave before he send any of my own chamber in foreign message whatsoever the occasion be.

Advances to the messengers were made by the auditor. Letters were written by the viscount's secretary, who headed the household's office. The description of his tasks begins:

> I will that my secretary give always diligent attendance upon me in respect that I shall oftentimes have cause to employ him as well as receiving into his custody such letters of weight as come into my hands, which he must safely keep filed up together in good order (as also in writing answers to such letters for mine own better easement) and such as are of importance he must transcript into a book, in the beginning whereof there must be an alphabetical table, containing the names of such as I have written unto, against which names there must be set figures, shewing in what pages or leaves letters to such persons shall be found.

Source: Scott, S.D., 'A Book of Orders and Rules'.

Appendix 4

Examples of costs of Tudor and Stuart postal routes

Statistics of costs for the Tudor and early Stuart posts begin in 1558 with the accounts of the Audit and Exchequer. Before that more random information can be found in Campbell, *State Papers Domestic and Foreign Henry VIII*, and in the Trevelyan Papers, which contain extracts from the household books of Henry VIII. Stone has prepared tables of daily wages for the posts after 1558, taken from the Audit Office rolls, and Fowler drew up tables of annual costs from the Exchequer rolls after 1590. Dr Stone kindly gave permission to draw on his research and Mrs Fowler has done the same for tables compiled by her late husband. The figures I give are approximate, as some additional allowances were made from time to time.

Postal route	**Postmasters**	**Annual cost**
London to Berwick 1558	28	£930
London to Berwick 1568	28 (½ wages)	£460
London to Berwick 1604	34	£1,432
London to Dover 1588	8	£262
London to Dover 1592	8	£252
London to Exeter 1579	11	£340
London to Bristol 1579	9	£213
London to Haverfordwest via Bristol 1605	16	£453
London to Portsmouth 1593	8	Daily cost 14s
London to Penrhyn via Exeter 1601 (plus monthly cost of a ship at Padstow £10)	21	£688
London to Holyhead via Chester 1602 (plus monthly cost of a ship and carriage of mail to Beaumaris £10)	21	£666
London to Harwich 1625	7	Daily cost 16s 6d

Source: Campbell, W. *Materials for a History of the Reign of Henry VII.* Rolls Series 60. 1873.

Appendix 5

Summary of postal accounts from June 1621 to May 1632

Received	£	s	d	**Paid out**	£	s	d
Michaelmas 1624	2002	1	8	Berwick Road	3833	6	6
Easter 1626	167	0	10	Dover Road	1045	7	0
Michaelmas 1626	219	19	10½	Holyhead Road	2283	7	9½
Easter 1628	99	0	0	Plymouth Road	1135	1	8
Michaelmas 1628	510	8	4	Harwich Road	538	10	0
Easter 1629	468	18	11	Falmouth Extension	209	17	6
Michaelmas 1629	524	5	0	Portsmouth Branch		515	12 0
Easter 1630	936	10	0	Postmaster Beaumaris	36	10	0
Michaelmas 1630	3800	11	8	Postmaster Cambridge	10	4	0
Easter 1631	914	5	4	Postmaster Hounslow	11	12	0
Progresses 1630–1	350	0	0	Court Postmaster	426	10	10
				Paymaster	137	0	0
				Clerk	20	0	0
				Auditor	8	0	0
Brought Forward	214	2	3	Postmaster Newmarket	5	14	0
TOTALS	10207	3	10½		10216	13	3½

Source: Fowler, K.A. *The Strategic Importance of the Post Roads.*

References

Chapter 1

1 Chevallier, pp.191–5. Ramsay, *Speed of Post*, p.60.
2 Rolfe, *Suetonius*, p.205. See also Ramsay, *A Roman Postal Service.*
3 Salway, *Roman Britain*, p.542 ff.
4 *Ordnance Survey Map of Roman Britain.* The standard work on Roman roads is Margary. See also Chevallier, H. Davies, Johnston, Jones and Mattingley.
5 Salway, pp.563–4.
6 For the *Itinerary* and *Cursus Romanus* see Black, Chapman, Chevallier and H. Davies.
7 Collingwood and Myres, *Roman Britain and the English Settlements*, p.241.
8 *Guide to Letocetum*, English Heritage (see Plate 1). See also Gould, *Letocetum.*
9 See Fig. 1.2.
10 Bowman and Thomas, *The Vindolanda Writing Tablets.*
11 Donaldson, *Signalling Communications in the Roman Imperial Army.*
12 Salway, p.520.
13 Wright, Hassell and Tomlin, *Inscriptions*, p.291.
14 Stevenson, *Literacy in Ireland.*
15 Stevenson, p.20.
16 Clanchy, *From Memory to Written Record*, p.315 and footnote.
17 Bede, *Ecclesiastical History*, book 2, ch. XI.
18 Bede, book 2, ch. XIX.
19 Stenton, *Anglo-Saxon England*, pp.174–5.
20 Chaplais, *Letter from Bishop Waldhere*; see Figure 1.5.
21 Douglas, *English Historical Documents*; vol. 1 discusses these early letters.
22 Chaplais, *The Royal Anglo-Saxon Chancery of the 10th century revisited.*
23 Pronay and Cox, *The Croyland Chronicle Continuations.*
24 Keynes, *Royal Government and the written word*, p.257.
25 Stenton, *Anglo-Saxon England*, p.272.
26 Stenton, p.402. For Cnut's *Letter to the people of England*, see Douglas, vol. 1 pp.452–4.
27 Keynes, p.241.
28 Stenton, p.478.
29 Harmer, *Anglo-Saxon Writs*, p.535.

Chapter 2

1 Fitz Nigel, *The Course of the Exchequer.*
2 Clanchy, *From Memory to Written Record*, pp.135–44 for an account of early rolls.
3 *CLR* 1240–5, p.169.
4 Devon, *Issues of the Exchequer Henry III to Henry VI*, p.83.
5 For the early medieval household, see Given-Wilson's Introduction in *The Royal Household and the King's Affinity.*
6 Gee and Hardy, *Documents illustrative of English Church History*, pp.59–60 Bettenson, *Documents of the Christian Church*, p.219.
7 Willard, *Dating & Delivery of Letters Patent and Writs in the 14th Century*, pp.3–4.
8 Willard, 2 November 1316.
9 Hall, *Red Book of the Exchequer*, vol. 3, pp.835–7.

10 Clanchy, p.58.
11 Clanchy, p.59.
12 Hoccleve, *The Regement of Princes*, pp.140, 145.
13 Clanchy, p.300.
14 *English Royal Signatures*, Public Record Office pamphlet no.^9.
15 Corner, *Grant per cultellum, pp.*213–16.
16 Taylor, p.224. See also *English Historical Documents*, vol. 4, p.497.
17 Cam, *The Hundred and the Hundred Rolls*, p.46.
18 Illustrated in *The Nation's Memory*, Public Record Office Handbook.
19 *Cam, The Hundred Rolls*, p.88.
20 *CLR* 1267–72, p.252.
21 Flower, *Public Works in Medieval Law*, vol. 1, p.XI.
22 Jenkinson, H. and Mills, M.H., *Rolls from a Sheriff's Office of the 14th Century.*
23 Mills, M.H., *The Medieval Shire House.*
24 Cam, p.137.
25 Cam, p.135.
26 *CIPM*, vol. 5, Edward II, item 83, p.40. See also item 89.
27 Welford, R., *History of Newcastle*, in vol. 3, p.140.
28 Steele, *Kings' Letters*, vol. 1, p.29.
29 Steele, *Kings' Letters*, vol. 1, p.258.
30 These examples taken from *Records of the Wardrobe & Household 1285–6.*
31 Larson, A., *The Payment of Fourteenth-Century Envoys.*
32 Johnston, H., *Letters of Edward Prince of Wales 1304–5*, Roxburghe Club, 1931.
33 Hill, *The Kings' Messengers*, p.16.
34 CCR, Edward I, vol. 3, p.145.
35 Perroy, E., *Diplomatic Correspondence.*
36 Ellis, 3rd series, p.54 discusses these letters.
37 For example, PRO Ref C219 1/13 for Edward I, 1302 returns.
38 Shirley, *Royal letters Henry H III.*
39 Printed in Riley, *Memorials of London Life*, p.285.
40 Taylor, p.229.
41 Powicke, *The Thirteenth Century*, p.336.
42 *Archaeologia*, vol. XVI, AD 1281–2.
43 *Archaeologia*, vol. XXVI for *Edward II Wardrobe Accounts.* MSS 120 and 121 in the Society of Antiquaries' Library.
44 MSS 121, vol. 1, pp.133–49.
45 CLR, Henry III, vol. 1, p.383.
46 *CIPM*, vol. 5, Edward II, item 250, p.135.
47 *CIMisc.*, vol. 1, item 2128, p.569.
48 Cam, p.154.
49 Sayles, *Select Cases in King's Bench*, p. XVII.
50 Hill, Appendix 1.
51 These examples taken from Devon, *Issue Roll of Thomas Brantingham.*
52 These examples taken from Hill, pp.92–3. Also Powicke, p.642.
53 Hill, pp.92–3.
54 *Foedera*, 3 April 1396, quoted in Jusserand, p.231.
55 Hill, p.98.
56 Byerley, *Records of Wardrobe and Household 1285–6*, Introduction, p. xxxviii.
57 13 Edward 1, ch. XLIV.

58 Queller, *Thirteenth-Century Envoys.*
59 See Wagner, *Heralds of England* for the following examples.
60 Taylor, p.224.
61 See Woolgar for Lancaster and Mortimer accounts.
62 Black Book of the household of Edward IV quoted in Douglas, *English Historical Documents 1327–1485*, p.955.
63 CPR, Richard II 1391–96, pp.712–13.
64 Hill, *English Historical Review*, vol. 57, 1942
65 Stretton, *Some Aspects of Medieval Travel*, p.77
66 Armstrong, *Some examples of the distribution and speed of the news etc.*
67 CCR, 1261–4, Henry III, p.381.
68 CCR, 1369–74, Edward III, p.389.
69 20 Richard II, ch. V.
70 CCR, 1392–6, Richard II, p.9.
71 28 Henry VI, ch. 2.
72 Armstrong, p.435.
73 Crawford, p.173.
74 Pronay and Cox, p.173.
75 Myers, see Douglas, *English Historical Documents*, vol. 4, p.1220.
76 CPR, 1374–7, Edward III, p.351.
77 CPR, 1408–13, Henry IV, p.213.
78 Furnivall, *Early English Meals and Manners*, p.75.
79 Figures taken from Wagner, *Heralds of England*.
80 CLR, Henry III, vol. 3, p.185.
81 Reports from the Select Committee appointed to enquire into the state of the public records of the Kingdom, vol. XV, 1800. 1st report of the Public Records, House of Lords, p.233.
82 For wages, see Hill, p.46.
83 Byerley, *Records of Wardrobe and Household 1285–6*, p.1700.
84 For clothing see Hill, ch. 2
85 PRO, Ref. E101 309/11.
86 Hill, pp.41–2 for descriptions of pouches.
87 Woolgar, *Household Accounts of Medieval England*, p.599.
88 CCR, Henry III, 1231–4, p.276.
89 Steele, Letters, vol. 1. p.213.
90 For care in illness see Hill, ch. 4.
91 CIMisc., vol. 4, p.167.
92 CCR, 1360–4, Edward III, p.318.
93 CCR, 1330–3, Edward III, p.581.
94 CCR, 1354–60, Edward III, p.389.
95 CChR, vol. 2, 1237–1300, 19 April 1258, p.5.

Chapter 3

1 Dickins, *Praemonstratensian Itineraries.*
2 Poole, *Domesday Book to Magna Carta*, p.79, footnote 1.
3 MacMahon, *Roads and Turnpike Trusts in East Yorkshire.*
4 Blackham for the Peace Guilds.
5 Poole, *Domesday Book to Magna Carta*, p.78.
6 Poole, *Domesday Book to Magna Carta*, p.79.

7 Bennett, *The Pastons and their England*, p.150.
8 CPR, 1232–72, p.498.
9 Cam, *The Hundred Rolls*, pp.104–5 for above examples.
10 Becker, *Rochester Bridge.*
11 For this and other examples cited, see Welch, *Worshipful Company of Paviours of the City of London.*
12 CSPDF 1509, vol. I, p.2.
13 13 Edward I, 1st Statute of Westminster, section 5
14 Statutes of the Realm, ex MSS Harl. 858, fo. 35.
15 CCR, 1381–5, p.517.
16 Sharpe, *London Letter Book 3*, pp.55–6.
17 Sharpe, p.140.
18 Davies, *History of Southampton*, p.120.
19 For an account of medieval streets, see Salisbury-Jones.
20 Map, *De Nugis Curialum*, p.207.
21 Given-Wilson, *The Royal Household*, p.22.
22 List and Index Society, vols. 132, 135; Kightly and Cyprien *Royal Roads*; Hindle has maps of routes.
23 Robertson, *Materials for the History of Thomas Becket*, vol. 3, p.29ff.
24 Map, p.261.
25 Steane, *King John's Itinerary*, p.84ff. Hindle, *Medieval Roads* has maps of some itineraries.
26 Moorman, *Church Life in the Thirteenth Century*, p.354.
27 Broome, *Exchequer Migrations to York.*
28 Ellis, *Original Letters*, series 1, vol. 1, preface.
29 Salzman, *Sussex Record Society*, vol. 55.
30 CLR, 1237–42, pp.192–3.
31 CSP *Venetian*, vol. 1, 1202–1509, 3 August 1402, p.42.
32 Parratt, *Ryedale Historian*, no.5, 1970.
33 Welford, *History of Newcastle*, vol. 2, p.16.
34 Ellis, *Letters*, series 1, vol. 2, p.253.
35 Leach, *Beverley Town Documents*, p.21 ff. for other references
36 Platt, *Medieval Southampton*, p.171.
37 Platt, *The English medieval town*, pp.71–2.
38 Hewitt, *Building Accounts of Vale Royal Abbey*, p.66.
39 Salzman, *English Trade in the Middle Ages*, ch.10.
40 Rogers, *The Economic Interpretation of History*, vol. 2, p.484.
41 Flower, *Public Works in Medieval Law*, vol. 1, p. xxiii.
42 Stenton, *The Road System of Medieval England*, p.244. See also Harvey, *Medieval Maps*, ch.6.

Chapter 4

1 Moorman, *Church Life in England in the 13th Century*, p.52.
2 Moorman, p.53.
3 Surtees, vol. 1. p. xxiii.
4 Douglas, *English Historical Documents 1327–1485*, p.956.
5 Moorman, p.169.
6 Moorman, p.272.
7 See Davies, J. C., *Journal of Historical Society of Wales*, vol. I, no.^9 for Bogo. Also

Giuseppi, *Wardrobe & Household Account of Bogo de Clare.*
8 Moorman, p.207.
9 Moriarty, *Voice of the Middle Ages*, p.112.
10 Keen, *English Society in the Late Middle Ages*, ch.9, p.236.
11 Bettenson, *Documents of the Christian Church*, p.217.
12 Gee and Hardy, *Documents illustrative of English church history*, pp.57–8.
13 Ritchie, *The Ecclesiastical Courts of York.*
14 The oath of an *apparitor* in the Coventry and Lichfield Diocese is known for November 1350. See Smith, D.M., p.56.
15 Woodcock, *Medieval ecclesiastical courts in the diocese of Canterbury.*
16 Timmins, *The Register of John Chandler 1404–17.*
17 Timmins, pp.256, 315, 583.
18 Pantin, *English Monastic Letter Books.*
19 See *The White Act Book. The Acts of the Dean and Chapter of the Cathedral Church of Chichester*, Sussex Record Society, vol. 52. This gives various references.
20 Cheney, *Notaries Public.*
21 Martin, C.T., *Register of John Peckham.*
22 Sheppard, *Literae Cantuarenses.*
23 Sheppard, vol. 3, p.304.
24 Edwards, K. and Owen, D.M., *Registers of Roger Martival.* For Itinerary see pp. xxxvii–xliii.
25 Moorman, p.176. Itinerary map, p.189.
26 Taylor, p.226.
27 Storey, *Register of Thomas Langley.*
28 Willard, *Dating and Delivery of Letters Patent and Writs in the 14th Century.*
29 Talbot, *Letters from English Abbots to the Chapter at Cîteaux.*
30 Cheney, *English Bishops' Chanceries.*
31 Cobban, *English Medieval Universities*, p.348.
32 Pollard, *The Clerical Organization of Parliament*, p.38.
33 Cheney, *English Bishops' Chanceries.*
34 Crawford, *Letters of the Queens of England*, p.39.
35 Moriarty, p.42.
36 Haskins, *Studies in Medieval Culture*, pp.2–3.
37 Davies, N., *Litera Troili and English Letters.*
38 Taylor J. discusses these early letters.
39 Lyell, pp.267–8.
40 Devon, *Brantingham Rolls*, p.207.
41 Devon, *Issue Rolls Henry III–Henry VI*, p.227.
42 Davis, *Medieval Cartularies of Great Britain.*
43 CChR, vol. 4, 1327–41, 25 March 1327.
44 Bennett, *The Pastons and their England*, p.163.
45 Taylor, p.227.
46 Taylor, p.227 footnote gives references in Pantin.
47 Anstey, *Epistolae Academicae*, vol. 1, p. xlvii.

Chapter 5
1 Douglas, *English Historical Documents*, vol. 2, p.1012.
2 Edward I, *Statutes of Merchants*, 1283 and 1285.
3 CChR, 1226–57, vol. 1, 20 January 1253.

4 CChR, 1226–57, vol. 1, 18 January 1257.
5 Palmer, *Cambridge Borough Documents*, p.36.
6 Cooper, *Annals of Cambridge*, p.209.
7 Bateson, *Records of Borough of Leicester*, vol. 2.
8 Cooper, p.394.
9 Sharpe, *London Letter Books*, vol. C, p.26.
10 Welford, *History of Newcastle*, vol. 1, pp.64–5.
11 *York Civic Records*, vol. 1, York's Archaeological Society Record Series, 1939, p.130.
12 Douglas, *English Historical Documents, 1327–85*, vol. 4, p.560.
13 Jacob, *The Fifteenth Century* gives these and other examples, p.392.
14 Keen, *English Society in the Later Middle Ages*, pp.87–8 gives estimates for 1377 and 1520. See also, Britnell *The Commercialisation of English Society.*
15 Poole, *From Domesday Book to Magna Carta*, table on p.96.
16 Coleman, O., *Collectors of Customs in London under Richard II.*
17 Welford, vol. 1, p.294.
18 Rymer, *Foedera*, 18 Edward II, 1324. Quoted in *Sec. Com.*, p.95.
19 *Sec. Com.*, p.95.
20 *Sec. Com.*, pp.95–7.
21 Taylor, pp.228, 234. See Keauper for *The Riccardi.*
22 PRO, Ref. El01/509/19.
23 Booth and Carr, *Chester Chamberlains' Accounts.*
24 Hill, *The King's Messengers*, p.152.
25 Bateson, *Bailiff's Minute Book of Dunwich.*
26 Devon, *Brantingham Rolls*, 1370.
27 See Sharpe's introduction to *Calendar of Letters from the Mayor etc.*
28 Sharpe, *Calendar of Letters from the Mayor etc.*, no.93.
29 Sharpe, *Calendar of Letters from the Mayor etc.*, no.169.
30 Thomas, *Calendar of Plean and Memoranda Rolls*, vol. 1, p.167.
31 Devon, *Brantingham Rolls*, p.191.
32 Devon, *Brantingham Rolls*, p.408.
33 Masters, *The Mayor's Household before 1600.*
34 Devon, *Brantingham Rolls*, p.225.
35 CPR, Richard II 1391–6, pp.712–13.
36 20 Richard II, Ch. 5.
37 Sharpe, *London Letter Book H*, 17 May 1392, 15 Richard II, p.375.
38 Sharpe, *London Letter Book K*, pp.234–5.
39 Pound, *The Social and Trade Structure of Norwich.*
40 Steer, *A History of the Scriveners.*
41 Beresford and Finsberg, *English Medieval Boroughs*, p.30.
42 Mackie, *The Earlier Tudors*, p.214.

Chapter 6

1 For Zouche see Payne and Barron. For literacy and early English letters, see Davies's introduction to the Paston Letters; Richardson, *Medieval English Vernacular Correspondence*; Coleman, J. *English Literature in History 1350–1400*; Taylor. J., *English Historical Literature in the Fourteenth Century.*
2 Kingsford, *Prejudice and Promise in Fifteenth Century England*, p.24.
3 Carpenter, *Stonor Letters*, no.260.

4 *Foedera* (1709 edn), ix, 427–30, quoted by Lyell in A *Medieval Postbag*, p.18.
5 Wagner, *Heralds of England*, p.43.
6 Steele, *Kings' Letters*, vol. 1, p.179.
7 Steele, vol. 1, p.185.
8 Stevenson, J., *Letters & Papers illustrative of the reign of King Henry VI*, vol. 2, part 1, pp. lviii–lix.
9 Stevenson, J., 21 August 1441, vol. 2, part 1, p.357.
10 Steele, vol. 1, pp.190–6.
11 Steele, vol. 1, p.209
12 Steele, vol. 1, p.239.
13 Steele, vol. 1, 11 April 1484, p.265.
14 Steele, vol. 2, p.2.
15 Steele, vol. 2, p.23.
16 Steele, vol. 2, p.43.
17 Gairdner, *Paston Letters*, May and June 1466, vol. 4, item 639, p.239ff and footnotes.
18 Gairdner, vol. 6, Letter 999, p.78.
19 Moore, *Shillingford Letters*, letter 23, 19 April 1448.
20 Moore, p.147.
21 Lyell, A *Medieval Postbag*, p.273, 19 March 1418. The five letters are quoted in Lyell.
22 Lyell, pp.293–4.
23 See Dow, Girling and Hudd.
24 Hanham, Letter 235.
25 Carpenter, letter 268.
26 Kirby, Letter 140.
27 Kirby, Letter 97.
28 Kirby, Letter 39.
29 Kirby, Letter 251.
30 Gairdner, vol. 3, nos 283, 284, pp.25ff.
31 Gairdner, vol. 2, no.117, p.142.
32 Gairdner, vol. 5, letter 917, p.296.
33 Gairdner, vol. 5, letter 842, p.196.
34 Bennett, *The Pastons and their England*, p.120.
35 Gairdner, vol. 2, letter 172, p.210.
36 Bennett, p.127.
37 Carpenter, letter 176.
38 Gairdner, vol. 5, letter 711, p.23.
39 Bennett, p.124.
40 Crawford, *Letters of Medieval Women*, pp.199–201.
41 Gairdner, vol. 2, letter 47, p.55.

Chapter 7

1 Miller, *Agrarian History*, vol. 3, p.32
2 Bracton, De *Legibus Angliae*, vol. 3, ch. XLVI, p.585.
3 Bailey, *The English Landscape*, p.32. See ch.6 for town populations.
4 Harris, *Account of the Great Household of Humphrey.*
5 Welford, *History of Newcastle*, vol. 2, p.57.
6 Tingey, *Norfolk Archaeology*, *vol.* XV, p.114.

7 Discussed in Lipson, *Economic History of England*, vol. 1, p.248.
8 Bennett, *The Pastons and their England*, p.121.
9 Salzman, *English Trade in the Middle Ages*, ch.10.
10 Bennett, p.106.
11 Seddon, *Letters of John Holles*, 1616, p.121.
12 Seddon, 1622, pp.261–2.
13 Seddon, 1622, p.263.
14 Poole, *Domesday Book to Magna Carta*, p.74.
15 Leach, *Beverley Town Documents*, p.21.
16 Mills, *The London Customs House*, pp.311–12.
17 Raine, *York Civic Records*, Yorkshire Archaeological Society Record Series, vol. 2, p.122.
18 Welford, vol. 2, p.107.
19 Keene, D., *Survey of Medieval Winchester*, vol. I, table 26.
20 Ruddock, *Italian Merchants and Shipping in Southampton*, p.90.
21 13 Edward I, *Statutes for the City of London*.
22 Sharpe, *Calendar of Early Mayor's Court Rolls of the City of London 1298–1307*, p.72.
23 Rogers, *History of Prices and Agriculture*, vols 1–2, ch. 27, p.660.
24 Leadham, *Select Cases in Star Chamber 1477–1509*, p.80.
25 Keene, D., p.330.
26 Rogers, vol. 5, p.763.
27 Rogers, vol. 5, p.769.
28 Rogers, vol. 5, p.773.
29 Crofts, p.4.
30 Rogers, vol. 4, p.709.
31 Bennett, p.164.
32 Lyell, *Medieval Postbag*, pp.293–4
33 Salisbury MSS, Part 2, 20 November 1582, p.533.
34 Pendrill, *London Life in the 14th Century*, for these details.
35 Crofts, p.30.
36 Childs, *Customs Accounts of Hull*.
37 Coleman and Lewis for Southampton Brokage Books.
38 Figures extracted from Coleman.
39 Leadam and Baldwin, *Select Cases before the King's Council 1243–1482*, p.67.
40 Chartres, *Internal Trade in England* discusses wagons, p.40.
41 Rogers, vol. 5, p.758.
42 RCM, 9th Report, Appendix, p.260.
43 Chartres, *Internal Trade in England*, p.10 ff.
44 Rogers, vol. 5, p.768.
45 CSPD, 1630, p.201.
46 Taylor, J., *Carriers Cosmography* p.1. The pages are not numbered.
47 Chartres, *Road carrying in the seventeenth century*, p.80.
48 Private collection.

Chapter 8

1 Campbell, *Materials for a History of Henry VII*, vol. 1, p.441.
2 Campbell, vol. 2, p.103.
3 Campbell, vol. 2, p.384.
4 Campbell, vol. 2, p.24.

5 Welford, vol. 2, p.83.
6 CSPDF, Henry VIII, vol. II, part 2, pp.1441–62.
7 Wagner, *Heralds of England*, p.183.
8 CSPDF, Henry VIII, vol. II, part 2, February 1512, p.1454.
9 CSPDF, Henry VIII, vol. I, p.710.
10 CSPDF, Henry VIII, vol. I, p.621.
11 CSPDF, Henry VIII, vol. I, part 2, p.925.
12 CSPDF, vol. XXI, part 2, p.140.
13 Patent in Sec. Com., p.21.
14 Sec. Com., p.21.
15 Sec. Com., p.36.
16 Ellis, *Letters*, series I, vol. 1, 23 June 1528, p.291.
17 Harleian MSS, in PRO, no.283, f.148; Nicholas, vol. 7, p.350.
18 Campbell, vol. 2, p.60.
19 Ferguson and Nanson, *Municipal Records of Carlisle*, p.47, and p.15 footnote.
20 CSPD, Addenda 1547–65, vol. 1, 19 June 1548, p.384.
21 See Figure 8.2.
22 RCM, 9th report, 1st part, p.263.
23 Anderson, *Letters of the 15th and 16th centuries*, 4 September 1550, letter 50, p.80.
24 APC, 1556–8, p.220.
25 Salisbury MSS, vol. 4, p.475.
26 Repertories 7, fo. 220.
27 Repertories 11, folios 75, 168b. It is a coincidence that hackney horses are here provided from Hackney. The word 'hackney' comes from the French.
28 Repertories, fos 386b, 471, 473b.
29 RCM, 9th report, 1st part, appendix, p.287.
30 Ellis, series I, vol. I. pp.239–40.
31 Masters, *Chamber Accounts.* Also Masters, *Mayor's Household before 1600* for the following details.
32 Repertories, vol. 17, fos 232b, 253b.
33 *City Archives*, report 18, fos 143, 159. Report 19, fo.462. Report 20, fo.320b.
34 Masters, *Chamber Accounts*, no.^968, p.100.
35 CSPD, Addenda, 1580–1625, 11 March 1590, p.304.
36 CSPD, Addenda, 28 September 1591, p.329.
37 CSPD, 1598–1601, 28 February 1594, p.444.
38 Salisbury MSS, Part 4, p.364; part 3, p.182.
39 CSPD, 1591–94, 8 April 1594, p.481.
40 Repertories, vol. 11, no.218 (in pencil), no.^941 (in ink), 1537–42.
41 APC, vol. 21, p.119, Stone p.27.
42 RCM, 14th report, appendix, part 8, p.30.
43 Bowle, *Henry VIII*, p.236.
44 Dance, *Guildford Borough Records*, p.57.
45 For details of Leicester's post see Bateson, *Records of the Borough of Leicester.*
46 RCM, 8th report, part 1, appendix, p.425.
47 Merson, *The Third Remembrance Book of Southampton*, vol. 2, 12 May 1558.
48 RCM, 9th report, part 1, pp.249–50.
49 Welford, vol. 2, p.40.
50 Welford, vol. 2, p.453.
51 Welford, vol. 3, p.69 ff. He gives various payments to messengers.

52 Blomefield, vol. 3, *Selected Records of Norwich*, pp.135–6.
53 Blomefield, vol. 3, p.294. Quoted from Assembly Book.
54 RCM, 9th report, part I, p.253.
55 RCM, 5th report, appendix, p.566.
56 RCM, 9th report, part I, p.248.
57 RCM, 9th report, part I, pp.248–9.
58 RCM, 13th report, appendix, part 4, p.88.
59 For the following correspondence, see Byrne, *Lisle Letters*, ch. 6.
60 Bell, *Handlist of British Representatives Abroad*.
61 *CSPD*, Addenda, 1547–65, p.425.
62 For many of the following references I am indebted to Allen, *Post and Courie Service*.
63 CSPF, Elizabeth 1558–9, 17 July 1559, p.383 footnote.
64 Allen pp.128–35.
65 CSPF, Elizabeth 1558–9, p.535.
66 CSPF, Elizabeth 1578–80, p.387.
67 CSPF, Elizabeth 1560–1, p.479.
68 See Chapter 9, pp.142–9.
69 CSPF, 1559–60, p.187.
70 CSPF, 1584, p.81.
71 CSPF, 1562, p.244.

Chapter 9

1 CPR, 1550–3, p.351.
2 CSPD, 1547–80, p.612.
3 CSPD, 1547–80, p.362.
4 CSPD, 1547–80, p.47.
5 CSPD, 1547–80, 4 February 1568, p.306.
6 APC 19, p.116.
7 APC, vol. 25, 20 April 1596, p.358.
8 CSPD, 1595–97, p.63.
9 CSPD, 1581–90, p.193
10 Stone, p.227.
11 Edwards, *The Horse Trade in Tudor and Stuart England*, Introduction, p.4.
12 APC, vol. 28, pp.561, 563.
13 APC, vol. 10, p.62.
14 Stevenson, *Records of Nottingham*, vol. 4, for various examples.
15 These references taken from Stevenson, vols 3 and 4.
16 Printed in full in Harrison, G.B., *An Elizabethan Journal*, vol. 2.
17 Salisbury MSS, vol. 5, p.214, p.211 for his examination and confession. Other cases in APC, vol. 25, pp.130, 210, vol. 27, p.137.
18 Salisbury MSS, vol. 10, p.252.
19 Salisbury MSS, vol. 11, p.192.
20 CSPD, Addenda, 1547–65, p.100.
21 CSPD, Addenda, 1601–3, p.296.
22 APC, vol. 13, p.351.
23 In full in Harrison, vol. 2, p.88.
24 APC, vol. 25, p.358.
25 CSPD, Addenda, 1547–65, p.383.

26 CSPD, Addenda, 1547–65, p.360.
27 APC, vol. 5, p.315.
28 *Second Report of the Postmaster General*, Post Office Records, p.38.
29 Stone, *The Philatelist*, vol. 4, no.6, p.257. Brayshay, *Knowledge, nationhood and governance; the speed of the Royal post.*
30 CSPD, Addenda, 1580–1625, pp.75–6.
31 CSPD, 1581–90, p.170.
32 See Stone, appendix 10.
33 CSPD, Addenda, 1547–65, p.337.
34 APC, 1556–8, p.385.
35 APC, vol. 6, p.261, 6 February 1558.
36 Ellis, *Original Letters*, 3rd Series, vol. 1. pp.206, 207.
37 CSP, *Venetian*, vol. 3, item 339, 22 September 1521.
38 Sec. Com., pp.99–101. This long letter is reproduced in full. Sampson's reply is printed in Ellis, 3rd series, vol. I, pp.347–58.
39 CSPDF, HVIII, vol. 4, part 3, p.2616.
40 APC, vol. 6, p.131.
41 APC, vol. 3, p.212.
42 CSPD, 1547–80, p.327.
43 CSP, Scotland 1509–1603, vol. 2, 30 September 1571, p.329.
44 Lodge, *Illustrations of British History*, vol. 2, p.65.
45 Stone, p.23.
46 Sec. Com., p.36.
47 Byrne, L.S.R., *The Fugger News Letters*, p.202.
48 Salisbury MSS, vol. 4, p.503.
49 Salisbury MSS, vol. 5, p.26.
50 Salisbury MSS, vol. 4, p.562.
51 CSPD, 1591–4, p.445.
52 CSPD, 1598–1601, p.48 also gives his expenses.
53 Hentzner, *Travels in England*, pp.1, 52, 82.
54 Clifford, *State Papers of Sir R. Sadler*, p.294 and later.
55 APC, vol. 10, p.128.
56 APC, vol. 11, pp.126, 156–7, 328.
57 APC, vol. 10, p.154.
58 Salisbury MSS, vol. 9, p.393.
59 Sainty, *Officers of the Exchequer* gives many references.
60 For the Elizabethan Chancery, see Jones, W.T., *The Elizabethan Court of Chancery.*
61 For James I see Misc. MSS, no 55, Inner Temple Library. For Charles I see Aylmer.
62 Crofts, *Packhorse, Waggon and Post*, p.54.
63 Tombs, *The King's Post*, p.1.
64 Tombs, p.2.
65 Salisbury Mss, vol. 7, p.285.
66 Salisbury Mss, vol. 9, p.152.
67 CSPD, 1598–1601, p.281.
68 APC, 1591, 1591–2, p.38.
69 CSPD, vol. 1, part 2, p.1188.
70 Winchester, *Tudor Family Portrait*, p.237.
71 Stone, p.230.

72 Many of the Corsini letters are illustrated in the Christie Robson Lowe auction catalogues.
73 For a general account of the Elizabethan Merchant Adventurers, see Bisson.
74 Burgon, *Life and Times of Sir Thomas Gresham*, p.72.
75 Smith, D.M., *Guide to the Archives of the Company of Merchant Adventurers of York.*
76 Sellers, *The York Mercers and Merchant Adventurers*, pp.180–1.
77 Sellers, p.183.
78 Sellers, p.40.
79 Sellers, p.43.
80 Livock, *City Chamberlain's Accounts*, pp.99, 111, 121.
81 Dendy, *Newcastle Merchant Adventurers*, vol. 2, p.161.
82 Lyell, *Acts of the Court of the Mercers Company.*
83 Lyell, p.641.
84 CSPD, *Milan*, 1385–1618, 8 September 1497, p.323, entry 540.
85 CSPD, HVIII, vol. 3, part 1, no 1130.
86 CSPD, vol. 4, part 1, nos 984, 985, 1741, 1864.
87 CSPD, 1547–80, pp.312, 313.
88 Salisbury MSS, vol. 5, p.112.
89 CSPF, 1547–53, 25 December 1551, pp.205–6.
90 Welford, *History of Newcastle*, vol. 2, p.208.
91 Welford, vol. 3, p.69.
92 Rogers, T., *History of Prices and Agriculture*, vol. 5, p.662.
93 Salisbury MSS, part 5, pp.346–7.
94 Salisbury MSS, part 4, p.243.
95 Archer, *The Philatelist*, March 1987.
96 Communar's Accounts, Chichester Chapter Archives, Cap 1/51/10, pp.16, 20, 21. Chichester Record Office.
97 RCM, Report 12, part 4, vol. I, p.84.
98 Batho, *Household Papers of Henry Percy.*
99 Hentzner, *Travels in England during the Reign of Elizabeth*, p.82.
100 British Library MS 18.D.111.

Chapter 10

1 See Harvey, *Maps in Tudor England*, and for books cited, Fordham, *Studies in Carto-Bibliography.* William Smith's MS was first published in 1879 by Wheatley & Ashbee.
2 Wallis, *Historians Guide to Early British Maps*, p.101.
3 Wallis says only used in London.
4 CSP, 1633–4, p.56.
5 Warrant in a private collection.
6 Hoskins, *English Provincial Towns* gives the yields.
7 Ordnance Survey, *Historical Map and Guide, Roman Britain.*
8 CSPD, 1547–80, p.286, no.71.
9 CSPD, Elizabeth, 1581–90, pp.83, 131.
10 Crofts, p.65. Also Brayshay *Royal post-horse routes.*
11 Stone, p.39.
12 Above references from Salisbury MSS, e.g. vol. 3, p.269.
13 Williams, C, *Thomas Platter's Travels*, p.148.
14 CSPDF, HVIII, vol. 2, p.1444.

15 CSPDF, HVIII, vol. 2, part 2, pp.1451, 1460.
16 CSPDF, HVIII, vol. 3, part 2, p.1423 (2 references).
17 Welford, *History of Newcastle*, vol. 2, p.82.
18 CSPD, HVIII, part 4, Correspondence Relative to Scotland and the Borders 1513–34, p.653.
19 APC, vol. 6, p.121.
20 APC, vol. 6, 19 October 1557, p.188.
21 Collier, *The Trevelyan Papers*, vol. 84, p.6 ff.
22 *APC*, vol. 6, p.385.
23 Sec. Com., p.35 refers to the route as existing in 1572.
24 Stone, p.21 prints the report.
25 *Calendar of Border Papers*, 1560–94, vol. 1, 28 December 1587, pp.299–300.
26 Stone, pp.218–22.
27 Salisbury Mss, part 2, p.214.
28 CSPD, 1581–90, p.153. Stone, pp.222–3.
29 Hemmeon, *History of Post Office*, p.98; ch.6 analyses speeds.
30 Salisbury MSS, vol. 12, p.625.
31 Salisbury MSS, vol. 15, p.124.
32 Allen, p.16.
33 Stone, p.209.
34 APC, vol. 7, p.302.
35 CSPD, 1547–80, p.625.
36 CSPD, 1547–80, p.677.
37 CSPD, 1598–1601, 24 February 1599, p.164.
38 Salisbury Mss, vol. 9, p.97.
39 APC, vol. 12, p.211.
40 Salisbury Mss, vol. 11, p.236.
41 Stone, p.211.
42 Stone, p.25; City of Exeter records; Cornelius, *Devon and Cornwall*, p.2.
43 Salisbury MSS, vol. 12, p.620.
44 Salisbury MSS, vol. 9, p.152.
45 Salisbury MSS, vol. 12, p.45.
46 APC, vol. 6, p.248.
47 APC, vol. 6, p.309.
48 Stone, p.10.
49 Salisbury Mss, vol. 7, p.358.
50 Stone, p.231.
51 Clifford, A., *The State Papers & Letters of Sir R. Sadler*, vol. 2, p.499.
52 Morris, J., *Letter Books of Sir Amyas Poulet*, p.15.
53 Morris, J., p.249.
54 24 Henry VIII, ch. 11.
55 Hughes and Larkin, vol. 1. p.85.
56 2 and 3 Philip and Mary, ch. 8.
57 5 Elizabeth, ch. 13.
58 27 Elizabeth, ch. 19.
59 14 & 15 Henry VIII, ch. 6.
60 22 Henry VIII, ch. 5.
61 18 Elizabeth, ch. 17.

Chapter 11
1 Guy, *Tudor England*, p.418.
2 Mackie, *The Early Tudors*, p.579; Moran, *Literacy and Education in Northern England 1350–1550.*
3 Harrison, *A Description of England*, p.258
4 Davies, G., *The Early Stuarts*, p.349.
5 Steele, 2nd Series, vol. 2, pp.220–6.
6 Byrne, *Letters of Henry VIII*, pp.304–6. For the execution, see Wagner, p.179.
7 Ellis, 2nd series, vol. I, letter LXXXIII.
8 Ellis, 2nd series, vol. II, pp.167–9.
9 Ellis, 1st series, vol. 2, pp.176–7.
10 Harrison, *Letters of Queen Elizabeth*, pp.19–21.
11 CSPD, 1547–80, p.677.
12 Harrison, p.121.
13 Harrison, p.250
14 Harrison, p.181.
15 Harrison, p.180.
16 Harrison, p.188.
17 Harrison, p.46.
18 Harrison, pp.125–6.
19 Harrison, p.178.
20 Astley, *Voyages and Travels*, vol. 1, pp.277–9.
21 Tenison, E. M., *Elizabethan England*, vol. 4, p.260.
22 Collier, *The Egerton Papers*, pp.292–301.
23 Jeaves, *Gawdy Letters*, 3 April 1591.
24 Jeaves, 4 February 1587.
25 Latham and Youings. Letter 219.
26 Ogle, *Copy Book of Sir Amyas Poulet's letters.*
27 Dickens, *Clifford Letters*, p.112.
28 Winchester, *Tudor Family Portrait*, p.13.
29 Winchester, p.38.
30 Winchester, p.269.
31 Winchester, p.248.
32 Winchester, p.277.
33 Winchester, p.296.
34 Winchester, p.237 and comments on the post.
35 Byrne, L.S.R, *The Fugger Newsletters.* Second Series, pp.107–8.
36 *The Philatelist*, July 1984, p.156.
37 Robson Lowe Christie's Sale, 2 September 1984, lot 12.
38 Sale 11, October 1988, lot 31.
39 Burgon, *The Life and Times of Sir Thomas Gresham*, p.366.
40 Burgon, pp.320–1.
41 CSPD, Addenda, 9 August 1574, p.467.
42 Burgon, p.406.

Chapter 12
1 Sec. Com., p.22, CSPD 1603–10, p.366.
2 CSP, 1603–10, p.9.
3 Sec. Com., p.38 prints both in full.
4 Haldane, *Three Centuries of Scottish Posts*, ch.1.

5 Stone, appendix 4.
6 Salisbury MSS, vol. 16, p.50.
7 See Haldane.
8 Sec. Com., pp.41–3.
9 CSP, 1603–10, p.512. Printed in full in Sec. Com., pp.41–3.
10 CSP, 1611–18, p.17.
11 CSP, 1611–18, p.44.
12 Stone, *The Inland Posts*, p.39.
13 CSP, 1611–18, p.17.
14 Stone gives costs, p.209.
15 CSP, 1611–18, p.126.
16 CSP, 1625–26, p.428.
17 CSP, 1619–23, p.517.
18 CSP, 1623–33, pp.145, 299.
19 CSP, 1631–33, p.298.
20 CSP, 1611–18, p.478.
21 CSP, 1611–18, p.562.
22 CSP, Addenda, 1594–1625, p.630.
23 CSP, 1611–18, p.601.
24 RCM, 15th report, appendix part 7, p.63.
25 APC, 1621–3, p.364. Printed in full in Stone, pp.232–4.
26 APC, 1621–3, p.473.
27 APC, 1623–5, p.46.
28 CSP, 1619–3, p.86.
29 CSP, 1625–6, 27 February 1626, p.261.
30 CSP, 1625–6,p.312.
31 CSP, 1625–6, p.346.
32 APC, 1627–8, p.452.
33 CSP, 1627–8, p.307.
34 Sec. Com., p.52.
35 CSP, 1631–3, p.30.
36 Stone prints in full, pp.239–41.
37 CSP, 1629–31, p.440, no.^99.
38 Stone, p.238.
39 CSP, 1631–3, p.241.
40 CSP, 1631–3, 8 August 1631, p.130.
41 CSP, 1631–3, p.257.
42 CSP, 1629–31, pp.199–200.
43 APC, 1629–30, para 601.
44 APC, 1629–30, para 921.
45 Cornelius, *Devon and Cornwall*, pp.7–8.
46 Described by Driver in an article in *Stamp Lover*, July–August 1967.
47 Cowper, *Coke Manuscripts*, part 2, p.26.
48 CSP, 1603–10, p.514.
49 CSP, 1623–5, p.161.
50 CSP, 1625–6, p.523.
51 Sec. Com., p.45
52 Seddon, *Letters of John Holies*, pp.125–7.
53 Probably began 22 March 1622.
54 CSP, 1623–5, p.131. Sec. Com., pp.45–7.

55 Sec.Com. p.48.
56 CSP, 1625–6, p.478.
57 CSP, 1627–8, p.6.
58 CSP, 1627–8, pp.436,591.
59 CSP, 1627–8, p.405.
60 CSP, 1627–8, p.573.
61 Sec. Com., pp.52–4.
62 CSP, 1631–3, p.242.
63 I, 1634–5, p.389.
64 Cowper, Coke MSS, part 1, p.478
65 Cowper, Coke MSS, part 2, p.6.
66 CSP, 1631–3, p.521.
67 CSP, p.197, August 1633. 'The King sequestered the place into the hand of Matthew de Quester. The Secretary is to send for John Hatt, an attorney, who has the legal interest in the place, and will him to assign it to Matthew de Quester.'
68 Sec. Com., p.58.
69 Barry, *The Tudor and Stuart Town*, p.123.
70 Chartres, *Internal Trade in England*, p.41.
71 CSP, 1633–4, p.464.
72 14 Car. II, ch. 6.
73 Stone, pp.248–50.
74 Sec. Com., p.55.
75 Sec. Com., p.57.
76 Cornelius, *Devon and Cornwall: A Postal Survey*, pp.7–8.
77 Cowper, Coke MSS, part 2, p.78.
78 Hyde, *Early History of the Post Office*, p.89.
79 The lengthy patent is quoted fully in Sec. Com., pp.52–4.
80 Sec. Com., p.68; and Hyde, p.90.
81 CSPD, 1661–2, p.610.
82 Hyde, pp.92–3; Coke MSS, part 2, p.163.
83 Hyde, p.142. He cites other cases.

Bibliography

Adamson, J.W., *The Extent of Literacy in the 15th and 16th Centuries*, The Library, series 4, vol. 10, 1929–30.

Allen, E.J.B., *Post and Courier Service in the Diplomacy of Early Modern Europe*, The Hague, 1973.

Anderson, R.C., *Letters of the 15th and 16th Centuries*, Southampton Record Society, 1921.

Anstey, H., *Epistolae Academicae*, Oxford Historical Society, vols 35 & 36, 1893.

Archer, M. S., 'Letters to London from the South Coast ports 1573–1601', *The Philatelist*, vol. 7, no.^9, March 1987.

Armstrong, C.A.J., 'Some examples of the distribution and speed of news in England at the time of the Wars of the Roses', *Studies in Medieval History Presented to F.M. Powicke*, ed. Hunt, R.W., Pantin, W.A., and Southern, R.W., OUP, 1948.

Aylmer, G.E. *The King's Servants. The Civil Service of Charles I.* Routledge and Kegan Paul, 1961.

Bailey, M., 'The English landscape' and 'Population and economic resources', chapters 1 & 2 in *An Illustrated History of Late Medieval England*, ed. Given-Wilson, C., Manchester, 1996.

Bailey, M., *The Bailiff's Minute Book of Dunwich*, Suffolk Records Society, vol. 34, 1992.

Baildon, W. P., 'Wardrobe accounts of King Richard II, 1393–4', *Archaeologia*, vol. LXII, 1910.

Barry, J., *The Tudor and Stuart Town 1530–1688*, Longman, 1995.

Bateson, M., *Records of the Borough of Leicester*, 2 vols, London, 1901.

Bateson, M., *Borough Customs*, 2 vols, Selden Society, London, 1904.

Batho, G.R., *The Household Papers of Henry Percy, Ninth Earl of Northumberland*, Camden Society, 3rd series, vol. 93, 1962.

Becker, M.J., *Rochester Bridge, 1387–1856*, Constable, 1930.

Bede, The Venerable, *The Ecclesiastical History of the English Nation*, Dent, Everyman's Library, 1927.

Bell, G.M., *A Handlist of British Diplomatic Representatives 1509-1688*, Royal Historical Society, 1990.

Bennett, H.S., *The Pastons and their England*, CUP edition, 1990.

Beresford, M.W., and Finsberg, H.P.R., *English Medieval Boroughs: A Handlist*, David and Charles, 1973.

Bernard, J., *Discours des plus mémorables faicts des Roys et grands Seigneurs d'Angleterre plus un traicté de la Guide des chemins … d'Angleterre*, Paris, 1576.

Bettenson, H., *Documents of the Christian Church*, Oxford, 1944.

Bindoff, S. T., *Elizabethan Government and Society: Essays Presented to Sir John Neale*, London, 1961.

Birley, A., *Garrison Life at Vindolanda*, Tempus, 2002.

Bishop, T.A.M., *Scriptores Regis*, Oxford, 1961.

Bisson, D.R., *The Merchant Adventurers of England*, Delaware, 1993.

Black E.W., 'Cursus Publicus', *Tempus Reparatum*, BAR British series, no.^941, Oxford, 1995.

Black, J.B., *The Reign of Elizabeth*, Oxford, 1945.

Blackham, R.J., *The London Livery Companies*, London, 1931.

Blagden, C., *The Stationers Company: A History*, Alien and Unwin, 1960.

Blomefield, E., *The County of Norfolk, vol. 3: History of Norwich*, 1806.

Booth, P.H.W. and Carr, A.D., *Chester Chamberlain's Accounts 1361–62*, Record Society of Lancashire and Cheshire, 1991.

Boutell's Heraldry, revised by Scott-Giles, C.W. and Brooke-Littel, J.P., Warne, 1966.

Bowle, J., *Henry VIII*, David and Charles, 1964.

Bowman, A.K., *Life and Letters on the Roman Frontier: Vindolanda and its People*, revised edition. British Museum Press, 2003.

Bowman, A.K., and Thomas, J.D., *The Vindolanda Writing Tablets*, Britannia Monographs, vol. 4, 1983. See also Britannia, vol. 18, 1987, vol. 21, 1990 and vol. 27, 1996.

Bowman, A.K. and Thomas, J.D., *The Vindolanda Writing Tablets, Tabulae Vindolandenses II*, British Museum Press, 1994.

Bowman, A.K. and Thomas J.D., *The Vindolanda Writing Tablets, Tabulae Vindolandenses III*, British Museum Press, 2003.

Bracton, *De Legibus Angliae*, 6 vols, ed. Twiss, T., Rolls series, 1878.

Brayshay, M., 'Knowledge, nationhood and governance: the speed of the Royal post in early-modern England', *Journal of Historical Geography*, 24.3 (1998) pp.265–88.

Brayshay, M., 'Royal post-horse routes of Hampshire in the reign of Elizabeth I', *Proc. Hampshire Field Club Arch. Soc.* 48 (1992) pp.121–34.

Brayshay, M., 'Royal post-horse routes in South West England in the reigns of Elizabeth I and James I', *Rep. Trans. Devon Ass. Advmt Sci.* 123, pp.79–103.

Brayshay, M, 'Royal post-horse routes in England and Wales; the evolution of the network in the later sixteenth and early seventeenth century', *Journal of Historical Geography*, 17.4 (1991) pp.373–89.

Brewer, T., *Memoir of the Life and Times of John Carpenter, Town Clerk of London*, 1856.

Britnell, R.H., *The Commercialisation of English Society*, MUP, 1996.

Broome, D.M., 'Exchequer Migrations to York', *Essays Presented to T.F. Tout*, ed. Little, A.G., and Powicke, F.M., 1925.

Burgon, J.W., *Life and Times of Sir Thomas Gresham*, London, 1839.

Byerley, B.J. and Byerley, C.R., *Records of the Wardrobe and Household 1285–6* and *1286–9*, HMSO, 1977.

Byrne, L.S.R., *The Fugger Newsletters*, 2nd series, Bodley Head, 1926.

Byrne, M.St C., *The Lisle Letters*, Chicago and London, 1981.

Byrne, M.St C., *Letters of King Henry the Eighth*, New York, 1936.

Cam, H.M., *The Hundred and the Hundred Rolls*, Methuen, 1930.

Campbell, W., *Materials for a History of the Reign of Henry VII*, 2 vols, Rolls series, 1873.

Carpenter, C., *Kingsford's Stonor Letters and Papers 1290–1483*, CUP, 1996.

Carus-Wilson, E.M., *Medieval Merchant Venturers*, Methuen, 1967.

Chaplais, P., 'Letter from Bishop Waldhere', *Medieval Scribes Manuscripts and Libraries: Essays Presented to N.R. Ker*, eds Parkes, M.B. and Watson, A.G., London, 1978

Chaplais. P., 'The Royal Anglo-Saxon Chancery Revisited', *Studies Presented to R.H.C. Davis*, ed. Meyr-Harting, H., and Moore, R.I., Hambledon, 1985.

Chapman. H.P.A., *The Archaeological and other Evidence for the Organization and Operation of the Cursus Publicus*, London, PhD thesis, 1978.

Chartres, J.A., 'Road Carrying in England in the 17th Century', *Economic History Review*, series 2, vol. 30, 1977.

Chartres, J.A., *Internal Trade in England 1500–1700*, Macmillan, 1977.

Cheney, C.R., *English Bishops' Chanceries*, Manchester, 1950.

Cheney, C.R., *Notaries Public in England in the 13th and 14th Centuries*, Oxford, 1972.

Chevallier, R., *Roman Roads.* Batsford. 1987.
Chichester Chapter Archives, *Communar's Accounts*, Cap 1/51/10, Chichester Record Office.
Childs, W.R., *Customs Accounts of Hull 1453–90*, Yorkshire Archaeological Society, 1986.
Childs, W.R., 'English Credit to Alien Merchants in the Mid Fifteenth Century', *Enterprise and Individuals in 15th-Century England*, ed. Kermode, J., Sutton, 1991.
City Cash 1632, vol. 1, mss vol. in Corporation of London Library.
Clanchy, M.T., *From Memory to Written Record*, 2nd edition, Blackwell, 1993.
Clifford, A., *The State Papers and Letters of Sir R. Sadler*, London, 1809.
Cobban, A.B., *The Medieval English Universities*, Scolar, 1988.
Coleman, J., *English Literature in History 1350–1400*, Hutchinson, 1981.
Coleman, O., *The Brokage Book of Southampton, 1443–44*, 2 vols, Southampton, 1960 and 1961.
Collier, J.P., ed., *The Egerton Papers*, Camden Society, old series, 1840.
Collier, J.P., ed., *The Trevelyan Papers inc. Extracts from the Household Book of Henry VIII*, Camden old series, 67, 84 and 105, 1857, 1863 and 1872.
Collingwood, R.G. and Myres, J.N.L., *Roman Britain and the English Settlements*, Oxford, 1945.
Cooper, C.H., *Annals of Cambridge*, 1842.
Cornelius, D.B., *Devon and Cornwall: A Postal Survey 1500-1791*, Postal History Society, 1973.
Corner, G.R., 'Grant per Cultellum of William the Second Earl of Warenne', *Sussex Archaeological Collections*, vol. VII, 1854.
Cowper, Earl, *Calendar of Coke Manuscripts*, 3 vols, Rolls series, 1888–9.
Crawford, A., *Letters of the Queens of England*, Sutton, 1994.
Crawford, A., *Letters of Medieval Women*, Sutton, 2002.
Crofts, J., *Packhorse, Waggon and Post*, Routledge Kegan Paul, 1967.
Crosby, R., 'Oral Delivery in the Middle Ages', *Speculum*, vol. XI, 1936.
Dance, E.M., *Guildford Borough Records*, Surrey Record Society, vol. XXIV, 1958.
Darby, H.C., *The Historical Geography of England before 1800*, CUP, 1951.
Dasent, J.R., *Acts of the Privy Council of England*, 45 vols, HMSO, 1890–1944.
Davies, G., *The Early Stuarts*, Oxford, 1952.
Davies, H., *Roads in Roman Britain*, Tempus, 2000.
Davies, J. C., 'The Inimitable Chancellor Bogo de Clare', *Journal of the Historical Society of Wales.* vol. I. no.2.
Davies, J.J., *A History of Southampton*, Gilbert, 1883.
Davies, N., 'The *Litera Troili* and English Letters', *Review of English Studies*, new series 16, 1965.
Davies, R., *Extracts from the Municipal Records of the City of York*, London, 1843.
Davis, G.R.C., *Medieval Cartularies of Great Britain*, Longmans, 1958.
Dendy, F.W., *Newcastle Merchant Adventurers*, vols 1 and 2, Surtees Society, 1895 and 1899.
Devon, F., *Issue Roll of Thomas de Brantingham, Lord High Treasurer of England, 1370.* Record Commissioners, 1835.
Devon, F., *Issues of the Exchequer: Henry III-Henry VI*, Record Commissioners. 1837.
Devon, F., *Issues of the Exchequer: James I*, HMSO, 1836.
Dickens, A.G., *Clifford Letters of the Sixteenth Century*, Surtees Society, vol. 172, 1962.
Dickins, B., 'Praemonstratensian Itineraries from a Tichfield Abbey', *Leeds Philosophical Society*, vol. IV, 1938.
Dietz, B., *The Port and Trade of Elizabethan London*, London Record Society, vol. 8, 1972.

Donaldson, G.H., 'Signalling Comunications in the Roman Imperial Army', *Britannia*, vol. 19, 1988.

Douglas, D.C., General Editor, *English Historical Documents*, vols 1–5, Eyre Methuen, 1969–81.

Dow, L., *Merchants Marks*, Harleian Society, vol. 108, 1959.

Edwards, P., *The Horse Trade in Tudor and Stuart England*, CUP, 1988.

Edwards, K. and Owen, D.M., *The Registers of Roger Martival*, 4 vols, Canterbury and York Society, 1959–75.

Ellis, H., *Original Letters*, series 1–4, London, 1846.

Ellis, H., *Original Letters of Eminent Men: 16th, 17th and 18th Centuries*, Camden Society, old series, 1843.

Ferguson, R.S. and Nanson, B.A., *Some Municipal Records of the City of Carlisle*, Carlisle and London, 1887.

Fitz Nigel, R., *Dialogus de Scaccario: The Course of the Exchequer*, Oxford, 1983.

Flower, C.T., *Public Works in Medieval Law*, 2 vols, Selden Society, 1915 and 1923.

Fordham, H.G., *An Itinerary of the 16th Century*, Cambridge Antiquarian Society, 1909.

Fordham, H.G., *Studies in Carto-Bibliography*, Dawsons, 1969.

Fowler, K.A., *The Strategic Importance of the Post Roads in England and Wales and their Management 1590-1635*. Thesis prepared for a London University doctorate but not entirely completed through ill health. Consequently not presented. In *Post Office Records*, 1990.

Fraser, C.M., *Newcastle on Tyne Chamberlain's Accounts*, Society of Newcastle Antiquaries, 1987.

Furley, J.S., *Winchester Records*, Oxford, 1923.

Furnivall, F.J., *Early English Meals and Manners*, Early English Text Society, 1868.

Gairdner, J., *The Paston Letters*, 6 vols, reprinted in microprint in one volume, Sutton, 1986.

Gee, H. and Hardy, J.H., *Documents Illustrative of English Church History*, Macmillan, 1896.

Gerhold, D., *Road Transport in the Horse-Drawn Era. Scholar Press.* 1996.

Girling, F.A., *English Merchants Marks*, Lion and Unicorn Press, London, 1962.

Giuseppi, M.S., *Guildford Records*, Surrey Record Society, vol. 24, 1926.

Giuseppi, M.S., 'Wardrobe and Household Accounts of Bogo de Clare 1284–86', *Archaeologia*, LXX, 1918–20.

Given-Wilson, C., *The Royal Household and the King's Affinity 1360–1413*, Yale and London, 1986.

Gould, J., *Letocetum. The Rise and Decline of a Roman Posting Station.* Published by J. Gould, 1998.

Grafton, R., *Chronicle or History of England*, 1569.

Gregory, J.W., *The Story of the Road*, London, 1931.

Green, A.S., *Town Life in the 15th Century*, Macmillan, 1895.

Griffiths, R.A., 'Public and Private Bureaucracies in England and Wales in the 15th Century', *TRHS*, 5th series, vol. 30, 1980.

Grundy, G.B., 'The Evidence of Saxon Land Charters on the Ancient Road System of Britain', *Archaeological Journal*, vol. 74, 1917.

Guy, D., *Tudor England*, Oxford, 1988.

Haldane, A.R.B., *Three Centuries of Scottish Posts*, Edinburgh, 1971.

Hall, H., *The Red Book of the Exchequer*, vol. 3, Rolls series, 1893.

Hanham, A., *Cely Letters 1472–88*, Early English Text Society, vol. 273, 1975.

Harmer, F.E., *Anglo-Saxon Writs*, MUP, 1952.

Harris, M., *The Account of the Great Household of Humphrey, 1st Duke of Buckingham for 1452–3*, Camden Society, 4th series, vol. 29, 1984.

Harrison, G.B., *An Elizabethan Journal*, Routledge, 1950.

Harrison, G.B., *The Letters of Queen Elizabeth I*, Funk & Wagnalls, 1969.

Harrison, W., A *Description of England*, ed. Lothrop Withington, London, n.d.

Harvey. P.D.A., *Maps in Tudor England*, British Library, 1993.

Harvey, P.D.A., *Medieval Maps*, British Library, 1991.

Haskins, C.H., *Studies in Medieval Culture*, Oxford, 1929.

Hearne, T., ed., *The Black Book of the Exchequer*, 1771.

Hemmeon, J.C., *The History of the British Post Office*, Cambridge, MA, 1912.

Hentzner, P., *Travels in England during the Reign of Elizabeth*, Cassell, 1894.

Hewitt, H. J., *Medieval Cheshire: Building Accounts of Vale Royal Abbey*, Chetham Society, new series, vol. 88, 1929.

Hey, D.G., *Packmen, Carriers and Packhorse Roads*, Leicester, 1980.

Hill, M.C., *The King's Messengers 1199–1377*, Arnold, 1961.

Hill, M.C., *The King's Messengers 1199–1377*, (a list of all known messengers), Sutton, 1994

Hill, M.C., Jack Faukes: King's Messenger, *English Historical Review*, vol. 57, 1942.

Hindle, B.P., *Roads and Tracks for Historians*, Phillimore, 2001.

Hoccleve, T., *The Regement of Princes*, Early English Text Society, extra series 72, 1897.

Holinshed, R., Harrison, W. *et al.*, *Chronicles of England, Scotland and Ireland*, 1577.

Hollaender, A.E.J. and Kellaway, W., eds, *Studies in London History Presented to P.E. Jones*, Hodder and Stoughton, 1969.

Holmes, T.R., *The Architect of the Roman Empire* (Augustus), 2 vols, Oxford, 1931.

Hoskins, W.G., 'English Provincial Towns in the Early Sixteenth Century', *TRHS*, 5th series, vol. 6, 1956.

Houlbrook, R., *Church Courts and the People during the English Reformation 1520–1570*, Oxford 1979.

Housden, J.A.J., 'The Merchant Strangers' Post in the 16th Century', *English Historical Review*, vol. 21, 1906.

Housden, J.A.J., 'Early Posts in England', *English Historical Review*, vol. 18, 1903.

Hudd, A.E., *Bristol Merchants Marks*, Clifton Antiquarian Club, part 1, vol. 7, 1909.

Hudson, W. and Tingley, J.C., *Records of the City of Norwich, 2* vols, 1906.

Hughes, P.L. and Larkin, J.E, *Tudor Royal Proclamations*, 3 vols, Yale, 1964–69.

Hyde, J.W., *Early History of the Post Office in Grant and Farm*, London, 1894.

Jacob, E.E., *The Fifteenth Century*, Oxford, 1961.

Jeaves, I.H., *Letters of P. Gawdy*, Roxburghe Club, 1906.

Jenkinson, H. and Mills, M.H., *Rolls from a Sheriff's Office in the 14th Century*', English Historical Review, vol. 43, 1928.

Johnston, D.E., *Roman Roads in Britain*, Spurbooks, 1979.

Johnstone, H., *Letters of Edward Prince of Wales 1304–05*, Roxburghe Club, vol. 194, 1931.

Jones, A.H.M., *The Later Roman Empire*, Blackwell, 1964.

Jones, B., and Mattingley, D., *An Atlas of Roman Britain*, Blackwell, 1990.

Jones, W.T., *The Elizabethan Court of Chancery*, Oxford, 1967.

Journals, indexes to, Corporation of London Library.

Joyce, H., *A History of the Post Office*, London, 1893.

Jusserand, J.J., *English Wayfaring Life in the Fourteenth Century*, Fisher Unwin, 1920.

Kaeuper, R.W., *Bankers to the Crown. The Riccardi of Lucca and Edward I*, Princeton, 1973.

Keen, M., *English Society in the Late Middle Ages*, Penguin, 1990.

Keene, D., *Survey of Medieval Winchester*, 2 vols, Oxford, 1965.

Kermode, J., *Enterprise and Individuals in 15th-Century England*, Sutton, 1991.

Keynes, S., 'Royal Government and the Written Word', *The Uses of Literacy in Medieval Europe*, ed. McKitterick, R., Cambridge, 1990.

Kightly C. and Cyprien, M., *A Traveller's Guide to Royal Roads*, Routledge and Kegan Paul, 1985.

Kingsford, C.L., *Stonor Letters and Papers*, Camden Society, 3rd series, vols 29 and 30, 1919.

Kingsford, C.L., *Prejudice and Promise in Fifteenth-Century England*, Cass reprint, 1962.

Kirby, J., *The Plumpton Letters*, Camden Society, 5th series, vol. 8, 1996.

Labarge, W.M., *Henry V the Cautious Conqueror*, Seeker & Warburg, 1975.

Larson, A., 'The Payment of Fourteenth-Century English Envoys', *English Historical Review*, vol. 54, 1939.

Latham A. and Youings J., *The Letters of Sir Walter Raleigh*, Univ. of Exeter Press, 1999.

Leach, A.F., *Beverley Town Documents*, Selden Society, 1900.

Leadham, I.S., and Baldwin, J.F., *Select Cases in Star Chamber, 1477–1509*, vol. 16, Selden Society, 1903.

Leadham, I.S. and Baldwin, J.E, *Select Cases before the King's Council 1243–1482*, Selden Society, vol. 35, 1918.

Leighton, A.C., *Transport and Communications in Early Medieval Europe*, David and Charles, 1972.

Leland, J., *Itinerary*, ed. Chandler, J., Alan Sutton, 1993.

Lewins, W., *Her Majesty's Mails*, London, 1865.

Lewis, E.A., *The Southampton Port and Brokage Books 1448–49*, Southampton Record Series, vol. 36, 1993.

Lipson, E., *The Economic History of England*, vol. 1, Black, 1945.

Livock, D.M., *City Chamberlain's Accounts*, vol. 24, Bristol Record Society, 1966.

Lodge, E., *Illustrations of British History, Biography and Manners*, 3 vols, 1791.

Lodge, E.C. and Somerville, *John of Gaunt's Register, 1379–83*, Camden Society, 3rd series, vols 56 and 57, 1937.

Lyell, L., *A Medieval Postbag*, Cape, 1934.

Lyell, L. and Watney, F.D., *Acts of the Court of the Mercers Company, 1453–1527*, Cambridge, 1936.

Lysons, S., 'Expenses of King Edward I at Rhuddlan Castle 1281–2', *Archaeologia*, XVI, 1812.

MacMahon, K., *Roads and Turnpike Trusts in Eastern Yorkshire*, East Yorkshire Historical Society, vol. 18, 1964.

Mackie, J.D., *The Earlier Tudors 1485–1558*, Oxford, 1952.

Mann, F.O., *Deloney's Works*, Oxford, 1912.

Map, Walter, *De Nugis Curialum*, Cymmrodorion Society, no.^9, 1923.

Margary, I.D., *Roman Roads in Britain*, 3rd edition, London, 1973.

Martin, C.T., *Registrum Epistolarum Johannis Peckham, 3* vols, Rolls series 77, 1882–5.

Masters, B.R., *Chamber Accounts*, London Record Society, vol. 20, 1984.

Masters, B.R., 'The Mayor's Household before 1600', *Studies in London History Presented to P.E. Jones*, eds Hollander, A.J., and Kellaway, W., Hodder and Stoughton, 1969.

McFarlane, K.B., *England in the Fifteenth Century*, Hambledon Press, 1981.

McKisack, M., *The Fourteenth Century, 1307-99*, Oxford, 1959.

McKitterick, R., *The Uses of Literacy in Mediaeval Europe*, Cambridge, 1992.

Merson. A.L., *The Third Remembrance Book of Southampton 1514–1602*, Southampton Record Society, 1952.

Miller, E., ed., *Agrarian History of England and Wales*, vol. 3, CUP, 1991.

Mills, M.H., 'The London Customs House in the Middle Ages', *Archaeologia*, LXXXIII, 1933.

Mills, M.H., 'The Medieval Shire House', *Studies Presented to Sir Hilary Jenkinson*, ed. Davies, J., OUP, 1957.

Moore, S.A., *Shillingford Letters*, Camden Society, new series, 1872.

Moorman, J.R.H., *Church Life in England in the 13th Century*, CUP, 1945.

Moran, J.H., 'Literacy and Education in Northern England 1350-1550', *Northern History*, 1981.

Moriarty, C., *The Voice of the Middle Ages*, Lennard, 1989.

Morris. J., ed., *The Letter Books of Sir Amias Poulet*, Burns & Gates, 1874.

Morris, W.A., 'The Office of Sheriff in the Early Norman Period', *English Historical Review*, vol. 33, 1918.

Morris, W.A., 'Sheriffs and the Administrative System of Henry I', *English Historical Review*, vol. 37, 1922.

Nicolas, Sir H., *Proceedings and Ordinances of the Privy Council of England*, 7 vols, Record Commission, 1834–37.

Ogilby, J., *Britannia*, vol. 1, 1675.

Ogle, O., *Copy Book of Sir Amyas Poulet*, Roxburghe Club, 1866.

Palmer, W.M., *Cambridge Borough Documents*, Cambridge, 1931.

Pantin, W.A., 'English Monastic Letter books', *Historical Essays presented to Tait, J.*, ed. Edwards, J.G., Manchester, 1933.

Pantin, W.A., *Documents Illustrating the Activities of the English Black Monks 1215–1540*, Camden

Society, 3rd series, 3 vols, nos 45, 47 and 54, 1931, 1933 and 1937.

Parkes, M.B., 'The Literacy of the Laity', *Scribes, Scripts and Readers*, Hambledon, 1991.

Parratt, T.W., 'On Northern Roads in the Middle Ages', *Ryedale Historian*, no.^9, June 1970.

Payne, P. and Barron, C. *The Letters and Life of Elizabeth Despenser, Lady Zouche*. Nottingham Medieval Studies 41 (1997) pp.126–56.

Pearson, P., 'The Paston Letters', *The London Philatelist*, nos 1171–6, 1990.

Pelham Letters, printed in *Collins Peerage*, vol. 8 from p. 95, 1779.

Pendrill, C., *London Life in the 14th Century*, Allen & Unwin, 1925.

Perroy, E., ed., *Diplomatic Correspondence of Richard II*, Camden Society 3rd series, 1933.

Platt, C., *The English Medieval Town*, Seeker & Warburg, 1976.

Platt, C., *Medieval Southampton 1000–1600*, Routledge, 1973.

Pollard, A.F, The Clerical Organization of Parliament', *English Historical Review*, vol. 57, 1942.

Pollard, A.F, 'The North Eastern Economy and the Agrarian Crisis of 1438–40', *Northern History*, vol. 25, 1989.

Poole, A.L., *Domesday Book to Magna Carta*, Oxford, 1951.

Poole, A.L., *Illustrations of the History of Medieval Thought and Learning*, SPCK reprint, 1932.

Poole, A.L., *Obligations of Society in the 12th and 13th Centuries*, Oxford, 1946.

Postan, M.M., *Medieval Trade and Finance*, CUP, 1973.

Pound, J.E, 'The Social and Trade Structure of Norwich 1525–75', *Past and Present*, July 1966.

Powicke, M., *The Thirteenth Century*, OUP, 1953.

Price, G., *The Languages of Britain*, Arnold, 1984.

Pronay, N. and Cox, J. *The Crowland Chronicle Continuations 1459–1486*, Sutton, 1986.

Public Record Office, *English Royal Signatures*, Museum Pamphlets, no.^9.

Queller, D.E., 'Thirteenth Century Envoys. Nuncii et Procuratores', *Speculum*, vol. 35, 1960.
Raine, A., 'Ordinances of the Porters', *Yorkshire Archaeological Society, Record Series*, York Civic Records, vol. 2, p.122, 1941.
Raine, J., *Historiae Dunelmensis scriptores tres*, Surtees Society, vol. 9, 1839.
Ramsay, A.M., 'The Speed of the Roman Imperial Post', *Journal of Roman Studies*, vol. XV, 1925.
Ramsay, A.M., 'A Roman Postal Service under the Republic', *Journal of Roman Studies*, vol. X, 1910.
Ramsey, N., 'Scriveners and Notaries as Legal Intermediaries in Later Medieval England', *Enterprise and Individuals*, ed. Kermode, J., Sutton, 1991.
Rashdall, H., *The Universities of Europe in the Middle Ages*, 3 vols, eds Powicke, F.M., and Emden, A.B., OUP, 1936.
Repertories, Indexes to, Corporation of London Library mss.
Richardson, M., 'Medieval English Vernacular Correspondence. Notes Towards an Alternative Rhetoric'. *Allegorica*. vol. 10. 1984.
Riley, H.T., *Memorials of London and London Life in the 13th, 14th and 15th Centuries*, Longmans, 1868.
Ritchie, C.I.A., *The Ecclesiastical Courts of York*, Arbroath, 1956.
Robertson, J.C., *Materials for the History of Thomas Becket*, vol. 3 of 7 vols, Rolls series, 1875–85.
Robinson, H., *The British Post Office*, Princeton and OUP, 1948.
Rogers, E.E, *The Correspondence of Thomas More*, Princeton, 1947.
Rogers, T., *History of Prices and Agriculture*, 6 vols, Oxford, 1856.
Rolfe, J.C., ed., *Suetonius: The Deified Augustus*, Heinemann, 1924.
Rowlands, R., *The Post of the World*, 1576.
Ruddock, A.A., *Italian Merchants and Shipping in Southampton 1270–1600*, Southampton, 1951.
Rymer, *Foedera*, ed. Clark, A., Record Commissioners, pubs 1–111, 1816–30.
Sainty, J.C., *Officers of the Exchequer*, List and Index Society, 1983.
Salisbury, *Calendar of Manuscripts of the Marquis of Salisbury* (contains mss of William Cecil, Lord Burghley and Robert Cecil, Earl of Salisbury), Historical Mss Commissioners, vols from 1883.
Salusbury-Jones, G., *Street Life in Medieval England*, Harvester, 1975.
Salway, P., *Roman Britain*, Oxford, 1991.
Salzman, L.E., *English Life in the Middle Ages*, Oxford, 1926.
Salzman, L.E., *English Trade in the Middle Ages*, Oxford, 1931.
Salzman, L.E., *Medieval Byways*, Constable, 1913.
Salzman, L.E., 'Minister's Accounts of the Manor of Petworth 1347–53'. *Sussex Record Society*, vol. 55, 1955.
Sayles, G.O., *Select Cases in the Court of King's Bench*, vol. 7, Selden Society, 1971.
Scott, S. D., 'A Book of Orders and Rules, Antony Viscount Montague in 1595', *Sussex Archaeological Collections*, 1854.
Secret Committee on the Post Office, Report of, HMSO, 1844.
Seddon, P.R., *Letters of John Holies*, vol. 1, 1587–1637, Thoroton Record Society, 1975.
Sellers, M., *The York Mercers and Merchant Adventurers*, Surtees Society, vol. 129, 1918.
Sellers, M., ed., *York Memorandum Book*, vols 1 and 3, Surtees Society, vols 120 and 125, 1912 and 1915.
Sharpe, R.R., ed., *Calendar of Letter Books of the City of London: A to Z*, Corporation of London from 1899.

Sharpe, R.R., ed., *Calendar of Letters from the Mayor and Corporation of the City of London circa 1350–70*, London, 1885.

Sheppard, J.B., ed., *Literae Cantuarienses: The Letter Books of the Monastery of Christ Church*, 3 vols, Rolls series, 1887.

Shirley, W.W., *Royal and Other Historical Letters Illustrative of the Reign of Henry III, from the Originals in the Public Record Office*, 2 vols, Rolls series, 1862–68.

Smith, D.M., *Guide to Bishops' Registers of England and Wales*, Royal Historical Society, Guide no.11, 1981.

Smith, D.M., *A Guide to the Archives of the Merchant Adventurers of York*, Borthwick Texts and Calendars 16, 1990.

Smith, W., *The Particular Description of England*, 1588.

Stapleton, T., 'Brief Summary of Wardrobe Accounts, 10th, 11th and 14th of King Edward II', *Archaeologia*, XXVI, 1836.

Statutes at Large, HMSO.

Steane, J., 'King John', A *Traveller's Guide to Royal Roads*, eds Kightly, C., and Cyprien, M., Routledge and Kegan Paul, 1985.

Steele, R., *Kings Letters*, 2 vols, Moring, 1903 and 1904.

Steer, F.W., *Scriveners' Company: Common Paper 1357-1628*, London Record Society, 1968.

Steer, F.W., *A History of the Worshipful Company of the Scriveners of London*, Philimore, 1973.

Stenton, F.M., *Anglo-Saxon England*, Oxford, 1943.

Stenton, D.M., 'The Road System of Medieval England', *Preparatory to Anglo-Saxon England: the Collected Papers of F M. Stenton*, OUP, 1970.

Stenton, Lady, Communications, *Medieval England*, ed. Poole, A.L., OUP, 1958.

Stevens, K.F. and Olding, T.E., *The Brokage Books of Southampton 1477–78 and 1527–28*, Southampton Record Society, vol. 228, 1985.

Stevenson, J., *Letters and Papers Illustrative of the Reign of Henry* VI, 2 vols, Rolls series, 1861–64.

Stevenson, J., 'Literacy in Ireland', The Uses of Literacy in Early Medieval Europe, ed. McKitterick, R., CUP, 1992.

Stevenson, W.H., *Records of the Borough of Nottingham*, Quaritch, 1882.

Stevenson, W.H., *Records of the Corporation of Gloucester*, 1893.

Stone, J.W.M., *The Inland Posts*, Christies Robson Lowe, 1987.

Stone, J.W.M., 'Great Britain: an Early Postmaster's Book', The Philatelist, vol. 4, no.^9, 1984.

Storey, R.L., The Register of Thomas Langley, Bishop of Durham 1406–37, Surtees Society, vol. 1, 1956.

Stow, J., *A Survey of London*, ed. Kingsford, C. L., Oxford, 1971.

Stretton, G., 'Some Aspects of Medieval Travel', TRHS, 4th series, vol. 7, 1924.

Surtees, R., History and Antiquities of the County Palatinate of Durham, 4 vols, London, 1816–40.

Talbot, C.H., Letters from the English Abbots to the Chapter at Cîteaux, 1442–1521, Camden Society, 4th series, vol. 4,1967.

Taylor, J., *English Historical Literature in the Fourteenth Century.* Oxford, 1987.

Taylor, J., The Carriers Cosmographie, London, 1637.

Tennison, E.M., *Elizabethan England*, vol. 4, published by author, 1933.

Thomas, A.H. and Jones, P.E., eds, Calendar of the Plea and Memoranda Rolls of the City of London, 6 vols, CUP, 1926.

Thomas, J.H., *Town Government in the 16th Century*, London, 1933.
Thompson, J.A.E., *The Transformation of Medieval England*, Longman, 1983.
Thrupp, S.L., *The Merchant Class of Medieval London*, Chicago, 1948.
Timmins, T.C.B., The Register of John Chandler Dean of Salisbury 1404–17, Wiltshire Record Society, vol. 39, 1984.
Tingey, J.C., 'Journals of John Dernell and John Boys', Norfolk Archaeology, vol. 15, 1904.
Tombs, R.C., The King's Post, Bristol, 1905.
Tout, T.E., 'The English Civil Service in the 14th Century', Bulletin of John Rylands Library, vol. 3, 1916.
Tout, T.E, *Chapters in the Administrative History of Medieval Englan*d, 6 vols, Manchester, 1920–33.
Unwin, G., 'The Merchants Adventurers Company in the Reign of Elizabeth', Economic History Review, vol. 1, 1926–27.
Wagner, A., *Heralds of England*, HMSO, 1967.
Wallis, H., Historian's Guide to Early British Maps, Royal Historical Society, 1994.
Wardrobe Accounts of K Edward II, vol. 2, mss 121, Society of Antiquaries.
Webb, S. and B., *The Story of the King's Highway*, Longmans, 1913.
Weber, R.E.J., *The Messenger Box*, Fraser, London, 1972.
Welch, C., *History of the Worshipful Company of Paviors*, London, 1909.
Welch, C., 'Fellowship Porters', Middlesex and Herts Notes and Queries vol. 1, 1895.
Welford, R., *History of Newcastle and Gateshead*, 3 vols, 1885.
Willan, T.S., *The Inland Trade*, Manchester, 1976.
Willard, C., The Use of Carts in the 14th Century', History, new series, XVII.
Willard, J.E, The Dating and Delivery of Letters Patent and Writs in the 14th Century', Bulletin of Institute of Historical Research, vol. x, 1932–3.
Willard, J.E, 'Inland Transportation in England during the 14th Century', Speculum, vol. 1, 1926.
Willcocks, R.M., *England's Postal History*, published by the author, 1975.
Williams, C., *Thomas Platter's Travels in England 1599*, Cape, 1937.
Winchester, B., *Tudor Family Portrait,* (the Johnson Correspondence), Cape, 1955.
Woodcock, B.L., Medieval Ecclesiastical Courts in the Diocese of Canterbury, OUP, 1952.
Woolgar, C.M., *Household Accounts of Medieval England,* 2 vols, OUP, 1992 and 1993.
Wordsworth, C., *Notes on Medieval Services in England*, London, 1898.
Wright, R.P., Hassell, M.W.C., and Tomlin, R.S.O., Inscriptions, vol. 6, Britannia, 1975.
Yates, R., *Monastic History of St Edmund's Bury*, London, 1843.
Youings, J., *Sixteenth Century England*, Penguin, 1984.

The Stuart Rossiter Trust Fund

(Registered Charity England & Wales Number 292076)

The Rossiter Trust is a charitable trust supporting research and publication relating to the history of communication through the postal systems of the world. The story of how people communicated with one another through the ages and across all the countries in the world is fundamental to a greater understanding of all types of history, particularly economic and social history.

Political and military history often affected the way in which postal systems were set up and the reasons for which they were set up. Speed in communicating information of all types was critical for business and commerce, and important for family purposes. The importance of post offices in the development and control of telegraph and telephone systems is often overlooked, yet these services affected and changed the nature of and need for postal communications.

While postal history is concerned with the role of the postal services to carry written or printed messages through the post, the study of the subject involves far more than just a study of stamps and postmarks, which, while important, are merely part of the mechanics that helped the postal systems to work. Thus it is important to recognise that postal history contemplates a period well before the issue of the Penny Black in 1840 and continues until the present.

The means by which mail was carried from one place to another, the cost of transmission of letters, the difficulties faced en route in wartime or by shipwreck, or in developing as yet unexplored countries is worthy of study. Indeed, changes in the British postal system currently contemplated because of regulation within the European Union will be the subject of study in the future. The impact of computer-driven communication on postal systems will probably be as profound as the reforms and development of postal systems which took place in the nineteenth century, particularly in 1840 and 1875.

Stuart Rossiter was a leading postal historian of his day and wanted, through setting up this charity with money from his estate, research to be devoted as much to the rapidly changing affairs of contemporary times as to those of the past. Stuart was a Fellow of the Royal Geographical Society and Chief Editor of the Blue Guides, as well as writing (for example) the classical Blue Guide to Greece, and was Editor of *The London Philatelist*. All these things brought together an interest in research and the publication of the useful results of such research.

The Trust intends to support research and publication projects by grant from 2005. Persons wishing to engage on a project within the objects of the charity, who need the financial support that the charity can give to approved projects, and who would benefit from the experience of the Trustees in helping people to get scripts fit for publication to an academic standard with the help of referees, should get in touch with the Corresponding Trustee, whose name and address are below, so that more details can be given.

The charity can help with the costs of research, such as photocopying in archives distant from the researcher, as well as publication costs. Applicants can be students seeking a higher degree at university, amateurs or professionals – provided the research is original, is approved and is likely to lead to publication for the benefit of a wider public and adds to the stock of publicly available material. The charity cannot support collecting but recognises that collections may have material, information and research resources that need to be recorded in support of its objectives.

The charity can help persons of any nationality wherever they live and whatever the subject, provided that subject is within the objectives set out in the charity's governing documents.

Persons who wish to support Stuart Rossiter's objectives financially by making a charitable gift or legacy of any amount should communicate with the Corresponding Trustee.

The Corresponding Trustee is Robin Pizer, 6 Drews Court, Churchdown, Gloucestershire. GL3 2LD. The Trust's website is www.rossitertrust.com

Index

If you are interested in purchasing other books published by Tempus, or in case you have difficulty finding any Tempus books in your local bookshop, you can also place orders directly through our website

www.tempus-publishing.com